A Publication Sponsored by
the Society for Industrial and Organizational Psychology, Inc.,
a Division of the American Psychological Association

Training
and Development
in Organizations

*Irwin L. Goldstein
and Associates*

Training
and Development
in Organizations

Jossey-Bass Publishers

San Francisco   •   Oxford   •   1989

TRAINING AND DEVELOPMENT IN ORGANIZATIONS
by Irwin L. Goldstein and Associates

Copyright © 1989 by: Jossey-Bass Inc., Publishers
350 Sansome Street
San Francisco, California 94104
&
Jossey-Bass Limited
Headington Hill Hall
London OX3 0BW

Library of Congress Cataloging-in-Publication Data

Goldstein, Irwin L., date.
    Training and development in organizations / Irwin L. Goldstein.
        p.   cm. — (Frontiers of industrial and organizational
psychology) (A joint publication in the Jossey-Bass management
series and the Jossey-Bass social and behavioral science series)
    Includes bibliographical references.
    ISBN 1-55542-186-5
    1. Employees—Training of. I. Title. II. Series. III. Series:
Jossey-Bass management series.   IV. Series: Jossey-Bass social and
behavioral science series.
HF5549.5.T7G542   1989
658.3'124—dc20   89-45587
                                                                CIP

Manufactured in the United States of America

The paper in this book meets the guidelines for
permanence and durability of the Committee on
Production Guidelines for Book Longevity of the
Council on Library Resources.

JACKET DESIGN BY WILLI BAUM

FIRST EDITION

Code 8960

A joint publication in
The Jossey-Bass Management Series
and
The Jossey-Bass
Social and Behavioral Science Series

Frontiers of Industrial and Organizational Psychology

Contents

ix

Contents

Foreword

One of the principal objectives of the Society for Industrial and Organizational Psychology, according to its bylaws, is to "advance the scientific status of the field." In 1982, Richard J. Campbell, then the president of the society, asked me to assume the chair of the Committee on Scientific Affairs, with the express charge of intensifying the society's pursuit of that objective. It was a charge that I, as well as the rest of the committee, embraced wholeheartedly.

Several new initiatives were undertaken during that year. The one that generated the greatest enthusiasm — not only in the committee but also widely throughout the society — was a plan to publish a series of volumes, each dealing with a single topic considered to be of major contemporary significance in industrial and organizational psychology. Each volume would present cutting-edge theory, research, and practice in chapters to be contributed by about ten individuals doing pioneering work on the topic.

The proposal was unanimously adopted by the society's executive committee in 1983, and its implementation was entrusted to an editorial board, which I agreed to chair. It is further testimony to the vitality of the idea that every one of the distinguished and busy psychologists who were asked to join the board accepted the invitation.

I think that plan has been so favorably received mainly because it is seen as filling a significant void in the media in which industrial and organizational psychologists advance their understanding of their field. Such volumes can be less kaleidoscopic than our journals, as well as more focused than review chapters and yearbooks that scan developments in broad sectors of the field. By aiming to identify significant recent developments that may not yet have fallen into articulated patterns, these books can be more current than texts and professional works that seek to present integrated pictures of their subjects. This is the special and important niche among the publications in industrial and organizational psychology that the Frontiers of Industrial and Organizational Psychology series is designed to occupy. The success of this endeavor should facilitate progress in theory and research on the topics presented, while also abetting the transition from science to practice.

The editorial board has further specified the plan in the following particulars. First, the volumes are to be aimed at the members of the Society for Industrial and Organizational Psychology, in the hope and expectation that scholars, professionals, and advanced students in cognate fields will also find them of value. Second, each volume is to be prepared by an editor who is a leading contributor to the topic it covers and will also prepare commentary to integrate the chapters into a broader context. Third, the choice of topics and editors will be made by the editorial board, which will also consult with the volume editors in planning each book. The chairperson of the editorial board will serve as series editor and will coordinate the relationships and responsibilities of the volume editors, the editorial board, the series publisher, and the executive committee of the society. Fourth, volumes are to be issued when timely, rather than on a fixed schedule, but at a projected rate of approximately one a year. The series is to be called Frontiers of Industrial and Organizational Psychology.

Among the first decisions that had to be made by the editorial board was the choice of a publisher. After careful consideration of several proposals, Jossey-Bass was chosen on the basis of editorial support, production quality, marketing capability, and pricing, among other criteria.

The first volume in the series, *Career Development in Organizations*, edited by Douglas T. Hall (1986), has amply achieved our objectives, to judge by the number of sales, the laudatory book reviews, and the requests for rights to translate the book into other languages. The demand for that book is still strong and reflects its cutting-edge emphasis. It is our expectation that, given such careful attention, each of our books will remain up to date for years. Our second volume, titled *Productivity in Organizations*, was edited by John P. Campbell and Richard J. Campbell (1988). Already there are clear signs of its success.

As with the earlier volumes, *Training and Development in Organizations* was chosen because of its practical and scientific significance. The rate and scope of changes in work and technology require the acquisition of new and complex information, skills, and attitudes on the part of much of the work force, including managers and professionals. Those trends are placing an increasing premium on design and implementation of effective training programs. Our editorial board therefore regarded as both important and timely the preparation of a volume that would highlight significant recent theory and research to guide the development, application, and evaluation of such programs. For the planning and editing of this important work, we were able to recruit a leading expert on the subject, Irwin L. Goldstein. He in turn lined up a distinguished group of contributors. We are pleased to make available in this volume the product of all that talent.

In the near future, readers can expect the publication of two more volumes in this series — one on organizational climate and culture, to be edited by Benjamin Schneider, and the other on the relationship between work and other aspects of workers' lives, to be edited by Sheldon Zedeck.

The present volume is the last for which I will serve as series editor. I am pleased to say that my place will be taken by Irwin L. Goldstein, whose many scholarly, administrative, and editorial achievements, including his responsibilities for the present book, admirably qualify him for the role.

Over the last six years, this entire undertaking has required the cooperation and efforts of many able and dedicated people, most of whom must remain unnamed because of space limitations. I hope they know who they are; they have our deep

thanks. Space notwithstanding, I cannot refrain from acknowledging my colleagues on the editorial board, whose contributions have amply fulfilled our high expectations. The assistance
and cooperation of the staff at Jossey-Bass also require grateful
mention.

September 1989   Raymond A. Katzell
                                                   New York University
                                                   Series Editor

Preface

Training is a multifaceted phenomenon. For individuals, training opportunities are very important, because they are instrumental in affording entry into and enjoyment of the satisfactions and rewards that are associated with the world of work. In
that sense, training represents a positive hope both for people in
their first jobs and for those who are changing their work
environment. For scientists and practitioners of industrial and
organizational psychology, training is a traditional topic that
has been associated with the discipline from the earliest times.

Few topics have as many other, different research topics
associated with them. Training is concerned with basic adult
learning processes. It focuses on the development of theories
and methods to describe and specify the training needs of
organizations. It concentrates on interventions and how they
can be evaluated in complex organizational environments, and
it is concerned with systemwide interactions, such as the inter-
relationship between organizational factors and the success of
training interventions. The topic also attracts individuals who
are concerned with factors involved in the design of training
methods. Finally, the research also concerns the interaction of
training and social issues such as those affecting the hard-core
unemployed, aging workers, and people entering nontraditional careers.

Another interesting characteristic of work in training is
that while many of the same interests discussed here existed
many years ago, theory and research have lagged far behind
them. Only in the last decade has there been any considerable

development in research and theory in these areas. This book appears at a point when more researchers are focusing their attention on training issues. In addition, members of the Society for Industrial and Organizational Psychology hope that training will increasingly give individuals positive opportunities to enter and adapt to ever more complex workplaces. The demands of society on the one hand and the growing number of researchers interested in training on the other make for exciting possibilities.

The goal of this book is to stimulate further thought and research on topics that focus on training systems in the workplace. This volume is intended for teachers, researchers, practitioners, and, most of all, for graduate students who may be stimulated to choose these areas as a focus for their energy and thoughts. As befits the diversity of topics in the training area, this volume is also aimed at a diverse audience of individuals in industrial and organizational psychology, organizational behavior, management, education, and allied disciplines.

In Chapter One, I offer a perspective on past, present, and future training issues and a description of how the chapters in the book address many of these issues. The remainder of the book is divided into four parts. Part One consists of three chapters that address systems issues. In Chapter Two, Cheri Ostroff and J. Kevin Ford discuss needs-assessment strategies, including organizational, task, and person analysis. They offer a levels-of-analysis approach, which looks at what type and levels of data need to be collected in order to produce effective needs-assessment systems. In Chapter Three, Wayne F. Cascio presents a model and research agenda for the use of utility approaches as an evaluation model for training systems. The part closes with Chapter Four by Richard D. Arvey and David A. Cole, who discuss alternative evaluation models with regard to power, sample size, and the reliability of measures.

Part Two addresses advances in cognitive and instructional psychology. In Chapter Five, William C. Howell and Nancy Jaworski Cooke discuss recent developments in instructional and cognitive psychology and the research implications these developments have for training in an increasingly complex workplace. Edwin A. Fleishman and Michael D. Mumford, in Chapter Six, consider learning taxonomies, the type of learning needed at various stages in the training process, and how these factors will affect workers who are likely to be transferring their abilities frequently from one task or job to another. The part closes with Chapter Seven, by Gary P. Latham, describing the development of cognitive and behavioral theory and its relationship to an increasing number of effective training interventions.

The third part of the volume relates training to social systems issues. It begins with Chapter Eight by Harvey L. Sterns and Dennis Doverspike on the older worker and training systems. It continues with Chapter Nine by Manuel London and Emily Bassman, describing issues in training, retraining, and career growth that individuals and organizations will be confronting. In Chapter Ten, Daniel C. Feldman adds a further perspective on how individuals learn and are trained, considering socialization, resocialization, and training. This chapter reminds us that individuals do not learn about jobs and organizations just from formal training programs. Part Three closes with Chapter Eleven, by Simcha Ronen, who introduces the reader to training issues that have begun to affect both organizations and individuals facing increasingly multinational work environments.

The final part, Part Four, offers a series of commentaries by individuals familiar to all who have actively followed training research. Paul W. Thayer offers a historical perspective on how the field has changed—or remained the same—between the time his original training volume with William McGehee was published in 1961 and the publication of the present collection. John P. Campbell analyzes the implications of the volume for research and theory development. Kenneth N. Wexley's chapter, which closes Part Four and the book, presents his view concerning the volume's contributions to practice in organizations.

The opportunity to edit this volume has in all ways been a rewarding experience. My appreciation goes first of all to the Society for Industrial and Organizational Psychology, which has had the foresight to sponsor a Frontiers volume series. The society's supportiveness in developing these volumes is one of the reasons for the great pride that so many industrial and organizational psychologists take in the society.

I am also grateful to the editorial board of the series, both for choosing this topic and for selecting me to be the volume editor. In this regard, I am especially thankful for the insightful thoughts and support of Raymond A. Katzell, the retiring editor of the series. Ray sets the highest standards of scholarship while at the same time being a caring and supportive person. He has made working on this volume a very meaningful experience for me.

I also want to personally thank William Hicks and his staff at Jossey-Bass for their assistance and cooperation. Since Bill was the editor who took a chance on me by publishing my first book in the training area, it was especially wonderful to work with him again.

My special thanks go to an unusual group of authors, all of whom were as excited about this volume as I am. The work and efforts of these extremely busy thinkers made being editor of this volume a joy. There is more than some truth to the adage that if you want something to be done extremely well, you should find the busiest person to do it.

I also want to thank William Kirwan, president of the University of Maryland, who often covered for me on assignments so that I could finish my work on this book. All universities should be fortunate enough to have people like him as their leaders.

Finally, I am deeply grateful to my wife, Micki, who continually provides the love and support that permit me to enjoy such opportunities to make a contribution.

College Park, Maryland   Irwin L. Goldstein
September 1989

The Authors

Irwin L. Goldstein is professor and chair of the Department of Psychology at the University of Maryland. He received his B.B.A. degree (1959) from City College of New York and his M.A. (1962) and Ph.D. (1964) degrees from the University of Maryland, all in psychology. His research interests have focused on needs assessment and job analysis, evaluation models, and personnel systems, including selection and training systems. He is the author of the text *Training in Work Organizations* (2nd ed., 1986) and of the chapter on training and development in the 1980 *Annual Review of Psychology*. He is also the author of the training chapter for the second edition of the *Handbook of Industrial and Organizational Psychology* (in press), edited by Marvin Dunnette. Goldstein has served as president of the Society for Industrial and Organizational Psychology and as associate editor of both the *Journal of Applied Psychology* and *Human Factors*. He has been elected a fellow of the American Psychological Association and the Human Factors Society. In 1988, he became the second editor, following Raymond A. Katzell, of the Frontiers of Industrial and Organizational Psychology series, of which this book is the third volume.

Richard D. Arvey is professor of industrial relations at the University of Minnesota. He received his B.A. degree (1966) from Occidental College and his M.A. (1968) and Ph.D. (1970) degrees from the University of Minnesota, all in psychology. His research interests include staffing and selection, training evaluation, job satisfaction, and organizational behavior. He is on the editorial boards of *The Journal of Applied Psychology* and *Personnel Psychology*. He is the author of *Fairness in Selecting Employees* (1979) and has published widely in many of the academic journals associated with human resource management.

Emily Bassman is a manager of human resources forecasting and planning at Pacific Telephone. From 1978 to 1989, she held positions at AT&T in the areas of organization development, market research, human factors, and human resources strategy development. She received her B.A. degree (1973) from Indiana University in psychology and her Ph.D. degree (1978) from Stanford University in experimental psychology.

John P. Campbell is professor of psychology and industrial relations at the University of Minnesota. He received his B.S. (1959) and M.S. (1960) degrees from Iowa State University and his Ph.D. degree (1964) from the University of Minnesota, all in psychology. In 1971 he authored the first chapter in training and development in the *Annual Review of Psychology*. He is the author of *Managerial Behavior, Performance, and Effectiveness* (1970, with M. Dunnette, E. Lawler, and K. Weick) and is co-editor with Richard J. Campbell of *Productivity in Organizations: New Perspectives from Industrial and Organizational Psychology* (1988). From 1976 to 1982 he served as editor of the *Journal of Applied Psychology*. Campbell is currently the principal scientist for the Army Selection and Classification Project (Project A).

Wayne F. Cascio is professor of management at the University of Colorado, Denver. He wrote his contribution to this volume while he was a visiting scholar at the Wharton School, University of Pennsylvania. He is the author of four texts on human resource management, including *Costing Human Resources: The Financial Impact of Behavior in Organizations* (2nd ed., 1987). He received his B.A. degree (1968) from Holy Cross College in psychology, his M.A. degree (1969) from Emory University in experimental psychology, and his Ph.D. degree (1973) from the University of Rochester in industrial/organizational psychology.

David A. Cole is a clinical psychologist and assistant professor of psychology at the University of Notre Dame. He received his B.A. degree (1976) from Saint Olaf College in psychology and his M.A. (1980) and Ph.D. (1983) degrees from the University of Houston in clinical psychology.

Cole's main research activities have been in the areas of research design, depression in childhood, and mental retardation. His methodological interests focus on the use of linear structural equation modeling in the behavioral sciences. Before his appointment at Notre Dame, he served as the associate research director of the Consortium Institute for the Integration of Severely Handicapped Learners at the University of Minnesota.

Nancy Jaworski Cooke is assistant professor in the Psychology Department at Rice University. She received her B.A. degree (1981) from George Mason University in psychology and her M.A. (1983) and Ph.D. (1987) degrees from New Mexico State University in cognitive psychology. Cooke's research interests span the areas of cognitive psychology, artificial intelligence, and human/computer interaction. She has published papers on expertise, knowledge representation, memory, attention, knowledge acquisition techniques, and interface design.

Dennis Doverspike is assistant professor of industrial/ organizational psychology in the Psychology Department at the University of Akron, where he is also a fellow at the Institute for Life-Span Development and Gerontology. He received his B.S. degree (1976) from John Carroll University in psychology, his M.S. degree (1979) from the University of Wisconsin, Oshkosh, in clinical psychology, and his Ph.D. degree (1983) from the University of Akron in industrial/organizational psychology. His research and teaching interests include personnel psychology, training, and industrial gerontology. He is the author of twenty articles or book chapters in addition to the chapter in this book, and he has served as a consultant to several private and public sector agencies.

Daniel C. Feldman is professor of management and Business Partnership Foundation Fellow at the University of South Carolina College of Business Administration. He has previously served on the faculties of the University of Florida Graduate School of Business, Northwestern University's J. L. Kellogg Graduate School of Management, the University of Minnesota Industrial Relations Center, and Yale College. He is the author of *Managing Careers in Organizations* (1987) and coauthor of *Individual and Institutional Responses to Job Loss* (1990, with C. Leana). Feldman received his B.A. degree (1972) from the University of Pennsylvania in sociology, his M.A. degree (1974) from Yale University in administrative sciences, and his Ph.D. degree (1976), also from Yale University, in organizational behavior.

Edwin A. Fleishman is Distinguished University Professor of Psychology at George Mason University, where he is also director of the Center for Behavioral and Cognitive Studies. He was the editor of the *Journal of Applied Psychology* and is past president of the American Psychological Association's Divisions of Industrial Organizational Psychology, Evaluation and Measurement, and Engineering Psychology and also of the International Association of Applied Psychology. In 1980 he was the recipient of the American Psychological Association's Distinguished Scientific Award for the Applications of Psychology. Fleishman received his B.S. degree (1945) from Loyola College in chemistry, his M.A. degree (1949) from the University of Maryland in psychology, and his Ph.D. degree (1951) from Ohio State University, also in psychology. In 1982 he was awarded an honorary Doctor of Science degree by the University of Edinburgh.

J. Kevin Ford is associate professor of psychology at Michigan State University. His major research interests include training, performance assessment, and decision making. He has published articles on training needs assessment and evaluation and has acted as a consultant on training issues for several corporations and governmental agencies. He has also taught a management studies course in Sweden and recently completed a research fellowship with the United States Air Force. He received his B.S. degree from the University of Maryland in psychology and his M.A. (1979) and Ph.D. (1983) degrees from Ohio State University in industrial/organizational psychology.

William C. Howell is Herbert S. Autrey Professor of Psychology and Administrative Science at Rice University. He graduated from the University of Virginia in 1954 with a B.A. degree in psychology and earned his M.A. (1956) and Ph.D. (1958) degrees in psychology from the same institution. Previous positions include the directorship of the Human Performance Center at the Ohio State University and a professorship in the Ohio State Psychology Department. He chaired the Psychology Department at Rice from 1970 to 1987 and has served as consultant to numerous corporations and government agencies. His research, which has been the basis for several papers and books, was recognized in 1979 by Division 21 of the American Psychological Association with the Franklin V. Taylor Award. Howell is a fellow of the American Psychological Association and has held a variety of offices in that and other professional and scientific organizations. He is associate editor of the *Journal of Applied Psychology* and of *Human Factors*, and is a consulting editor for *Organizational Behavior and Human Decision Processes* and for *Human Performance*.

Gary P. Latham is Ford Motor Research Professor, chairman of the Department of Management and Organization in the Business School, and adjunct professor in the Department of Psychology at the University of Washington. He is a fellow in both the American and Canadian Psychological Associations and in the Academy of Management. He received his B.A. degree (1967) from Dalhousie University (Halifax, Nova Scotia) in psychology, his M.S. degree (1969) from the Georgia Institute of Technology, also in psychology, and his Ph.D. degree (1974) from the University of Akron in industrial/organizational psychology.

Manuel London is director of the Center for Labor/ Management Studies and professor in the W. A. Harriman

School for Management and Policy at the State University of New York, Stony Brook. From 1977 to 1989, London held a variety of human resources, organizational effectiveness, management development, and training positions at AT&T. He received his B.A. degree (1971) from Case Western Reserve University in psychology and philosophy and his M.A. (1972) and Ph.D. (1974) degrees from the Ohio State University in industrial and organizational psychology. He taught in the Department of Business Administration at the University of Illinois, Urbana, from 1974 to 1977.

Michael D. Mumford is associate professor of psychology at George Mason University. He received his B.A. degree (1979) from Bucknell University in psychology. His M.A. (1981) and Ph.D. (1983) degrees he received from the University of Georgia in industrial psychology and psychometrics.

Mumford's research interests include applied differential psychology, measurement, adult development, training, personnel selection, and job analysis. His experience in the training area includes the development of performance predictor models for the United States Air Force. He has also constructed management development systems for the U.S. Army and taught at the Georgia Institute of Technology. His books include *Patterns of Life Adaptation: The Ecology of Human Individuality* (1989, with others). He is currently working on two other books concerned with background data and innovation.

Cheri Ostroff is assistant professor in the Industrial Relations Center at the University of Minnesota. She received her B.A. degree (1982) from the University of Texas in psychology and both her M.A. (1985) and Ph.D. (1987) degrees from Michigan State University in psychology.

Simcha Ronen is professor of organizational psychology and comparative management at the Graduate School of Business Administration, Tel Aviv University, and previously was on the faculty of the Graduate School of Business, New York University. He received an engineering degree (1963) from the University of New Brunswick (Fredericton, New Brunswick) and a Ph.D. degree (1973) from New York University in psychology.

Harvey L. Sterns is professor of psychology and director and senior fellow of the Institute for Life-Span Development and Gerontology at the University of Akron. He is research professor and co-director at the Western Reserve Geriatric Education Center, Northeastern Ohio Universities College of Medicine. He received his B.A. degree (1965) from Bard College in biology and psychology, his M.A. degree (1968) from the State University of New York, Buffalo, in psychology, and his Ph.D. degree (1971) from West Virginia University in life-span developmental psychology. His research and teaching interests include industrial gerontological psychology, training and retraining, career development, and cognitive intervention. Sterns has published more than forty book chapters and articles. He has served as a consultant at the national, state, and local levels.

Paul W. Thayer has been professor and head of the Psychology Department at North Carolina State University since 1977. From 1954 to 1977 he rose from training researcher to senior vice-president at the Life Insurance Marketing and Research Association. He is a fellow of both the American Association for the Advancement of Science and the American Psychological Association and past president of the Society for Industrial and Organizational Psychology. He received B.S. degrees from the United States Merchant Marine Academy (1948) in marine engineering and from Pennsylvania State University (1950) in psychology and a Ph.D. degree (1954) from Ohio State University in industrial psychology.

Kenneth N. Wexley is professor of psychology and management at Michigan State University. He received his B.A. degree (1964) from the State University of New York, Buffalo, and his M.A. degree (1965) from Temple University, both in psychology, and his Ph.D. degree from the University of Tennessee in industrial/organizational psychology. His main research activities and experiences as a practitioner have been in the areas of personnel training, management development, and performance appraisal systems. In 1976, he was awarded the status of fellow by the American Psychological Association. He has coauthored five books, including *Developing Human Resources in Organizations* (1981, with G. Latham), and has written over sixty professional articles.

Training
and Development
in Organizations

1

Critical Training Issues: Past, Present, and Future

Irwin L. Goldstein

Training represents a positive hope, both for persons first entering the world of work and for individuals changing their work environments. When training is well designed, it gives individuals opportunities to enter the job market with needed skills, to perform in new functions, and to be promoted into new situations. This emphasis on training opportunities is consistent with the concept of work and its value as an activity of daily life. For most persons, training is instrumental for earning entry into and enjoying the satisfactions associated with the world of work.

At this time, employees, managers, and organizations are more and more frequently turning to training as a solution to work issues. This increased emphasis is reflected in a variety of ways. For example, labor unions insist that new contracts include opportunities for training, so that workers can meet technological changes in the workplace, and training is frequently offered as a court-imposed solution for individuals who have been victims of discrimination, to give them opportunities for equal employment. Well-designed training programs are likely to accomplish these goals, and there are expectations that training should be able to accomplish these purposes. To the degree that it is based on careful needs assessment, well-designed instructional strategies, and research strategies that will permit

1

the collection of data to provide feedback on necessary revisions, training is more likely to meet everyone's expectations.

Demographic trends (Cascio & Zammuto, 1987) make it clear that the rate of growth in the work force will seriously decline during the next decade. This will make it increasingly important for each individual to have opportunities to reach their maximum potential and will result in increased emphasis on the use of training programs, both for entry-level workers and for the more experienced. In addition, jobs are likely to become more technologically complex and to result in increased cognitive demands on individual workers. This situation is also likely to result in increased emphasis on the use of training as a way of preparing individuals for jobs. For persons involved in training research and design, these events present both a great opportunity and a challenge. The goal of this book is to present research and ideas that will stimulate further training research to meet the challenges of the future.

The purpose of this introductory chapter is to provide a context for the chapters in this volume. First, background on previous books and reviews, which have examined theory and research in the area of training and development, is presented. Next is a summary of the major research and theories that authors of these previous efforts have felt needed to be addressed. The chapter then discusses future changes facing work organizations that have implications for the direction of research and theory development on training issues. The chapter explores predicted changes in population demographics, as well as changes in organizations and workplaces. The final section readdresses the question of training issues in the context of these predicted changes.

A Short History of Training Texts and Reviews

While it is not feasible to discuss each of the research and theoretical articles that have had training as a primary focus, it is possible to present a short history of the major texts and review articles that have appeared in the industrial and organizational psychology literature, followed by a summary of the major training themes discussed by these authors and researchers. By reviewing those efforts, the interested reader can trace the research on many training topics. It is also important, however, to realize that the area of training is extremely broad; researchers in business and management, cognitive psychology, education, educational psychology, human factors, industrial and organizational psychology, instructional psychology, and organizational behavior have all contributed to the literature. For example, work regarding criterion-referenced measures has a long history in educational psychology, while research on machine simulators stems from the human factors literature. Each of these disciplines has its own research and practice journals. In addition, there are a number of societies that devote themselves exclusively to research and practice issues in the training area, including the American Society for Training and Development and the Instructional Systems Association. The emphasis in this chapter is on reviews and materials published in the industrial and organizational psychology literature that focus on critical issues relevant to training in work organizations, but any reader who refers to the reviews noted here will discover that they include important literature from all these different disciplines.

Training as a topic was introduced early in the history of psychology and scientific management. As noted by Latham (1988), Taylor's principles of scientific management, which date from 1911, discussed both selection of the best workers and extensive training, while at the same time Munsterberg, in 1913, focused on training as well as selection issues, first in the civilian sector and later in military populations during World War I. Chapters on training also appeared in most early industrial and organizational psychology textbooks (for example, Viteles, 1932). Nevertheless, most modern researchers trace the first systematic treatment of the major issues in training and development, as a topic in industrial and organizational psychology, to 1961, when McGehee and Thayer published their now classic text *Training in Business and Industry*. Many of the issues discussed today were originally introduced in that text, including such topics as the three-part approach to job analysis, which presented organizational analysis, task analysis, and person analysis as the critical components of training. One year later, Glaser (1962) edited a text that contained chapters on many issues still of concern, including needs assessment, criterion development, and learning processes for various tasks (complex skills, perceptual motor learning, and foreign language learning). Bass and Vaughan (1966) followed with a text that tended to focus heavily on the traditional learning issues involved in training programs.

In 1971, Campbell completed the first invited chapter on training in the *Annual Review of Psychology*. Campbell systematically examined the research and evaluation issues involving training systems. His thoughtful presentation, consistent with the views of McGehee and Thayer (1961), found that the work on training systems was lacking in the areas of needs-assessment and evaluation methodology. Campbell made the following observation: "By and large, the training and development literature is voluminous, non-empirical, non-theoretical, poorly written, and dull. As noted elsewhere, it is faddish to an extreme" (p. 565). This comment led other observers to offer a decade of complaints about the faddish nature of training, the design of training systems without needs assessment, and the failure to evaluate training systems. Campbell's observation also proved to be a challenge to a whole group of researchers who became interested in the very topics that he noted as missing from the research.

Goldstein's (1974) text was the first since McGehee and Thayer's (1961) to focus heavily on a systems view of training, with particular emphasis on needs assessment and evaluation. His book adopted a problem-solving approach to needs-assessment and evaluation methodology, focusing on what types of models could be used to gain information about the introduction of training systems. In that same year, Gagné and his colleagues published the first of a number of volumes (Gagné & Briggs, 1974, 1979; Gagné & Dick, 1983) on instructional psychology and on what would be eventually called cognitive learning principles and their potential relationship to instructional design.

Two years later, Hinrichs (1976) presented his work on

personnel training, in the first *Handbook of Industrial and Organizational Psychology* (Dunnette, 1976). This chapter was one of the first efforts to conceptualize training as a subsystem within all of the other systems in organizations. This work led other authors to begin considering systems issues, such as the interaction between selection and training systems. Also in that year, the American Society for Training and Development published the second edition of its *Training and Development Handbook* (Craig, 1976). This greatly expanded edition of the handbook had forty-seven chapters, with heavy emphasis on the practice and implementation issues involved in training and development.

Four years after that, Goldstein followed his text with the second invited *Annual Review of Psychology* chapter in 1980. He argued that while some of the literature did fit Campbell's description, there was nevertheless a growing substantive research literature. Goldstein pointed to positive developments in needs-assessment procedures, evaluation models appropriate for use in work organizations, and theory development and research on a number of techniques, such as behavioral role modeling. In 1981, Wexley and Latham published their text on training, which was followed in 1984 by Wexley's *Annual Review* chapter. These authors' efforts further contributed to a discussion of the issues in training, with particular emphasis on research issues and approaches concerning management training.

Goldstein's (1986) revision of his earlier book updated the literature on needs-assessment, evaluation, and training techniques. Also included in this volume were sections that related training systems to social system issues, such as fair employment, the hard-core unemployed, older workers, and women in nontraditional careers. Two years later, Latham (1988) emphasized the theoretical and research developments in training and specifically noted that it was time to be more optimistic about the progress being made on central issues. Similarly, Campbell (1988) commented, "Contrary to my somewhat negative view some eighteen years ago, the field of training and development has entered an exciting age and promises to become even more intense in the future" (p. 208). Campbell also noted important developments in cognitive and instructional psychology, which soon may prove useful for designing instructional systems related to behaviors that are to be learned. Goldstein (in press) has further updated information on the progress in training literature, for the second *Handbook of Industrial and Organizational Psychology*.

Past and Recent Training Themes

What are the recent summary themes that these commentators and analysts discuss, with respect to directions for training research?

The importance of needs assessment, as input for the development and evaluation of training techniques, continues to be emphasized, but analysts no longer lament the absence of methodology for needs assessment. Rather, the focus is on the outcomes expected as a result of the methodology and on how information should be collected about the job, the performer, and the organization.

Campbell (1988) notes the difference between a description of training needs and the performance capabilities expected to be the results of a training program. He says that it is necessary to become more explicit about what we mean by *competent* or *expert performance* and that we are likely to need systems for collecting data about expert performance. Goldstein (1986) also observes that one area of needs assessment that has an extremely limited theoretical and empirical base is organizational analysis. He maintains that there is little information available to help determine whether well-trained individuals will actually be able to transfer their learning into organizations. Wexley (1984) expresses a similar lament.

Goldstein (1974) has been concerned about several topics: the understanding of what behaviors are essential to the performance of job tasks, what type of learning is necessary for acquiring those behaviors, and what type of instructional content is best suited to accomplishing that form of learning. Goldstein's criticisms have taken various forms. He has rejected data related to basic learning variables as not relevant to adult learning in training situations, and he has called for the development of instructional systems relevant to adult learning. More recently, Campbell (1988) and Latham (1988) have noted promising theoretical developments in the cognitive and instructional areas. In particular, Latham (1988) points to the importance of self-efficacy in training, which stresses active participation that leads to accomplishment, extrinsic reinforcement, and goal setting. Similarly, Campbell (1988) points to the importance of evaluating learning methods in terms of whether they allow the trainer to actively produce the required performance and to receive feedback that is timely, accurate, and positive. Instructional models based on cognitive principles of learning are very recent developments, but for the first time there is a glimmer of hope that research is actually targeted on important instructional variables.

All reviewers have noted progress in thoughtful evaluation methodology. In particular, Latham and Saari (1979), Frayne and Latham (1987), and Komaki (1977) have been cited for their innovative use of evaluation designs in organizational environments. Nevertheless, most commentators (Campbell, 1988; Goldstein & Gessner, 1988) continue to call for research on other types of methodology, including the development of content-validity strategies, utility strategies, and research on the usefulness of various quasi-experimental designs.

Goldstein and his colleagues (Goldstein, 1986; Goldstein & Gessner, 1988; Goldstein & Gilliam, in press) have reminded readers about the complex systemic interactions that exist when training programs are used in interventions that involve fair employment, the hard-core unemployed, and older workers. They stress the careful matching that is required between training systems and organizational support systems. Unfortunately, research is lacking in many of these areas, and the issues are not yet well defined.

Wexley (1984) and Latham (1988) have noted changes in society, such as the increasingly international flavor of organizations and the increasing use of technology in the workplace. However, these authors lament the fact that little research or theoretical effort is available for discussion.

Given these current themes, it is interesting to speculate about what future training issues are likely to be. To do so, however, we must reflect on forthcoming changes in work organizations and on the persons who will be working in them.

Social Issues and Training

Coming changes in society are likely to have important implications for training. In some instances, such as the technological revolution, the changes have already started, but they are only beginning to stimulate researchers and commentators. For convenience's sake, it is possible to categorize these changes, although it is important to recognize that the categories are not necessarily independent of one another. The first category involves changes related to population demographics, including changes related to both the entry-level work force and the older work force. The second category involves changes in the workplace.

Demographic Changes

Entry-Level Workers. On the basis of past trends in the labor force, it is possible to project future trends with relative accuracy (Fullerton, 1985). The individuals who will enter the labor force in the year 2000 have already been born. Projections clearly indicate that the work force is changing (Fullerton, 1985) and thus will impact human resource management in a way never before seen (Cascio & Zammuto, 1987). According to the U.S. Bureau of Labor Statistics (Fullerton, 1985), the labor force will increase from its 1984 total of 114 million persons to 129 million by 1995, but the rate of growth will seriously decline over that time. One of the most important aspects of these trends is change in the composition of the work force.

Data reveal that the proportion of entry-phase youth will decline in later decades (Fullerton, 1985; Odiorne, 1986; Cascio & Zammuto, 1987). Summatively, what these age–work-force projections suggest is that the rate of increase in the work force will decline significantly in the upcoming decades, and that the number of new entrants, or those primarily between the ages of sixteen and twenty-four, will decrease substantially. Therefore, the number of individuals usually making up the entry pool and serving as selectees for industry will be dismal at best (Cascio & Zammuto, 1987). Of further interest is the age and ethnic composition of the future work force. Most people entering the labor force heretofore have been white and between the ages of sixteen and twenty-four, but decreases in this specific segment of the population will be substantive in the decades to come. By contrast, minority groups (such as blacks) between the same ages will increase in participation, from 13.5 percent in 1980 to an estimated 17.5 percent in future years (Fullerton, 1985). Therefore, of the reduced entry-pool population, it is estimated that minorities will represent an increasingly higher proportion (Cascio & Zammuto, 1987).

More Mature Workers. By the year 2000, 36 million people will be between the ages of forty-five and fifty-four (Sandell, 1987). Thus, while the proportion of entry-phase youth will decline in the decades to come, the percentage of the middle-aged labor force will increase substantially as the baby boomers of the past decades enter those age groups.

As compared to people between the ages of forty-five and fifty-five, workers fifty-five and older will be on the decline. Trend data indicate that what was an expanded older work force in 1970 began to diminish in 1980 and should continue diminishing (Fullerton, 1985). Several factors lead to this conclusion. For one thing, people acquire the largest gains in pension plans at the onset of their retirement eligibility. Thus, as more people become covered by pension plans, there will be a consistent drop in the number of available older workers (Wise, 1984–1985). Even if people over fifty-five take advantage of pension plans to retire, data indicate that their absence will be more than compensated for by the increase in workers between forty-five and fifty-five. Thus, the total proportion between the ages of forty-five and sixty-four will increase by the year 2020, to over 25 percent of the labor force (it was 20 percent in 1980). If the predictions about retirement prove incorrect, then these groups will obviously make up an even larger part of the work force.

Another important aspect of these projections involves the entry of women into the work force. Career aspirations, enhanced opportunities, and such supportive factors as child-care and flexible work arrangements have contributed to the participation of women in the labor force (Vaydanoff, 1987). Data show that during the early 1970s, entry-level participation by women between the ages of twenty and twenty-nine rose rapidly. By the late 1970s and early 1980s, that entry-level participation rate had dropped to a more moderate rate, which is projected to continue for women in this age group (Fullerton, 1985). This change in the trend for women entering the work force, from rapid to moderate, is partly related to changing norms encouraging women to be active parts of the work force even in areas previously considered nontraditional. Many analysts also believe that women and their spouses will reach a salary plateau, where earnings will no longer steadily increase. Therefore, to maintain their standard of living, women between thirty and forty-five may further increase their activity in the labor force. Taken as a whole, the female work force is expected to steadily increase in the coming decade. Before we consider how these data will influence training, it is important to examine what the world of work will probably be like in the year 2000 and how it will affect work organizations' dependence on work populations and training systems.

Changes in the Workplace

Technology and the World of Work. Prognostications concerning what the world of work is likely to be beyond the year 2000 are harder to judge than demographic changes. While virtually everyone who will be working in the year 2000 has already been born, data regarding the workplaces of the future must obviously be based more on educated guesses and opinions. Nevertheless, a few trends make it possible to speculate. There is a clear trend, for example, toward more highly technological and sophisticated systems. According to Cascio and

Zammuto (1987), its advocates believe that technology will increase productivity and product quality and, as a result, will permit America to regain its competitive edge. Computer-aided design and engineering, robots, and other automation systems are already transforming the workplace. It is extremely unlikely, however, that automation will make the country less dependent on workers. Increased technology requires a highly trained work force to design and operate the systems, and demographic predictions are that there will be relatively fewer such persons entering the work force in the year 2000 and beyond.

Shifts from Manufacturing to Service. There also appears to be a shift in our economy, from a manufacturing to a service orientation. The manufacturing share of our economy has decreased, from 33.7 percent in 1950 to 22.4 percent in 1980 (Cascio & Zammuto, 1987). Most service jobs are very labor-intensive and are not particularly amenable to automation. If this change results in increased demand for employees, it implies even more competition for entry-level workers. If technology does turn out to have an impact on service-oriented jobs (witness the use of automated banking services), then increased technology will have a major impact there as well as on manufacturing jobs.

Organizations and Global Markets. A future-oriented look at jobs and organizations clearly reveals growth in fluid market arrangements worldwide, and this development includes the need of organizations to learn how to function with individuals from cultures around the world. Add to these interesting and complicated interactions the fact that it is no longer unusual for a manufacturer to produce a product (for example, an automobile) that is partially manufactured in the United States and partially manufactured in a foreign country. Sometimes these enterprises involve arrangements between liaison teams that direct the overall efforts of different employees in different organizations in different countries, all contributing to the manufacture of a single final product.

Impact of Population and Work Changes on Training

We have already seen what various analysts have viewed as the major issues currently facing training researchers and theorists. It is interesting to consider what other issues will be facing training analysts, given the previously mentioned analyses of population and work changes.

Increased Emphasis on Instructional System Design. It is apparent that any description of future work organizations must view them as being more competitive and as operating in a more complex technological environment. Growth in technology and machine responsibility paradoxically increases demands on human beings. It gives individuals responsibility for increasingly "smart" machines, thereby also increasing the cognitive complexity for the human being. Instead of doing simple procedural and predictable tasks, people will become responsible for inferences, diagnoses, judgments, and decision making, often under severe time pressure. This development underscores Campbell's (1988) call for an understanding of expert performance and Goldstein's (1986) plea for research on types of instructional systems that can support different types of learning performance. It will also be necessary to understand learning abilities, as well as types of ability needed at different points in the learning process. Given that individuals are also likely, as a result of technology shifts, to respond to many job changes, it will be important to understand types of ability and how transfer of learning can occur. Finally, needs-assessment systems will have to become increasingly flexible in order to provide the required information. If job requirements will indeed be shifting quickly, it may become necessary, as argued by Schneider and Konz (1988), to figure out how to determine training requirements for jobs that do not yet exist.

Strategic Planning for Training. The kinds of concerns reflected in rapidly changing technologies involve a whole set of individual, organizational, and social issues. This point is clear in a statement concerning executives' expectations for workers at a new Mazda plant in Michigan: "They want their new employees to be able to work in teams, to rotate through various jobs, to understand how their tasks fit into the entire process, to spot problems in production, to trouble shoot, articulate the problems to others, suggest improvements, and write detail charts and memos that serve as a road map in the assembly of the car" (Vobejda, 1987, p. A14).

The implications for training systems' design are enormous. Added to this issue, however, is the rapid obsolescence of individuals who previously had very advanced training. If one considers the possible decline in the entry-level population, the importance of retraining and reeducating workers is even more obvious. It is also important not to overlook the interactions of this topic with research on training older populations. Our relative lack of knowledge concerning older workers is, in light of this topic, especially disheartening. At this point, strategic planning, retraining, and career planning are overlooked skills in the training process.

Cross-Cultural Training Issues. Wexley (1984) remarks on the dearth of recent research on cross-cultural issues. He cites a survey of 105 American companies with overseas units, where 68 percent of the branches have no training programs to prepare individuals for work abroad. The absence of such programs is often cited as a partial explanation for the relatively high failure rate (approximately 30 percent) of Americans abroad (Hays, 1971). A future-oriented look at jobs and organizations cannot help noting the growth in fluid market arrangements worldwide. Obviously, cross-cultural aspects of training programs are a topic about which we shall hear more in the future. This is another area for which needs-assessment procedures will have to be reconsidered, with organizational analysis becoming of even more concern than usual.

Increased Emphasis on Accountability. Competitive organizational environments have increased the number of questions about the utility of training programs and about what organizations gain from the resources they spend. It is not unusual for organizations to accept contracts with school systems, whereby payment is directly related to the degree of improvement that students show on standardized achievement tests. In management circles, it is becoming more common to question the effects of expensive training and development programs. This is a trend that will test the ingenuity of training analysts to determine the effectiveness of their programs—in terms of performance improvements, costs, and other subsidiary benefits—through the establishment of systematic evaluation.

Training and Available Work Populations. It is clear from demographic analysis that more attention will need to be given to the population of available workers. At the entry level, the decline in available individuals will probably mean that it will become more important for each person already to have the skills necessary for employment. At present, young people who are undereducated typically make up the largest portion of the unemployed. These people, who are labeled as hard-core unemployed, often are poor, undereducated, and members of minority groups.

Society will not be able to afford to lose this population from the world of work. There has been very little research on instructional strategies for successful interventions with this group. One of the few large-scale successful efforts was conducted in the military (Sticht, Armstrong, Hickey, & Caylor, 1987) and concluded that such basic skills as reading, writing, and arithmetic are best learned if practice material comes from the intended job. This study also featured very careful instructional design and support systems for the individual. More research in this area, including work that examines the possibility of increasing the formal ties between work organizations and public school systems, will be needed.

There are similar concerns about the lack of knowledge concerning training and older workers. It should be apparent that, with increased technology and the likely need for workers, many of the barriers that deter people from entering nontraditional careers (for example, barriers against women entering management or technologically oriented fields) will continue to disappear. Nevertheless, there is still a need for research on and analysis of constraints in the work environment. It does not help if an organization has a very successful training program, only to discover that people are prevented from using what they have learned because of constraints in their work environment. Goldstein and Gilliam (in press) indicate that there is no evidence for women's needing any special training different from that offered to men, if women are to succeed in work organizations. There is increasing evidence, however, that organizations that invite women into the world of work may need training to understand what types of support systems permit people to survive in and contribute to organizations.

Again, we need research and theory development in organizational analysis, as a component of needs analysis. We also need research on socialization and entry into work organizations. We have much to gain from examining training, both as socialization to work and as a program for learning skills and abilities relevant to job performance.

Plan of the Book

Part One: Training Systems Issues. Following the present chapter, which is designed to provide an overview of training issues, this book is divided into four parts. The three chapters in the first part explore needs-assessment and evaluation issues that have been a focus of concern ever since McGehee and Thayer (1961), Campbell (1971), and Goldstein (1974) noted that training systems require systematic research attention before energy can be profitably focused on particular training methods. Certainly, the growing emphasis on accountability, as well as the expectations that training approaches will be available to resolve future workplace issues, increases the need for understanding systems.

In Chapter Two, Cheri Ostroff and J. Kevin Ford refocus attention on McGehee and Thayer's original job-analysis strategy, consisting of organizational analysis, task analysis, and person analysis. They note that examination of these components requires different levels of analysis. This approach has implications for the type of data collected, for the type of questions asked in collecting data, and for determination of who the respondents should be in various phases of needs assessment. Ostroff and Ford also identify research questions that should be addressed when one is considering a levels-of-analysis perspective on needs assessment.

Chapter Three, by Wayne F. Cascio, concerns utility approaches for examining training programs. For years, researchers have been calling for an examination of procedures that can be used to establish the utility (or lack thereof) of training systems. Cascio presents models for these analyses and expresses gains from the use of training programs in a number of different measures, including dollars, percentage increases in output, and reductions in the size of the work force in order to accomplish work and dollar savings in payroll costs. He also examines assumptions and research questions that involve utility in a number of situations, including those where training effects remain strong each year or where the benefits decline over time.

In Chapter Four, Richard D. Arvey and David A. Cole extend the consideration of experimental designs used in evaluating training programs. They ask which methods can be used to assess change and what the advantages and disadvantages of these models are as used in field settings. Arvey and Cole explore such issues as sample-size requirements for each of these designs in order to detect change and the impact of unreliable measures on the assessment of change. In addition, they identify research areas that are increasingly becoming a focus of attention, including assumptions of measurement error in the choice of designs and the effects of selection bias on the choice of individuals undergoing training.

Part Two: Learning and Cognitive Issues. This part discusses cognitive and instructional psychology and its relationship to adult learning in training programs. The examination of basic learning variables and their relationship to training systems has a sad history. Until now, most commentators have concluded that little is known about adult learning, and that there is not enough information for either a research or an implementation agenda. The last decade has seen the beginning of a revolution in instructional and cognitive psychology, however.

Chapter Five, by William C. Howell and Nancy Jaworski Cooke, analyzes developments in these areas and their implications for training systems. Howell and Cooke examine the increase in cognitive complexity resulting from the technological revolution, and they discuss its implications for training. In addition, they introduce the reader to a number of instructional constructs that deserve further research attention. For example, most organizational psychologists have never heard the term *advanced organizers*, but this type of construct is likely to have more implications for understanding human learning in training systems than have such time-honored constructs as ratio schedules of reinforcement. Moreover, changes in the workplace, along with the limited number of new entrants to the job market, make it likely that older workers will increasingly need retraining.

In Chapter Six, Edwin A. Fleishman and Michael D. Mumford explore learning abilities and the types of ability needed at various points in the learning process. They also discuss types of abilities and how transfer of learning can occur. Fleishman and Mumford consider several decades of studies on learning taxonomies and their implications for training research. Unraveling these mysteries will probably become increasingly important for researchers as job incumbents are expected to transfer their learning from one complex cognitive task to another.

In Chapter Seven, Gary P. Latham reviews behavioral approaches to training and learning in organizations. This chapter clearly demonstrates how theory, in conjunction with empirical investigations, can contribute to the development of instructional techniques. Latham also explores early developments in behavioral analysis, traces the development of techniques such as behavioral role modeling, and concludes with a discussion of other strategies, including self-management techniques, which are only beginning to be explored.

Part Three: Social System Issues in Training Research. In Chapter Eight, Harvey L. Sterns and Dennis Doverspike offer the first chapter ever published in organizational psychology literature on aging and training issues. Previous articles have emphasized aging and performance on basic laboratory tasks, such as flicker fusion and memorization of nonsense syllables. Sterns and Doverspike report on what is known about training effects when the focus is on training and performance in the workplace. Given the aging work force and the coming changes in technology, this chapter is probably only the beginning of a series of discussions on this important topic.

Closely related to these issues is Chapter Nine, by Manuel London and Emily Bassman on training and retraining. The authors focus on what retraining issues we are likely to face in the future. They discuss the changing workplace, the future of work organizations, and the implications of these changes for research and theory development.

In Chapter Ten, Daniel C. Feldman continues the discussion of entry, training, and retraining by presenting a perspective on socialization, resocialization, and training. It has been clear to many observers that learning and training for individuals in organizations occurs in a variety of ways, only some of which involve formal training programs. Feldman explores the kind of learning that occurs through socialization, along with its implications for the individual entering a work organization. These issues are also important for understanding what occurs when minorities and women enter organizations. Feldman's research agenda for these issues could keep investigators busy for many years.

The final formal chapter in this volume is Chapter Eleven, where Simcha Ronen challenges the organizational community to consider global trends that will require individuals to work in an international environment. He asks research questions about international assignees, including who should be trained, what they need to learn, how training should occur, and who should conduct it. This chapter, along with Chapter Eight, offers the first systematic exploration of themes that are likely to be increasingly important to the future of work organizations.

Part Four: Commentaries on the Training Issues. Three commentators offer their perspectives on the chapters in this book. First, Paul W. Thayer (coauthor, with McGehee, of the first major text exploring training issues) offers a historical perspective. He asks what is new, what has changed, and where we have been going since their book was published in 1961.

Next, John P. Campbell explores what the book offers to the development of theory and research. He offers his perspective on whether the present volume takes a step forward in presenting relevant issues for the research community and on whether the issues discussed here will stimulate theory and research among industrial and organizational psychologists concerned with research training and development.

In conclusion, Kenneth N. Wexley examines the contributions of this book for the industrial/organizational psychologist concerned with practice, asking how they are likely to affect the future of training programs in organizations.

References

Bass, B. M., & Vaughan, J. A. (1966). *Training in industry: The management of learning*. Belmont, CA: Wadsworth.

Campbell, J. P. (1971). Personnel training and development. *Annual Review of Psychology, 22*, 565–602.

Campbell, J. P. (1988). Training design for performance improvement. In J. P. Campbell & R. J. Campbell (Eds.), *Productivity in organizations* (pp. 177–215). San Francisco: Jossey-Bass.

Cascio, W. F., & Zammuto, R. F. (1987). *Societal trends and staffing policies*. Denver: University of Colorado Press.

Craig, R. L. (Ed.). (1976). *Training and development handbook*. New York: McGraw-Hill.

Frayne, C. A., & Latham, G. P. (1987). The application of social learning theory to employee self-management of attendance. *Journal of Applied Psychology, 72*, 387–392.

Fullerton, H. N., Jr. (1985). The 1995 labor force: BLS' latest projections. *Monthly Labor Review, 117*, 17–25.

Gagné, R. M., & Briggs, L. J. (1974). *Principles of instructional design*. New York: Holt, Rinehart & Winston.

Gagné, R. M., & Briggs, L. J. (1979). *Principles of instructional design* (2nd ed.). New York: Holt, Rinehart & Winston.

Gagné, R. M., & Dick, W. (1983). Instructional psychology. *Annual Review of Psychology, 34,* 261–295.

Glaser, R. (1962). *Training research and education.* Pittsburgh, PA: University of Pittsburgh Press.

Goldstein, I. L. (1974). *Training: Program development and evaluation.* Monterey, CA: Brooks/Cole.

Goldstein, I. L. (1980). Training in work organizations. *Annual Review of Psychology, 31,* 229–272.

Goldstein, I. L. (1986). *Training in organizations: Needs assessment, development, and evaluation* (2nd ed.). Monterey, CA: Brooks/ Cole.

Goldstein, I. L. (in press). Training in work organizations. In M. D. Dunnette (Ed.), *Handbook of industrial and organizational psychology* (2nd ed.). Palo Alto, CA: Consulting Psychologists Press.

Goldstein, I. L., & Gessner, M. J. (1988). Training and development in work organizations. In C. L. Cooper & I. Robertson (Eds.), *International review of industrial and organizational psychology* (pp. 43–72). London: Wiley.

Goldstein, I. L., & Gilliam, P. (in press). Training system issues in the year 2000. *American Psychologist.*

Hays, R. D. (1971). Ascribed behavioral determinants of success/ failure among U.S. expatriate managers. *Journal of International Business Studies, 2,* 40–46.

Hinrichs, J. R. (1976). Personnel training. In M. D. Dunnette (Ed.), *Handbook of industrial and organizational psychology* (pp. 829–860). Skokie, IL: Rand McNally.

Komaki, J. L. (1977). Alternative evaluation strategies in work settings: Reversal and multiple-baseline designs. *Journal of Organizational Behavior Management, 1,* 53–77.

Latham, G. P. (1988). Human resource training and development. *Annual Review of Psychology, 39,* 545–582.

Latham, G. P., & Saari, L. M. (1979). The application of social learning theory to training supervisors through behavioral role modeling. *Journal of Applied Psychology, 64,* 239–246.

McGehee, W., & Thayer, P. W. (1961). *Training in business and industry*. New York: Wiley.

Odiorne, G. S. (1986). The crystal ball of HR strategy. *Personnel Administrator, 31*, 104.

Sandell, S. H. (1987). Prospects for the older workers: The demographic and economic context. In S. H. Sandell (Ed.), *The problem isn't age: Work and older Americans*. New York: Praeger.

Schneider, B., & Konz, A. M. (1988). *Strategic job analyses*. Unpublished manuscript, Department of Psychology, University of Maryland, College Park.

Sticht, T. G., Armstrong, W. B., Hickey, D. T., & Caylor, J. S. (1987). *Cast-off youth*. New York: Praeger.

Vaydanoff, P. (1987). Women's work, family and health. In K. S. Koziara, M. H. Moskow, & L. D. Tanner (Eds.), *Working women: Past, present, and future*. Washington, DC: Bureau of National Affairs, Inc.

Viteles, M. (1932). *Industrial psychology*. New York: Norton.

Vobejda, B. (1987, April 14). The new cutting edge in factories. *The Washington Post*, p. A14.

Wexley, K. N. (1984), Personnel training. *Annual Review of Psychology, 35*, 519–551.

Wexley, K. N., & Latham, G. P. (1981). *Developing and training human resources in organizations*. Glenview, IL: Scott, Foresman.

Wise, D. A. (1984–1985). Labor aspects of pension plans. *HBER Reporter*, 23–25.

PART ONE

Training Systems Issues

2

Assessing Training Needs: Critical Levels of Analysis

Cheri Ostroff
J. Kevin Ford

Advancements in personnel research are likely when the concepts and theoretical perspectives of organizational psychology
are integrated into the concepts and perspectives of the personnel literature (Schneider & Schmitt, 1986). The personnel
research–related area of training has been particularly singled
out as being faddish and technique-oriented, with little concern
for the development of theories (Goldstein, 1986; Hinrichs,
1976; Moore & Dutton, 1978). Hinrichs (1976) concludes that
the content and emphasis of training may have changed, but the
way in which training is developed and evaluated has evolved
very little.

The focus of this chapter is on the assessment of training
needs, since this step provides critical input into the development and evaluation of training programs. It is our contention
that the emerging literature in organizational psychology on
levels-of-analysis issues (Roberts, Hulin, & Rousseau, 1978; Rousseau, 1985) provides a theoretical framework for viewing the
anlaysis of training needs. The levels perspective forces training

Note: The authors would like to thank Richard D. Arvey, Raymond Noe, Irwin
L. Goldstein, and Raymond A. Katzell for their helpful comments.

researchers to explicitly acknowledge the importance of understanding relationships among characteristics of organizations, groups, and individuals. The integration of levels concepts with the traditional concepts of needs assessment forms a theoretical perspective that provides a framework for more systematic research on needs-assessment issues.

This chapter is divided into four sections. First, the literature on training needs assessment is reviewed and critiqued. Second, the levels-of-analysis perspective is introduced. Third, a conceptual model of training needs assessment, which incorporates levels issues within the traditional concepts of needs assessment, is developed. The fourth section presents new research directions derived from the conceptual model of training needs assessment, as well as practical guidelines for conducting needs assessment from the levels perspective.

Training Needs Assessment

There is little disagreement among training researchers (for example, Bass & Vaughan, 1966; Goldstein, 1986; McGehee & Thayer, 1961; Wexley & Latham, 1981) that a thorough assessment of the organization's needs is of utmost importance and should be conducted before the development of a training program. Training needs assessment provides information on where training is needed, what the content of the training should be, and who within the organization needs training in certain kinds of skills and knowledge (Wexley, 1984). In this section, McGehee and Thayer's (1961) framework, which has structured the needs-assessment literature, is reviewed, and the need for a new and expanded theoretical perspective on training needs assessment is addressed.

Framework for Training Needs Assessment. McGehee and Thayer (1961) introduce a framework for understanding the needs-assessment process. It identifies three critical and interrelated components: organizational analysis, operations (or task) analysis, and person analysis. Organizational analysis emphasizes the study of the entire organization, its objectives, its resources, and the allocation of those resources, as they are related to the organizational objectives (McGehee & Thayer, 1961). It involves the examination of a number of factors, such as efficiency indexes and productivity records, to determine the extent to which organizational goals are being met. An assessment must also be performed to determine whether training is a viable strategy for accomplishing organizational goals.

Once an organizational analysis has been conducted to identify where training is needed (for example, in a department or a work group), a task analysis determines the activities performed on the job and the conditions under which the jobs are done (Goldstein, 1986). Information is often collected regarding the knowledge and skills needed for effectiveness on the job.

A person analysis focuses on determining which employees need training and what kinds of training are required (McGehee & Thayer, 1961). This step involves the determination of how well employees are doing their jobs, through such measures as performance evaluation and job-knowledge tests. When individuals perform below standard levels, analyses must be conducted to determine whether training will be the solution to the performance problems.

The framework developed by McGehee and Thayer (1961) has been the major contributor to the ordering of the complex problems that surround training needs assessment. The framework has been praised as the most comprehensive and sophisticated one for considering training needs (Wexley, 1984). Moore and Dutton (1978) use the framework to categorize the various techniques employed for determining training needs. Recent reviews of the training literature have used the framework for organizing and discussing the needs-assessment literature (Goldstein, 1980; Wexley, 1984).

A New Perspective. It has been over twenty-five years since the introduction of the tripartite system for identifying training needs. Since then, the needs-assessment literature in the training area has focused on the expansion, formalization, and creation of specific techniques for data collection (Moore & Dutton, 1978). Consequently, organizational, task, and person analyses can best be viewed as descriptive labels for groups of related data-collection methods, rather than as a conceptual framework that drives research on training needs assessment. The lack of conceptual development in the needs-assessment literature has persisted despite McGehee and Thayer's (1961) caveat that their framework is only one of many possible approaches to the understanding of training needs analysis.

Training researchers and analysts have implicitly acknowledged the importance of incorporating both macro (organizational) and micro (group and individual) perspectives into training research (Goldstein, 1986; Moore & Dutton, 1978). For example, Hinrichs (1976) conceptualizes the training system as existing on three levels: those of the individual, the training department, and the organization. Of more specific relevance to needs-assessment issues is McGehee and Thayer's (1961) contention that individual and organizational goals may be the results of inadequate skills, insufficient knowledge, or inappropriate attitudes. McGehee and Thayer also state that the examination of organizational climate must begin with the "unity" level of the company and continue through the departmental and divisional levels, until an adequate picture of the training situation emerges. Moore and Dutton (1978) suggest that research on training needs has focused mainly on the individual as the relevant unit of analysis and has ignored work groups and internal group processes.

The notion of multiple levels of analysis is implicit in training research, but it has not been given explicit consideration (Dansereau & Markham, 1987); failure to recognize levels-of-analysis concepts explicitly can result in confusion, misinterpretation of data, and inefficiency in utilizing resources. In fact, a more rigorous and scientific consideration of levels-of-analysis issues has been cited as essential to the advancement of social science (Mossholder & Bedeian, 1983; Roberts, Hulin, & Rousseau, 1978; Rousseau, 1985).

Over the last decade, the levels-of-analysis literature has expanded, and the concepts underlying that approach have been clarified. Explicit use of the levels perspective on training needs analysis can lead to advances, both in the conceptual and in the operational domains. This perspective also reflects more adequately the complexity and the structuring of the training function and of the organization. In the next section, we briefly review the important components of the levels perspective that are most relevant to the development of a new theoretical perspective for training needs assessment.

Components of the Levels-of-Analysis Perspective

The levels-of-analysis perspective is an extension of the general systems paradigm. It posits that events should be viewed within their larger contexts; it is impossible to understand complex events by reducing them to their individual elements (Von Bertalanffy, 1975, 1980). Any particular system must be viewed as a subsystem of some still larger system (Lewin, 1951). The systems are seen as interrelated, such that the properties of the system and its components are changed if the system is disassembled in any way (Ashmos & Huber, 1987).

These general assumptions form the basic elements of the levels perspective. To build a research model from the levels perspective, several steps need to be taken. First, the system being studied must be decomposed into subsystems or levels. Second, the conceptual variables of interest must be identified for each level of analysis. Third, operational measures of the conceptual variables of interest must be specified for each level. Finally, information gathered on the relationships among variables in the model must be interpreted at the appropriate level(s) of analysis.

Identification of Levels. A paradox of the general systems paradigm is that the notion of systems' interrelatedness makes it impossible to test any models, since nothing can be separated from the larger system (James, Muliak, & Brett, 1982). From the levels perspective, a system is viewed as nearly decomposable (Simon, 1973), which means that it can be divided into relatively independent subsystems, or levels, yet maintain the original system's characteristics. Interactions among subsystems are viewed as weak but not negligible. Therefore, while mechanisms at any particular level can be studied as relatively autonomous functions within the hierarchical system, interactions among levels are also important considerations.

Vertical differentiation of levels is also possible, because the time processes at any given level differ from those at other levels. Higher levels are said to have slower time scales than lower levels do (Simon, 1969; Mesarovic, Macko, & Takahara, 1970). Adjacent levels have more similar time scales for processes than do levels that are farther apart.

From the levels perspective, hierarchical structure allows for the vertical segregation of hierarchical levels (Rousseau, 1984). Organizational researchers typically have used the terms *organizational, subunit,* and *individual* to denote the hierarchical ordering of organizational levels (for example, Indik, 1968). The *organizational* level refers to the entire system, without reference to specific individuals or groups. The *subunit* level refers to each formal work group in the organization, without consideration of individual workers. The *individual* level refers to a single person in a work group.

Conceptualization. The levels perspective requires the specification of constructs for each level (organizational, subunit, and individual). Once the constructs of interest have been determined, consideration must be given to the development of theories that specify how the constructs or variables are related within and across levels. The levels issues relevant to the conceptualization of variables include isomorphism, bond strength, constraints, and the distinction between parts and wholes.

In developing a conceptual model from the levels perspective, one must consider the functional similarities that exist across levels, and particularly across adjacent levels (Indik, 1968). *Isomorphism* (Van Gigh, 1978; Von Bertalanffy, 1980), a basic element of the levels perspective, refers to the generalizability of constructs across levels; that is, there are general characteristics, exhibited by all systems, that represent similar processes in all the systems. Isomorphic constructs have also been labeled "composition models" (see Rousseau, 1985).

For mechanisms to be generalized across levels, the constructs of interest must have similar meanings across levels (Roberts, Hulin, & Rousseau, 1978). A construct at one level is therefore related to another form of the construct at a different level (James, 1982). Functionally similar or isomorphic constructs (for example, goals, tasks, or climate) must be determined independently for each level. Moreover, concepts at higher levels should be defined more broadly than those at lower levels (Mesarovic, Macko, & Takahara, 1970) and may include more elements than a similar concept does at a lower level. As an illustration, the general objectives at the organizational level (for example, "increase quality") must be translated into individual-level objectives that are much more specific ("reduce scrap by 10 percent over the next month").

Relationships among variables can operate at multiple levels simultaneously. Mechanisms at any particular level can be conceptualized as relatively autonomous functions within the hierarchical system, but it is also important to specify interactions among levels. Behavior and relationships across levels can be viewed as bonded together, such that variables at one level may affect or be affected by variables at an adjacent level (Indik, 1968; Rousseau, 1984).

The notion of *bond strength* (Simon, 1973) refers to the degree of interaction between components or levels, such that the behavior of one influences another. Bond strength is greatest between systems or levels closest to each other in the hierarchy (Rousseau, 1984). For example, technology at the subunit or group level has a greater influence on individual task design than does the more general notion of technology at the organizational level.

Consideration must be also given to variables that constrain or limit the freedom of an outcome of any component in the system (Pattee, 1973); that is, conceptual models should be developed to specify the variables that may influence or constrain the constructs of interest.

Constraints can be of two types—exteroceptive and interoceptive (Borich & Jemelka, 1982). Exteroceptive constraints, often referred to as *cross-level effects*, reflect the impact that variables or phenomena at one level have on variables at a lower level. For example, the surrounding technology of the work environment constrains both task design and the tasks needed for the performance of individual jobs (Griffin, 1982). Interoceptive constraints (sometimes referred to as *level-specific effects*) represent influences in processes within a single level, such as those found in means-end chains or in causal links among variables within a level. An example of an interoceptive constraint is an individual's motivation to learn, which affects the acquisition of knowledge.

It is also important to consider theories where levels of analysis are concerned (Dansereau, Alluto, & Yammarino, 1984; Roberts, Hulin, & Rousseau, 1978). Dansereau and his colleagues contend that a distinction must be made between *parts* and *wholes*. In developing theoretical frameworks, researchers must explicitly consider whether they are interested in differences between whole entities (say, differences between individuals) or in differences within an entity (say, differences in an individual's skill levels across various tasks).

Operationalization. With the levels perspective, once the appropriate constructs have been conceptualized, the operationalization of these variables must be made consistent with the levels for which they were conceptualized. A growing body of literature on empirical procedures for examining research incorporates levels-of-analysis issues (see Dansereau, Alluto, & Yammarino, 1984; Dansereau & Markham, 1987; James, 1982; James, Demaree, & Wolfe, 1984). Rather than describe the data-analysis techniques used in levels research, in this section we shall focus on some important issues that researchers must consider when operationalizing variables from the levels perspective. The two major considerations are the unit of theory and the issue of aggregation.

The *unit of theory* refers to the organizational level on which a theory is based (Roberts, Hulin, & Rousseau, 1978). From the levels viewpoint, the unit of theory should dictate the level or levels selected for observation and measurement (Mossholder & Bedeian, 1983); for example, a goal that each group should be producing at a certain level represents a group-level goal, and the operations of each group should be assessed to determine whether the group as a whole is meeting this objective. Individual performance on tasks is not a concern, since the group mean is the level of analysis that matches the level of conceptualization. Only when goals are couched in individual terms (for example, person A should be producing x units) should individual performance be the focus of attention. Consequently, researchers must clearly identify the unit of theory for the constructs of interest and measure the variables at the appropriate level(s) of analysis.

Ensuring congruence between conceptualization and operationalization is not easy and may pose some difficulties for the assessment of constructs and the examination of relationships. The preferable approach is to develop constructs and corresponding operationalizations at the same level of analysis (Glick, 1985; Roberts, Hulin, & Rousseau, 1978; Rousseau, 1984). When this approach cannot be used, *aggregation of responses* may be an appropriate strategy. Aggregation of responses occurs when measures are derived from one level (say, from the individual level) and then aggregated or averaged to represent another level (say, the subunit level). For example, a measure of organizational climate would ask individuals about their perceptions of the climate for their units as a whole, rather than in relation to their individual situations, and then aggregate those perceptions, to represent climate at the organizational level (Schneider, 1985).

Interpretation. Once data have been gathered to test theoretical perspectives, inferences congruent with the unit of theory must be made. For example, if the interest is in an organizational-level variable (such as organizational technology), then inferences drawn from the measures of this construct should represent the organizational level. One potential interpretational pitfall involves *cross-level inference*, which refers to the common error of inferring relations among variables at one level from analyses performed at a different level. Such inferences often occur when data are gathered from one level and then aggregated and interpreted to represent a construct at another level. For example, in job analysis, incumbents are often asked to rate the importance of the tasks they perform. Responses are then aggregated across individuals, to determine the importance of each task for each job.

Aggregation is often a useful strategy, but inappropriate conclusions may be drawn when constructs are not appropriately measured and are interpreted at levels of analysis to which they are not related. In particular, there is the danger of fallacious reasoning when the unit to which an inference refers is smaller or larger than the unit of theory. This has been termed the "fallacy of the wrong level" (Mossholder & Bedeian, 1983).

In drawing cross-level inferences, it is crucial to ensure that interpretations drawn from aggregated data represent the unit of theory upon which the construct of interest is based. Aggregations should represent high levels of agreement among perceivers in a common context (Jones & James, 1979) before the aggregated data are interpreted to represent a unit of theory.

Summary of Levels Issues. Table 2.1 presents a summary of the levels-of-analysis issues relevant to training needs assessment. The system must first be decomposed into its hierarchical levels (organizational, subunit, and individual). The relevant constructs are then identified, with attention given to the conceptual issues of isomorphism, bond strength, constraints, and parts versus wholes. Operationalization of these constructs follows, and unit of theory and aggregation are considered. Finally, interpretations are drawn from the operationalizations, with attention paid to cross-level inferences. Throughout this process, it is crucial that variables be conceptualized, measured, and interpreted to reflect appropriate levels of analysis. Careful adherence to levels issues will promote appropriate conclusions about relationships within and across levels.

A Model of Training Needs Assessment from the Levels Perspective

The literature on training needs assessment has traditionally focused on the development of better techniques and

Table 2.1. Summary of Levels Issues.

Identification of Levels	
Organizational	the entire organizational system, without reference to specific individuals or groups
Subunit	each formal work group operating in the organization, without consideration of individual workers
Individual	a single person performing in a work group
Conceptualization	
Isomorphism	the functional similarity of constructs across levels
Bond strength	the degree of interaction between variables at different levels
Constraints	the impact that variables at one level have on variables within and across levels
Wholes/parts	the specification of differences between whole entities or differences within an entity
Operationalization	
Unit of theory	the unit on which a theory is based, dictating the level(s) selected for observation and measurement
Aggregation	appropriate aggregation of responses from one level to represent a construct at a different level
Interpretation	
Cross-level inference	the appropriate inferring of relations among variables at one level from measures derived from a different operational level

methods for improving the quality of information collected about organizational, task, and person analyses. Numerous variables and techniques have been identified, but they have yet to be placed in a theoretical framework. The differentiation of training needs by levels is crucial to understanding training needs assessment, as is the incorporation of any issues of conceptualization, operationalization, and interpretation that are relevant to levels of analysis. This section presents a model of training needs assessment from the levels-of-analysis perspective. The isomorphic constructs relevant to this new model of training needs assessment are also described.

Figure 2.1 presents a model for considering training needs assessment from the levels perspective. The model casts

Figure 2.1. A Model of the Levels Perspective
on Training Needs Assessment.

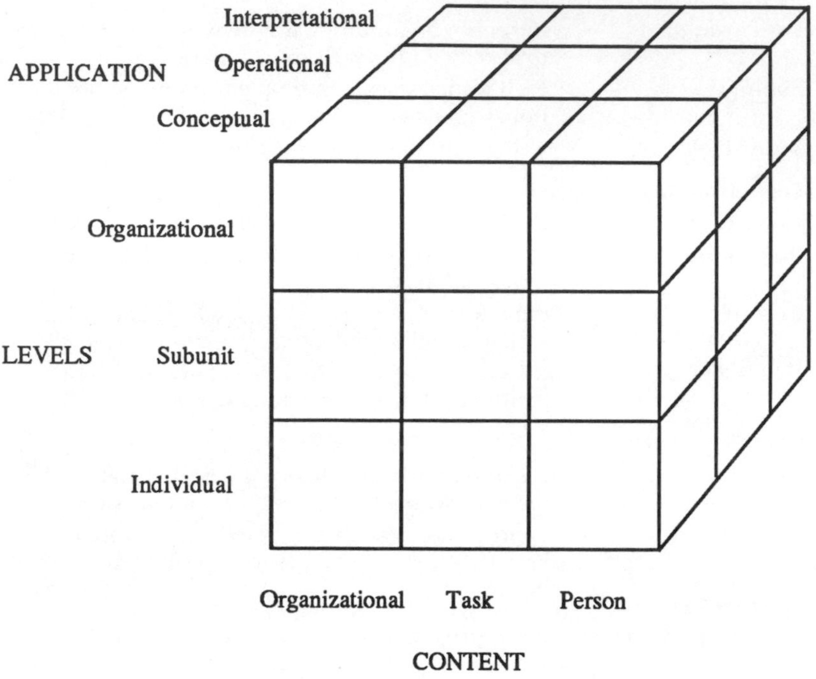

training needs assessment within a tripartite framework that involves a training content, organizational level, and application.

The first component of the new model is its three content
areas (organizational, task, and person analysis). We retain the
labels used by McGehee and Thayer (1961), because these three
content areas are entrenched in the training literature and,
more important, they capture the major types of information
that can be collected during a training needs assessment.

The second component of the model expands the basic
framework of McGehee and Thayer by differentiating the three
content areas according to organizational, subunit, and individual levels of analysis. (It is possible, of course, to identify
more than three levels of analysis, since the total depends on the
number and types of groups in the organization. For example,

work groups may be identified as belonging to a lower echelon, and functional departments as belonging to a higher echelon, when the group level is examined as an entity. The environment surrounding the organization can also be considered as another level of analysis.) This differentiation makes explicit the notion that a needs assessment must deal with issues at the organizational, subunit, and individual levels of analyses. For example, a task analysis at the organizational level would involve determining the basic tasks performed or technology used by all the people in an organization, while the same analysis at the individual level would focus on the tasks that each individual performs in the organization. A subunit-level task analysis would focus on the tasks performed or technology used by each work group.

The third component of the model adds depth by incorporating the issues of conceptualization, operationalization, and interpretation. Constructs relevant to training needs assessment across the three levels and the three content areas (that is, the nine cells on the front face of the twenty-seven-cell matrix of the figure) must be identified and defined. In the identification of the constructs, the conceptual issues of isomorphism, bond strength, constraints, and parts versus wholes must be considered. Operationalization concerns the development of measures that adequately tap the constructs of interest for each level and content area (that is, the middle nine cells of the matrix, relevant to the intersection of levels, content, and operationalization). When one is developing measures for use in a training needs assessment, the unit of theory and the aggregation of responses become important considerations. Interpretation is concerned with ensuring that the inferences drawn from a training needs assessment (see the last row of nine cells in the matrix) are consistent with the conceptual definitions and operational measurements, regardless of the level of analysis or content area addressed. In interpreting information from a needs analysis, the appropriateness of cross-level inferences must be examined.

To summarize, this new model of training needs assessment indicates that aspects of the individual, subunit, and organizational levels must be taken into account with respect to variables that involve organizational, task, and person analysis. The model also requires the specification of constructs, operationalizations, and interpretations, which are clearly defined for each organizational level and content area.

Conceptualization and the Identification of Isomorphic Constructs. Figure 2.1 shows that training needs can be more fully delineated when constructs and their relationships are mapped across the three training content areas and the three organizational levels. In developing our typology of training needs constructs, we reviewed the organizational psychology and training literatures to identify characteristics relevant to training needs across the three levels of analysis. This section presents a framework that specifies the key organizing constructs for organizational, task, and person analysis. In each of these three content areas, we develop isomorphic constructs for the organization, subunit, and individual levels of analysis.

The needs-assessment literature on training has defined *organizational analysis* as the study of the entire system in terms of its goals, resources, and performance. The integration of the levels perspective into needs assessment demonstrates how limited a view of organizational analysis this is, since it ignores issues across multiple levels of analysis.

It has been proposed that organizational analysis is composed of two basic dimensions or constructs. One dimension pertains to the examination of the goals, objectives, and values of the unit that is the focus of the analysis (Etzioni, 1964; Goldstein, 1986; McGehee & Thayer, 1961). As is consistent with past research, goals are considered to be sets of constraints that limit an entity's scope of action (Simon, 1964). The other dimension of organizational analysis involves time orientation (Lawrence & Lorsch, 1967; McGrath & Kelley, 1986). On the basis of recent work by McGrath and his associates (McGrath & Kelley, 1986; McGrath & Rotchford, 1983), we contend that entities (organizations, groups, and individuals) develop different conceptualizations toward time, and that these affect their behavior in organizations.

At the organizational level of analysis, organizations differ in their predominant objectives and goals. For example, Blau and Scott (1962) say that different types of organizations (service, or business) differ in the social roles that they play, and those roles in turn affect the goals that different types of organizations attempt to meet. Goals within one type of industry may also differ. For example, an organizational goal may involve an increase in market share, continuous innovation, productivity, high quality, profitability, managerial performance, or human resource development (Drucker, 1954). Further, organizations may have multiple, conflicting goals. There may also be priorities for goals, with some goals seen as more important during organizational declines or crises (Thompson, 1967).

Subunits of an organization have also been found to create specific cultures, with their own goals and values, but in ways that reflect cross-organizational commonalities (Katz & Kahn, 1978). Such differentiation within an organization occurs because each functional unit deals with a particular aspect of the organizational environment. For example, sales departments must be concerned with marketing objectives, while manufacturing departments pay close attention to cost reductions and process efficiency (Lawrence & Lorsch, 1967).

At the individual level, people bring their own unique patterns of needs, values, and goals to organizations (Porter, Lawler, & Hackman, 1975). People actively seek to satisfy their own personal needs (Locke, 1976) and to achieve their own goals within the constraints of the subunits and organizations to which they belong. For example, one individual may be oriented toward achievement through work, while another in the same subunit may be oriented toward family or other nonwork issues.

The failure, during needs analysis, to analyze goals from each operational level has important implications for effective training. If goals are not specified across levels, it is unlikely that goal-related information will be available when decisions are made about who should be trained. For example, the goals of the unit or the department may determine what type of training is desired. At the individual level, analysis may reveal that an individual does not perceive a particular training program's potential to help him attain his goals. In this case, training may be ineffective for enhancing his performance, since he is not motivated to learn the material or to transfer new skills to the job. Instead, strategies to enhance his perception of the training program's value may be needed (see Hicks & Klimoski, 1987, for an example of a realistic preview for potential trainees). More-over, when a subunit has goals beyond or in conflict with organizational goals, and when the subunit's goals are not identified, training will be deficient and ineffective (Goldstein, 1986; Lynton & Pareek, 1967).

Organizations can be differentiated not only in terms of their goals and values but also according to the time frames within which goals and priorities are set. Time, of course, is inherently scarce and immutable (McGrath & Rotchford, 1983); nevertheless, cultures and the organizations within them develop dominant conceptions of time, and these create temporal problems (McGrath & Kelley, 1986). Organizations have to resolve three critical, time-related problems: uncertainty, conflicts of interest, and scarcity. The solutions to these problems involve the need for scheduling actions, the need for synchronizing or coordinating actions, and the need for allocating time in an efficient and rational way that maximizes organizational goals and priorities (McGrath & Rotchford, 1983). This idea implies that an organization's conception of time may be largely a function of its culture, but how the organization's approaches to scheduling, coordination, and allocation of time may differ. McGrath and Rotchford (1983) assert that these issues are at the heart of organizational efficiency, cost, and productivity; they reflect the organization's goals, purposes, and priorities, as well as its effectiveness in attaining its goals.

At the subunit level of analysis, Lawrence and Lorsch (1967) view time orientation as a key factor that differentiates among departments in an organization. They see time as a span or interval for receiving definitive feedback about the results of work efforts and behavior. For example, sales and production personnel deal with problems that provide rapid feedback about results. Consequently, they tend to focus their attention on short-term matters. By contrast, research and engineering personnel have longer-range concerns, since tangible feedback on their work is often a long-delayed result (Lawrence & Lorsch, 1967).

At the individual level, McGrath and Rotchford (1983) note that anyone who belongs to a large, formal organization will share the organization's conception of time, to some degree. Nevertheless, just as subunits may vary from the organization's dominant values, individuals also have different conceptions of time. These conceptions of how work should be scheduled and coordinated, and of how time should be allocated, may result in conflicts between the individual and the subunit or organization to which he or she belongs. These and other conflicts about time can lead to dysfunctional consequences, such as role ambiguity, role conflict, or role overload (McGrath & Rotchford, 1983).

Thus, there is theoretical support for the levels perspective on time orientation. Individuals, subunits, and organizations do not face the same issues in matters of time; the solution to a temporal problem for one entity may constitute a new problem for another. While different organizational levels may not face the same temporal issues, however, they do face the parallel set of issues that revolve around scheduling, synchronization, and allocation of time. Therefore, training needs analysis must include examination of how organizations, subunits, and individuals schedule, coordinate, and allocate time, as well as of the effects that these actions have on behavior and performance. For example, role ambiguity, role conflict, and role overload may reflect how time issues are addressed within an organization more than they reflect skill deficiencies that call for individual- or subunit-level training.

Task analysis has been defined in the training literature as analysis of the job to be performed by a trainee upon completion of a training program. Task analysis may also include analysis of the organizational setting in which the job is done (Goldstein, 1986). Here, we propose that the two constructs relevant to task analysis across levels of analysis are the technical environment and situational constraints.

There exists much confusion about the conceptualization and operationalization of technology (Stanfield, 1976), but most researchers agree that technology can be viewed as techniques used to transform inputs into outputs on a predictable basis (Hage & Aiken, 1969; Rousseau, 1983; Scott, 1975; Slocum & Sims, 1980). For the purposes of this chapter, we define *technical environment* as the processes through which physical and informational inputs are transformed into outputs (see Katz & Kahn, 1978).

Rousseau (1983) makes explicit the notion that technology exists and should be studied at three organizational levels, with attention focused on isomorphic constructs and the development of composition models. At the organizational level, the focus is on the modal or most typical processes used to perform work (that is, the predominant technology of the organization). For example, the modal technology of a manufacturing firm may be routine and long-linked (Thompson, 1967). Moreover, large firms may employ multiple types of technical processes. Rousseau (1983) argues, in such cases, for the examination of the organization's core conversion-process technology (that is, the technology that directly yields a product or service) and of the support technologies that aid it (that is, supply and quality assurance).

Departments and work groups in an organization have technologies that differ from the core technology of the firm. Studies have found that subunits can be differentiated in terms of work flow and technical processes (Lynch, 1974; Overton, Schneck, & Hazlett, 1977). Subunit technology is also qualitatively different from the individual jobs that each unit contains, since subunit technology reflects the characteristics of individual jobs as well as the interactions among jobs (Rousseau, 1983). For example, Comstock and Scott (1977) find that aggregated measures of individual tasks can be distinguished from subunit-level technology in terms of work flow. Thus, subunit technology is not simply the aggregation of the tasks from individual jobs within the subunit.

At the individual level, the technical process concerns individual jobs. The focus is on describing a job (including its equipment and surrounding conditions). The tasks performed (or the knowledge, skills, abilities, and other personal characteristics required for the job) are the fundamental unit of analysis.

The research on task analysis reported in the training literature has typically focused on the individual level of analysis, aggregating responses to task inventories to provide comprehensive analysis of particular jobs or clusters of jobs (see Ford & Wroten, 1984; Goldstein, Macey, & Prien, 1981). Training researchers have tended to ignore the subunit and organizational levels of analysis. By simply aggregating tasks, however, training analysts may miss important aspects of subunit or organizational technology, which in turn will be neglected in the design of training programs. From the levels perspective, the interaction and coordination of tasks must be identified at the subunit (or organizational) level. For example, a task analysis at the subunit level must identify not only the people with whom individuals interact but also the informational requirements of those interactions and the skills required for effective interaction within and across work units.

The second construct identified for a task analysis, *situational constraints*, we define as the work-setting characteristics that directly affect organizational, subunit, or individual performance. A variety of factors can affect work performance. Peters and O'Connor (1980) highlight eight such factors: adequate job-related information; tools and equipment; materials and supplies; financial and budgetary support; services and help from others; personal preparation through education, training, or experience; availability of necessary time; and physical comfort and conditions necessary for doing the job. These factors have been found to hinder or otherwise affect individual performance (Peters, O'Connor, & Eulber, 1985).

At the individual level, willingness and ability to perform may not necessarily lead to success, because of situational constraints (Campbell & Pritchard, 1976; Schneider, 1978). Empirical evidence supports the idea that situational constraints beyond the individual's control hinder task performance (see Peters, Fisher, & O'Connor, 1982; Peters, O'Connor, & Rudolf, 1980). Situational constraints may also lead an individual to modify how a task is completed, so as to minimize the impact of constraints.

The same situational constraints are readily observed at the subunit or organizational levels. At the subunit level, work-group norms are an additional situational factor that may constrain the performance of the group's members (Hackman, 1976). Norms may also affect what tasks are completed by which members of the work group. At the organizational level, organizations can be differentiated in terms of the degree to which situational constraints affect organizational effectiveness. For example, Rousseau (1983) contends that various input factors (such as the availability of resources, materials, supplies, and information) affect the technological transformation process, which in turn has an effect on output characteristics (such as the number of unique and innovative products or services provided by an organization).

In training research, some situational constraints (often called the conditions under which work is performed) are identified for individual jobs. A typology of situational constraints (Peters & O'Connor, 1980) provides training researchers with a framework for systematic study of task analysis across levels of analysis. For example, managers are often asked to assess their own or others' skills across a variety of managerial areas, to determine training needs (see Ford & Noe, 1987). Since the lack of training and experience is only one of many possible constraints, researchers may want to ask managers about the extent to which relief from other constraints is likely to lead to significant changes in job performance. Training can then focus on problems that are due to the lack of skills and experience, rather than focusing on other factors. For example, a performance deficiency may not be due to inadequate skills; rather, it may be the result of inadequate budgetary support or of a poor physical environment. Similar analysis can differentiate work groups that require training from work groups that require other interventions to improve their performance.

In training needs research, *person analysis* focuses on the knowledge, skills, abilities, motivations, and attitudes of individuals. From the levels perspective, we view person analysis as involving two major constructs: skills and climate. Like the traditional approach to person analysis, the first construct concerns an inventory of knowledge, skills, abilities, and motivations. The levels approach diverges from the traditional approach, however, in that this skills inventory must also be taken at the organizational and subunit levels.

One type of skills inventory at the organizational and subunit levels of analysis has been called "human resource analysis" (for example, see McGehee & Thayer, 1961). A human resource analysis describes the current skills of workers and projects what skill needs will exist in the future. This analysis also involves projection of the types and numbers of people who will be needed to fill positions in the future. Analysis of the adequacy of current and projected skill levels for the organization can help in understanding training needs.

An assessment of the organization's and its units' overall performance is also important. Such an assessment can include efficiency indexes or profitability, growth, and productivity measures. In the identification of a training need, the organization's or the unit's performance can be gauged against the extent to which the organization or unit is meeting its performance goals. Unmet goals may indicate the need for training or for some other intervention.

The levels perspective explicitly incorporates the idea that organizations and subunits can be differentiated in terms of the skills mix of their employees (Mann, 1965). For example, one company may employ a number of skilled and professional employees, while another company that manufactures a similar product may rely more on unskilled labor. (The effects of the skills mix on the use of training as a solution to performance problems has not been addressed.)

Typically, person analysis (for example, Klimoski, 1982) has focused on the individual level. An individual's knowledge and skills are assessed and compared to some standard of performance. Discrepancy between the assessed skills and the criterion of success calls for an examination of whether training could reduce the discrepancy. Training researchers have not conducted person analysis across levels of analysis and have ignored its implications for training. For example, subunits may differ in skill levels, and this situation may call for different types of training programs (say, a refresher course for one subunit, and more basic training for another).

The second construct of person analysis is *climate*, which focuses on the attitudinal or perceptual component of person analysis, across multiple levels. From the levels perspective, the climate is defined as a set of attributes that can be perceived about the work unit. A number of dimensions of climate can be studied, but one basic dimension of overall climate is the quality and style of interpersonal relations (impersonal, supportive, warm, open, or stressful) among work-group members (Porter, Lawler, & Hackman, 1975). Such perceptions, because they may have major impacts on people's reactions to events in an organization, may affect their behavior and performance.

From the levels perspective, organizations can be differentiated according to the climates that develop in them. For example, one marketing firm may have a highly participative, supportive management style; another has a highly centralized, high-pressure management style. The climate that develops may affect how the organization views its human resources. In fact, recent work at the organizational level of analysis (that is, work on organizational strategy) indicates that some industries are more oriented toward developing human resources than others are (Schuler & Jackson, 1987). Thus, the basic orientation of an organization may affect how it views the importance of training and development versus other strategies (say, selection or retrenchment) for enhancing organizational effectiveness.

Lawrence and Lorsch (1967) believe that organizational subunits are also differentiated by the kinds of interpersonal relationships found among their members. They suggest that, to be effective, subunits should develop interpersonal orientations that are related to the nature of particular tasks. For example, production subunits with great time pressure and highly routinized tasks may foster a style of interpersonal relations (impersonal and stressful) different from the style found in research and development departments, which deal with longer-term projects and perform fairly unstructured tasks. Conflicts in an organization may be partly due to the different climates that exist in different units.

At another level of analysis, individuals differ in their perceptions of and reactions to events that occur in subunits. People's reactions can affect their attitudes toward their subunits and ultimately can affect their relationships with other members of their subunits (Schneider, 1985). Thus, an individual in the "out group" may perceive the climate of a subunit differently and interpret events in a different way from an individual in the "in group."

The levels perspective implies that climates differ according to whether organizations are oriented toward training and development or toward other types of solutions to their problems. The training literature has ignored issues at this level of analysis and has typically measured organizational climate only to ensure that the work environment will accept changes in the behavior of trainees. While this issue is important, the levels perspective also implies that support for new skills should be examined across levels. For example, it is important to consider whether a particular training program (say, training in participative management skills for subunits that are oriented toward developing people) may be successful in one subunit but unsuccessful in others, where the climate may not be so supportive. For such unsupportive subunits, other interventions may have to precede training.

Operational and Interpretational Issues. The foregoing discussion has identified key constructs and isomorphic variables for the three *content areas* of organizational, task, and person analysis and for the three *levels* of analysis. The key constructs constitute an organizing framework for understanding training needs assessment.

The next step is to develop or identify relevant measures for each of the constructs in the framework. This step, which is beyond the scope of this chapter, is certainly complex; industrial and organizational psychology is still struggling with operationalization across levels of analysis. Nevertheless, when collecting and interpreting data, one should remember that there is no single unit of analysis that is appropriate for the measurement of all constructs. Measures, as well as the interpretations derived from them, should be consistent with the units of theory for each construct.

Specification beforehand of appropriate units of theory, analysis, and interpretation is rarely provided in needs-assessment research. Consequently, there has generally been a lack of correspondence between the conceptual and operational variables from each of the three content areas. Since the individual typically has been chosen as the relevant unit of analysis for the three content areas (Moore & Dutton, 1978), researchers have failed to consider whether the unit of theory, the unit of measurement, and the inferences drawn from these measures are all congruent. The potential impact of this situation on the quality of training programs—that is, poor design due to use of the wrong kind of analysis—has not been explored.

Consider the cell of Figure 2.1 defined by the level of the subunit, the content of task analysis, and the operational application. One approach to the measurement of subunit technology might be to aggregate measures of individual tasks, in order to represent the technology of the subunit. When one moves to the corresponding interpretational cell, however, there is danger of using the wrong level, since subunit technology may not be qualitatively represented by the simple aggregation of tasks. Here, the unit of theory and the unit of measurement and interpretation may not be congruent. A more appropriate strategy might be to use a global measure of group technology, such as Thompson's (1967) typology, that could more clearly reflect a unit-level technological construct.

Implications of the Levels Perspective
for Research and Practice

McGehee and Thayer (1961) provided the training field with a useful framework for describing the content of training needs assessment. This framework, comprising organizational, task, and person analysis, has stimulated research and organized the conduct of training needs assessment. The levels-of-analysis perspective presented in this chapter provides a new model of training needs assessment. The levels perspective deals explicitly with issues that were either implicit or ignored in the original framework and in subsequent research on needs assessment. The implications of this new model, both for research and for the practice of training needs assessment, are discussed in the following sections.

Research Directions

Since McGehee and Thayer's (1961) work, there has been an increase in the sophistication of methods for identifying the content of training needs (Wexley, 1984). The levels perspective represents a conceptual advancement that has implications for what kind of research needs to be done. From the levels perspective, research is needed about training needs assessment at the macro (organizational) level of analysis, about cross-level effects on the needs-assessment process, and about the development of within-level frameworks.

Needs Assessment at the Organizational Level of Analysis. Wexley (1984) notes the paucity of research on the training area of organizational analysis. From the levels perspective, it is clear that there is little research on training needs assessment at the organizational level, regardless of the content area (organizational, task, or person analysis).

One research direction concerns the development of methodologies that measure organizations in terms of goals, time orientations, technical environment, situational constraints, skills inventories, and climate. With such measures, differences across organizations could be related to differences in how training needs are assessed and to differences in types of training needs identified. For example, one manufacturing company may emphasize gaining market share, while a similar company focuses on short-term profits as a key goal. Given these goals, it is likely that the company with the market-share orientation would have a longer-term time orientation than the company that has the goal of immediate profits (with feedback from quarterly reports).

Research could address the extent to which differences in goals and time orientations affect the types of knowledge and skills that are identified by each company for training. Companies oriented toward market share, with relatively long time frames for analyzing feedback on meeting their goals, would probably be more interested in identifying people-related skills (participation, delegation, or teamwork) that might need improvement. Companies that focus on short-term profits would probably be oriented toward identifying specific task-oriented training needs, such as statistical process control and machine maintenance. Similarly, an organization with an overall supportive climate would be likely to focus more on identifying people-related skills for training than would an organization with a less supportive climate.

Another research direction might involve examining the interface between organizational-level variables and the organization's environment. The needs-assessment literature on training has only recently acknowledged the importance of examining how well training systems identify and respond to changes in order to meet future standards and expectations (see Camp, Blanchard, & Huszczo, 1986). Empirical research is needed on the process by which training systems identify environmental and organizational-level changes (for example, changes in goals, constraints, or climate) and on how this information is translated into the identification of training needs.

For example, research could focus on the different types of strategies for scanning and acquisition that training staff members use to identify environmental and organizational-level changes. A proactive strategy would be to actively seek and acquire information before some crisis arises. With a reactive strategy, by contrast, information is acquired in response to a crisis or is searched for as a result of upper management's directives (for example, a new technology is introduced, and management tells the training staff to develop a program for updating skills). Studying the effects of proactive versus reactive strategies for identifying training needs, as these strategies may be related to the effectiveness of a training system, would be a fruitful research direction.

Cross-Level Effects. The focus of the needs-assessment literature on training, with respect to the content of organizational, task, and person analysis, has resulted in relative inattention to interrelationships among variables. Such interrelationships across levels are explicitly accounted for in the levels framework when bond strength and constraints are examined. Conceptualizing the needs-assessment process for training in terms of these links is another potentially productive line of research.

One line of possible research in this area would be the study of isomorphic variables across levels of analysis and of the constraining effects of higher-level factors on lower-level factors. For example, the goals of one work group in an organization may be to increase efficiency continually and remain technically up to date. A second work group in the same functional specialty may focus attention on maintaining good working relationships among employees. Examining the effects of these different group goals on individual goals (for example, the amount of variance in individual goals that is attributable to the group's goals) has important implications for determining whether training would be an appropriate response to a performance problem.

Another research direction would be to examine time issues across levels of analysis. From the levels perspective, higher levels have slower time frames than lower levels do. For example, personal goals and objectives tend to change more rapidly than group and organizational goals. This means that higher-level processes can be analyzed less often than processes at lower levels, and that manifestations of change that is due to interventions at higher levels will appear more slowly than signs of change from interventions at lower levels.

Research is needed on appropriate intervals for collecting information relevant to processes at different levels of analysis. For example, studies could focus on examining optimal time intervals for conducting training needs analysis with respect to individual versus group versus organizational performance. It would also be useful to examine how long it takes for changes at higher levels to affect lower-level processes (for example, how long it takes for changes in work technology to influence such individual-level variables as job perceptions and work performance). Such research would provide preliminary information that is needed in the development of strategies for when and how to conduct training needs assessment.

Within-Level Issues. The research on training needs assessment has tended to examine only one content area at a time. From the levels perspective, the constructs relevant to organizational, task, and person analysis are not independent entities. Therefore, research is needed on interrelationships among constructs within levels of analysis. This type of research requires the development of models that show how the constructs relevant to training needs assessment are related.

For example, research could examine the different types of training needs that are identified when technical aspects as well as person-analysis aspects are considered. Regardless of the level of analysis, there should be some degree of compatibility between the technical system and the social system (Griffin, 1982; Indik, 1968; Mealiea & Lee, 1979). Different degrees of compatibility may result in different sets of training needs. Thus, a routine technology will probably provide jobs with low variety and autonomy, in terms of tasks (Griffin, 1982), and this low degree of job scope may result in negative perceptions of the work environment. In such a case, training in human relations and interpersonal skills may be needed, to offset the dysfunctional aspects of routine jobs. Similarly, the number of situational constraints in a job may greatly affect individuals' levels of motivation or their perceptions of their units and of the organization. It would be useful to identify which situational constraints result in particular types of training needs and which constraints call for other interventions.

Research could also examine the implications of identifying training needs in one content area for identifying training needs in another. For example, how do a group's long- and short-term time frames for receiving feedback affect not only situational constraints in the group but also the skills that group members have for dealing with the scheduling, synchronization, and allocation of time? As another example, identifying training needs on the basis of technological factors may result in different types of person-centered training. Different technologies clearly require different types of skills training, but certain technologies (for example, those that require interdependence, coordination, and sharing of resources) may create greater needs for interpersonal skills and participative climates.

One purpose of conducting a training needs assessment is to determine whether there are performance problems and, if so, whether training is a possible solution. The development of within-level models (if one keeps in mind the constraints placed on those variables from higher-level variables) can aid in such analysis.

Training Practice

Viewing needs assessment at the organizational, subunit, and individual levels of analysis provides a framework that highlights the need for congruence among construct definition, construct measurement, and interpretation of data. The following steps for conducting a needs assessment are based on the levels-of-analysis perspective. It is useful to consider the steps before actually collecting data during the needs-assessment process.

Identify the Level(s) of Analysis Relevant to the Current Needs Assessment. It is quite possible for training needs to exist at one level but not at others. The training analyst must determine what level of analysis is relevant to the needs assessment. For example, an analysis may focus on the subunit level and determine the extent to which each subunit is meeting its goals, but problems that require a multilevel perspective may arise. Consider the case of an organization that is planning to centralize the training of its new employees. This training, rather than taking place informally on the job, will occur before the new employees are placed into work groups. In this case, the training analyst may need to examine not only the organizational goals relevant to the training but also the norms, values, and behaviors of the work groups into which the new employees will be placed. Group norms (for example, "Do not believe what they tell you in the training course") can have a major impact on the transfer of skills from training to the workplace. In this situation, the needs assessment would have to examine organizational as well as group-level factors. Another level of complexity is added if one also perceives the need to examine the expectations and goals of the individuals who are entering the training program.

Identify the Conceptual Variables of Interest for the Appropriate Levels of Analysis. Once the relevant levels of analysis are identified, the specific conceptual variables of interest must also be identified. The training analyst must consider whether information relevant to goals and values, time orientation, technical environment, situational constraints, skills inventories, or climate must be measured and, if so, what types of information will be required. For example, the adoption of organizational policies on sexual harassment may require the development of a training program, to impart knowledge about the policies as well as to provide supervisors with role-playing practice in handling complaints. In addition to collecting needs-assessment information on the organization's objectives for adherence to these new policies, it may be important to collect information on individual values (for example, attitudes toward women as managers), as well as on the overall climate of the organization (or of its subunits) with respect to perceptions of fairness and equality.

After the critical variables have been identified, it is also important to consider the constraining influences of isomorphic or similar variables at higher levels of analysis. In the preceding example, individual values or attitudes about women may be affected by the norms and values of work groups. This situation may call for analysis of the strength and intensity of group norms before attention is focused on individual values and beliefs.

Develop Causal Pathways or Models That Link Variables Within and Across Levels of Analysis. After identifying the relevant variables, the training analyst must explicitly provide a framework for showing how the variables are linked to affect training needs. In this way, informed choices about the types of information to gather and about how to interpret the results of the needs-assessment process can be made beforehand.

For example, the introduction of robotics into a workplace often focuses immediate attention on necessary changes in skills, as a function of technological change. A simple model of this process is as follows: *Introduction of robotics → Assessment of necessary skills → Skill-based training → Positive attitudes of workers toward robotics.* An alternative model for conducting a needs assessment in response to the introduction of robotics could look like this: *Organizational goals for increased productivity → Technological process/efficiency analysis → Assessment of work-group climate for change → Examination of individual attitudes toward robotics → Assessment of necessary skills → Introduction of robotics → Skill-based training.* The second model indicates that an assessment of the need for new skills may not be sufficient; in that case, the analyst should consider the organization's productivity goals and efficiency concerns, as well as organizational or work-group climate and attitudes toward the new technology. Inappropriate attitudes and climates may hinder the introduction of an innovation (Chao & Kozlowski, 1986). In the second model, information on whether an intervention is necessary must be gathered before the introduction of the new technology and the skill-based training program.

By developing pathways, the individual who conducts a training needs assessment not only makes explicit his or her view of the process but also must explore the feasibility of alternative processes. This stage of needs assessment is critical, since the model that ultimately frames the needs-assessment process affects the types of variables examined, not to mention the interpretation of results.

Measure Variables and Interpret Results at the Appropriate Levels of Analysis. Once a model has been chosen, the measurement of its constructs must be considered. The advantage of the levels perspective is that it forces the analyst beforehand to consider the appropriate level(s) of measurement and interpretation. The analyst must consider what questions should be asked, as well as how they should be asked, to be consistent with the appropriate unit of analysis. It may be inappropriate to ask individuals what their particular job duties are and then aggregate the responses to identify group tasks. If the analyst wants to make inferences about group-level tasks, then questions should be framed at that level of analysis.

Similarly, the analyst must examine the level of agreement among individuals before aggregating responses at a higher level of analysis. Unless individual perceptions or responses are similar within a work group, aggregation and interpretation of responses at the higher level of analysis may lead to inappropriate conclusions about training needs.

Use the Levels Perspective to Guide Training Design and Evaluation. Goldstein (1986) has indicated the importance of linking needs-assessment information to training design and evaluation strategies. From the levels perspective, it is important that the level of analysis from which inferences about training needs are drawn match the level chosen for the design and evaluation of the training program. For example, team training and the analysis of learning at the group level, or of improvements in work-group performance, are necessary when entire work groups (or subunits) are found to need training. Thus, the levels-of-analysis perspective is also an organizing framework for considering the complete process of training needs assessment, training design, and program evaluation.

Conclusions

The idea that training spans multiple levels of analysis is not new (see Goldstein, Macey, & Prien, 1981; Hinrichs, 1976; McGehee & Thayer, 1961). Nevertheless, until now a well-articulated framework has not been developed from the levels perspective. In this chapter, we have integrated the traditional content issues of training needs assessment with the levels per-spective on organizations, to provide a useful framework for describing and understanding training needs assessment. The framework has resulted in our mapping of the needs-assessment constructs and their relationships across levels of analysis. We believe that this new levels-of-analysis framework can lead to advances, both in the research and in the practice of training needs assessment.

References

Ashmos, D. P., & Huber, G. P. (1987). The systems paradigm in organizational theory: Correcting the record and suggesting the future. *Academy of Management Review, 12*, 607–621.

Bass, B. M., & Vaughan, J. A. (1966). *Training in industry: The management of learning.* Belmont, CA: Wadsworth.

Blau, P. M., & Scott, W. R. (1962). *Formal organizations.* San Francisco: Chandler.

Borich, G. D., & Jemelka, R. P. (1982). *Programs and systems: An evaluation perspective.* Orlando, FL: Academic Press.

Camp, R. R., Blanchard, P. N., & Huszczo, G. E. (1986). *Toward a more organizationally effective training strategy and practice.* Englewood Cliffs, NJ: Prentice-Hall.

Campbell, J., & Pritchard, R. (1976). Motivation theory in industrial and organizational psychology. In M. D. Dunnette (Ed.), *Handbook of industrial and organizational psychology* (pp. 63–130). Skokie, IL: Rand McNally.

Chao, G. T., & Kozlowski, S.W.J. (1986). Employee perceptions of the implementation of robotic manufacturing technology. *Journal of Applied Psychology, 71*, 70–76.

Comstock, D., & Scott, W. R. (1977). Technology and the structure of subunits: Distinguishing individual and work-group effects. *Adminsitrative Science Quarterly, 20*, 177–202.

Dansereau, F., Alluto, J. A., & Yammarino, F. J. (1984). *Theory testing in organizational behavior: The variant approach.* Englewood Cliffs, NJ: Prentice-Hall.

Dansereau, F., & Markham, S. E. (1987). Levels of analysis in personnel and human resources management. In K. M.

Rowland & G. R. Ferris (Eds.), *Research in personnel and human resources management: Vol. 5* (pp. 1–50). Greenwich, CT: JAI Press.

Drucker, P. F. (1954). *The practice of management.* New York: Harper & Row.

Etzioni, A. (1964). *Modern organizations.* Englewood Cliffs, NJ: Prentice-Hall.

Ford, J. K., & Noe, R. A. (1987). The effects of attitudes towards training, managerial levels, and function. *Personnel Psychology, 40,* 39–54.

Ford, J. K., & Wroten, S. P. (1984). Introducing new models for conducting training evaluation and for linking training evaluation to program design. *Personnel Psychology, 37,* 651–665.

Glick, W. H. (1985). Conceptualizing and measuring organizational psychological climate: Pitfalls of multilevel research. *Academy of Management Review, 10,* 601–616.

Goldstein, I. L. (1980). Training in work organizations. *Annual Review of Psychology, 31,* 229–272.

Goldstein, I. L. (1986). *Training in organizations: Needs assessments, development, and evaluation* (2nd ed.). Monterey, CA: Brooks/Cole.

Goldstein, I., Macey, W., & Prien, E. (1981). Needs assessment approaches for training development. In H. Meltzer & W. R. Nord (Eds.), *Making organizations humane and productive* (pp. 41–52). New York: Wiley.

Griffin, R. W. (1982). *Task design: An integrative approach.* Glenview, IL: Scott, Foresman.

Hackman, J. R. (1976). Group influences on individuals. In M. D. Dunnette (Ed.), *Handbook of industrial and organizational psychology* (pp. 1455–1525). Skokie, IL: Rand McNally.

Hage, J., & Aiken, M. (1969). Routine technology, social structure, and organizational goals. *Administrative Science Quarterly, 14,* 366–376.

Hicks, W., & Klimoski, R. (1987). Entry into training programs and its effects on training outcomes: A field experiment. *Academy of Management Journal, 30,* 542–552.

Hinrichs, J. R. (1976). Personnel training. In M. D. Dunnette

(Ed.), *Handbook of industrial and organizational psychology* (pp. 829–860). Skokie, IL: Rand McNally.

Indik, B. P. (1968). The scope of the problem and some suggestions toward a solution. In B. P. Indik & F. K. Berrien (Eds.), *People, groups, and organizations* (pp. 3–26). New York: Teachers College Press.

James, L. R. (1982). Aggregation bias in estimates of perceptual agreement. *Journal of Applied Psychology, 67*, 219–229.

James, L. R., Demaree, R. G., & Wolfe, G. (1984). Estimating within-group interrater reliability with and without response bias. *Journal of Applied Psychology, 69*, 85–98.

James, L. R., Muliak, S. A., & Brett, J. M. (1982). *Causal analysis: Assumptions, models, and data.* Newbury Park, CA: Sage.

Jones, A. P., & James, L. R. (1979). Psychological climate: Dimensions and relationships of organizational and aggregated work-environment perceptions. *Organizational Behavior and Human Performance, 23*, 201–250.

Katz, D., & Kahn, R. L. (1978). *The social psychology of organizations* (2nd ed.). New York: Wiley.

Klimoski, R. J. (1982, August). *Needs assessment for managerial development.* Paper presented at the 90th annual American Psychological Association convention, Washington, DC.

Lawrence, P. R., & Lorsch, J. W. (1967). Differentiation and integration in complex organizations. *Administrative Science Quarterly, 12*, 1–47.

Lewin, K. (1951). *Field theory in the social sciences.* New York: Harper & Row.

Locke, E. A. (1976). The nature and causes of job satisfaction. In M. D. Dunnette (Ed.), *Handbook of industrial and organizational psychology* (pp. 1297–1350). Skokie, IL: Rand McNally.

Lynch, B. P. (1974). An empirical assessment of Perrow's technology construct. *Administrative Science Quarterly, 19*, 338–356.

Lynton, R. P., & Pareek, U. (1967). *Training for development.* Homewood, IL: Dorsey Press.

McGehee, W., & Thayer, P. W. (1961). *Training in business and industry.* New York: Wiley.

McGrath, J. E., & Kelley, J. R. (1986). *Time and human interactions: Towards a social psychology of time.* New York: Guilford Press.

McGrath, J. E., & Rotchford, N. L. (1983). Time and behavior in organizations. *Research in Organizational Behavior, 5,* 57–101.

Mann, F. C. (1965). Towards an understanding of the leadership role in formal organizations. In R. Dubin, G. C. Homans, F. C. Mann, & D. C. Miller (Eds.), *Leadership and productivity* (pp. 83–124). San Francisco: Chandler.

Mealiea, L. W., & Lee, D. (1979). An alternative to macro-micro contingency theories: An integrative model. *Academy of Management Review, 4,* 333–345.

Mesarovic, M., Macko, D., & Takahara, Y. (1970). *Theory of hierarchical multilevel systems.* Orlando, FL: Academic Press.

Moore, M. L., & Dutton, P. (1978). Training needs analysis: Review and critique. *Academy of Management Review, 2,* 532–545.

Mossholder, K. W., & Bedeian, A. S. (1983). Cross-level inference and organizational research: Perspectives on interpretation and application. *Academy of Management Review, 8,* 547–558.

Overton, P., Schneck, R., & Hazlett, C. (1977). An empirical study of the technology of nursing subunits. *Adminstrative Science Quarterly, 22,* 203–219.

Pattee, H. H. (1973). The physical basis and origin of hierarchical control. In H. H. Pattee (Ed.), *Hierarchy theory: The challenge of complex systems* (pp. 71–108). New York: Braziller.

Peters, L. H., Fisher, C. D., & O'Connor, E. J. (1982). The moderating effect of situational control of performance variance on the relationship between individual differences and performance. *Personnel Psychology, 35,* 609–621.

Peters, L. H., & O'Connor, E. J. (1980). Situational constraints and work outcomes: The influences of a frequently overlooked construct. *Academy of Management Review, 5,* 391–397.

Peters, L. H., O'Connor, E. J., & Eulber, J. R. (1985). Situational constraints: Sources, consequences, and future considerations. In K. M. Rowland & G. R. Ferris (Eds.), *Research in personnel and human resources management: Vol. 3* (pp. 79–114). Greenwich, CT: JAI Press.

Peters, L. H., O'Connor, E. J., & Rudolf, C. J. (1980). The behavioral and affective consequences of situational variables relevant to performance settings. *Organizational Behavior and Human Performance, 25,* 79–96.

Porter, L. W., Lawler, E. E., & Hackman, J. R. (1975). *Behavior in organizations.* New York: McGraw-Hill.

Roberts, K. H., Hulin, C. L., & Rousseau, D. M. (1978). *Developing an interdisciplinary science of organizations.* San Francisco: Jossey-Bass.

Rousseau, D. M. (1983). Technology in organizations: A constructive review and analytic framework. In S. Seashore, *Assessing organizational change* (pp. 229–255). New York: Wiley.

Rousseau, D. M. (1984, August). *Theories of levels in organizational science.* Paper presented at the 92nd annual American Psychological Association convention, Toronto, Ontario, Canada.

Rousseau, D. M. (1985). Issues of level in organizational research: Multilevel and cross-level perspectives. In L. L. Cummings & B. Staw (Eds.), *Research in organizational behavior: Vol. 7* (pp. 1–38). Greenwich, CT: JAI Press.

Schneider, B. (1978). Person-situation selection: A review of some ability-situation interaction research. *Personnel Psychology, 31,* 281–297.

Schneider, B. (1985). Organizational behavior. *Annual Review of Psychology, 36,* 573–611.

Schneider, B., & Schmitt, N. (1986). *Staffing organizations* (2nd ed.). Glenview, IL: Scott, Foresman.

Schuler, R., & Jackson, S. (1987). Organizational strategy and organizational level as determinants of human resource management practices. *Human Resource Planning, 10,* 123–141.

Scott, W. R. (1975). Organizational structure. *Annual Review of Sociology, 1,* 1–20.

Simon, H. A. (1964). On the concept of organizational goals. *Administrative Science Quarterly, 9,* 1–22.

Simon, H. A. (1969). *The sciences of the artificial.* Cambridge, MA: MIT Press.

Simon, H. A. (1973). The organization of complex systems. In H. H. Pattee (Ed.), *Hierarchy theory: The challenge of complex systems* (pp. 1–28). New York: Braziller.

Slocum, J. W., & Sims, H. P. (1980). A typology for integrating

technology, organization, and job design. *Human Relations,*
33, 193–213.

Stanfield, J. D. (1976). Technology and organizational structure
as theoretical categories. *Administrative Science Quarterly, 21,*
489–493.

Thompson, J. D. (1967). *Organizations in action.* New York:
McGraw-Hill.

Van Gigh, J. P. (1978). *Applied general systems theory.* New York:
Harper & Row.

Von Bertalanffy, L. (1975). *Perspectives on general systems theory.*
New York: Braziller.

Von Bertalanffy, L. (1980). *General systems theory.* New York:
Braziller.

Wexley, K. N. (1984). Personnel training. *Annual Review of Psychology, 35,* 519–551.

Wexley, K. N., & Latham, G. P. (1981). *Developing and training
human resources in organizations.* Glenview, IL: Scott, Foresman.

3

Using Utility Analysis to Assess Training Outcomes

Wayne F. Cascio

As the demands of the "second industrial revolution" spread, companies are coming to regard training expenses as no less a part of their capital costs than plant and equipment. Total training outlays by U.S. firms are now $30 billion and rising (American Society for Training and Development, 1986).

At the level of the individual firm, Motorola is typical. It budgets about 1 percent of annual sales (2.6 percent of payroll) for training. It even trains workers for its key suppliers, many of them small- to medium-size firms without the resources to train their own people in such advanced specialties as computer-aided design and defect control. Taking into account training expenses, wages, and benefits, the total cost amounts to about $90 million. The results have been dramatic, according to a company spokesperson: "We've documented the savings from the statistical process control methods and problem-solving methods we've trained our people in. We're running a rate of return of about 30 times the dollars invested—which is why we've gotten pretty good support from senior management" (Brody, 1987, p. 87).

A recent report by the American Society for Training and Development (1988) is even more emphatic. To regain their competitive edge in world markets, U.S. employers will have to invest at least 2 percent of annual payroll in training and development activities. This figure represents a $15 billion increase over current spending levels. Translating human effort into corporate goals requires that organizations be viewed as learning systems, and not just as production systems, but important shifts in orientation are necessary for this to occur. First, training must be treated as an investment, with the same promise of payoff as investments in research and development. Second, training and development must be incorporated explicitly into strategic planning efforts devoted to finding new markets, improving product quality, and applying new technology (American Society for Training and Development, 1988).

By the year 2000, 75 percent of all workers currently employed, young and old alike, will need to be retrained because of job changes that will require improved skills. As a result, many companies and unions have stepped into the workplace as educators, offering programs that include remediation and high school equivalency courses. For example, classes that teach English as a second language are on the rise because of the growing number of Hispanic and other workers whose native language is not English. Hispanics are expected to account for 22 percent of the growth in the labor force between now and the year 2000.

Many companies are providing training in basic mathematics, reading, and writing. The Polaroid Corporation is typical. It has installed computers and computerized machinery throughout its operations. Polaroid's employees are increasingly being asked to enter data into computers, read computer displays, and analyze data. To respond to workers' deficiencies in the skills needed for such tasks, the company set up a tutorial program to cover educational material typically taught in the first through twelfth grades. Over a three-year period, three thousand of the company's ten thousand employees took the courses. As one Polaroid executive noted, "We view this as absolutely necessary to be effective today in the workplace and necessary to move into the future" ("Businesses Teaching . . ." 1988, p. 29).

There is evidence that retraining pays off. A study by the Work in America Institute (cited in Brody, 1987) found that retraining workers for new jobs is more cost-effective than firing them and hiring new workers—not to mention the difference that retraining makes to employees' morale. In shrinking industries where there are no alternatives to furloughs, unions are working with management to retrain workers in marketable job skills. In short, every available indication is that training is now and will continue to be big business in the United States and abroad. In Japan, for example, when a manager hires a new employee, the manager commits the firm to investing hundreds of thousands of dollars in that employee over his or her career. Training and retraining, learning and relearning, operate continually.

In the past, companies were often chided for spending billions on training, but not one cent for evaluation. That situation is changing, as it must. Given current outlays for training, together with ongoing pressures for cost control, an inevitable question on the part of operating managers is "What are we getting for all this money and time?"

Continued growth of the training enterprise in all kinds of organizations suggests that many competing programs will be proposed. These programs will compete in turn with other worthwhile investments. In an era of limited resources, difficult choices will have to be made. Assessments of the costs and benefits of competing projects will become more important, and proposed training programs are no exception. The purpose of this chapter is to illustrate how cost-benefit analysis can be applied to training.

In the following pages, we will consider the application of cost-benefit (utility) analysis to the assessment of training outcomes. We also will discuss how break-even analysis and meta-analysis can be used in this process, as part of an effort to help human resource managers compete for resources in the broader organizational arena. In terms of directions for future research, we also will examine several theoretical issues on which there is little information. These include the length of training effects and the rate of decay or enhancement of these effects. On two other relevant issues, there is considerable information available: the rate of employee attrition and the impact of multiple employee cohorts. This chapter presents methods that take these factors explicitly into account in the overall determination of the economic impact of training and development efforts. Let us begin by examining the use of utility analysis in the assessment of training outcomes.

Utility Analysis

Utility analysis is a powerful tool for expressing the outcomes of personnel programs in terms of dollars (Boudreau, 1983; Cascio, 1980, 1987; Cascio & Ramos, 1986; Schmidt, Hunter, McKenzie, & Muldrow, 1979; Schmidt & Hunter, 1981, 1983). To date, utility analysis has been used to demonstrate to the firm the economic value of its personnel programs, principally in the area of selection, but it also has been extended to encompass "employee separations and acquisitions" (Boudreau & Berger, 1985), turnover (McEvoy & Cascio, 1985), and training and development (Landy, Farr, & Jacobs, 1982; Schmidt, Hunter, & Pearlman, 1982).

Linear regression-based decision-theoretic utility models have been available since the 1940s (Brogden, 1949; Cronbach & Gleser, 1965), but in many ways this area is still in its infancy. This fact will presently become apparent, as we examine the economic impact of training and development activities. Many areas lack empirical data, and many theoretical issues remain to be explored.

Methods for determining the economic impact of training are nevertheless available. Human resource professionals are interested in applying these methods to their work in organizations, because such methods allow them to express the outcomes of what they do in terms that top managers are able to understand — dollars. Those outside (and many within) the field of human resource management are often uncomfortable when the impact of training and development programs is expressed only in statistical or behavioral terms; for example, a common question is "What does the 0.05 significance level really mean in practical terms?"

It is convenient to be able to speak in terms of net dollars gained from the implementation of a well-designed training program. Nevertheless, the real question, from a broader organizational perspective, is this: Given the firm's financial objectives, on the one hand, and an array of alternative investment opportunities, on the other, how can one invest the firm's money in programs that will yield the returns most consistent with the financial objectives? Such programs may include the acquisition of new plants and equipment, technological improvements, financial assets (stocks and bonds), new selection programs, or training and development activities, just to name a few possibilities.

If human resource professionals are to compete with sales, marketing, production, and other functional areas for scarce resources, then the expected dollar returns (utility) of personnel programs must be evaluated against the utility of alternative investments. Decision rules are necessary for assessing how sensible it is to invest the firm's dollars in personnel programs, as opposed to capital improvements, financial assets, or other investments. In other words, if human resource professionals wish to have a meaningful impact on general business decisions, with regard to proposed personnel programs, they cannot regard utility estimates as simply the end result of evaluating the proposals; rather, they must see such estimates as the first step in a broader determination of whether the proposed programs will increase the market value of the firm. Unless the financial return from proposed personnel programs exceeds what the firm considers the minimum return necessary to justify its investment, such programs (for example, selection or training) will continue to be viewed as costs of doing business, rather than as investments to increase the productive value of the firm's human resources. Decision rules also are necessary for helping human resource professionals assess which of several proposed programs will be likely to produce sufficient returns to make them attractive to decision makers outside human resource management.

To help answer these questions, utility theory must be integrated with capital budgeting theory. Similarities between these two areas have already been identified (Boudreau, 1983,

1984; Cronshaw & Alexander, 1985), but an overall framework for integrating them is still lacking.

A major objective of this chapter is to bridge that gap. This chapter presents a three-step process: (1) the use of capital budgeting methods to analyze the minimum annual benefits, in dollars, required as the return on investment in any proposed personnel program; (2) the use of break-even analysis, which employs the general utility equation to estimate the minimum effect size (degree of departure from the null hypothesis) for a proposed personnel program that will produce the necessary returns; and (3) the use of meta-analysis results from similar programs, to estimate the expected actual payoff from the proposed program.

Next, this chapter considers the effects on payoff of employee attrition, decay or enhancement of the effect size associated with training, and multiple cohorts of trainees. Pieces of the overall framework have already been developed in the applied psychology literature. The objective here is to tie those pieces together, identify gaps in our theoretical and empirical knowledge base, and encourage future research in these areas. This chapter illustrates the overall framework with an example from the literature on training and development—namely, an example that shows the implementation of a goal-setting and feedback program.

Capital Budgeting Analysis of Training Programs

When we evaluate an investment in a training program, using a capital budgeting framework, we must specify the cost of the program, the incremental benefits derived during each period, the duration of those benefits, and the discount rate that represents the firm's minimum expected return on the investment. (Discounting is the reverse of compounding. It reflects the fact that a dollar received in the future is worth less than a dollar received today, because today's dollar can be invested to earn interest. Discounting is used to express the present value—that is, in terms of today's dollars—of future cash flows.)

The acceptance criterion to be applied to the training

program is that the net present value (*NPV*) of the program must be greater than zero; that is,

$$NPV = -C_0 + \sum_{t=1}^{n} B_t(1/1+i)^t > 0,$$

where C_0 is the cost of the program, B_t denotes the program benefits (in incremental cash flow) in period t, i is the discount rate, and n is the number of periods over which the program benefits last.

The cost of the program, C_0, is the amount of cash (after taxes) committed to the personnel program at t_0 (the beginning). If there are cash outlays over several periods, C_0 is the present value of these outlays. If the cost of the program is a tax-deductible expense, the after-tax cash outlay would be as follows:

$$C_0 = \text{program expense } (1 - T)$$

where T denotes the firm's income tax rate.

From the perspective of capital budgeting, any benefits from the program ultimately must be stated in terms of direct, measurable changes in the firm's cash flows. Without such tangible evidence of benefits, we cannot know whether the program meets the firm's investment criterion. Hence, rigorous ongoing assessment of training outcomes, in end-result terms (for example, increases in sales or decreases in defects), is necessary in order to justify adoption of the framework advocated here. In this case, the benefits of the program should be measured by the incremental cash flow, B_t, generated by the program during each period (t). (For the sake of simplicity, we assume that the cash flows are received at the end of period t.)

With regard to the discount rate, i, in the first equation, many different approaches could be used (see Brealey & Meyers, 1985; Brigham, 1985). To a great extent, one's approach depends on the amount of risk (uncertainty) associated with the benefits that will be generated by a proposed investment. The risk associated with a proposed personnel program would almost certainly be higher than, say, the risk associated with the purchase of an industrial robot used to weld metal parts. The estimation of systematic, or market, risk—and, ultimately, of the discount rate associated with proposed personnel programs—is best left to financial professionals; certainly, it is beyond the scope of this chapter. Therefore, human resource professionals in any organization are advised to consult financial officers to determine appropriate discount rates. Alternatively, since there is likely to be substantial uncertainty associated with the estimation of a single discount rate (a point estimate), a range of discount rates might be used (see Rich & Boudreau, 1987).

Example: Evaluation of a Proposed Training Program

To see how the capital budgeting framework can be applied to the evaluation of a proposed training program, consider the following example. Assume that Sunshine National Bank wishes to improve performance in its commercial loan department by using a goal-setting and feedback program. One cohort of fifty employees will be trained at a cost of $1,000 per person. If we assume that these costs are incurred at t_0, are tax-deductible, and are subject to a corporate tax rate of $T = 46$ percent, the after-tax cost of the program is as follows:

$$C_0 = n(\text{cost per person})(1 - T)$$
$$= 50(\$1,000)(1 - .46)$$
$$= \$27,000,$$

where n denotes the number of employees in the cohort that is trained.

Accurate cost data are important to the kinds of analyses described here. For the sake of simplicity, we have not identified the individual components of the total costs of training. Readers who are interested in doing that should consult the training cost model presented by Mirabal (1978). His model includes specific cost elements in four categories: course development, participants, instructors, and facilities.

The benefits of this program are expected to last for four

years. As a first approximation for our analysis, assume that the benefits do not decline each year; hence, they are the same amount, B, each year over the four-year horizon.

Phase 1: Computation of Minimum Annual Benefits Required. The first question we can ask is this: Given that the firm's required return on investments with this level of risk is, say, $i = 0.20$ (20 percent), what minimum level of annual benefits must be generated by the goal-setting and feedback program to justify the investment? If we assume that the benefits are expected to be the same amount, B, each year, the criterion for the net present value (*NPV*) requires

$$NPV = -C_0 + B \sum_{t=1}^{4} (1/(1+i))^t \geq 0$$

or

$$NPV = -\$27,000 + B \sum_{t=1}^{4} (1/1.20)^t \geq 0$$
$$NPV = -\$27,000 + B(2.5887) \geq 0,$$

where $\sum_{t=1}^{4} (1/1.20)^t = 2.5887$ is the present-value factor for an annuity of \$1 per year for four years, at a discount rate of 20 percent. Solving for the minimum required annual benefit, B, yields $B \geq \$10,430$.

This means that in each of the four years, there must be a total increment in the bank's cash flow of at least \$10,430. If the benefits resulting from the goal-setting and feedback program are expected to be less than this, then the program will not meet the bank's investment objective. The \$10,430 per year must be the result of increased revenues generated by the participating employees or of reductions in operating costs. In our bank example, such training could result in a greater number of loans being made or in a reduction in the time spent on processing each loan.

Calculation of the minimum annual benefits, *B*, also specifies what the minimum annual net payoff (ΔU) from the intervention must be. For example, if we express the general utility model in annual terms, the expression is

$$\Delta U = n(d_t)\text{SD}_y,$$

where ΔU must be at least $10,430 per year. Costs of the program are not subtracted from this figure, because they have been considered already in the net-present-value calculation that forms the basis of estimating *B* in the first equation. This objective determination of ΔU can then serve as a basis of determining the minimum acceptable effect size in the general utility equation (shown in the second equation).

Phase 2: Use of Break-Even Analysis to Determine the Minimum Effect Size (d_t) That Will Yield the Minimum Required Annual Benefit. The use of break-even analysis in the context of proposed personnel programs was first proposed by Boudreau (1984). The method about to be shown follows a similar logic. Let us assume, as before, that fifty employees will be trained ($n = 50$) at a cost of $1,000 per person and that their average salary is $35,000. Schmidt and Hunter (1983), examining empirical estimates of the variability of employees' productivity as a percentage of average salary, found that the standard deviation varied from about 40 percent to 60 percent of average salary. To be conservative, we will use the lower bound (that is, 40 percent of $35,000, or $14,000). Hence, $\text{SD}_y = \$14,000$. Certainly there are many other ways to estimate SD_y (see Cascio, 1987, chap. 8, for a review), but to keep our discussion simple, we will use 40 percent as a rule of thumb. Substituting these values into the second equation, we have

$$\$10,430 = 50(d_t)\$14,000$$

or

$$\$10,430/(50 \times \$14,000) = d_t$$
$$d_t = 0.015.$$

This means that each employee's annual job performance would have to improve 0.015 standard deviation units (approximately one-half of 1 percent) (that is, in a normal distribution, if one standard deviation above or below the mean encompasses approximately 34 percent of the total area under the curve, then $0.015 \times 0.34 = 0.0051$). This is a very small required improvement in job performance projected as a result of the training program.

To put this issue into perspective, consider that at the outset of a training program, the null hypothesis to be tested is that there will be no difference between the job performance of the trained and the untrained groups. To the extent that the training has any discernible effect, the mean job performance of the trained group should exceed that of the untrained group. This is shown graphically in Figure 3.1. The extent of the departure from the null hypothesis (no mean difference in job performance between the trained and the untrained groups), expressed in standard deviation units, represents the effect size d. When this estimate of the effect size is corrected for unreliability in the criterion measure $(d/\sqrt{r_{yy}})$, the result is an estimate of the true difference in job performance between the trained and the untrained groups, d_t.

Phase 3: Use of Meta-Analysis Results to Determine Expected Effect Size and Expected Payoff from the Intervention in Question. Meta-analysis involves a class of analytical techniques that permit quantitative cumulation of empirical results across multiple studies. Two uses of the methodology can be distinguished: to draw scientific conclusions, and to employ the results of validity evidence obtained from prior studies to support testing in a new situation (Green & Hall, 1984; Hunter, Schmidt, & Jackson, 1982). Such quantitative techniques can be applied to any area that has two or more empirical studies bearing on the same relation.

In estimating the expected payoffs from proposed train-

Figure 3.1. Standard Score Distributions of Job-Performance Outcomes of Trained and Untrained Groups.

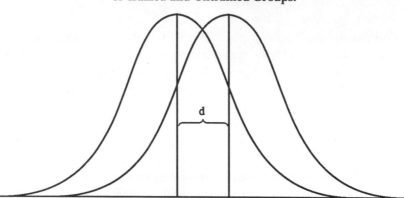

$$\overline{Z}_u \qquad \overline{Z}_t$$

ing and development, the first use of meta-analysis is appropriate (that is, for drawing scientific conclusions). The specific conclusion that we are interested in is related to the following question: Across all available studies, what is the average effect size of the intervention in question? As we have seen, effect size (d) refers to the differences between the mean performance of the trained and the untrained groups in standard (z) score form. Nevertheless, studies typically report results in terms of statistics, such as t, F, or r. Fortunately, each of these terms can be transformed into d, and vice versa. With small correlations, for example, d is approximately equal to $2r$, and r is approximately equal to $d/2$ (Hunter, Schmidt, & Jackson, 1982, p. 98).

Meta-analytical results are beginning to appear for a large number of selection methods (Hunter & Hunter, 1984) and training/development interventions (Guzzo, Jette, & Katzell, 1985; Landy, Farr, & Jacobs, 1982; McEvoy & Cascio, 1985). These data make it possible to determine the expected effect size for a proposed intervention. For example, Guzzo, Jette, and Katzell (1985) report the expected effect size for a goal-setting and feedback program to be 0.75. For purposes of estimating an expected payoff, however, use of a point estimate probably is inappropriate, for two reasons.

First, some human resource development programs will be better designed and implemented than others. Hence, in some instances, effect sizes may be higher than 0.75, while in other instances they may be lower. An interval estimate of effect size, expressed in terms of a 95 percent or 99 percent confidence interval, will capture this variability in expected effect size, while a simple point estimate will not. Guzzo, Jette, and Katzell (1985) present 95 percent confidence intervals for alternative interventions in human resource development. For goal setting, the upper bound of the 95 percent confidence interval is 0.93, and the lower bound is 0.57. Substituting these values into the general utility (second) equation, along with the parameters specified earlier for Sunshine National Bank, allows us to compute an interval of estimated actual payoffs per year (ΔU):

$$\Delta U = 50 \times 0.57 \times \$14,000$$
$$\Delta U = \$399,000$$

and

$$\Delta U = 50 \times 0.93 \times \$14,000$$
$$\Delta U = \$651,000.$$

Comparison of the minimum expected payoff ($399,000) with the minimum payoff necessary to justify the program ($10,430, to produce a net present value of $0.00) shows the goal-setting and feedback program to be well worth the money. Indeed, if the annual benefits are $399,000, then the net present value of the program over four years, on the basis of the first equation, is $1,005,891 ($1,032,891 − $27,000), where the annual benefits are discounted at the 20 percent required return. Of course, as Boudreau (1983) has shown, the expected payoff must be adjusted for the combined effects of discounting (previously considered in the computation of B), variable costs, and corporate taxes before meaningful comparisons can be made. To do this, we must modify the general utility equation as follows:

$$\Delta U = n(\text{SD}_y)(1 + V)(1 - T)d_t.$$

When the values assumed earlier are substituted into the latter equation, along with the following assumed values (tax rate = 46 percent; variable costs = − 5 percent), the unadjusted payoff of $399,000 is reduced as follows:

$$\Delta U = 50 \times \$14,000 \times (0.95) \times (0.54) \times 0.57$$
$$\Delta U = \$204,687.$$

The total payoff over four years, with a discount rate of 20 percent, is $529,880. These values are only 51 percent as high as the unadjusted values, but they are arguably more realistic. They clearly exceed the minimum payoffs required by the firm ($10,430 per year, and a present value of $27,000 over four years, discounted at 20 percent). The goal-setting and feedback program seems well worth the money.

But is it? In actual practice, many human resource development programs will be proposed. The task of the training and development department is to estimate the expected payoffs of each one and to set priorities for the proposed programs, in terms of their expected returns and in terms of the strategic objectives of the firm. The highest-priority proposals should then be submitted to the firm's decision makers, to be considered along with other, competing projects.

A related issue is validation of the expected payoffs. Some may feel that meta-analysis absolves them of any further responsibility for evaluation, but that is not true. In fact, while meta-analysis results do provide a useful starting point, evaluation of actual payoffs, in terms of dollars, is both expected and necessary, in order to justify the use of the capital budgeting framework. In short, meta-analysis results that indicate an expected effect size are useful at the front end of a human resource development program. They allow us to estimate expected payoffs by means of the general utility equation. Rigorous evaluation of actual results is necessary at the back end, so that the increment to cash flows that results from training can be specified.

Alternative Measures of Training Outcomes

Until now, we have focused on expressing the outcomes of training in terms of dollars. Some organizations, however, particularly those in the public, not-for-profit sector, may find it more useful to express outcomes in terms of increases in output per trainee. To do this, it is necessary to express d_t in terms of the percentage improvement in job performance. As we saw earlier, this outcome can be expressed by means of the area under the normal curve. Thus, if 34 percent of the area under the normal curve lies within one standard deviation above or below the mean, and if $d_t = 0.57$, then the expected improvement in job performance among new trainees is 0.34 (0.57), or 19.4 percent.

Suppose a decision is made to take the productivity gains from improved selection in the form of reduced hiring—that is, in terms of a smaller work force and lower payroll costs. For example, in the situation just described, where new trainees can be expected to have 19 percent greater output, the number of employees selected can be reduced by about 15 percent, with no decline in output $(0.19/(1 + 0.19) = 0.1597)$. Let us assume that one hundred new hires are added each year, all doing the same job for which the gains in output have been demonstrated empirically, as a result of goal setting and feedback. With training, only eighty-five new hires would be needed to produce the same amount of output as one hundred hires untrained in goal setting and feedback did previously. Further, if each new hire is paid an average of $20,000 per year, the payroll savings would be expected to be $15 \times \$20,000$, or $300,000 per year. There would be additional savings, to the extent that overhead costs also were reduced (for example, costs of equipment and supplies). An analysis using this methodology was applied to the entire federal work force by Schmidt, Hunter, Outerbridge, and Trattner (1986). Despite its appeal, however, it is important to recognize that this metric is not appropriate for all jobs, especially those where personnel requirements are fixed by the design of equipment to be used (say, requirements for airplane cockpit crews). For mechanics, word-processing operators, or many types of clerical workers, however, this metric may make sense.

A further benefit of expressing utility in terms of potential reductions in personnel requirements is that this metric allows us to relate expected job performance to human resource forecasts of supply or demand. For example, suppose that an integrated human resource forecast (that is, a forecast that includes estimates of human resource supply as well as demand) indicates that five hundred new word-processing operators will be needed five years hence. Assuming that all will be trained in the goal-setting and feedback program, and that their output will increase by 19 percent, we will need 15 percent fewer operators than are forecast. Thus, instead of five hundred new word-processing operators, we need seventy-five fewer. We are now able to link expected improvements in job performance to human resource requirements, as reflected in human resource forecasts. Of course, we should do this by job or by strategic business unit, thus acknowledging that the metric of reduced work-force requirements is appropriate only for certain jobs and that different levels of effect size can be observed in different jobs.

We now have the ability to express gains from effective training and development in at least four different metrics: dollars, percentage increases in output, reductions in the size of the work force, and savings in payroll costs associated with the reduced work force. While the particular circumstances associated with certain jobs may preclude the use of some of these metrics, judicious choice of the metric that best fits the situation may help us communicate training benefits in language easily understood and appreciated by decision makers.

Employee Attrition, and Decay in
Strength of Training Effects

The payoff shown earlier for the Sunshine National Bank refers to just one cohort of trainees. It assumes that the training effect remains equally strong each year and that the effect lasts for four years. This may be too simplistic, because later some trainees may quit, while others will be transferred or promoted out of their current jobs and into other jobs where the training in question will be irrelevant. Moreover, the effects of such training may change over time, and several cohorts may be trained over a period of years. This section considers the effects of employee attrition and of decay in the strength of training effects.

    In terms of change over time, training effects may decay, so that at some (unknown) rate the benefits dissipate, perhaps as a result of new technology or of failure to reinforce on the job what was learned in training. Alternatively, to the extent that material learned in training is applied to and reinforced on the job, the benefits of a training program may actually increase over time. This is an important issue that has not been investigated empirically, yet it is essential to the use of utility analysis as an evaluation model for training programs. Further, when we use the word *decay*, we are referring to the dissipation of the specific effects of the training program itself. Job performance may increase or decrease, but for reasons that have nothing to do with the training. As always in program evaluation, the task of experimental research is to pinpoint the specific impact of the program while controlling for or ruling out rival explanations for results. Consideration of such issues is beyond the scope of this chapter (but see Arvey and Cole's chapter in this volume).

    We begin by analyzing the example of a single cohort, where the benefits decline over time. Assume that the Sunshine National Bank program will suffer not only employee attrition but also decay in training effects. Assume further that the number of employees participating in the training program is $n_1 = 50$, but that in each subsequent period proportion $a = .20$ of these employees quit or are transferred to other jobs, so that the number of trained employees remaining at the end of period t is

$$n_t = n_1(1 - a(t - 1))$$

for $t < 1/a$. In addition, assume that the beneficial effects of the training decay at a rate of $h = .25$ per year, so that

$$b_t = b_1(1 - h(t - 1))$$

Table 3.1. Value of Training Program with Declining Payoffs
for a Single Cohort.

1	2	3	4	5	6
Period t	Number of Employees Remaining n_t	Benefits per Employee b_t	Total Benefits for Cohort (B_t)	Present-Value Factor $1/(1.20)^t$	Present Value of Annual Benefits
1	50	$7,980	$399,000	.833	$332,367
2	40	5,985	239,400	.694	166,143
3	30	3,990	119,700	.579	69,306
4	20	1,995	39,900	.482	19,232
5	10	0	0	—	0
6	0	0	0	—	0
Present value of total benefits					$587,048
Cost of the program					−27,000
Net present value of the program					$560,048

for $t < 1/h$, where $b_1 = \$7,980$ (that is, the total payoff of $399,000 divided by the fifty employees who were trained). Table 3.1 shows the number (n_t) of employees remaining at the end of each period, the benefits per employee (b_t), and the total benefits for all employees in the cohort (B_t).

In the table, the number of employees remaining declines by 20 percent each period, as shown in column 2. After the fifth year, none remain. Column 3 shows the benefits per employee, b_t, earned from the program each year. Because of the 25 percent annual decay in the strength of the training effect, the benefits of the goal-setting and feedback program are exhausted after the fourth year. Column 4 shows the total benefits,

$$B_t = n_1(1 - a(t - 1))b_1(1 - h(t - 1))$$
$$= (n_t) \times (b_t),$$

earned in each year, taking account of employee attrition and decay in the strength of the effect of the training. Column 6 shows the present value (discounted at 20 percent) of each year's benefits; the $587,048 near the bottom of the table represents the present value of the program. To get the net present value

(*NPV*), we must subtract the cost of the program. Thus, the net present value of this program for one cohort is

$$NPV = -C_0 + \sum_{t=1}^{4} B_t(1/1 + i)^t$$

$$= -C_0 + \sum_{t=1}^{4} n_1 b_1(1 - a(t-1))(1 - h)(t-1)(1/1 + i)^t,$$

which is \$560,048, taking into account employee attrition, decay in benefits, the time value of money, and the \$27,000 cost of the program.

Multiple-Cohort Effects

Most successful training and development efforts would involve several cohorts over several periods. In terms of the use of utility analysis in program evaluation, the analysis should consider the costs and benefits of implementing a sequence of programs. Whether we train a single cohort or several, the method of analysis and the criterion for acceptance are essentially the same: We must compare the present values of the costs and benefits to determine whether the net present value is positive. Remember that only programs with *NPV* > \$0 are worth undertaking, from the perspective of capital budgeting. In terms of multiple-cohort effects, we will consider two possible cases. The first assumes that all cohorts are identical in terms of costs and benefits; the second assumes initial set-up costs and identical cohorts. An analysis similar to this has been presented by Boudreau and Berger (1985).

Case 1. If several cohorts are to be trained in sequence, if every program and cohort is identical in terms of expected costs and benefits, and if the program run with the first cohort is acceptable, then all are acceptable. In fact, the net present value of the sequence of cohorts will simply be the discounted value of the net present values of all individual cohorts; that is,

$$\sum_{j=0}^{n} NPV_j 1/(1+i)^j,$$

for a sequence of $n+1$ cohorts, where NPV_j refers to the class that starts at time j.

For example, suppose the Sunshine National Bank plans to train fifty additional employees each year for four years, starting at time t_0, with the last class starting at time t_3. As in the previous example, each class of fifty will cost \$27,000 after taxes, and the benefits per class will be the same as described for the case with employee attrition and decay of benefits.

With the same costs and benefits, each class will yield a net present value of \$560,048, evaluated at the date each class begins. Column 2 of Table 3.2 shows the number of employees trained each year. Column 3 shows the total number of employees remaining at the end of each year, after attrition is accounted for. Column 4 shows the total incremental cash flow earned from the total program each year, taking account of both attrition and decay of benefits per employee. Column 5 shows the present value of those benefits, discounted at 20 percent per year: \$1,823,946. All four classes, whose costs total \$108,000, have a present value of \$83,876 at t_0, and the net present value is \$1,740,070.

The alternative approach to evaluating this sequence of identical cohorts is to determine the present value of the net present values of training for all cohorts. For all four, this would amount to

$$PV = \sum_{j=0}^{3} NPV_j(1/(1+i))^j = \$560,048 \sum_{j=0}^{3} (1/1.20)^j$$
$$= \$560,048\ (3.107)$$
$$= \$1,740,070,$$

where 3.107 is the present value of an annuity of \$1 to be received in each of four periods, starting at t_0 and ending at t_3, at a discount rate of 20 percent.

Table 3.2. Value of Training Program for Four Successive Cohorts, with Declining Benefits.

1 Period t	2 New Cohort Trained	3 Number of Employees Remaining	4 Total Benefits for All Cohorts	5 Present Value of Annual Benefits @ $i = .20$
1	50	50	$399,000	$ 332,370
2	50	90	638,400	443,050
3	50	120	758,000	438,854
4	50	140	798,000	384,875
5		100	399,000	160,258
6		60	159,600	53,403
7		30	39,900	11,136
8		10	0	0
9		0	0	0
Present value of total benefits				$1,823,946
Minus present value of program cost				− 83,876
Net present value of program				$1,740,070

Case 2. The second (and more interesting) case to consider involves fixed costs incurred at the beginning of the entire program. These do not depend on the number of cohorts. They are set-up costs, and they are quite common in applied behavioral science (for example, in assessment centers, career development programs, or any other situation where equipment must be acquired or materials developed before training begins). After the set-up costs have been incurred, a sequence of classes is run through the program, with each separate class incurring an investment cost that depends on the number of participants. The utility of the overall program would be

$$\Delta U = - \text{set-up cost} + \sum_{j=0}^{n} NPV_j(1/(1+i))^t.$$

For example, suppose that Sunshine National Bank is considering a training program that involves an initial set-up cost of $1 million, incurred at time zero. Each year a new cohort of fifty employees will be trained, at a total investment cost of

$27,000 per class. As before, each class is expected to yield a net present value of $560,048, before the $1 million set-up cost is considered. For three cohorts, starting at t_0, t_1, and t_2, the overall utility of the program would be

$$\Delta U = -\$1,000,000 + \$560,048 \ (2.528)$$
$$= \$415,801,$$

at a discount rate of 20 percent. Obviously, the utility of the program will tend to increase as more cohorts are trained, so as to offset the fixed set-up cost. A possible difficulty, however, is that as more cohorts are trained, the beneficial effects of the training may tend to dissipate.

    For example, in the early 1970s, the Xerox Corporation provided racial-awareness training to multiple cohorts of managers over a two-year period (Bass, Cascio, McPherson, & Tragash, 1976). During that time, the effect for cohorts that were trained later was not as strong as the effect for cohorts that were trained earlier (Cascio, 1976). Major reasons for this discrepancy seemed to be that trained and untrained employees interacted on the job and that society in general moved from a lower to a higher level of awareness of the need to integrate blacks into the work environment.

    If we anticipate some dissipation of benefits or other interaction of benefits between or among cohorts, we can easily consider these effects in our analysis, without making it unduly complicated. Beyond these considerations, however, is the fact that training programs may sometimes be justified on grounds that are not simply financial. In the example just cited, Xerox trained several thousand of its white employees on the need to consider problems of race in the work environment. This decision was not based on a net-present-value analysis; rather it was made on social grounds. As a result of the company's vigorous affirmative action program, blacks were being hired and promoted at all levels. Xerox provided the training in reaction to, and in anticipation of, continuing major changes in the social environment of the workplace.

Conclusions

Training programs are investments. They require the commitment of a firm's financial resources and can generate future benefits. As investments requiring the commitment of resources, training programs must compete for necessary resources with other investment opportunities. Consequently, if at all feasible, proposed programs should be presented in terms of economic costs and benefits.

The approach described in this chapter integrates expected payoffs from training and development with a firm's capital investment decisions. The methodology to do this is available now, but many pressing research questions remain to be investigated, particularly questions associated with the duration of program effects and the decay or enhancement of effects over time.

Computational formulas can be computerized, so that a manager of human resources need only input values corresponding to each of the critical parameters. These include the following:

- Cost (the present value of the after-tax cash outlays incurred over the life of the program)
- Benefits (the incremental cash flows generated as a result of the program; these cash flows are derived from the utility parameters)
- Number of employees trained
- Expected effect size (d_t), determined by meta-analysis
- Estimated SD_y
- Duration of the program and its benefits
- Discount rate representing the organization's minimum required return on investment
- Corporate tax rate
- Percentage of variable costs associated with the program

Once these parameters are specified, the following values can be computed:

- Minimum payoff required by the firm, from the perspective of capital budgeting
- Minimum effect size necessary to yield the required payoff (determined by break-even analysis)
- Expected payoff of the training program over the duration of the program's effects

If the expected payoff exceeds the minimum payoff, then the human resource manager can submit, with economic justification, a proposal for training and development to higher-level decision makers. It is crucial to recognize, however, that the outcomes of a training program must be linked to the incremental cash flow that will result from it. If outcomes are expressed only in terms of improvements in job satisfaction, turnover, motivation, productivity, or even sales, with no link to incremental cash flow, the results will not be comparable to those of competing investment proposals. Furthermore, upper management may have difficulty understanding why training and development should use the firm's scarce resources. Nevertheless, the evidence to date indicates that returns on investments in human resources can be surprisingly high. This kind of evidence must be presented to top managers in the most forceful, convincing, and concrete manner possible.

Resources

American Society for Training and Development. (1986). *Serving the new corporation*. Alexandria, VA: American Society for Training and Development.

American Society for Training and Development. (1988). *Gaining the competitive edge*. Alexandria, VA: American Society for Training and Development.

Bass, B. M., Cascio, W. F., McPherson, J. W., & Tragash, H. J. (1976). PROSPER—Training and research for increasing management awareness of affirmative action in race relations. *Academy of Management Journal, 19*, 353–369.

Boudreau, J. W. (1983). Economic considerations in estimating the utility of human resource productivity improvement programs. *Personnel Psychology, 36*, 551–576.

Boudreau, J. W. (1984). Decision theory contributions to HRM theory and practice. *Industrial Relations, 23*, 198–217.

Boudreau, J. W., & Berger, C. J. (1985). Decision-theoretic utility analysis applied to employee separations and acquisitions. *Journal of Applied Psychology, 70*, 581–612.

Brealey, R., & Meyers, S. (1985). *Principles of corporate finance* (2nd ed.). New York: McGraw-Hill.

Brigham, E. F. (1985). *Financial management: Theory and practice* (4th ed.). Chicago: Dryden.

Brody, M. (1987, June). Helping workers to work smarter. *Fortune*, pp. 86–88.

Brogden, H. E. (1949). When testing pays off. *Personnel Psychology, 2*, 171–183.

Businesses teaching 3 R's to employees in effort to compete. (1988, May 1). *New York Times*, pp. 1, 29.

Cascio, W. F. (1976). An empirical test of factor structure stability in attitude measurement. *Educational and Psychological Measurement, 36*, 847–854.

Cascio, W. F. (1980). Responding to the demand for accountability: A critical analysis of three utility models. *Organizational Behavior and Human Performance, 25*, 32–45.

Cascio, W. F. (1987). *Costing human resources: The financial impact of behavior in organizations* (2nd ed.). Boston: Kent.

Cascio, W. F., & Ramos, R. A. (1986). Development and application of a new method for assessing job performance in behavioral/economic terms. *Journal of Applied Psychology, 71*, 20–28.

Cronbach, L. J., & Gleser, G. C. (1965). *Psychological tests and personnel decisions* (2nd ed.). Urbana: University of Illinois Press.

Cronshaw, S. F., & Alexander, R. A. (1985). One answer to the demand for accountability: Selection utility as an investment decision. *Organizational Behavior and Human Decision Processes, 35*, 102–118.

Green, B. F., & Hall, J. A. (1984). Quantitative methods for literature reviews. *Annual Review of Psychology, 35*, 37–53.

Guzzo, R. A., Jette, R. D., & Katzell, R. A. (1985). The effects of psychologically based intervention programs on worker productivity: A meta-analysis. *Personnel Psychology, 38,* 275–291.

Hunter, J. E., & Hunter, R. F. (1984). Validity and utility of alternative predictors of job performance. *Psychological Bulletin, 96,* 72–98.

Hunter, J. E., Schmidt, F. L., & Jackson, G. B. (1982). *Meta-analysis: Cumulating research findings across studies.* Newbury Park, CA: Sage.

Landy, F. J., Farr, J. L., & Jacobs, R. (1982). Utility concepts in performance measurement. *Organizational Behavior and Human Performance, 30,* 15–40.

McEvoy, G. M., & Cascio, W. F. (1985). Strategies for reducing employee turnover: A meta-analysis. *Journal of Applied Psychology, 70,* 342–353.

Mirabal, T. E. (1978). Forecasting future training costs. *Training and Development Journal, 32*(7), 78–87.

Rich, J. R., & Boudreau, J. W. (1987). Effects of variability and risk in selection utility: An empirical comparison. *Personnel Psychology, 40,* 55–84.

Schmidt, F. L., & Hunter, J. E. (1981). Employment testing: Old theories and new research. *American Psychologist, 36,* 1128–1137.

Schmidt, F. L., & Hunter, J. E. (1983). Individual differences in productivity: An empirical test of estimates derived from studies of selection procedure utility. *Journal of Applied Psychology, 68,* 407–414.

Schmidt, F. L., Hunter, J. E., McKenzie, R. C., & Muldrow, T. W. (1979). Impact of valid selection procedures on work-force productivity. *Journal of Applied Psychology, 64,* 609–626.

Schmidt, F. L., Hunter, J. E., Outerbridge, A. N., & Trattner, M. H. (1986). The economic impact of job selection methods on size, productivity, and payroll costs of the federal work force: An empirically based demonstration. *Personnel Psychology, 39,* 1–29.

Schmidt, F. L., Hunter, J. E., & Pearlman, K. (1982). Assessing the economic impact of personnel programs on productivity. *Personnel Psychology, 35,* 333–347.

4

Evaluating Change
Due to Training

Richard D. Arvey
David A. Cole

Our inspection of several books concerning training and development, which were written for academic and practitioner audiences, reveals a somewhat casual approach to describing and summarizing how to measure change that results from formal interventions. For example, Goldstein (1986) provides a fairly short description of internal and external validity considerations (see Cook & Campbell, 1979) and outlines several experimental designs that can be used to assess change. These designs include, for example, the one-group posttest-only design, the classic pretest-posttest control-group design, the Solomon four-group design, the time-series design, and the nonequivalent-control-group design. Similarly, Wexley and Latham (1981) provide a brief review of these designs (including the posttest-only control-group design and multiple time-series designs). A recent book by Camp, Blanchard, and Huszczo (1986) also briefly describes a number of evaluation designs.

In none of these texts, however, is there any sophisticated statistical treatment of the measurement and detection of change that results from training interventions. One exception is the text by Cascio (1987), where three pages are devoted to these issues. Where do investigators who are interested in evaluating the effectiveness of training and development learn how to measure change? Moreover, where do they learn about some of the particularly thorny issues associated with the measurement of change, such as statistical power, sample-size requirements, and so forth?

The purpose of this chapter is to provide a somewhat more sophisticated treatment of change that results from training. We start from the premises that the evaluator has or will be able to use a fairly standard, classic evaluation design, that data are or will be available from treatment groups and control groups (with members randomly assigned), and that pre- and posttest data are or may be available. With these assumptions we will deal with the following issues in detecting change: (1) the choice of the statistical method to evaluate change (Which kinds of statistical methods can be used to assess change, and what are the advantages and disadvantages of each?) (2) power (What are the sample-size requirements for detecting change, given these designs?) (3) reliability (What is the impact of unreliable measures on the assessment of change, when one uses the methods specified?) and (4) alternative approaches (Are there some alternative methods for evaluating change, other than the classic methods?)

Data Set

To help illustrate several of the points we make in this chapter, we constructed an artificial training-outcome data set. We imagined a classroom training situation in which students were taught fundamental principles of statistics and research design (for example, analysis of variance, regression, power, and so forth). The hypothesis was that students in this class would learn these principles and concepts (a modest assumption, indeed), but we also might have expected them to vary widely with regard to their prior knowledge of this area. We also imagined a second class, in which very different materials were taught. Our goal was to assess the effectiveness of training in the class on research and design.

To conduct this study, we randomly "assigned" twenty of

Table 4.1. Sample Data Set for a Two-Group, Pretest-Posttest Design.

Subject	Group[a]	Pretest	Posttest
1	1	31	38
2	1	35	29
3	1	25	34
4	1	18	24
5	1	23	26
6	1	17	23
7	1	24	30
8	1	19	23
9	1	25	21
10	1	19	27
11	2	22	23
12	2	28	25
13	2	31	23
14	2	23	21
15	2	20	18
16	2	23	32
17	2	28	25
18	2	16	20
19	2	21	17
20	2	31	33

[a] 1 = experimental group; 2 = control group

our hypothetical students to one of the two classes (imaginary students can be very compliant). Members of the class on statistics and design were dubbed the *experimental group*; members of the other class were the *control group*. Because the students were randomly assigned, we did not expect the two groups to differ on any prior characteristics.

We prepared a fifty-itcm multiple-choice test, designed to tap all the major content areas taught in the class on statistics and design. Each group of ten students was administered the questionnaire twice, once on the first day of class and again on the last. The resulting scores for this study are presented in Table 4.1.

The means and standard deviations for the various cells are as follows (the standard deviations are shown in parentheses):

	Pretest	Posttest	Gain Scores
Experimental group ($N = 10$)	23.6 (5.8)	27.5 (5.4)	3.9 (5.2)
Control group ($N = 10$)	24.3 (5.0)	23.7 (5.4)	$-.6$ (4.8)

The correlation between the pre- and posttest scores across all subjects was .53. Visual inspection of these data suggests that the training intervention had a positive effect. On the average, the experimental group's scores increased about four points from pretest to posttest, whereas the control group's average remained relatively constant. Note also that the standard deviations are relatively stable across time.

Choice of Statistical Method

How might a researcher begin to analyze these data to determine whether the training intervention had a statistically significant effect? There are several possibilities.

Posttest-Only Design. One fairly simple procedure is to use a posttest-only design, where only the posttest scores are analyzed to determine whether a significant difference can be observed. Thus, an independent t test could be computed, to test the hypothesis that the two groups differed on the posttest scores. When such a test is performed on these data (using the SPSS PC package), the t-test value obtained is 1.59 (df = 18), which is not statistically significant (p > .10). Here, we are faced with a classic but awkward situation: The lack of statistical significance may reflect the possibility that the null hypothesis is true; that is, training has no effect. The four-point difference between pretest and posttest may be due to sampling error. Alternatively, the results may constitute a Type II error; that is, training really did have an effect, but our study lacked sufficient power to detect it. Along these lines, we should note that in the posttest-only design, a substantial number of data have been ignored (of course, we are referring to the pretest).

Gain-Score Design. Another obvious strategy is to use a gain-score procedure, whereby the differences between the pretest and the posttest scores are computed. The experimental and control groups are then compared on the gain-score variable via a *t*-test analysis. With these data, the average difference between the pretest and the posttest scores for the experimental group is 3.9 (SD = 5.2), whereas the average difference for the control group is − .6 (SD = 4.8). The resulting independent *t* test for the difference between the groups was $t(18) = 2.06$, which was close to being significant (p ≤ .055). Thus, inclusion of the pretest in this analysis did help to account for (or control) prior differences among the subjects on the variable of interest, to some extent. Nevertheless, this strategy was not quite helpful enough to enable us to detect what might have been a true difference between the groups.

Repeated-Measures ANOVA. Another frequently used procedure is the repeated-measures analysis of variance (ANOVA). In this analysis, the between-subjects source of variance is represented by a group variable (experimental versus control), and the within-subjects source of variance is represented by time (the pretest and posttest levels). The interaction between the group factor (experimental and control) and the time factor (pretest and posttest) is examined. There has been some debate concerning this issue (see Huck & McLean, 1975), but it turns out that the results are equivalent to those obtained via gain-score analysis. In fact, when the within-subjects factor has only two levels, the procedures are mathematically equivalent. To illustrate this point, Table 4.2 presents the relevant sources of variance and the statistical tests for such a repeated-measures design on the data presented in Table 4.1. When one examines the *F* test for the interaction, the resulting value is 4.23 (df = 1.18; p ≥ .055). The square root of this value is 2.06, which is exactly equivalent to the *t*-test value obtained via the gain-score procedure already described. Indeed, the procedures are identical and, as such, they share the same potential shortcoming: Both the gain-score and repeated-measures approaches are based on the assumption that there is a perfect relation between the pretest and the posttest. This is apparent in that the pretest implicitly receives a weight of 1.0 in the calculation of the gain scores: gain score = posttest – (1.0) pretest. In most data sets, however, the correlation between pretest and posttest is not perfect. For the current data, recall that the pretest-posttest correlation was only .53. To the extent that this is true, the gain-score or repeated-measures approach lacks a certain degree of precision.

Analysis of Covariance. Another, perhaps less common, procedure for addressing this problem is to incorporate the pretest score as a covariate and use analysis of covariance (ANCOVA). In many respects, the ANCOVA approach resembles the gain-score approach, insofar as the researcher partials out or controls for the effect of the pretest while examining the difference between the experimental and control groups on the posttest. Unlike the gain-score approach, however, ANCOVA assigns a weight to the covariate, a weight that reflects the extent of correlation between pretest and posttest. A very effective discussion of how ANCOVA can be used for analyzing data in pretest and posttest designs is provided by Huck and McLean (1975). It should be noted, however, that this technique may be less than optimal if there is little or no correlation between the pretest and posttest scores (a matter we will discuss in more detail later).

In conducting the ANCOVA, we again used the SPSS PC version of the covariance procedure. The results are presented

Table 4.2. Repeated-Measures ANOVA for Evaluating
Pre- and Posttest Design.

Source of Variation	df	SS	MS	F
Between subjects				
Group	1	24.03	24.03	.52
Subjects (groups)	18	831.45	46.19	
Within subjects				
Time	1	27.23	27.23	2.27
Group × Time	1	50.63	50.63	4.23[a]
Subjects (Group × Time)	18	215.65	11.98	

[a] $p \le .055$

Table 4.3. Analysis of Covariance (ANCOVA) for Evaluating
Pretest and Posttest Designs.

Source of Variation	df	SS	MS	F
Covariate: pretest	1	178.70	178.70	8.99[a]
Group main effect	1	88.06	88.06	4.43[b]
Residual	17	337.90	19.88	

[a] $p < .01$
[b] $p < .05$

in Table 4.3. These data indicate that the covariate (that is, the pretest) was indeed significantly related to the posttest ($F = 8.99$; $p < .01$) and, more important, that the differences between the experimental and control groups on the posttest were also significant after we controlled for the pretest ($F = 4.43$; $p \leq .05$).

An alternative but equivalent method of performing the covariance analysis can be accomplished by use of regression procedures, whereby the pretest and a dummy-coded variable for the group (for example, experimental = 1; control = 2) are entered as independent variables predicting posttest scores. The standardized and unstandardized regression weights obtained with these data are as follows:

	Unstandardized Beta	Standard Error	Standardized Beta
Pretest	.58	.19	.55
Group	− 4.21	2.00	− .39

The t value for the beta corresponding to the group variable is 2.11 ($p < .05$). This constitutes a test of the null hypothesis that $b = 0$. Squaring this value gives us 4.43, corresponding to the F value obtained by means of the ANCOVA procedure.

Yet a third approach to covariance analysis involves the use of hierarchical regression procedures. One constructs two regression models—a full model, and a reduced model. The reduced model consists only of the posttest regressed onto the pretest variable: Posttest $= \beta_0 + \beta_1$ pretest. The full model includes the dummy-coded group variable as a predictor of posttest as well: Posttest $= \beta_0 + \beta_1$ pretest $+ \beta_2$ group. Then one examines the R^2 values for each of these models. If the R^2 for the full model is significantly larger than the R^2 for the reduced model, one concludes that group membership predicts posttest, over and above the pretest variable. In other words, we find group differences on the posttest (controlling for the pretest). In this instance, the F value associated with the change in R^2 between the two models is 4.43 ($p < .05$), the same as the F value obtained via a simultaneous-regression approach. All of this illustrates that there are several methods for accomplishing a covariance analysis, and all are equivalent.

In summary, a researcher can use several procedures to test for the significance of a training intervention: the posttest-only design, the gain-score design, and the ANCOVA design. Using the data provided here for illustrative purposes, we obtained statistical significance only with the ANCOVA approach or its equivalent. Why might this have been so? One reason has to do with the statistical power of the ANCOVA procedure, as compared to the other designs.

Statistical Power

Factors Affecting Power. The *power* of a statistical test refers to the probability of correctly rejecting the null hypothesis when it is false. For example, if the null hypothesis is that there is no effect due to some kind of training intervention, then a test's power has to do with its ability to help us accept the alternative hypothesis: that a real effect, due to training, did result.

The power of a statistical test is affected by three components: the effect size, the choice of alpha level, and the standard error of the statistic. Effect size consists of the actual magnitude of the difference between the experimental and control groups. To the extent that a training intervention produces large differences in the dependent variable, statistical power is correspondingly greater. Cohen (1977) suggests an index of effect size, d, as a ratio of the raw group difference (expressed in units of the dependent variable) and the common within-group standard deviation. Somewhat arbitrarily, Cohen also defines three levels of effect size for the social sciences: small $(d = .2)$, medium $(d = .5)$, and large $(d = .8)$. All other things being equal, the power of a statistical test is greater when d is large.

Increasing the alpha level also affects the power of a design. For a given effect size, increasing the alpha level (for example, from .05 to .10) increases power. Of course, alpha is the probability of making a Type I error, and so increasing the probability of a Type I error directly results in a decrease in the probability of a Type II error. Similarly, using a one-tailed test, as opposed to a two-tailed test, increases power, if the overall alpha is held constant and the direction of the effect is correctly anticipated.

Finally, any procedure that reduces the standard error of the statistic will enhance power. The most widely recognized method for decreasing the standard error is to increase the sample size. However, this procedure is often impossible, especially at sites where relatively few employees undergo training at one time. (Under certain circumstances, a nonparametric statistic may be more powerful than its parametric counterpart. These circumstances have nothing to do with sample size, however. See Blair, 1981, for a fairly readable account.) A second and less recognized way to reduce the standard error involves employing statistical designs that use pretest information. In certain cases, measures of preexisting differences between subjects (such as pretest scores on the dependent variable) can be used to account for within-group variance. Such procedures typically shrink the standard error of the statistic and thereby increase power. We can best see how inclusion of pretest information affects the standard error by reexamining the three basic approaches already described. These three approaches can be differentiated with regard to their use of pretest information. The posttest-only design ignores pretest information altogether. The gain-score design analyzes the differences between the pretest and the posttest. The ANCOVA design treats the pretest as a covariate in a between-group design.

Testing the Same Null Hypothesis. It may not be obvious at first that these three approaches all test the same null hypothesis. However, the effect size differs dramatically from one approach to another. To understand this point, let E be the experimental (or training) group, C be the control group, X be the pretest, and Y be the posttest. For the sake of simplicity, homoscedasticity is assumed (that is, $\sigma_{YE} = \sigma_{YC} = \sigma_{XE} = \sigma_{XC}$). Given this assumption, the null hypothesis (H_0) of the posttest-only design can be expressed as $\mu_{YE} = \mu_{YC}$. For the gain-score design, the H_0 is $\mu_{YE} - \mu_{XE} = \mu_{YC} - \mu_{XC}$. We have assumed, however, that $\mu_{XE} = \mu_{XC}$. Therefore, the H_0 is simplified as $\mu_{YE} = \mu_{YC}$, which is identical to the expression for the posttest design. Finally, for the ANCOVA design, the H_0 can be expressed as $\mu_{YE} - \beta_E \mu_{XE} = \mu_{YC} - \beta_C \mu_{XC}$, where β is the coefficient of the pretest (X) when the posttest (Y) is regressed onto X. Assuming homogeneity of regression (that is, $\beta_E = \beta_C$), this expression for the H_0 is reduced to $\mu_{YE} = \mu_{YC}$. Again, this is identical to the null hypothesis for the posttest-only design. Therefore, all three designs test the same null hypothesis.

Comparing Power in Posttest, Gain-Score, and ANCOVA Designs. Although these three approaches test the same hypothesis, they vary considerably in their power. These differences occur because the potential inclusion of the pretest (X) directly affects the error variances. Recalling that one index of effect size, d, is a ratio of the raw effect size over the within-group error, we can compare the d's for each of these approaches. For the posttest-only design, the effect size (d_p) is simply

$$d_p = \frac{|\mu_{YE} - \mu_{YC}|}{\sigma_Y},$$

since $\sigma_{YE} = \sigma_{YC} = \sigma_Y$ (Cohen, 1977, p. 40). For the gain-score design, the effect size (d_g) can be expressed as

$$d_g = \frac{|\mu_{(Y-X)E} - \mu_{(Y-X)C}|}{\sigma_{(Y-X)}},$$

which, after a bit of unnecessarily complicated calculation, becomes

$$d_g = \frac{|\mu_{YE} - \mu_{YC}|}{\sigma_Y \sqrt{2(1 - \rho_{XY})}},$$

where ρ_{XY} is the correlation between the pretest (X) and the posttest (Y). The interested reader is referred to Arvey, Cole, Hazucha, and Hartanto (1985) for the details of these calculations. Finally, the ANCOVA effect size, d_a, is represented by

$$d_a = \frac{|\mu_{Y'E} - \mu_{Y'C}|}{\sigma_Y},$$

where $Y' = Y - b(\overline{X} - X)$ (see Cohen, 1977, p. 379). After even more and stickier calculations (see Arvey, Cole, Hazucha, & Hartanto, 1985), this becomes

$$d_a = \frac{|\mu_{YE} - \mu_{YC}|}{\sigma_Y \sqrt{1 - \rho_{XY}}}.$$

Some intriguing insights into the relative power of these three designs may be derived by comparison of d_p, d_c, and d_a. First, in the gain-score and ANCOVA designs, power always increases as the correlation between pretest and posttest increases (because of the increase in effect size). Thus, for programs in which variables are fairly stable across time, the inclusion of pretest data is particularly advantageous.

Second, when $\rho_{XY} > .5$, the gain-score analysis will be more powerful than the posttest-only analysis. Nevertheless, a little-known point is that when $\rho_{XY} < .5$, the reverse is true. That is, t tests on posttests only (ignoring pretests) will be more powerful than t tests on gain scores (see Maxwell & Howard, 1981). When $\rho_{XY} = .5$, gain-score and posttest-only analyses are equally powerful. Clearly, the correlation between the pretest and the posttest plays an important role in the choice between a posttest-only and a gain-score design.

Third, for most cases, ANCOVA will always be at least as powerful as either the posttest-only or the gain-score design (Huck & McLean, 1975). The extent of the ANCOVA approach's superiority depends on two things. One factor is the correlation between the pretest and the posttest. As this correlation increases, the advantage of ANCOVA over the gain-score approach actually diminishes. Alternatively, when r_{XY} is very small, the advantage of ANCOVA over the gain-score approach is substantial, but the advantage over the posttest-only approach becomes negligible or even nonexistent. A second factor affecting the relative superiority of ANCOVA is degrees of freedom. In ANCOVA, one degree of freedom is lost for the inclusion of a covariate in the analysis. This factor increases the critical value of the statistic at any particular alpha level. When the sample size is relatively large, the loss of one degree of freedom is negligible. For small-group research, however, a difference in one degree of freedom corresponds to a greater change in the critical value of the statistic and may mean the difference between rejecting the null hypothesis and not. Cohen (1977) suggests that the lost degree of freedom ceases to affect power substantially once sample sizes are as large as fifteen or twenty, but the point at which the loss of one degree of freedom renders ANCOVA less powerful than other approaches has not been demonstrated.

Power in Small-Sample Research. Because many training interventions involve relatively small sample sizes, Table 4.4 was constructed to further clarify the differences among designs. Power calculations are included for two different effect sizes ($d_p = .5$ and .8), corresponding to Cohen's (1977) definition of medium and large differences. Power was computed for a variety of relatively small sample sizes—n's ranging from 3 to 24. For the gain-score and ANCOVA designs, power is further broken down according to the correlation between pretest and posttest (ρ_{XY}). In determining the power of the ANCOVA, we took the loss of one degree of freedom into account (unlike Cohen, in his 1977 tables). Consequently, the point at which ANCOVA becomes less powerful than the gain-score approach is evident (that is, where ρ's = .7 and .9; see Table 4.4).

Thinking back to the example data presented earlier in this chapter, we find that one could use Table 4.4 to estimate the

Table 4.4. Approximate Power of Posttest-Only, Gain-Score, and ANCOVA Approaches, Broken Down by n, ρ_{XY}, and Effect Size ($\alpha = .05$).

n[a]	Posttest Only	Gain Score					ANCOVA				
		.1[b]	.3	.5	.7	.9	.1	.3	.5	.7	.9
		Medium Effect Size (d = .5)									
3	.11	.09	.10	.11	.14	.27	.11	.11	.12	.14	.25[c]
4	.14	.11	.12	.14	.18	.37	.14	.14	.16	.19	.37
6	.19	.16	.18	.19	.27	.54	.21	.22	.24	.30	.55
8	.25	.17	.20	.25	.34	.67	.24	.25	.28	.36	.69
10	.29	.20	.23	.29	.40	.78	.28	.29	.33	.43	.79
12	.33	.23	.27	.33	.46	.84	.33	.34	.39	.50	.85
16	.40	.28	.32	.40	.56	.92	.39	.42	.48	.61	.93
20	.46	.31	.36	.46	.64	.96	.46	.49	.56	.70	.97
24	.53	.36	.42	.53	.71	.98	.53	.55	.62	.77	.99
		Large Effect Size (d = .8)									
3	.18	.13	.15	.18	.25	.52	.16	.17	.19	.24[c]	.47[c]
4	.24	.17	.19	.24	.34	.70	.23	.24	.27	.36	.69[c]
6	.35	.25	.29	.35	.49	.87	.36	.37	.42	.54	.87
8	.46	.31	.36	.46	.63	.96	.44	.46	.53	.67	.96
10	.53	.36	.43	.53	.72	[d]	.52	.55	.62	.77	.99
12	.60	.41	.49	.60	.79	[d]	.59	.63	.70	.83	[d]
16	.72	.51	.59	.72	.88	[d]	.71	.75	.81	.92	[d]
20	.80	.59	.68	.80	.94	[d]	.80	.83	.88	.96	[d]
24	.86	.66	.74	.86	.96	[d]	.86	.89	.93	.99	[d]

[a] Represents total sample size (both experimental and control group).

[b] Correlation between pretest and posttest (ρ_{XY}).

[c] ANCOVA power is less than change-score power.

[d] Power is greater than .995.

power of these three statistical approaches. In that example, we had a sample size of $n = 20$. We estimated the pretest-posttest correlation at $r_{XY} = .53$ (we shall assume it was .5). If the true effect size were $d = .80$, the posttest approach would have had a power of .80. The power of the gain-score approach would also have been .80, but the ANCOVA approach would have had a slightly superior power of .88. Alternatively, if the true effect size were only $d = .50$ (a medium effect size), the posttest-only and gain-score approaches would have had a power of only .46, whereas the ANCOVA approach would have had a power of .56. If we estimate our effect size from the sample data, we see that $d_p = (27.5 - 23.7)/5.36 = .71$. Therefore, the actual power of these tests lies somewhere between the estimates based on $d = .5$ and $d = .8$.

Closer examination of Table 4.4 reveals some other interesting issues. Although the general superiority of the ANCOVA approach is apparent, the advantage of ANCOVA over the gain-score approach is small when ρ_{XY} is large (that is, greater than .7 for relatively small samples). Conversely, the difference between the ANCOVA and posttest-only approaches is negligible when ρ_{XY} is small (that is, less than .3). One may be tempted to develop a decision tree on the basis of this information. Depending on the magnitude of ρ_{XY}, one should make a choice among the posttest-only, the gain-score, and the ANCOVA approaches. Life need not be so complex, however. Even when ρ_{XY} is small, ANCOVA is about as powerful as the posttest-only approach. Similarly, in most cases when ρ_{XY} is large, ANCOVA is as powerful as the gain-score approach. Consequently, one can almost recommend ANCOVA in all cases, if power is the primary consideration.

Another point concerns the impact of the lost degree of freedom in ANCOVA. In general, using one degree of freedom for the pretest-only approach slightly attenuates the superiority of ANCOVA over the other two approaches. This reduction in degrees of freedom actually makes ANCOVA less powerful than the gain-score approach, but only under certain very limited circumstances. In particular, this occurs when n is extremely small ($n \leq 4$) and r_{XY} is very large ($\rho_{XY} > .7$), and even then the difference in power is not large. Thus, the advantage of including a covariate is often substantial and is only rarely offset by the cost of one degree of freedom.

There are, however, some disadvantages associated with the use of pretest data on the evaluation of training programs. The first and most obvious disadvantage is the research effort, in terms of the time, money, and other resources needed to gather these data. A more efficient but less powerful option may be to use the posttest-only procedure. Another potential problem is that administration of a pretest may sensitize subjects to the training context and initiate differential learning. This problem, as well as some possible solutions to it, are described by Cook and Campbell (1979).

Reliability of Measures

Still another issue to consider in the analysis of pretest-posttest training interventions has to do with the reliability of measures. Reliability can be affected in at least two primary ways: via a change in the total amount of true variance, and/or via a change in the total amount of error variance. The first case is represented by a situation in which the variability of true scores (in the population) actually changes. This can occur when the experimenter redefines the population of interest to include a more (or less) heterogeneous set of subjects. In this scenario, the total variance of the measure (σ_X^2) would be increased, not because of a change in the error variance but because of the change in the true variance (or reliability, ρ_{XX}) of the measure. The second case is represented by a situation in which the variability of true scores remains constant, but the error variance changes. One relatively straightforward way to affect reliability in this manner involves changing the length (for example, the number of items) of the instrument that measures the outcome variable. Let us consider that, instead of the fifty-item questionnaire in our imaginary study, we have two other possible measures. One is a two-item questionnaire, and the other is a twelve-item questionnaire. Let us also assume that all the items are interchangeable (that is, they are equally reliable indices of the same training variable). All other things being equal, the twelve-item measure will be more reliable than the two-item instrument. The Spearman-Brown formula for reliability of a lengthened test (Lord & Novick, 1968, p. 112) can be written as

$$\rho_t = \frac{k\rho_i}{[1 + (k-1)\rho_i]},$$

where ρ_t is the reliability of the test, ρ_i is the reliability of each item, and k is the number of items in the instrument. Thus, if

$\rho_i = .6$, ρ_t for a two-item instrument would be .75, while ρ_t for a twelve-item measure would be .95. Another general formula for reliability is $\rho_t = \sigma^2_T/(\sigma^2_T + \sigma^2_E)$, where σ^2_T is the true variance and σ^2_E is the error variance. Since the true variance (σ^2_T) is not affected by an increase in the test's length (that is, we have not made the population more heterogeneous), the difference in reliability of the test corresponds to a reduction in the error variance (σ_E^2).

Reliability and Power. In the literature, there has been considerable discussion concerning the impact of test reliability on the power of a significance test. On the one hand, Overall and Woodward (1975, 1976) note that a decrease in reliability can produce an increase in power. This occurs when reliability is increased in the first manner just described, via an increase in the true variance (that is, by means of a more heterogeneous population). In this way, the total variance of X (σ_X^2) is increased. Since σ_X appears in the denominator of the equations for effect size, the net result is a reduction in power. By contast, Zimmerman and Williams (1986) note that increased reliability can also produce an increase in the power of a significance test. This occurs when reliability is affected in the second manner described here, via a reduction in the error variance (σ^2_E). If we assume that the true variance remains constant, a reduction in σ^2_E will reduce the total variance (σ^2_E), thereby producing an increase in effect size and an increase in statistical power. In the remainder of this section on reliability, we shall be concerned only with the second way in which reliability can be affected (that is, we assume that the true variance remains constant).

Posttest Design. Concerning the power of the posttest design, the effect of increasing reliability is fairly straightforward. From the formula

$$d_p = \frac{|\mu_{YE} - \mu_{YC}|}{\sigma_Y},$$

we see that the effect size for the posttest approach is clearly a function of σ_Y. Increasing the reliability of Y (for example, by moving from a two-item to a twelve-item posttest) will directly reduce σ_Y, thereby increasing the effect size. Of course, larger effect size means greater statistical power.

Gain-Score and ANCOVA Designs. Interestingly, the impact of reliability on the gain-score and ANCOVA designs is more complex. Recalling the formulas for these two designs (see pp. 98–99), we note that effect size is a function of both σ_Y and ρ_{XY}. As in the posttest design, a more reliable measure will have smaller variance. Thus, the power of either the gain-score or the ANCOVA design will be at least as great as the posttest-only design. We say "at least as great" because the reliability of the measures also affects the correlation between pretest and posttest. Increasing the reliability of the measures will have the effect of disattenuating (that is, increasing) the expected correlation between pretest and posttest. Mathematically, the expected value of the correlation between X and Y would be

$$E(r_{XY}) = \rho_{XY}\rho_{XX}\rho_{YY},$$

where ρ_{XX} and ρ_{YY} are the pretest and posttest reliabilities, respectively. If $\rho_{XY} = .80$ and $\rho_{XX} = \rho_{YY} = .75$ (for a two-item measure), then the expected r_{XY} would be .60. If $\rho_{XX} = \rho_{YY} = .95$ (for a twelve-item measure), however, the expected r_{XY} would be .76. Using these values in Table 4.4 would lead to very different estimates of power for both the gain-score and the ANCOVA design, with greater power associated with higher estimates of ρ_{XY}. Thus, greater reliability is associated with greater power in all three designs, but the benefits will be more substantial in the gain-score and ANCOVA designs than in the posttest-only approach.

Measuring Change under Conditions That Are Less Than Ideal

Until now, we have focused on measuring change in situations over which the experimenter has a great deal of control. At many training sites, however, this will not be the case. In this section, we will discuss three of the many ways in which conditions for measuring training outcomes may be less than ideal. For each of these circumstances, we also present one possible way of handling the problem.

When Sample Sizes Are Small. Earlier in this chapter, we compared the power of the posttest-only, gain-score, and ANCOVA designs under the condition that n was small. Our discussion revealed that more extensive use of pretest information (as in ANCOVA) can enhance the power of the significance test. Nevertheless, recent Monte Carlo studies (Maxwell, Delaney, & Dill, 1984) suggest that still more extensive use of the pretest can further enhance even its power, especially in small-group research.

This procedure involves the combined use of alternate ranks and ANCOVA, thus making double use of the pretest. First, subjects are rank-ordered on the pretest. Second, instead of being randomly assigned to experimental or control groups, subjects are assigned according to an ABBAABB . . . scheme, in which the top-ranked person is assigned to the experimental group (A), the second-ranked person is assigned to the control group (B), and so on (Dalton & Overall, 1977). In this fashion, groups will be more closely matched before training begins. This procedure reduces the possibility that the traditional random assignment will fail, leaving nonequivalent groups at pretest. Third, the pretest is used as a covariate in the data analysis, by means of the ANCOVA approach described in this chapter.

Results of Maxwell, Delaney, and Dill's (1984) study revealed that alternate-ranks assignment, coupled with ANCOVA, is substantially more powerful than ANCOVA or alternate-ranks assignment alone, especially for small samples. For example, with $n = 12$ and $\rho_{XY} = .3$, ANCOVA plus the alternate-ranks approach is 5.2 percent more powerful than ANCOVA alone and 6.8 percent more powerful than the use of alternate ranks alone. Similar patterns emerged for other sample sizes and other values of ρ_{XY}.

When Self-Report Criteria Are Used. In many training-outcome studies, the variables of interest are relatively straightforward and reliable indices of behavior. For example, we may be interested in workers' productivity, assembly errors, number of sick days, and so forth. Sometimes we are interested in the effect of training on more subjective outcomes, such as workers' satisfaction or morale. To measure subjective variables, self-report methods (for example, questionnaires, interviews, and so forth) must be used. Self-report measures can greatly complicate the assessment of change due to training, not so much because of problems with the statistical approaches described here, but rather because of problems in the definition of change itself. For example, Golembiewski, Billingsley, and Yeager (1976) describe three kinds of change that can occur with self-report data. They label these *alpha*, *beta*, and *gamma* change.

Alpha change occurs when the observed difference between a pretest and a posttest represents a true change on the construct of interest. Presumably, this change is due to the training intervention.

Beta change refers to a case in which true (alpha) change is confounded by a recalibration of the scale(s) used to measure the construct of interest. Howard and Dailey (1979) describe a relatively common kind of beta change, called *response-shift bias*. A classic example of response-shift bias may be helpful here: At pretest, a supervisor regards herself as being of average competence. After a training program, two things occur: She is in fact a more competent supervisor, and she now realizes how much more there is to being a good supervisor than she has previously imagined. Consequently, after training, she again rates herself as average, giving the spurious impression that the training has had no effect. In reality, however, true change has occurred, but the measurement of this effect has been confounded by concomitant changes in the meaning and/or calibration of the rating scale.

Gamma change refers to a subject's reconceptualization of the construct of interest; that is, the subject's personal understanding of, say, job satisfaction may change qualitatively as a result of training. Consequently, the subject's score on a questionnaire (designed to tap this construct) reflects different things at pretest as compared to the posttest period.

What makes matters even more complicated is that alpha,

beta, and gamma change are not mutually exclusive; all of them may affect a single subject. Considerable discussion has centered on methods of disentangling these types of change (Lindell & Drexler, 1979; Zmud & Armenakis, 1978). One of the more noteworthy accounts is presented by Terborg, Howard, and Maxwell (1980). These authors recommend the collection of another piece of information, called the "retrospective pretest" (also called the "then score"; see Howard & Dailey, 1979). For example, let us assume that we have an intervention designed to increase job satisfaction, among other things. Before the intervention, the traditional pretest will be administered, to assess each employee's degree of job satisfaction. After the intervention, the subjects will be asked to rate their job satisfaction as it was (that is, retrospectively), before the intervention. Of course, each subject will also be asked to rate his or her current (posttest) job satisfaction.

Comparing these three measures, Terborg, Howard, and Maxwell (1980) describe how alpha, beta, and gamma change can be assessed. A critical point, however, is that these comparisons must be made for each subject one at a time. For example, to assess beta change, the average of a respondent's items on the pretest is compared to his or her own average on the retrospective pretest. If no response-shift bias (or beta change) has occurred, these means should be identical. Terborg, Howard, and Maxwell (1980) recommend using a t score to indicate the degree of beta change for each subject. Similarly, one assesses alpha change by comparing posttest scores to retrospective pretest scores. The combined influences of both alpha and beta change are represented in the difference between posttest and pretest scores. Gamma change is a bit more complex. It stands to reason that if the subject's understanding of the construct changes, then the correlation and/or dispersion of responses to the various items should change from pretest to retrospective pretest (but not from retrospective pretest to posttest). To measure each subject's degree of gamma change, Terborg, Howard, and Maxwell (1980) recommend computing the correlation and change in variance between pretest and retrospective pretest items.

These indices (*t* values, correlations, and standard deviations) should not be treated as statistics in their own right, because they are computed on multiple items taken from single subjects (which violates the assumption of independence). Instead, they should be treated as index variables in a non-parametric version of one of the previously described designs. For example, *t* values (or correlations, or standard deviations) can be rank-ordered and subjected to a Mann-Whitney U analysis, the nonparametric counterpart to a *t* test on posttest scores. In this fashion, the researcher can test for and distinguish among all three kinds of change (alpha, beta, and gamma) when self-report measures of training effectiveness are used.

Several methods have been developed to assess alpha, beta, and gamma change, other than the method specified by Terborg, Howard, and Maxwell (1980). An interesting comparison of these methods is described by Schmitt, Pulakos, and Lieblein (1984), who discuss the advantages and disadvantages of each procedure. The possibilities inherent in these approaches are intriguing, but the major conclusion is that much additional use and more comparisons of these methodologies will be necessary before researchers or practitioners can interpret the practical significance of beta and gamma changes.

When Experimental and Control Groups Differ on the Pretest. Implicit in all that has been presented here is the assumption that the experimental and control groups are equivalent at pretest. Traditionally, this situation is arranged via random assignment. Unfortunately, however, training evaluators often lack this kind of control in their settings. The existence of nonequivalent groups at pretest has a devastating impact on all the designs so far discussed (Linn & Slinde, 1977).

If groups are not equivalent at pretest, the posttest-only approach will not test a hypothesis of interest, in most training evaluations. The discovery at posttest of differences between the experimental and control groups does not necessarily mean that training has been effective; the groups may have differed to the same extent, and in the same direction, even before training began. Reciprocally, the discovery of no difference at posttest does not necessarily mean that training has been ineffective; pretest scores for the experimental group may have been lower than those for the control group. Therefore, effective training may be reflected in the absence of group differences at posttest.

At first glance, the analysis of gain scores or the analysis of covariance may seem to avoid such problems. Pretest information can be used to adjust posttest scores for preexisting group differences. Even though these procedures do at least test a hypothesis of interest, certain relatively common circumstances often lead to spurious results.

The problems are twofold. First, we may not have equated the two groups statistically on all the essential variables. Second, even if we have corrected for the essential characteristics, our measures of these variables may not be perfectly reliable. The first problem is most clearly depicted by Lord (1967, 1969), in reference to situations where no treatment effects and/or large preexisting differences exist. If the proper adjustments are not made, rather remarkable (and misleading) conclusions may be reached. The second problem arises because preexisting differences will not be completely accounted for if the pretest measure is itself fallible. To the extent that the pretest is an imperfect (unreliable) measure of the construct of interest, the effect of training on the dependent variable will be over- or underestimated, depending on the direction of the pretest differences (Fortune & Hutson, 1984). Problems such as these have led to considerable pessimism about the prospects for detecting change in designs that use nonequivalent control groups (Meehl, 1970; Cronbach & Furby, 1970).

Nevertheless, three alternative procedures have been described by Fortune and Hutson (1984). A randomized block model (Myers, 1972) involves blocking on levels of the pretest as a mechanism for balancing groups at pretest. Unfortunately, this procedure requires a rather large sample size and does little to account for the fallibility of the pretest. Alternatively, Rubin (1973) recommends direct matching and bias calibration. In this procedure, matched subsamples of each group are selected for the comparison; but, again, this design requires large samples of generally overlapping populations. The third approach establishes a combined-groups regression model, from which comparisons can be made between the experimental and control groups. The regression-discontinuity design (Campbell & Erlebacher, 1970; Reichardt, 1979) is an example of this kind of approach. All three of these models provide reasonable tests for group differences, at least when the sample sizes are relatively large, but none of these tactics provides adjusted scores for individual subjects. Consequently, with these models, more refined analysis of change is impossible.

One very interesting new development is described by Dwyer (1984). In a sense, the nonequivalence of groups at pretest represents a measurement problem. The groups differ on a set of variables for which we have only imperfect measures. As we have seen, such measurement error can have devastating effects on the statistical conclusion validity of many training-outcome designs. These have all been manifest-variable approaches, however. Dwyer (1984) recognizes that latent-variable statistics offer a method for handling measurement problems.

By means of linear structural-equation modeling and such computer programs as LISREL (Jöreskog & Sörbom, 1986), latent-variable models can be constructed and tested. In such a model, an unmeasured (or imperfectly measured) latent variable affects both the assignment of subjects to groups and the outcome variable of interest. Controlling the latent variable (instead of particular, fallible operationalizations of that variable), we can assess the effect of training, over and above the effect of the confounding variable. Unfortunately, this procedure also requires relatively large samples of experimental and control subjects.

Conclusions

In the assessment of training outcomes, researchers frequently face a variety of threats to their investigations. Sample sizes may be small; measures may be biased or lack high reliability; the experimental and control groups may not be equivalent before the intervention.

In our discussion of statistical power, we presented three

traditional research designs and one relatively new one. Special attention was given to research on small samples. Many investigators may shy away from more complex designs (given small samples), but our review indicates that more sophisticated use of pretest information has a profound impact on power, especially in small-group research.

In our review of four research designs, the posttest-only design was found to lack power in cases where the pretest-posttest correlation was greater than .5. The gain-score design was found to be weak when the pretest-posttest correlation was less than .5. The ANCOVA design (using the pretest as the covariate) was generally more powerful than either the posttest-only or the gain-score design, even when the loss of one degree of freedom (because of the covariate) was taken into account. The fourth approach involved the combined use of ANCOVA and alternate-ranks assignment. (In this approach, subjects are rank-ordered on a pretest and assigned to groups on the basis of rank. Then the pretest is entered as a covariate in the analysis of the outcome measures.) This procedure has greater power than even the ANCOVA procedure and is especially recommended for small-group designs.

In our discussion of reliability, we described two basic ways in which reliability can be affected. One involves a change in the variance of subjects' true scores, as might occur if restriction-of-range problems were encountered. The other has to do with the amount of error variance in the instrument itself, as might occur in the comparison of a long questionnaire to an abbreviated one. In the latter case, we noted that diminished reliability differentially affects the power of different designs. In general, the gain-score and ANCOVA approaches appeared to suffer greater reductions in power than did the posttest design.

We also presented a procedure that seems to hold particular promise in cases where training outcomes are assessed by means of self-report measures only. Three different kinds of change on such measures are described (alpha, beta, and gamma change). Procedures are outlined for teasing apart true (alpha) change from changes in the recalibration of the scale (beta change) and changes in the subjects' conceptualization of the construct (Terborg, Howard, & Maxwell, 1980).

Finally, we discussed situations in which the researcher faces experimental and control groups created by nonrandom assignment. Obviously, differences at pretest can confound the results of many traditional training-outcome designs. We presented innovative approaches that can be of assistance: Myers's (1972) randomized block model, Rubin's (1973) matching and bias-calibration procedures, Reichardt's (1979) regression-discontinuity method, and Dwyer's (1984) linear structural-equation modeling. Each design has its strengths as well as drawbacks.

In this chapter, we have necessarily limited ourselves to only a few of the possible designs and analyses that can be applied to research on training outcomes. Without a doubt, the frontiers for measuring change are moving forward all the time, leaving us with new and more sophisticated options. Several procedures have been discussed in the recent literature.

Hierarchical Linear Models for Assessing Change. A two-stage model of change was proposed by Bryk and Raudenbush (1987). It essentially tracks growth curves for individuals, as a function of differences among subjects in background characteristics or instructional experiences and treatments. Thus, this model specifies how different growth trajectories for subjects are related to different training exposures.

Sensitivity Analyses for Evaluating Change. Lipsey (1983) presents an interesting scheme for assessing whether the chosen measure is sensitive enough to treatment effects, as well as robust in the face of procedural irregularity, inconsistency of treatment implementation, and subjects' heterogeneity. The procedure uses analysis-of-variance (ANOVA) methods associated with generalizability theory (Cronbach, Gleser, Nanda, & Rajaratnam, 1972).

Incorporation of Measurement Error Directly into Evaluation Design and Analysis. A number of authors (Wolfe & Ethington, 1986; Dwyer, 1983) have illustrated how measurement error can be incorporated into designs investigating change, by means of LISREL methods and procedures.

Time-Series Designs and Exponential Smoothing Methods. Time-series and data-smoothing techniques are being used to evaluate programmatic interventions. For example, Mandell and Bretchneider (1984) illustrate possible forms that intervention can have on time-series data. They also present methods for teasing out the effects of an interruption in a time-series data set (such as an interruption due to training).

Each of these four topics could furnish material for an entire chapter in the present book. It is clear that the frontiers are being pushed forward in the evaluation of change due to training interventions. One obvious implication of these developments is that professionals in training and development will need increased sophistication in and knowledge of complex statistical models to keep abreast of innovations.

References

Arvey, R., Cole, D., Hazucha, J., & Hartanto, F. (1985). Statistical power of training evaluation designs. *Personnel Psychology, 38,* 493–507.

Blair, C. (1981). A reaction to "Consequences of failure to meet assumptions underlying the fixed-effects analysis of variance and covariance." *Review of Educational Research, 51,* 499–507.

Bryk, A. S., & Raudenbush, S. W. (1987). Application of hierarchical linear models to assessing change. *Psychological Bulletin, 101,* 147–158.

Camp, R. R., Blanchard, P. N., & Huszczo, G. E. (1986). *Toward a more organizationally effective training strategy and practice.* Englewood Cliffs, NJ: Prentice-Hall.

Campbell, D. T., & Erlebacher, A. E. (1970). How regression artifacts in quasi-experimentation can mistakenly make compensatory education look harmful. In J. Hellmuth (Ed.), *Compensatory education: A national debate: Vol. 3. The disadvantaged child.* New York: Brunner/Mazel.

Cascio, W. (1987). *Applied psychology in personnel management* (3rd ed.). Reston, VA: Reston Publishing Co.

Cohen, J. (1977). *Statistical power analysis for the behavioral sciences* (rev. ed.). Orlando, FL: Academic Press.

Cook, T. D., & Campbell, D. T. (1979). *Quasi-experimentation: Design and analysis issues for field settings.* Skokie, IL: Rand McNally.

Cronbach, L. J., & Furby, L. (1970). How should we measure "change" — or should we? *Psychological Bulletin, 374,* 68–80.

Cronbach, L. J., Gleser, G. C., Nanda, H., & Rajaratnam, N. (1972). *The dependability of behavioral measurements: Theory of generalizability for scores and profiles.* New York: Wiley.

Dalton, S., & Overall, J. (1977). Nonrandom assignment in ANCOVA: The alternate-ranks design. *The Journal of Experimental Education, 46,* 58–62.

Dwyer, J. H. (1983). *Statistical models for the social and behavioral sciences.* New York: Oxford University Press.

Dwyer, J. H. (1984). The excluded-variable problem in nonrandomized control-group designs. *Evaluation Review, 8,* 559–572.

Fortune, J. C., & Hutson, B. A. (1984). Selecting models for measuring change when true experimental conditions do not exist. *Journal of Educational Research, 77,* 197–206.

Goldstein, I. L. (1986). *Training in organizations: Needs assessment, development, and evaluation* (2nd ed.). Monterey, CA: Brooks/Cole.

Golembiewski, R. T., Billingsley, K., & Yeager, S. (1976). Measuring change and persistence in human affairs: Types of change generated by OD designs. *Journal of Applied Behavioral Science, 12,* 133–157.

Howard, G. S., & Dailey, P. R. (1979). Response-shift bias: A source of contamination of self-report measures. *Journal of Applied Psychological Measurement, 64,* 144–150.

Huck, S., & McLean, R. (1975). Using a repeated-measures ANCOVA to analyze data from a pretest-posttest design: A potentially confusing task. *Psychological Bulletin, 82,* 511–518.

Jöreskog, K. G., & Sörbom, D. (1986). LISREL VI: Analysis of linear structural relationships by maximum likelihood, instrumental variables, and least squares methods. Mooresville, IN: Scientific Software, Inc.

Lindell, M. K., & Drexler, J. A. (1979). Issues in using survey methods for measuring organizational change. *Academy of Management Review, 4,* 13–19.

Linn, R. L., & Slinde, J. A. (1977). The determination of the significance of change between pre- and posttesting periods. *Review of Educational Research, 47,* 121–150.

Lipsey, M. W. (1983). A scheme for assessing measurement sensitivity in program evaluation and other applied research. *Psychological Bulletin, 94,* 152–165.

Lord, F. M. (1967). A paradox in the interpretation of group comparisons. *Psychological Bulletin,* 68, 304–305.

Lord, F. M. (1969). Statistical adjustments when comparing pre-existent groups. *Psychological Bulletin,* 72, 336–337.

Lord, F. M., & Novick, M. R. (1968). *Statistical theories of mental test scores.* Reading, MA: Addison-Wesley.

Mandell, M. B., & Bretchneider, S. I. (1984). Using exponential smoothing to specify intervention models for interrupted time series. *Evaluation Review, 8,* 663–691.

Maxwell, S., Delaney, H., & Dill, C. (1984). Another look at ANCOVA versus blocking. *Psychological Bulletin, 95,* 136–147.

Maxwell, S., & Howard, G. (1981). Change scores—necessarily anathema? *Educational and Psychological Measurement, 41,* 747–756.

Meehl, P. E. (1970). Nuisance variables and the ex post facto design. In M. Radner & S. Winokur (Eds.), *Minnesota studies in the philosophy of science: Vol. 4* (pp. 310–372). Minneapolis: University of Minnesota Press.

Myers, J. L. (1972). *Fundamentals of experimental design* (2nd ed.). Newton, MA: Allyn & Bacon.

Overall, J. E., & Woodward, J. A. (1975). Unreliability of difference scores: A paradox for measurement of change. *Psychological Bulletin, 82,* 85–86.

Overall, J. E., & Woodward, J. A. (1976). Reassertion of the paradoxical power of tests of significance based on unreliable difference scores. *Psychological Bulletin, 83,* 776–777.

Reichardt, C. S. (1979). The statistical analysis of data from nonequivalent group designs. In T. Cook & D. Campbell (Eds.), *Quasi-experimentation: Design and analysis issues for field settings* (pp. 147–206). Skokie, IL: Rand McNally.

Rubin, D. B. (1973). The use of matched sampling and regression adjustment to remove bias in observational studies. *Biometrics, 29*, 185–203.

Schmitt, N., Pulakos, E. D., & Lieblein, A. (1984). Comparison of three techniques to assess group-level beta and gamma change. *Applied Psychological Measurement, 8*, 249–260.

Terborg, J. R., Howard, G. S., & Maxwell, S. E. (1980). Evaluating planned organizational change: A method for assessing alpha, beta, and gamma change. *Academy of Management Review, 5*, 109–121.

Wexley, K. N., & Latham, G. P. (1981). *Developing and training human resources in organizations*. Glenview, IL: Scott, Foresman.

Wolfe, L., & Ethington, C. A. (1986). Within-variable, between-occasion error covariances in models of educational achievement. *Educational & Psychological Measurements, 46*, 571–591.

Zimmerman, D. W., & Williams, R. H. (1986). Note on the reliability of experimental measures and the power of significance tests. *Psychological Bulletin, 100*, 123–124.

Zmud, R. W., & Armenakis, A. A. (1978). Understanding the measurement of change. *Academy of Management Review, 3*, 661–669.

PART TWO

Learning and
Cognitive Issues

5

Training the Human Information Processor: A Review of Cognitive Models

William C. Howell
Nancy Jaworski Cooke

The nature of work has undergone dramatic changes over the past decade as the impact of computer technology has penetrated ever more deeply into the functioning of organizations. Typists have become word-processor operators; clerks manage their files electronically; designers rely heavily on computer graphics; managers use powerful software in planning, organizing, and decision making. From assembly line to boardroom, scarcely a function remains untouched by the ubiquitous microchip.

It is difficult to tell where all this will lead, or how fast: Futurists have had a field day predicting all sorts of dire and utopian social consequences. One need not resort to crystal balls or tea leaves to read certain trends, however. In particular, it is perfectly obvious that the relationship of people to machines will continue to change as the machines' physical and computational capabilities draw closer to those of people (Christensen, 1987; Norman, 1984; Van Cott, 1984). Advances in robotics and artificial intelligence (AI) will force frequent redefinition of once clearly defined roles. Machines will continue to shoulder more of the physical workload and more of the burdensome mental operations characteristic of well-defined, repetitive tasks. The storehouse of information and the software available to people who have complex responsibilities will continue to expand. Most important, machines will become increasingly involved in what we now consider uniquely human intellectual functions: those that require cognition, or thought (Sheridan, Charney, Mendel, & Roseborough, 1986; Sheridan, Kruser, & Deutsch, 1987).

Of course, frequent changes in even the most pedestrian of tasks can put a tremendous burden on the training establishment, if such changes affect a significant segment of the work force. Thus, finding efficient ways to impart procedural knowledge and to modify existing skills will undoubtedly assume more economic importance as time goes on (Goldstein, 1986). Tullis (1983), for example, estimated that a one-second improvement in the average response time of operators in a national computer-based repair network would save fifty-five person-years annually. As we shall see, recent developments in educational technology offer considerable promise in this regard, although their impact on training in the workplace appears so far to have been quite limited (Wexley, 1984).

The most significant implication of technology-driven change for training, however, lies well outside the realm of simple procedural tasks. It involves the shift in the fundamental roles that have been assigned to humans and machines. Somewhat paradoxically, increasing the scope of machines' responsibilities and capabilities often increases, rather than reduces, demands on human operators. The burden of the more routine and predictable functions is relieved, but the operator is left to grapple with the more unpredictable and poorly defined ones. Moreover, the operator must control an increasingly powerful and complex subordinate. If one is to manage a "smart," powerful machine effectively, one must understand what it is supposed to do, how it works, and the various ways in which it can fail (Davis, 1987). Often under considerable time pressure, one must use fallible information to decide whether a machine has indeed failed and, if so, what action to take. That action may well include calling temporarily on infrequently practiced manual skills and assuming the machine's role (Fischhoff, 1987). In short, work requirements at all levels are becoming cognitively more demanding. What once were highly structured tasks may now call for inference, diagnosis, judgment, and decision making. Skill in monitoring and communicating with semiautomated systems has become essential.

What all this means for training, obviously, is that workers generally will need to acquire and refine somewhat different kinds of skills from those they have used in the past. Rather than just developing appropriate response repertoires for application to well-defined sets of stimulus alternatives, they will have to gain conceptual understanding of the automated processes under their control. Further, they will find it increasingly advantageous to have well developed problem-solving and reasoning skills.

With notable exceptions, the predominant educational philosophy underlying today's training programs derives from the behavioristic tradition that dominated the psychology of learning until the 1960s (Pintrich, Cross, Kozma, & McKeachie, 1986; White and Zsambok, 1987). The emphasis has been on observable behavior and its relation to environmental variables, including stimuli, conditions of practice, and reinforcement. For the most part, the principles that have evolved have been strictly empirical, based on laboratory research, itself of variable or undetermined external validity (Gagné, 1970). Neither theory nor "mentalistic" integrative concepts has been available to guide practitioners in generalizing from learning principles to training practice. Nevertheless, to the extent that the tasks for which people are trained have imposed relatively limited cognitive demands, and when means have been available for validating programs, this strict empiricism has not been a severe handicap, and many demonstrably successful programs have evolved. In fact, explicit methodologies have been developed to provide the essential strategic guidance lacking in the basic learning literature. One good example is Goldstein's (1974) systematic approach to program development and evaluation. Another is the Instructional System Development (ISD) methodology that has been in wide use by the military since 1970 (Ryder, Redding, & Beckschi, 1987).

As task demands depart from the routine, however, and as successful performance increasingly depends on what people contribute at the cognitive juncture between observable inputs and outputs, the traditional behavioristic philosophy—even when buttressed by modern training methodology—becomes seriously deficient. Ryder, Redding, and Beckschi (1987) underline this point with reference to the inappropriateness of the current ISD model for today's military and industrial tasks, which are "primarily cognitive in nature" and thus require "new approaches to training" (p. 1261). They go on to suggest modifications in ISD, based on the analysis of cognitive skill requirements and application of what is now known about the nature and development of such skills. In essence, they call for replacement of the behavioristic with a cognitive orientation in the design of training programs, to address more adequately the kinds of learning demanded by modern work.

Advances in cognitive psychology and related disciplines over the past three decades provide a rich theoretical foundation on which to erect the proposed training edifice (White and Zsambok, 1987). Basic psychology, of course, long ago abandoned radical behaviorism in favor of a more cognitive emphasis, and the spirit of this paradigm shift has had a profound impact on most applied fields of psychology. In human factors today, for example, there is much more interest in the design of effective cognitive links between humans and computers than in demonstrations of the superiority of one set of "knobs and dials" over another (Mark, Warm, & Huston, 1987). In instructional psychology, where the chief objective is hardly distinguishable from that of training, "conceptions of the learner, the task, the medium, and instruction are being reformulated as parallel interacting processes grounded in cognition" (Pintrich, Cross, Kozma, & McKeachie, 1986, p. 617). Training applications, it seems, have simply lagged behind. In this one arena, the "black box," rather than the intelligent information processor, remains (implicitly, at least) the model of choice.

What are these alternative cognitive models? What do we know about human cognition that is of potential value in the design and implementation of training programs for work settings? On what basis can we claim that in the future a cognitive focus on training is likely to be superior to the traditional behavioristic one? Is it just another fad, of the sort for which the training establishment has shown such affinity in the past (Campbell, 1971)? Or does the cognitive focus have demonstrable value?

The purpose of this chapter is to address these questions in light of recent developments in three principal (and closely related) areas: basic research on human cognition and its relation to learning and transfer; AI and its involvement in instructional technology; and illustrative applications of cognitive principles to real-world educational and work problems. The underlying thesis here is that, in excising the mind from the human learner, behaviorism greatly restricted the tools available for training purposes; restoring the mind enlarges the toolbox. Some of the new tools may offer better ways of implementing ordinary procedural learning, but the most significant advantage is to be found where technological change has made simpler tools obsolete. Cognitive tasks require cognitively oriented training tools. Traditional learning principles and training prescriptions have little to say about how to make people better diagnosticians, how to increase their available attention capacity, or how to help people create appropriate mental models for the complex processes under their control. Inference, monitoring, and problem solving will be core skills in workplaces of the future, and cognitive psychology has a lot to say about all of them. We turn now to a consideration of some of these basic cognitive concepts.

An Overview of Cognitive Psychology

Information-Processing Models. The discipline of cognitive psychology is concerned with the study of such mental processes as attention, perception, pattern recognition, memory, language, reasoning, and problem solving. For the last three decades, information processing has been the dominant paradigm of this discipline. According to this paradigm, at least some human behavior can be conceptualized as the manipulation of symbols. Because the computer can also be considered a symbol manipulator, it has provided the paradigm with a rich source of analogies (Lachman, Lachman, & Butterfield, 1979). Consequently, such concepts as *input, storage, buffer,* and *working memory* have been used to explain various aspects of human thought.

Numerous information processing models similar to the one presented in Figure 5.1 have been proposed (Card, Moran, & Newell, 1983; Dodd & White, 1980; Newell & Simon, 1972; Shiffrin & Atkinson, 1969; Wickens, 1984), and all share some basic features. These models describe the cognitive structures and processes that occur from the time stimulus information impinges on the senses until a response to that stimulation is executed. Measures of reaction time and errors are employed to isolate particular stages of processing (Posner & McLeod, 1982). Different processing stages and memory stores are indicated by boxes, and arrows connecting the boxes signify the transfer of information from one stage or store to another. Feedback loops usually allow the outputs of stages to act as inputs to other stages. For instance, in Wickens's (1984) model (Figure 5.1), the output of the response-execution stage (for example, the sound of a key press) is also an input to the perception stage.

There are also several "bottlenecks" in the system, which constrain the amount of information that can be processed at once. In Figure 5.1, there is a limited pool of "attention resources" allocated to various components of the model. This conceptualization of attention—as a processing capacity or reservoir of allocatable processing resources (Kahneman, 1973; Navon & Gopher, 1979; Norman & Bobrow, 1975)—can be contrasted with the view that attention is a "selective filter," which allows only a portion of environmental stimulation to enter consciousness at one time (Broadbent, 1958; Treisman, 1964). Both the selection and capacity concepts are currently used to

Figure 5.1. A Human Information-Processing Model.

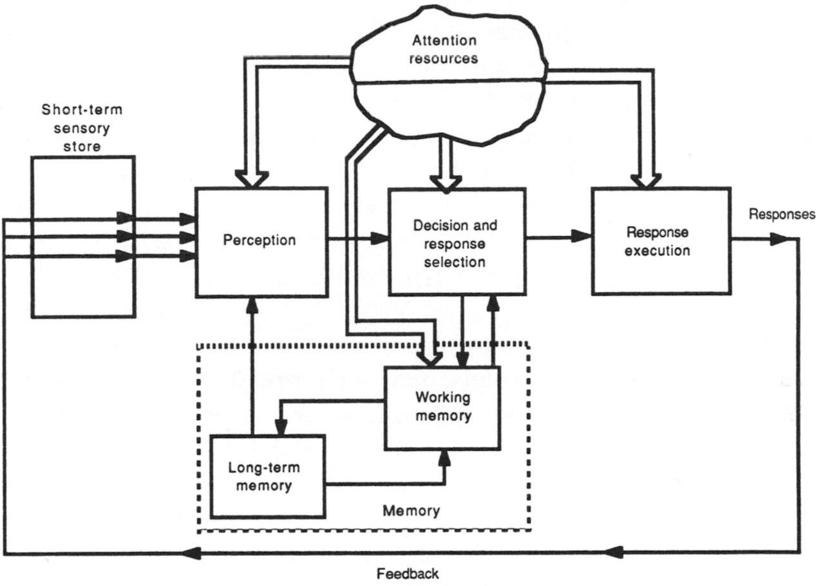

Source: Wickens, 1984.

explain different sets of attentional phenomena. Another "bottleneck" is the store that Wickens (1984) identifies as "working memory," which is used to hold only information that is needed for immediate processing (see Figure 5.1). For instance, in solving arithmetic problems mentally, working memory can be used to hold values and partial results. The amount of information that can be held is limited to about seven, plus or minus two units of information; this capacity can be increased, however, by the organization of to-be-remembered information into meaningful chunks (Miller, 1956).

The view that information undergoes transformations between input and output has resulted in a major emphasis on the cognitive code, or the representation of information in memory. Much research has been concerned with whether the code is visual (Paivio, 1971) or verbal (Clark, 1974) in nature, or both (Anderson, 1983; Begg & Paivio, 1969). Another concern has to do with how particular concepts or categories, such as *dog* or *furniture*, are represented in memory. Some researchers have argued that each instance of a category is stored in memory (Hintzman & Ludlam, 1980; Medin & Schaffer, 1978); others have argued that what is stored is a prototype or average that has been abstracted from the instances of a category (Posner & Keele, 1968, 1970). Other issues revolve around the structure of the cognitive code, as well as questions of similarity and typicality (Collins & Loftus, 1975; Smith, Shoben, & Rips, 1974; Tversky, 1977).

Cognitive psychologists have become aware of some limitations of flowchart models, such as the one shown in Figure 5.1. Neisser (1976), for instance, emphasizes that perception should be thought of as a cycle, rather than as a series of discrete stages: Information already stored in memory guides the perception of particular events in the environment; in turn, this perceptual activity modifies the existing knowledge. Numerous studies (Biederman, Mezzanotte, & Rabinowitz, 1982; Bransford & Johnson, 1972; Schvaneveldt & McDonald, 1981) have supported Neisser's view and have resulted in increased emphasis on such "top-down processing," in addition to the stimulus-driven or "bottom-up processing" emphasized in flowcharts. Moreover, flowchart models are often oversimplified and lack detailed descriptions of various components of the system. Nevertheless, they are useful in suggesting interesting research questions, which can then be investigated in detail and modeled with more formal mathematical procedures or computer-aided simulation techniques.

Without minimizing the importance of the controversy surrounding the precise structure and operation of human information-processing models, let us move on to a consideration of the components that have the greatest potential significance for training. Memory, of course, is fundamental to learning; and the organization of the basic processes involved in such higher-order skills as language comprehension and problem solving is clearly more salient than the detailed nature of component processes. Thus, we shall concentrate on remembering and on the so-called complex cognitive processes.

Remembering. Memory, or the ability to retain information over time, is central both to the other basic functions (for example, attention and perception) and to the more complex cognitive processes. Information-processing theorists often divide memory into three major processes: encoding, storage, and retrieval. *Encoding* refers to the transformation of incoming information into the internal cognitive representation, or code. *Storage* generally refers to such properties as memory capacity and duration. Different memory structures, or stores (sensory, long-term, and working or short-term stores), have been distinguished on the basis of their functional properties (Stern, 1985). A great deal of information can be held almost indefinitely in long-term memory, whereas short-term (working) memory is capable of holding only a few items for a few seconds. Sensory storage involves the very brief (lasting less than one second) preservation of the stimulus impression. Finally, retrieval has to do with accessing the information held in long-term memory, a process vital to the performance of many tasks, particularly those of a more complex nature.

Years of memory research have established several recurring concepts, which are useful in explaining various memory phenomena. One such concept is *depth of processing*, which implies qualitatively different levels or forms in which material may be stored. Craik and Lockhart (1972) suggest that material encoded at "deep," or semantic, levels of processing (where meaning is attached) will be better remembered than information encoded at more shallow levels (where only phonetic information is involved). In a study that supports this hypothesis, Hyde and Jenkins (1973) worked with subjects who were unaware that they were going to be tested on a list of words. Those who were given semantic-orienting tasks (such as rating the pleasantness of each word) recalled more than subjects who were given nonsemantic-orienting tasks (such as detecting the occurrence of a specified letter in each word). Although there have been numerous explanations for this effect, it seems that information is more memorable when encoding activities are meaningful or appropriate to later retention tasks (Morris, Bransford, & Franks, 1977). Clearly, an important implication for the design of training programs involves the need to create contexts conducive to effective encoding.

Another concept that recurs in much of the memory literature is the idea that organization facilitates recall (Bower, 1972). For instance, the list "rose, daisy, marigold, ruby, sapphire, diamond" should be easier to remember than the list "daisy, fish, shirt, truck, ruby, sparrow," because the first list is organized according to two familiar categories. It has also been found that, in the absence of any obvious external organization, people will impose their own organization on material, in order to remember it (Tulving, 1962). It is thought that particular organization of a list facilitates learning because the list corresponds more closely to the individual's knowledge, which is similarly organized. Caramazza, Hersh, and Torgerson (1976) and Schwartz and Humphreys (1973) found that pairwise ratings of similarity (a measure of memory organization) for a set of items were highly correlated with the recall order of those items, results that support this contention.

Network and featural models have both been proposed as descriptions of memory organization. According to network models (Collins & Quillian, 1969; Collins & Loftus, 1975), such concepts as *robin* and *bird* are represented by nodes in a network, and associations between pairs of concepts are represented by links between the nodes. Labels are attached to links, to specify the nature of relations. For instance, the link between *robin* and *bird* would be labeled "is a," indicating that *bird* has a superordinate relation to *robin*. Alternatively, in featural models of memory (Rips, Shoben, & Smith, 1974), concepts are represented as sets of defining and characteristic features. Defining features are shared by all members of a category (wings, for example, in the case of birds), whereas characteristic features are shared by many members (for example, flying, in the case of birds). Thus, although cognitive psychologists generally agree that the information stored in memory is organized, they disagree on the particular form of organization. Nevertheless, it is apparent that the organization of to-be-learned material should be another important consideration in the design of training programs.

Not only are levels of processing and organization interesting from a theoretical standpoint; research results in these areas also often suggest techniques that could be used to aid or improve memory. For instance, the chunking or grouping of related items has already been mentioned as a strategy that can be used to overcome working-memory limitations. Likewise, mnemonic techniques can improve memory by providing well-learned structures or frameworks, on which the individual can attach the to-be-remembered items. For example, in the "method of loci," a person associates each item with a familiar geographical location; retrieval then becomes just a matter of mentally scanning the locations. In general, these techniques involve one's making the material more meaningful or accessible by actively promoting the formation of mental images and associations (Baddeley, 1982).

Complex Cognitive Processes. The processes discussed up to this point (attention, perception, encoding, storage, and retrieval) are involved in the processing of all incoming information. By contrast, such complex processes as language comprehension, problem solving, and reasoning operate on an "as needed" and, to some extent, "top-down" basis. These processes are typically composed of combinations of several basic processes and thus are considered complex. For instance, the comprehension or understanding of a sentence entails attending, perceiving, encoding, retrieving meaning, resolving ambiguities, and drawing inferences, all precisely orchestrated in a continuous flow of activity.

One prominent model of comprehension, Anderson's (1976) ACT model, has been successful in accounting for a variety of behavioral data. In it, Anderson distinguishes between *declarative*, or factual, knowledge ("knowing that") and *procedural* knowledge ("knowing how"). Declarative knowledge is represented in a propositional network similar to the Collins and Loftus (1975) model described earlier. Procedural knowledge is represented in a production system, consisting of condition-action (if-then) rules. The production system interacts with the active factual knowledge in the network, as an interpreter. Anderson (1982) has also used ACT to explain changes that occur in knowledge during the acquisition of a cognitive skill. Over time, declarative knowledge is proceduralized, or transformed into production rules. In addition, groups of rules that are frequently used together become chunked, or compiled, which increases the efficiency of the system. Anderson's concept of compiled knowledge is very similar to a concept put forth by Shiffrin and Schneider (1977), which they call "automaticity." Both concepts imply that in certain circumstances (extensive practice on a task in which responses are consistently mapped to stimuli), processing that once required active control can become automatic, thus minimizing demands on the processor's limited attentional capacity (see Figure 5.1). As we shall see, the automatization process is a fundamental consideration in training design: Task components that can be "automated" offer obvious targets of opportunity.

The ability to draw inferences and to go beyond the literal interpretation of language is a critical aspect of comprehension. Bartlett (1932) points out that subjects often make inferences and elaborate on details of stories that they are asked to recall. He introduced the notion of a schema—a body of stored knowledge related to a particular set of experiences—to explain the constructive nature of cognition. Recently, the schema construct has been formalized, to provide machines with inferencing capabilities. Two such formalizations involve scripts and frames. Scripts (Schank & Abelson, 1977), or cognitive representations of events that occur in typical scenarios (visiting a doctor, going to a restaurant), are stored in a temporal sequence. Frames (Minsky, 1975), which are also schemalike structures, consist of slots that can be filled with information about the particular situation or concept in question. Each slot can be associated with constraints and a default value. For instance, a frame representing information about a birthday party might have a slot for "party food." The default value for this slot, or type of food typically expected, might be "cake." Thus, if no information about party food were given explicitly in a description, the default value, "cake," would be assumed. The presence of structured stereotypical knowledge, both in scripts and in frames, provides them with inferencing capabilities.

Bartlett's (1932) schema concept has received much attention in cognitive psychology, as well as in such related areas as social cognition. In addition, learning has been described in terms of schemata. Rumelhart and Norman (1981) conceive of learning as the creation and modification of schemata, which entail accretion, tuning, and restructuring processes. *Accretion* refers to the use of a schema to guide the encoding of new information. This type of learning can be thought of as the instantiation of an existing schema. *Tuning*, which is qualitatively different from accretion, refers to the gradual evolution of the schema through modifications and refinements. This type of learning is thought to occur during the acquisition of expertise. Some learning involves *restructuring*, which refers to the actual creation of new schemata. Development of schemata, or mental models, lies at the very heart of the cognitive approach to training.

Problem solving is another cognitive process that is composed of many basic processes, among which memory plays a central role. For example, in their theory of problem solving, Newell and Simon (1972) emphasize the importance of the "problem space," or the way in which a problem is represented by a subject. Such factors as previous experience with similar problems, instructions, and plans in memory influence the construction of the problem space. According to Newell and Simon (1972), once the problem space is constructed, problems are often solved by a strategy called means/end analysis, in which the solver strives to reduce the distance between the initial state and the goal state of the problem. Problem-solving strategies such as this constitute a principal content domain for cognitively oriented training.

One underlying theme that has emerged in the study of complex cognitive processes is that people do not always behave optimally, especially when they are faced with incomplete or uncertain information. They often run up against cognitive limitations and, as a result, they "satisfice" (Simon, 1981) — that is, they strive for a satisfactory, rather than an optimal, solution. Kahneman and Tversky (1973), for instance, have identified various decision-making heuristics, or rules of thumb, that people employ under tasks involving uncertainty. These heuristics lead to accurate solutions most of the time, but occasionally they lead to serious errors. For example, people frequently make judgments about the probability that an event or an object belongs to a particular class, on the basis of the similarity, or *representativeness*, of the object to the class. Biases result because such factors as prior probabilities and sample size affect probability, but not similarity. Thus, in considering similarity, but not prior probability and sample size, people misjudge the true likelihood of an event.

Finally, in order to study complex cognitive processes, it is necessary to identify problem-solving strategies, plans, facts, mental models, and heuristics that people use. Such measures as reaction time and error, although useful for decoupling the stages of information processing, are less helpful for uncovering this type of information. Consequently, investigators have turned to more subjective techniques, such as protocol analysis, which have their own shortcomings. Therefore, there is a critical need in cognitive psychology for new methods of eliciting knowledge, a point we shall develop further in the last section of this chapter. Interestingly, there is a similar need in AI, especially with respect to the design of intelligent, knowledge-based systems (Cooke & McDonald, 1986).

Applications to Education and Human Factors

As we said earlier, the training community has generally been slow to respond to the cognitive trends in work requirements and in the psychology of learning. The same cannot be said for the education community, where instructional research and program design have been dominated for some time by mental constructs and theories (Shuell, 1986; Gagné & Dick, 1983; Pintrich, Cross, Kozma, & McKeachie, 1986). Central to this orientation is the information-processing model of the learner, with its emphasis on basic knowledge structures and mental operations (as illustrated in the last section). In this view, the design of instructional programs requires consideration of learner as well as task characteristics, from the standpoint of component information-processing functions (Glaser, 1984). One needs to know what demands particular tasks place on the component mental structures and operations, as well as how people in general, or the learner in particular, handle such demands. More specifically, one needs to know how the learner progresses from a lower to a higher level of skill on the critical functions.

Certainly, many advances in the field of instructional design have direct implications for training. In this section, we shall examine a sample of them. Closely related, in a conceptual sense, are advances in work design, which have as their primary objective improved system performance through the human factors approach: better allocation of functions to humans and machines, better interfaces, better software, or combinations thereof. The conceptual link is the centrality of the information-processing model and of the idea that operator and machine interact in defining the characteristics of a task. One can improve software design by making it compatible with the operator's mental model of the task, for example, or one can compensate for known deficiencies in the human cognitive system by providing "machine aids" that reduce task demands, or one can simply make it easier for the operator and the machine to communicate with each other about the task (Fotta, 1987; Kramer & Schumacher, 1987). It is not uncommon, incidentally, for engineers to think in terms of replacing the human entirely in advanced systems, although sound arguments can be offered that artificial intelligence can never completely substitute for the real thing (Davis, 1987; Wiener, 1987).

In any event, while they share their cognitive foundations with modern instructional design, these efforts in human factors have sought improvement through better task design, rather than through better learning. Only recently have they begun to deal seriously with the fact that, in designing tasks for the human user, one is often aiming at a moving target. Thus, it becomes important to determine how the operator's conceptualization of the task changes as he or she acquires knowledge and skill, and to discover whether such changes interact with individual-difference variables, such as intelligence or age. If one is designing a system to maximize the performance of novices, care must be taken to ensure that it does not hamper their development beyond that stage or interfere with their performance when they become experts. Rasmussen (1980) has suggested that many skills progress through three stages: a knowledge-based stage, which involves a considerable amount of cognitive effort; a rule-based stage, which requires less; and a skill-based stage, which approaches the level of automatic processing (discussed earlier). This progression does not reflect just improved execution of the same cognitive routine; rather, it shows a qualitative change, toward more efficient processing.

Such cognitive changes must be taken into account, whether one is concerned with optimizing system performance (human factors) or skills learning (instructional design). Therefore, we shall explore a sample of applications from the cognitive, human factors, and AI literatures, as well as from the educational domain. The former applications are best illustrated within the real-world contexts of monitoring, trouble shooting (fault diagnosis), and judgment or decision-making tasks — all domains of the sort that we cited earlier as increasingly representative of modern work. It happens that they are also domains in which people are known to have serious shortcomings; hence, they offer considerable room for improvement, either through training or through system-design interventions. First, however, let us consider the educational domain.

Cognition in Education

There are many points where cognitive notions have influenced modern educational thought and practice. Three broad and overlapping themes seem particularly relevant for training applications: the recognition that human learning involves multiple processes, each of which obeys somewhat different laws (and therefore carries somewhat different instructional implications); the articulation and use of individual-difference variables in the design of instructional programs (personalization, in terms of mental models); and the identification of general strategies that can be taught, in order to enhance performance on very broad ranges of cognitive tasks (problem-solving skills, or even generalized thinking skills).

The *multiple-process* theme emphasizes the importance of cognitively oriented task analyses, and those that have evolved draw heavily on the basic concepts introduced in the previous section: working memory, encoding processes, knowledge organization, automaticity, schema formation, and the like. We shall have more to say on this theme in a moment.

The *individual-differences* theme emphasizes the importance of analyzing cognitive traits or tendencies of the learner, including those more properly regarded as states that characterize the learner at a particular stage in the learning process. Expert tutoring, for example, a fundamental element of all intelligent computer-assisted instruction (ICAI) programs, requires an understanding of the ways in which the particular learner is likely to go astray in dealing with a class of problems, as well as the ability to diagnose the particular error that the learner is currently encountering.

The *general-strategies* theme emphasizes the lability of intellectual skills that have been regarded in traditional psychometric theory as relatively fixed. Controversy still rages about the extent to which the most general of cognitive skills, those typically used to define the construct of intelligence, can be improved through instruction (Mayer, 1983; Nickerson, Perkins, & Smith, 1985). Space does not permit exploration of the complex set of issues surrounding this debate. Suffice it to say here that a number of successes have been reported in programs designed to improve thinking skills for application to very broad ranges of problems (Baron & Sternberg, 1987; Nickerson, Perkins, & Smith, 1985). Whether one chooses to say that this is improving intelligence, teaching thinking skills, or simply preparing people to deal more efficiently with a certain (broad) class of problems encountered in school or at work is largely a matter of theoretical preference. From a practical standpoint, the critical issue is the same: How broad is the category of tasks within which one can demonstrate significant positive transfer, and how does one define that category? At the end of this section, we shall examine a few of the reported successes from this perspective.

Multiple Processes and Task Analysis. The multiple-process notion and its task-analysis corollary are by no means new to the education field. The argument for taxonomies of education tasks goes back at least to the middle of this century (Bloom, 1956; Miller, 1953). Several influential papers over the next two decades elaborated on this theme, emphasizing the need for a better link between learning principles and instructional or training design than was customary at the time (Briggs, 1970; Gagné, 1962, 1970; Glaser, 1964, 1966, 1972). Gagné's (1970) taxonomy, for example, distinguished eight types of learning, five of which (verbal association, discrimination, concept, rule, and problem solving) involved a hierarchical progression of cognitive processes. Glaser (1966) clarified the steps necessary to go from psychological theory to instructional application — "(a) analyzing the characteristics of subject-matter competence, (b) diagnosing preinstructional behavior, (c) carrying out the instructional process, and (d) measuring learning outcomes" (p. 14) — while Briggs (1968) articulated an explicit model for implementing the approach.

The work of Glaser, Gagné, Briggs, and their colleagues has continued to play a leading role in the evolution of modern instructional theory. Building on this general idea — that effective instruction requires a detailed understanding of the desired learning outcomes (what the learner should know or be able to do) and the steps or processes by which that result can best be achieved — their approach has incorporated many of the newer insights from the cognitive literature. The most recent version of Gagné's (1984) taxonomy of learning outcomes, for example, includes intellectual skills (procedural knowledge), verbal information (declarative information), and cognitive strategies among its five categories. Glaser (1986) identifies categorization, principled knowledge, mental models, automatization, proceduralization, and metacognition (or monitoring one's own learning) as critical elements in the development of expertise.

As we noted earlier, the information-processing revolution was fueled largely by problems and discontent with the behaviorist paradigm. Cognitive psychologists rejected many of the assumptions and methodologies of the old paradigm and generally abandoned the study of learning. Only recently have cognitive psychologists, such as John Anderson (1981), become interested in questions of learning and knowledge acquisition per se. Nevertheless, the study of high-level information processes has revealed information very relevant to learning and thus has contributed significantly to education. As is characteristic of the information-processing approach, researchers interested in such complex human behaviors as problem solving or comprehension have attempted to decompose tasks that involve these behaviors into smaller and more manageable processes or stages. This type of approach also allows for comparison of tasks that are based on shared cognitive processes. In addition, this approach provides a useful framework for those interested in education.

Along these lines, Greeno (1978) describes a typology in which he classifies problems according to the cognitive processes and abilities needed to solve each one. For instance, anagrams and cryptarithmetic problems are both problems of arrangement and involve a constructive search process. This particular process requires a variety of cognitive abilities, including the generation of possibilities and the application of principles that constrain search. Given that the typology is psychologically valid, instruction should focus on these particular abilities in order to improve performance on problems of arrangement. Other, more specific tasks, such as solving physics problems (Chi, Feltovich, & Glaser, 1981; Larkin, McDermott, Simon, & Simon, 1980) or math problems (Brown & Burton, 1978), have also been analyzed in attempts to understand the knowledge structures and processes associated with them. Resnick (1983) points out that instructional objectives are in fact byproducts of cognitive research directed at understanding tasks.

Some of Greeno's (1983) work on geometric proofs illus-

Figure 5.2. A Proof-Checking Problem.

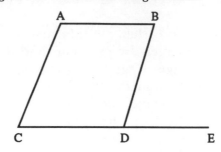

Given: $\overline{AB} \mathbin{/} \overline{CE}$ and $\overline{AB} \cong \overline{CD}$

Prove: $\angle ACD \cong \angle ABD$

Statement	*Reason*
1. $\angle ACD \cong \angle BDE$	Corresponding $\angle$s
2. $\angle BDE \cong \angle ABD$	Alternate interior $\angle$s
3. $\angle ACD \cong \angle ABD$	Transitive property

Source: Greeno, 1983.

trates the identification of educational objectives. Greeno not only identifies objectives but also incorporates them into instructional materials, in order to evaluate the objectives and, in a sense, the general approach of cognitive task analysis. In this particular project, Greeno defines *proof understanding* in terms of the features necessary for a series of statements to be a proof. The task used to study this type of knowledge involves checking geometry proofs for correctness and, in cases where they are judged incorrect, explaining why. Proofs are displayed as a series of statements, each of which is accompanied by a reason for that statement, as illustrated in Figure 5.2.

In the first phase of the project, Greeno interviewed high school geometry students at two points during the year. He gave the students proofs to check, and he observed their performance on the task. In general, students performed poorly. In some cases, there was little or no improvement in performance over time. These results verify the task difficulty and the need for instructional intervention. In addition, Greeno's observations revealed particular sources of errors that suggest possible intervention needs. For instance, students often failed to detect errors in proofs that involved missing assertions.

In the next part of the study, Greeno developed a psychologically plausible computational model of proof checking. He did not model errors that the students made; instead, he simulated correct performance. This model served as a specific hypothesis about the knowledge that was necessary to perform the proof-checking task correctly: It was, in other words, a cognitive task analysis. Each of the six steps in the proof-checking procedure was applied to every statement of the proof. The first step involved checking to determine whether the reason given was a theorem, a definition, or a postulate. The next step involved retrieving the explicit rule (antecedent and consequent) behind the reason; for instance, the reason "Corresponding angles" is associated with a postulate, and the explicit rule is "*If* angles X and Y are corresponding angles, with lines L and M as sides, and lines L and M are parallel, and line N contains their other sides, *then* X and Y are congruent." The next steps involved instantiating the antecedent and the consequent in a formal statement, using objects in the problem statement, and, finally, determining whether the statement matched the problem goal.

Greeno incorporated the computational model into instructional material in a series of "if-then" rules. He gave this instructional material to a group of college students, along with a general geometry review. A control group received the review only. Subjects then performed a series of proof-checking problems, along with three proof-construction problems. The training and the first problem set involved proofs that dealt with the congruence of triangles. In addition, transfer to geometry problems in a different domain was also investigated. The results indicate that the group given instructional material detected significantly more errors than the control group did, that the training benefits occurred in proof construction as well as in checking, and that training transferred to problems in a different domain. Verbal protocols (a subject's verbalizations of ongoing thought processes), collected while subjects solved the problems, reveal that the steps suggested in the instructional materials were used more by the experimental group than by the control group. Greeno argues that this use of the proof-checking procedure is evidence of implicit understanding of a proof, and that, consequently, the instructions generated by the cognitive task analysis improved proof understanding.

In summary, Greeno used a combination of empirical observation and computer simulation to analyze the proof-checking task. The analysis revealed several steps, which were then incorporated into instructional materials. Subjects who studied these materials outperformed subjects who did not have access to the information on the proof-checking and proof-construction tasks. It is encouraging that the instruction was transferred to a different set of geometry problems. This finding suggests that educational objectives uncovered by cognitive task analyses are not necessarily restricted to the specific tasks analyzed.

Individual Differences. Along with the information-processing revolution came an emphasis on nomothetic explanation, in preference to the investigation of cognitive variation among individuals. Recently, however, researchers involved in the modeling of problem-solving processes have recognized the need to address some major sources of individual variation, such as experience (Adelson, 1981; Chase & Simon, 1973; Chi, Feltovich, & Glaser, 1981; McKeithen, Reitman, Rueter, & Hirtle, 1981). One construct that has been used to explain expert-novice differences is the mental model (Gentner & Stevens, 1983), to which we have referred before. Mental models, in the broad sense of the term, are like schemata in that they are structures in memory that contain related chunks of knowledge. Viewed narrowly, mental models are descriptions of people's conceptualizations of physical devices or systems, which can be used to explain and predict the systems' behavior. Mental models are typically characterized as qualitative, incomplete, and inaccurate, although an expert's model should approximate reality more closely than a novice's.

Cognitive research on mental models and individual differences has materialized in the education literature in the guise of student models in intelligent tutoring systems, or Intelligent

Computer-Assisted Instruction (ICAI). A student model is a mental model that an individual student possesses about a particular task at a particular time. One of the objectives of intelligent tutoring systems is to identify the student model and to focus the tutoring interaction on misconceptions, or "bugs," in the model. Consequently, the tutoring session is individually tailored. Sleeman and Brown (1982) distinguish between this current knowledge-based approach to computer-assisted instruction and the older approach, which is based on performance on tasks that are selected to differentiate subskills. The older approach illuminates the student's weaknesses but affords no explanation of the misconceptions in knowledge underlying those weaknesses. This shift from behaviorally based models to knowledge-intensive models parallels the shift from behaviorism to information processing.

There are numerous examples of intelligent tutoring systems, many of which are described by Sleeman and Brown (1982). Burton's (1982) DEBUGGY system is described here as a specific illustration. DEBUGGY is a system that diagnoses students' errors in three-digit subtraction problems and is based on BUGGY, a model of students' errors in simple procedural skills (Brown & Burton, 1978). Students' knowledge is represented in the form of goals and methods for accomplishing the goals. The methods may be correct or incorrect ("buggy"). Given a student's solutions to a set of subtraction problems, DEBUGGY attempts to uncover the student's misconceptions by searching through a stored list of "bugs" until one is located that produces the answers that best match the student's answers.

Burton (1982) discusses several complications that arise from this type of diagnosis. For example, students often behave inconsistently, because of such factors as fatigue, boredom, or errors in primitive skills (for example, the belief that $13 - 7 = 8$). An even more complex problem arises when misconceptions are tied to combinations of several "bugs," which greatly increases the size of the list of "bugs" that is to be searched. Burton managed to circumvent some of these difficulties by using heuristics to constrain the search and by carefully selecting a set of test problems that distinguished among many of the "bugs." In fact, the DEBUGGY system is capable of measuring the diagnostic capability of a particular problem. This feature is useful in an interactive version of DEBUGGY, which can select the problems given to a student according to current hypotheses about that student's misconceptions.

DEBUGGY has been used to diagnose subtraction misconceptions in over one thousand students, and it illustrates the state of the art in current ICAI systems, which rely heavily on adequate models of individual students and on cognitive modeling research in general. Sleeman and Brown (1982) note several shortcomings of ICAI, many of which hinge on future research on knowledge acquisition and representation. They point out that current systems make assumptions about the student's model and fit the student's performance into that framework, rather than discovering the actual model. Thus, although the goal is to base each tutoring session on the cognitive model of the individual student, it is not at all clear how to obtain this model; therefore, these concessions must be made.

General Strategies. Much of the problem-solving research in cognitive psychology has been directed toward the discovery of general problem-solving strategies that are used to solve a wide variety of problems. Probably the best-known example of such an approach is the work of Newell and Simon (1972). According to their theory of problem solving, a problem is internally represented by a problem solver in a problem space, which is composed of various states and of operators that enable movement through the states. General strategies take the form of heuristics, such as subgoal analysis and working backwards, that are used to search through the problem space. Newell and Simon found evidence to support their theory, in verbal protocols that were collected while subjects worked through a variety of problems. Other evidence for general strategies or skills, which underlie not only problem solving but also intelligence, creativity, and metacognition, is summarized by Nickerson, Perkins, and Smith (1985).

Numerous instructional programs (Baron & Sternberg, 1987; Nickerson, Perkins, & Smith, 1985) revolve around the notion of general problem-solving strategies. These programs apply many of the findings from the study of problem-solving strategies in cognitive psychology. The IDEAL program, described by Bransford and Stein (1984), illustrates this approach. The letters of the acronym IDEAL stand for specific components of the generic problem-solving process: I = identify the problem, D = define and represent the problem, E = explore possible strategies, A = act on the strategies, and L = look back and evaluate the effects of your activities. Strategies include Newell and Simon's (1972) subgoal analysis and working backwards, as well as imagery and mnemonics to aid memory. Nickerson, Perkins, and Smith (1985) point out that programs like IDEAL, which concentrate on very general strategies, tend to ignore such complex tasks as writing and mathematical problem solving. In addition, the effectiveness of this approach is difficult to evaluate, because it usually depends on extensive practice on diverse tasks, as well as frequent testing—characteristics that tend to benefit the student, regardless of the specifics of the program.

Recently, the importance of domain-specific knowledge has been emphasized over general strategies in the study of problem solving, although Nisbett, Krantz, Jepson, and Kunda (1983) challenge this emphasis. Support for the former view has come from studies comparing experts and novices, in which problem-solving skills were shown to reflect domain-specific knowledge and the organization of that knowledge in memory (Adelson, 1981; Chase & Simon, 1973; Chi, Feltovich, & Glaser, 1981; McKeithen, Reitman, Rueter, & Hirtle, 1981). In addition, work in AI on the development of expert systems (computer programs that solve problems typically requiring human expertise) has focused on the knowledge base in which domain-specific facts and rules are stored (Waterman, 1986). Finally, other researchers have found that subjects in many cases experience difficulty in transferring the general strategies they have learned in one set of problems to different, isomorphic problems (Hayes & Simon, 1977; Reed, Ernst, & Banerji, 1974; Simon & Hayes, 1976). Therefore, some studies demonstrate the importance of domain-specific knowledge but do not rule out the

existence of general problem-solving strategies. Some researchers emphasize such strategies, while others (for example,
Simon, 1980) have suggested that general strategies be taught in
the context of specific problem areas. The question of identifying the proper level of specificity, however, remains one of the
issues that make the application of cognitive principles to training problematic.

Schoenfeld's (1979, 1980) work on teaching heuristics in
the domain of mathematical problem solving exemplifies the
context-specific approach to general strategy development. In
one experiment, Schoenfeld compared the problem-solving
performance of four math majors, who were taught specific
heuristics, to a control group of three majors, who were not. The
five heuristics relevant to solving the math problems used in this
study were to draw a diagram, if at all possible; when there was
an integer parameter, to look for an inductive argument; to
consider arguing by contradiction or contraposition; to consider similar problems, with fewer variables; and to try to establish subgoals.

All students were pretested with one set of math problems, given instructions, and then posttested with a different set
of problems. The instruction session for all students called on
them to work through example problems, each of which was
followed by the presentation of a good problem-solving process.
This process incorporated the heuristics implicitly. The experimental group, in addition, was presented with the list of
heuristics at the beginning of instruction, and they were mentioned explicitly as they were used in the problem-solving instructional process. The experimental group was also presented
with instruction problems grouped by heuristic, along with a list
of heuristics to use during the posttest. Results indicated that
the students explicitly exposed to the heuristics solved significantly more problems than the control group did. In addition,
verbal protocols indicated that students in the experimental
group were applying the heuristics that they had learned.

Schoenfeld's work provides support for the teaching of
strategies in a specific problem context. Nevertheless, the extent
to which these learned strategies would transfer to other math

problems, or to other domains, remains unclear. Investigation of the transfer of training, and the identification of a transfer-appropriate level of instruction, are clearly topics that require additional research. In summary, the success of various approaches like Schoenfeld's, in which problem-solving strategies are explicitly taught, is encouraging and instructive. Such approaches show that this kind of instruction can be effective, and they suggest ways of accomplishing that goal. General principles regarding level of specificity are still lacking, however.

Cognition in Human Factors

From its very beginning, during World War II, human factors (engineering) psychology has relied heavily on cognitive models. In fact, many of the basic concepts described in this chapter, such as that of humans as capacity-limited information channels and attention as a selective filter, originated in research aimed at solving "man–machine system" design problems (Mark, Warm, & Huston, 1987; Wickens, 1984).

While they are primarily concerned with achieving safer, more efficient, and more error-free designs, human factors researchers have always recognized the importance of training considerations. On the one hand, training represents an alternative strategy to design, the relative costs and benefits of which must be taken into account in any design decision. On the other, ease of learning and transfer are themselves important dependent variables that help to define the effectiveness of any design (Howell & Goldstein, 1971).

In the design of training simulators, for example, a continuing issue is that of psychological fidelity, or the extent to which the training device preserves the functionally salient characteristics of the operational system (Flexman & Stark, 1987). As system tasks have changed, from analog-manual tasks to executive-control tasks (from the learner's perspective), those salient characteristics have become increasingly cognitive. To design a good simulator, one needs the same kind of basic understanding of the learner's evolving mental model of the task, and of the considerations regarding such underlying processes as metacognition, automaticity, and heuristic processing, as one does to design a good instructional program. The ultimate test of that design is whether practice on it transfers to the operational system itself.

The remainder of this section is devoted to illustrating how researchers in human factors have envisioned the application of cognitive concepts to specific training issues. Before we proceed with examples, however, let us recall that the overarching theme here is exactly the same as the one discussed earlier, in connection with educational applications—namely, cognitive task analysis. One must identify the overall objectives of the task, decompose them into elements that have meaning from the learner's perspective (and from what we know about the underlying cognitive processes), and only then decide what elements to feature in the training program, and in what order (Montague, 1986). This is in marked contrast to both the traditional engineering approach, which focuses on sequential behavioral elements, and structured job-analysis techniques, which include cognitive elements, but at a level of analysis that fails to capture the underlying structure of human cognition. It would be very difficult to use either the SAINT methodology (a prominent example of the engineering approach to task analysis) or the PAQ methodology (a prominent example of job analysis) to identify what aspects of a to-be-learned content domain are the most promising targets for automaticity training, or in what fashion the organization of that domain should be represented in a training program (Meister, 1985). (We shall have more to say about task analysis in the final section.)

Monitoring and Vigilance. Joint monitoring of automated systems by humans and machines (the human–computer monitoring concept) is now commonplace in commercial aircraft, air traffic control, industrial inspection, and process control contexts (Parasuraman, 1987). Some forty years of research have produced over one thousand studies on how people function in this role and, in particular, on the potential problem of diminished attention with sustained watchkeeping (Mackie, 1987). Despite some controversy regarding its practical significance

(Adams, 1987), this so-called vigilance decrement has been the subject of numerous investigations, many aimed at evaluating possible remediation strategies (Mackie, 1987). Some have involved training.

The most notable example, from a training standpoint, is a study by Fisk and Schneider (1981), which follows directly from the qualitative distinction between automatic and controlled processing (Shiffrin & Schneider, 1977). Automatic processing, as noted earlier, involves highly overlearned skills that require little investment of attentional resources (for example, normal driving). Controlled processing is effortful, in the sense that it is conscious, intentional, and interferes with other mental activities (Posner & Snyder, 1975). Two critical variables that determine whether training will result in automatization of a skill (most skills, incidentally, begin in the controlled state) are the consistency with which the stimulus and response elements of a task are paired during practice, and the amount of practice.

Drawing on these principles, Fisk and Schneider (1981) were able to show that the vigilance decrement is attributable almost exclusively to controlled processing. Consistent pairing of to-be-detected target stimuli with detection responses and feedback ("consistent mapping") was sufficient, over four thousand training trials, to automatize the subject's detection response. Transfer to a standard vigilance paradigm, in which only eighteen of six thousand presentations contained the target stimulus, resulted in virtually no decrement over time. By contrast, similar training in which only some of the four thousand trials contained target stimuli produced a typical 65 percent vigilance decrement over the six-thousand-trial (fifty-minute) test session.

A particularly noteworthy aspect of these findings is that the ineffective variable-mapping paradigm was the one in which training conditions most closely approximated the transfer conditions. Consistent mapping, however, which offered seemingly unrealistic preparation for a task whose most salient feature is low target frequency (relative to nontarget events), produced sustained performance. On the basis of the traditional consideration of similarity between training and transfer conditions, one would have predicted exactly the opposite results. Only through understanding of the cognitive processes involved (automatic versus control) was it reasonable to predict such a counterintuitive finding.

The message, of course, extends well beyond the vigilance phenomenon. Intensive training on certain procedural elements of a task—training designed to make these subroutines cognitively automatic, and thereby to free up capacity for handling more unpredictable or creative task demands—seems to be a potentially useful strategy for training people to deal with today's complex work assignments. The trick, once again, is to identify those elements of the total task that are particularly amenable to automatization. Of course, even if all suitable elements were so trained, the remaining elements would still require controlled processing. It is to these so-called higher mental components that our remaining examples apply: problem solving, as represented in trouble shooting (fault diagnosis), and various kinds of judgment and decision-making (J/DM) tasks.

Trouble Shooting. As systems become more complex, there are more things to go wrong and more ways for that to happen. Further, as dramatically illustrated by the Three Mile Island, Chernobyl, Challenger, and Vincennes accidents, small failures can have a large impact. Generally speaking, the ultimate responsibility for diagnosing faults rests with humans, although with the aid of increasingly sophisticated machines. Often a specific problem will be one that someone has never seen before; the pattern of symptoms will be interpretable only through a comprehensive understanding of the system (an appropriate store of declarative knowledge, or an appropriate mental model) and a well-developed set of diagnostic skills (the appropriate procedural knowledge). The central training issue thus becomes how to prepare people to deal with unfamiliar, infrequent, and idiosyncratic problems.

Viewed from a cognitive perspective, the learning issue clearly has many aspects. First, there is the matter of instilling the necessary domain-specific knowledge. Second, there is the question of determining how broadly to define the domain of procedural skills and how best to develop it: What sorts of problem-solving skills does one need, and how specific are they to the present context? Third, there is the issue of engagement: How does one learn to draw on the right knowledge and select the right procedures for the problem at hand? Each of these issues poses many subissues as well.

Despite its complexity, however, and despite the arguments that persist over the nature of its various components, the question of how to train trouble shooters has begun yielding to research evidence, from both laboratory and real-world settings. It draws on the long tradition of problem-solving research in psychology (Mayer, 1983; Reed, 1988), on the more recent attempts to teach general problem-solving skills (Nickerson, Perkins, & Smith, 1985; Baron & Sternberg, 1987), and on a growing literature on fault diagnosis per se (Gitomer, 1988; Rouse, 1978; Rouse & Hunt, 1984; Bond, 1987). It is from the last of these categories that we draw our examples.

Rouse and his colleagues (1978, 1984) have conducted extensive research on maintenance trainees, using trouble-shooting tasks that ranged from abstract simulations to actual systems. In all cases, the basic problem consisted of finding faulty components in a malfunctioning physical system (electronic network, automobile engine), on the basis of system-performance information and whatever problem-solving skills the subjects brought to that situation. Among the many variables manipulated were system complexity, level of abstraction, display representation, computer aiding, and context specificity (hence, the relevance of preexperimental knowledge).

A principal objective of the work was to determine the appropriate role for humans in such tasks, by manipulating the kinds of machine aiding provided and by inferring from detailed analyses of performance what mental operations were being affected. More important for present purposes, however, is that the various manipulations presented an opportunity to examine transfer effects and thus to develop generalizations about training requirements. Several findings are particularly noteworthy in this regard, and our description of them requires a brief account of two key variables: task realism and aiding. Realism was varied by use of a very abstract (hence, context-free) network simulation (designated TASK), a realistic and familiar (hence, context-specific) simulation (designated FAULT), and several actual systems. Aiding was also provided at three different levels: to relieve the operator of capacity-draining "bookkeeping" operations, to furnish graded feedback (reinforcement) on the quality of individual choices, and to provide feedback on conceptual errors in context-specific terms.

The first finding of interest is that both the "bookkeeping" and conceptual feedback aids improved performance during practice and showed positive transfer to the unaided condition. The reinforcement aid, however, degraded performance on both practice and transfer trials. The general message here seems to be that it is possible to improve fault-diagnosis skills through training under aided conditions, but one must be careful to preserve the conceptual integrity of the task, no matter what kind of aid is provided. Knowledge of results must be consistent with an appropriate mental model, or else utility may be zero or even negative.

The second relevant finding concerns transfer from the aided to the unaided versions of the same task, versus unaided tasks of greater or lesser realism (context specificity). In general, all these conditions produced positive transfer, but the greatest amount resulted between unfamiliar systems, irrespective of the realism level. Thus, it appears that neither high fidelity nor concreteness (in terms of specific context) is essential for effective training in fault diagnosis—provided, once again, that certain conceptual properties of the task are preserved. We must qualify this conclusion, however, by recalling both the positive and the negative evidence of context-specificity effects in the general problem-solving literature (Reed, 1988).

The key to understanding the role of context in the learning and transfer of problem-solving skills may well lie in identifying more precisely the mental models or schemata by which individual learners represent particular problem domains. An interesting footnote, in this regard, is that individual differences in cognitive style are better predictors of problem-solving performance than are common measures of ability and aptitude. Although they are very tentative, these findings suggest that impulsive problem solvers did not benefit much from practice; and field-dependent problem solvers, initially inferior to their field-independent counterparts, gradually narrowed the gap.

Our next example illustrates an approach aimed explicitly at identifying mental models for different classes of problem solvers — in this case, those classified as distinctly different in proficiency level on a particular task domain. The reader will recognize this approach as a version of the expert-versus-novice comparisons that are currently enjoying great popularity in the AI and problem-solving literatures. In this case, however, the differences were not so extreme, and so the comparison is more conservative.

Gitomer (1988) developed a technique for inferring characteristics of a subject's mental model in an electronics trouble-shooting task from patterns of errors on carefully devised problem sets and supporting verbal reports (an approach similar to that described earlier for DEBUGGY, in the educational context). He then compared two groups of trained technicians, classified independently as higher or lower in proficiency level, both on model characteristics and on performance on another set of trouble-shooting problems.

The principal results suggest that the more proficient subjects were guided by mental models that were much more consistent with the true functional properties of the device than were their less proficient counterparts. The more proficient group's basic declarative knowledge was more complete and more appropriately organized. Superficial features of the task environment (context) had much less of an effect on their performance than they did on the performance of the less skilled subjects. System knowledge was not the whole story, however. The skilled subjects were also better at selecting and implementing appropriate strategies (procedural knowledge). Naturally, both of these cognitive advantages were reflected in the more proficient group's superior performance on the common test problems. Errors produced by skilled subjects tended to be computational, while those of the less proficient subjects were largely conceptual.

This research did not directly study training issues, but the implications are provocative: Starting with a theory of expertise for a problem domain, one can "isolate precise deficiencies in an individual's mental model of a device [and] . . . determine whether an individual's procedural skills are weak because of a lack of knowing how to do something versus an inefficiency in executing or accessing that knowledge under certain conditions" (Gitomer, 1988, p. 25). Training can then be focused on the areas of greatest deficiency. Most important, this research illustrates a successful approach to the knotty problem of identifying component processes. It does not, however, take the next steps: designing an intervention program guided by these findings, and demonstrating its effectiveness in upgrading the skills of the less proficient technicians.

Judgment and Decision-Making Tasks. Among the general thinking and problem-solving skills that have been targeted for training, the effective use of heuristics, or inexact rules of thumb that can be applied to broad problem domains, ranks high on the list, as we saw earlier. In one problem domain, however— judgment and decision making (J/DM)—heuristic processing has been suggested as constituting a major problem, rather than a solution (Kahneman, Slovic, & Tversky, 1982; Tversky & Kahneman, 1974; but see Hogarth, 1981, for a conflicting viewpoint).

As already noted, descriptive decision research has identified a number of heuristics, such as representativeness, that seem to reflect distorted mental models, or nonoptimal strategies, that people apply to common tasks of judgment and choice. The question from the standpoint of training is whether—and, if so, how—either the models or the resulting behavior can be made more optimal. Can people be debiased through systematic training?

The key to addressing this issue, of course, lies in precise identification of the manner in which the mental model (heuristic process) deviates from the proper algorithm for the particular judgment or decision problem. There are many kinds of J/DM problems; hence, there are many candidates for training aimed at debiasing. Those that have received the most attention have been problems for which quantitative algorithms exist, notably statistical problems. This may represent something of an overemphasis (perhaps even a misdirection), as Einhorn (1982) has argued, but there is no doubt that such problems constitute an important part of modern work. Managers must aggregate day-to-day observations into overall performance judgments (descriptive statistics). Any interview is partly an information-integration and inference task. Strategic decisions by an executive, and tactical decisions by the lowest-level machine operator, involve the consideration of risk and utility.

We shall not attempt to catalogue either the inventory of J/DM tasks on which research has found humans to be seriously wanting or the growing list of heuristic processing models used to account for such shortcomings. Compendia are readily available (Einhorn & Hogarth, 1981; Kahneman, Slovic, & Tversky, 1982). Unfortunately, although debiasing efforts can be found throughout the more than twenty-year history of this research, the results have not been encouraging. Our nonoptimal mental models seem extraordinarily resistant to modification through training—not too surprisingly, perhaps, when one considers that we have spent a lifetime overlearning them, and that they have often produced satisfactory (if not always optimal) results. Besides, the normatively correct models may be inherently difficult to conceptualize or instantiate (Einhorn, 1982; Lopes, 1982). Some debiasing successes have been reported, however, and we shall direct our attention to examples of these.

Lopes (1982) addresses the well-established, far-reaching, and practically important bias through which people tend to average items of evidence in drawing inferences, rather than applying the appropriate *multiplicative* rule. (The normative rule, embodied in Bayes's theorem, says that one's prior beliefs should be modified, in light of diagnostic evidence, through multiplication of those beliefs by the diagnostic impact of the evidence.) A result of this bias is the tendency to produce conservative revisions of opinions and, hence, to give undue weight to preconceptions (for example, stereotypes) or initial evidence (for example, first impressions) in drawing conclusions. Lopes's explanation of previous failures to reduce this bias centers on the claim that insufficient attention has been paid to why or how averaging occurs. Her suggestion is that people may use an anchoring-and-adjustment heuristic (Tversky & Kahneman, 1974), which, although quantitatively equivalent to averaging, is cognitively a very different kind of process. On the basis of this cognitive model, she has devised training procedures designed to improve the (deficient) mental adjustment process. The results of two laboratory studies using a very realistic decision problem (industrial quality control) show dramatic improvement in the performance of subjects trained in the experimental (cognitive) mode, relative to the performance of normally trained control subjects.

Without going into the details of this simple yet impressive demonstration, we shall note several key principles. First, in contrast to previous (unsuccessful) attempts to effect debiasing by training people to recognize the normative model (Bayes's rule) or their deficiencies relative to it (averaging instead of multiplying), the focus was on the learner's own conception of the task and probable intuitive strategy for dealing with it (anchoring and adjustment). Second, the training design was aimed at providing the learner with alternative procedures, which, when applied to his or her existing model, would produce a result more consistent with that of the normative rule. Third, the approach illustrates a general point: that simply because a problem falls within a formal domain (statistical, quantitative, algebraic, geometric, or whatever), which provides convenient and even optimal representational and computational tools, that does not mean that those tools are the only ones or even necessarily the best ones, from a training standpoint. The training produced significant movement toward formally optimal solutions to problems that are typically couched in quantitative terms, without having made any reference whatsoever to quantitative operations or models. The distinction is subtle but perhaps vital. It represents the difference between trying to get learners to see a problem and their own procedural options more normatively (restructuring), on the one hand, and recasting the problem in ways that will allow learners to build constructively on their existing perceptions (tuning), on the other. The latter approach seems to offer considerable promise; the former, to date, has produced mostly frustration.

One factor that may well be important in the efficacy of cognitively oriented training is the nature of the J/DM task itself. This possibility is the main focus of Hammond's (1986) "cognitive continuum theory," which posits that tasks vary in their propensity to elicit more intuitive or more analytical processing modes. Tasks situated toward the intuition-inducing end of the continuum tend to produce fast, holistic processing of predictive cues; weighted averaging; inconsistency; and systematic biases in the resulting criterion judgments. Those situated toward the analysis-inducing end tend to encourage slower, systematic (often serial) processing of cues; more consistent and deliberate use of organizing rules; and, hence, more nearly optimal judgments.

Hammond has devoted considerable attention to identifying and attempting to verify the specific features of J/DM tasks that characterize particular points along the continuum. Prominent among those held to induce intuitive cognition are unfamiliarity, time constraint, complexity of relationships among cues and between cues and criteria, and uninformative outcome feedback. The analysis-inducing list is composed largely of opposite features: well-understood task structure, sufficient time, less complex relationships (or well-defined principles of organization), and informative process feedback.

It is no easy matter to test a notion as comprehensive and, in some respects, loosely defined as the cognitive continuum theory. Nevertheless, certain of its predictions have received empirical support. For example, in one recent study, Hamm (1985) was able to show marked differences in the approaches that highway engineers took toward expressing their knowledge of how the esthetics, safety, and capacity of highways were related to sets of relevant factors (landscaping, terrain, road conditions, lane width). Esthetic factors were handled more intuitively, and capacity factors were handled more analytically, both factors in accordance with well-operationalized predictions.

Of particular relevance to the issue of cognitive training is the role of feedback in continuum theory. As already noted, feedback is considered an important item of the task-features list, which collectively influences the individual's processing mode. If, however, other task features preclude an analytical approach, feedback will be relatively useless, irrespective of how potentially informative it may be. In fact, it may even degrade performance (Rouse, 1978; Rouse & Hunt, 1984) by encouraging the individual to abandon the only feasible strategy for these circumstances: heuristic (intuitive) processing. Heuristics, as we have noted, are theoretically nonoptimal, but they are still generally quite functional.

When collective task features permit (and, indeed, encourage) analytical processing, however, the role of feedback information — as well as "feedforward," or prior, information — becomes central. Here, the circumstances are conducive to improving performance through the development and use of an appropriate mental algorithm (an organizing principle, a set of rules, or some other analytical device). Theoretically, one can do considerably better than the heuristic strategy. Whether that happens is largely a function of the informativeness and perceived salience of feedback. Mere outcome feedback, which says little about either the individual's present strategy or the optimal strategy, repeatedly has been shown to be of dubious value. Only if the learner already has a very clear picture of the underlying task structure (an appropriate mental model) can one expect outcome feedback to foster improved performance. By contrast, process feedback, which supplies information related to how one's strategy deviates from that called for by an appropriate rule, can promote both strategy development and improved future performance (Adelman, 1981; Hoffman, Earle, & Slovic, 1981).

Translated into the language of debiasing efforts, Hammond's (1986) thinking suggests limiting conditions under which it makes little sense to consider cognitive training: Intuition will not be improved through techniques designed to enhance analysis. In terms of training, attention may be better turned to improving task design. When task conditions permit, however, training should be oriented toward building in an appropriate cognitive model, through both process-analytical instruction and feedback.

Hammond's work has concentrated on tasks that involve the prediction of criterion values from multiple cues (the policy-capturing and multiple-cue probability-learning paradigms), but his theory clearly has implications for other kinds of J/DM problems. As Lopes (1982) has shown, however, one cannot take for granted that the formally optimal organizing principle or model is the most salient mental representation of a problem. It may be, in the case of cue-criterion relationships; it may not be, in other types of problems. This means, of course, that one must carefully choose the form and substance of the model that one uses to convey process feedback. One must attempt to understand the problem from the learner's perspective, as well as from the standpoint of "objective reality." The failure of many past debiasing efforts may be attributable either to the misapplication of analytical methods to intuitive problems, or to misinterpretation (or neglect) of the learner's model in providing process feedback on analytic problems.

Conclusions

Our goal in the preceding sections was chiefly to show that recent advances in cognitive psychology have relevance for training, and to reinforce that argument with illustrative applications from the closely related fields of instructional design and human factors. We have barely mentioned explicit procedures by which trainers can put this body of knowledge to use; nor, in the space remaining, can we fully explore the vast territory of potential applications. It seems appropriate, however, to close on a practical note, if only to provide strategic guidance for those inclined to pursue these matters. Thus, we shall end with a brief look at the issues involved, the strategies available, and some explicit suggestions for implementing a cognitive approach to training. We shall approach these topics in order, from the more general to the more specific.

Following the lead of the instructional theorists, we suggest that two methodological hurdles must be cleared before cognitive concepts can be applied to training design. These are task analysis and knowledge elicitation. Neither topic is easy; both constitute prime targets for continuing research. Unless one can decompose the particular task, in terms of desired learning outcomes and cognitive-process elements, however, there is almost no point to understanding knowledge structures, and unless one can gain access to those knowledge structures, in both the particular and the generic learner (expert, novice, or whatever), there is no dependable way to translate theory into practice. In short, one must know not only what learning operations the task requires but also what operations the learner is and should be executing at each stage of the learning process.

We have already discussed and illustrated some of the principles involved in cognitive task analysis. Several analytical frameworks based on these principles have been put forth. Probably the most explicit derives from the most explicit instructional theory (Gagné & Briggs, 1979). Tasks or task elements are classified according to the five major learning categories (intellectual skill, cognitive strategy, information, attitude, and motor skill), and each category is differentiated in terms of recommended techniques that correspond to a classification of instructional events (for example, presenting the stimulus material, or providing feedback). Thus, an overall instructional (training) program can be devised if one combines, in the proper order, the techniques called for by the particular task elements. A good source of practical advice on this whole approach is Gagné and Driscoll (1988).

Another analytical approach involves an instrument known as the Instructional Quality Inventory (Wulfeck, Ellis, Richards, Wood, & Merrill, 1978). Five content categories (fact, concept, procedure, rule, and principle) are combined with three task categories (remember, use–unaided, use–aided) to analyze objectives, presentation, and test characteristics for any training program. Since its purpose is to measure program quality, it can serve as a template for use in program design.

Earlier, we mentioned suggestions for modifying the widely used military system of training design (ISD) by incorporating cognitive elements. One such suggestion is representative of the state of the art in cognitive task analysis. Ryder, Redding, and Beckschi (1987) simply cite the components missing from ISD (knowledge organization, mental models, automaticity, and metacognition) and point out that better techniques are needed for analyzing these aspects of tasks. Royer (1986) proposes a somewhat more explicit model, which begins with an analysis of the transfer domain and incorporates analysis of the learner's background knowledge with a set of strategic options (mnemonics, analogies, advance organizers, and concrete advance organizers), to define the appropriate instructional technique. We shall have more to say about these options in a moment.

Summing up the status of the task-analysis issue, we can say that one probably can derive some guidance from existing taxonomies and systems, but a great deal is left to the ingenuity of the designer in any particular application. If, however, the designer understands the nature of the cognitive mechanisms through which learning presumably occurs, decomposition of a task into meaningful elements becomes possible.

With respect to the knowledge-elicitation issue, the reader will recall that such information is necessary for determining an individual's misconceptions or deficits, so that interventions can be appropriately directed (as illustrated in intelligent tutoring, debiasing, and electronic trouble shooting). It is useful to identify the knowledge possessed by the trainee. Moreover, the knowledge of experts in the domain is also necessary, to provide a goal state for the training program. Of course, knowledge can take the form of mental models, facts, rules, strategies, or heuristics. The most commonly used method in both cognitive psychology and AI has involved the analysis of verbal protocols (Ericsson & Simon, 1984). Generally, subjects are observed as they solve problems. While they do so, they are asked to think aloud, or verbalize their thought processes. The problem is that verbal reports are often incomplete and inaccurate (Nisbett & Wilson, 1977). At least part of the difficulty is probably due to the fact that much knowledge, particularly in experts, is compiled (Anderson, 1982) or automatic (Shiffrin & Schneider, 1977). In short, it is difficult for subjects to observe and report on their mental processes. Even when they can, it is difficult for them to translate these processes into verbal statements. In addition, the number of data produced with this methodology is typically enormous and difficult to analyze objectively.

A recently developed alternative to verbal protocols is based on psychometric scaling techniques, such as multidimensional scaling and cluster analysis (Butler & Corter, 1986; Cooke & McDonald, 1986, 1987; Gammack & Young, 1985). This technique involves eliciting knowledge from individuals, in the form of relatedness judgments, and then applying scaling techniques to construct structural representations of that knowledge. It was used in two recent studies, to elicit knowledge from fighter pilots (Schvaneveldt et al., 1985) and computer programmers, (Cooke & Schvaneveldt, 1988) respectively. In both cases, it successfully distinguished experts from novices, on the basis of their knowledge representations. Most important, it revealed the misconceptions in the novices' knowledge. While it is still relatively new, this methodology shows promise for overcoming several problems inherent in protocol analysis.

One final approach is illustrated by the work of Gitomer (1988) on electronic trouble shooting. In essence, it consists of tasks structured in such a way that particular kinds of errors in the knowledge or procedural domains can be diagnosed and classified on the basis of overt responses. While it is extremely useful for certain kinds of applications in well-defined contexts, this technique is limited by the necessity for all cognitive options to be represented unambiguously, in identifiable response patterns. For many cognitive tasks, this level of control is simply not feasible. Perhaps the most valuable use of this approach, apart from its application to well-defined task domains, comes after a more subjective technique has provided a preliminary account of the cognitive activities.

Knowledge elicitation, like cognitive task analysis, is still evolving. Progress in both areas, however, coupled with a solid grasp of underlying cognitive principles, affords the designer of training programs considerable guidance for addressing the challenges of future work requirements. Perhaps the best way to appreciate just how such guidance may occur is to review the specific implications of the principles described in the foregoing pages. We shall conclude, therefore, with a summary of implementation techniques.

The first point to be made is that the goal of most cognitively oriented training programs is a level of understanding that transcends the specific context of the learning situation; that is, since one distinguishing characteristic of anticipated work roles is greater uncertainty about the problems that will arise and about exactly how to deal with them, learning must be generalized to a wide range of transfer conditions. For example, a radar technician must understand the principles by which the system works (form an appropriate mental model) if he or she is to become an effective trouble shooter. Learning must ultimately be demonstrated through the learner's ability to apply his or her understanding (models, principles, rules, concepts) to a variety of conceptually similar problems in a variety of relevant contexts (Royer, 1986). This means that items designed to gauge the transferability (decontextualization) of learning are crucial parts of the training paradigm. In essence, such items — together with the various self-report techniques already discussed — define the scope and nature of understanding.

The specific cognitive principles discussed earlier, while generally aimed at increasing the learner's understanding, do so through somewhat different means. Some, such as model development, are very direct; others, such as automaticity training, do so indirectly, by freeing up mental capacity for use in understanding. Let us consider these techniques in a bit more detail.

Automatic Processing. Obvious efficiencies can be gained through identifying task elements that involve consistent stimulus-response mapping and then providing intensive (part-task) training on them. The resulting automatization (or shift from knowledge-based to skill-based processing) enhances proficiency in execution of the trained elements but also conserves mental capacity for application to other elements that are not so easily automated (for example, planning and decision making). Such training requires the learner to practice each element actively and repeatedly, under conditions that ensure correct responses. The correct response should be clearly identified. Any confusing or stressful aspects of the normal (transfer) setting in which it occurs should be removed. (Recall that vigilance training did not preserve the low-frequency aspect of the actual task; see Fisk & Schneider, 1981.)

Organizing Structures for Working Memory. The limitations imposed by short-term memory can be partially offset by artificial schemes for organizing material into chunks (mnemonics). Once task analysis has identified where the learner must temporarily retain more than about seven items of information, as well as what the nature of that material is, an integrating structure can be devised and explicitly taught through any traditional method. One of the best compendia of such techniques is found in Lorayne and Lucas (1974). Of course, where standardization is not required, acquisition can be enhanced through the use of personalized schemes (mnemonics that are already meaningful to the learner) and, in many cases, through imagery.

Organizing for Long-Term Memory. Discovering the manner in which recognized experts on a task organize the relevant knowledge domain can be useful as a basis for training novices in mastery of the same content. The training program is simply designed in accordance with the experts' classification scheme. First the structure and rules are made explicit for the learner (by means of outlines, graphics, or whatever best conveys the principles), and then they are reinforced by organized presentation of the content to be learned (declarative knowledge). Drill and practice, or other standard learning programs, can be used to instantiate the knowledge. Of course, care must be taken to establish at the outset that the experts' structure actually offers clear advantages and is not idiosyncratic. Experts are only one source of potentially useful organizing structures.

Mental Models and Schemata. The organization of declarative knowledge is actually a special case for a more general application: training people in the formation and use of efficient conceptualizations, or mental models, of a task, system, or process. The number of ways this notion can be used in training is large, and the potential payoff, as demonstrated in instructional applications to date, appears great. Again, the basic objective is to establish in the learner an accurate or efficient mental representation of what must be understood before he or she can perform well on the task or set of tasks associated with that particular knowledge system. The desired representation (sometimes called the *conceptual model*) may be based on experts' models, provided that there is some consistency among those models and that they differ substantially from nonexperts' models. It may also derive from formal or literal properties (geometric principles, actual system architecture). In any case, the conceptual model is the goal of training, and the learner's model defines both the initial need state (what needs to be changed) and the progress toward that goal as training proceeds. As illustrated in Greeno's (1978, 1983) research, one can also use computer modeling to diagnose learners' errors and provide corrective feedback during learning.

The specific approach and format may vary considerably, depending on the material, the learner, the context, computer facilities, and a host of other factors. Several common tactics can be articulated, however (Gagné & Glaser, 1987). First, familiar analogies from everyday life can help convey the conceptual message (graphics may also be effective), particularly in the early stages of training (Carroll & Mack, 1982). This technique provides a meaningful starting point (context), from which training can proceed in the direction of greater generality, or decontextualization. Without some such reference, the learner may become lost in a sea of abstraction. Second, if a typical progression from novices' to experts' models can be identified, this knowledge can be used to program the training sequence. Moreover, it can provide clues for the interpretation and correction of errors. Third, by determining the learner's initial model for the system in question, or for similar systems, the trainer can build on or shape that conceptualization to be more functional, through examples and counterexamples for relevant situations. In short, the tuning rather than the restructuring approach may be used, as was illustrated in Lopes's (1982) work on the conservatism bias. (In that instance, tuning the learner's nonoptimal anchoring-and-adjustment model produced better results than trying to restructure it into the formally optimal Bayesian model.)

It is not hard to conceive of useful ways to incorporate mental-model information into a training program, and we have every reason to believe that it is both possible and practical to do so. What is more difficult is finding ways to extract that information—from experts, novices, or anyone in between.

Metacognition and Strategic Skills. One key to successful mental-model building—in fact, to almost any rule-based or knowledge-based learning—is for learners to appreciate, at any given stage, what they do and do not know. This self-monitoring capability (called metacognition), together with a number of other strategies involved in reasoning and problem solving, distinguishes proficient from nonproficient learners. Most important, metacognition and strategic skills can themselves be taught. If-then rules, subgoal analysis, working backwards, and various domain-specific heuristics are among the examples already described.

Argument persists about how best to teach these skills—in particular, about how important specific context is for learning them. Most evidence suggests, however, that if the learner is fairly naïve, it is best to provide considerable context at the outset and then work toward generalization as skill develops (much as we suggested for mental-model building). Metacognition can be promoted through the embedding of explicit diagnostic probes and suggestions for implicit test procedures into the primary learning material. Active involvement (for example, the working of illustrative problems) and diagnostic feedback (what strategy the learner used, why it produced the wrong result, and what he or she might have done instead) together constitute important components of any attempt to develop strategic skills.

Expert Systems and ICAI. Growth in the power, sophistication, and general usefulness of computer technology has greatly expanded the horizons of automated training aids (Eberts & Brock, 1987). From the simple programmed instruction of the 1950s, which relied entirely on prestructured stimulus-response sequences, to today's computer-assisted and computer-managed instruction, which provides much greater flexibility and individualization (but at considerable cost), we have now entered an era in which the computer will play a central role in directing, monitoring, and shaping the entire learning process. Moreover, it is capable of doing so at the very conceptual or cognitive levels to which this chapter has been devoted. (We identified this capability earlier as ICAI and illustrated its application in the context of individualized instruction in math.)

The point here is that developments in the AI field of expert systems, although originally undertaken to aid or replace (rather than instruct) human operators, are now beginning to influence training, in much the same way that ICAI has influenced education. Of course, the contributions of both to industrial training applications still lie mainly in the future.

The common objective of expert systems and ICAI applications is to instill in learners the level of understanding necessary for carrying out complex, knowledge-based operations (such as problem solving or decision making) in an effective manner, despite wide variations in problem context. The underlying principle involves shaping the learner's knowledge base (procedural as well as declarative knowledge) to some approximation of the ideal state, by means of a variety of aids, supplied in an ongoing, interactive fashion. Thus, the computer must be able to recognize the desired end state (conceptual or expert model, appropriate strategies, metaknowledge, and so on), diagnose the learner's present level of understanding through inference from responses (novice or learner models, heuristics, metaknowledge), and provide feedback or guidance in a timely and useful form. The learner must have the opportunity to try out ideas, ask questions, and receive informed responses from the computer—in short, to interact and participate actively in the shaping process.

In the case of ICAI, as we saw earlier, the emphasis has been on programming the system to recognize and correct students' models. In expert-system applications, it has been on developing the knowledge bases and expertise (including expert models and metaknowledge, or self-understanding) to permit informed diagnosis and shaping. The former is most useful under circumstances (for example, with mathematical problem solving) where tasks and strategies are reasonably well understood. The latter has more to contribute when conceptual principles or strategies must themselves be articulated.

A good illustration of the training potential of expert systems is provided by Goldsmith and Schvaneveldt (1985) in connection with development of an air-combat simulator. This system maintains expertise on air-to-air combat maneuvers found in a large data base of scenarios. It can select an appropriate maneuver, given the specifics of a scenario, and display the consequences of that selection graphically. It can also do the same for a trainee's selection, thereby affording the learner an opportunity to compare selections directly and meaningfully and thus promoting "cognitive understanding of the mapping of conditions into actions" (Goldsmith & Schvaneveldt, 1985, p. 15).

It is easy to see how a similar approach could be effective in training process controllers, trouble shooters, or any number of operators of complex, semiautomated systems in tomorrow's workplace. The key, in this instance, is direct interactive experience, to provide an understanding of the processes by which the learner's (incorrect) and the expert's (correct) strategies produce their respective results.

Another feature of most expert systems is their ability to learn from experience (update their knowledge bases, acquire new rules, compare their knowledge bases to others, and so on). This feature, too, has important training implications as a source of insight into the expert process of acquiring meta-knowledge. To the extent that learners have access to the techniques or rules used by the expert—have them made explicit or see them in operation—they are in a better position to develop or refine their own.

Of course, the optimal training applications will eventually be those in which the explicit instructional techniques of ICAI are combined with the massive knowledge-base and adaptability capabilities of future expert systems. A current example of such a blend is SOPHIE, a system for training electronics technicians, in which the learner interacts with a large knowledge base while debugging a piece of malfunctioning electronic equipment (Brown, Burton, & de Kleer, 1982). In the process, the learner is provided with a variety of tutoring aids (from ICAI) that assist understanding of the state of his or her own knowledge, as well as that of the expert system.

To apply either set of techniques to a given training situation, of course, is no simple matter. ICAI, in particular, requires a thorough understanding of the knowledge and rule domain through which tasks are accomplished, a substantial computer facility, and a massive programming effort. As progress in expert systems continues, however, these limitations can be expected to shrink, since fewer and fewer parameter values will need to be prespecified.

Organizers and Present Knowledge. The fact that new material is more easily encoded, retained, and used when it builds on an existing knowledge framework has a number of training implications. A good example is the use of what are known as *advance* and *comparative organizers*, which afford the learner a means of classifying and incorporating the to-be-learned material into his or her present knowledge base (Ausubel, 1963; Ausubel, Novak, & Hanesion, 1978; Gagné & Driscoll, 1988). An organizer is essentially a verbal, quantitative, graphic, conceptual, or other type of cue that identifies the present knowledge to which the new material relates. Presented in advance of learning, it promotes understanding and long-term memory (comparative organizers clarify subsequent distinctions). In addition, it can serve to enhance the learning of rules and strategic applications (for example, in problem solving) by suggesting that a particular (unique, unfamiliar) problem actually calls for an already available heuristic or algorithm. In fact, advance organizers have been used to help learners decontextualize learned strategies while becoming more general problem solvers. Of course, application of this approach requires some understanding of what the learner's knowledge framework consists of, or at least of what the typical learner can be expected to know at the particular stage of training where the organizer is to be used.

The reader will recognize that many of the techniques already discussed (mnemonics, knowledge organization, analogies, and so on) involve the principle of advance organizers. The key points to be stressed here are, first, that the trainer should actively search for appropriate organizers in planning the training; second, that doing so requires consideration of both the learner and the task; third, that to link old and new knowledge requires organizers at a higher level of abstraction than the to-be-learned material; and, fourth, that the practical utility of organizers has now been rather convincingly demonstrated. Mayer and his colleagues (Mayer, 1975; Mayer & Bromage, 1980), for example, show that a simplified diagram of the functional architecture of a computer—a conceptual model, if you will—presented at the outset of a college course in computer programming, and couched in familiar language ("ticket window," "memory scoreboard," "shopping list"), greatly enhance both learning of the more technical terms and rules as well as transfer to other problems. Certainly, it would be hard to find a more timely or compelling argument for the relevance of advance organizers, in particular, and the cognitive approach, in general, to modern training demands than is offered by Mayer's research. It is thus a fitting note on which to end the present chapter.

References

Adams, J. H. (1987). Criticisms of vigilance research: A discussion. *Human Factors, 29,* 737–740.

Adelman, L. (1981). The influence of formal, substantive, and contextual task properties on the relative effectiveness of different forms of feedback in multiple-cue probability learning tasks. *Organizational Behavior and Human Performance, 27,* 423–442.

Adelson, B. (1981). Problem solving and the development of abstract categories in programming languages. *Memory and Cognition, 9,* 422–433.

Anderson, J. R. (1976). *Language, memory, and thought.* Hillsdale, NJ: Erlbaum.

Anderson, J. R. (1981). *Cognitive skills and their acquisition.* Hillsdale, NJ: Erlbaum.

Anderson, J. R. (1982). Acquisition of cognitive skill. *Psychological Review, 89,* 369–406.

Anderson, J. R. (1983). *The architecture of cognition.* Cambridge, MA: Harvard University Press.

Ausubel, D. P. (1963). *The psychology of meaningful verbal learning.* Orlando, FL: Grune & Stratton.

Ausubel, D. P., Novak, J. D., & Hanesion, H. (1978). *Educational psychology: A cognitive view* (2nd ed.). New York: Holt, Rinehart & Winston.

Baddeley, A. (1982). *Your memory: A user's guide.* New York: Macmillan.

Baron, J. B., & Sternberg, R. J. (1987). *Teaching thinking skills: Theory and practice.* New York: W. H. Freeman.

Bartlett, F. C. (1932). *Remembering: A study of experimental and social psychology.* Cambridge, England: Cambridge University Press.

Begg, I., & Paivio, A. U. (1969). Concreteness and imagery in sentence meaning. *Journal of Verbal Learning and Verbal Behavior, 8,* 821–827.

Biederman, I., Mezzanotte, R. J., & Rabinowitz, R. J. (1982). Scene perception: Detecting and judging objects undergoing relational violations. *Cognitive Psychology, 14,* 143–177.

Bloom, B. S. (1956). Taxonomy of educational objectives: The classification of educational goals. In B. S. Bloom (Ed.), *A taxonomy of educational objectives: The classification of educational goals: Handbook 1. Cognitive domain.* New York: McKay.

Bond, N. A., Jr. (1987). Maintainability. In G. Salvendy (Ed.), *Handbook of Human Factors* (pp. 1328–1355). New York: Wiley-Interscience.

Bower, G. H. (1972). A selective review of organizational factors in memory. In E. Tulving & W. Donaldson (Eds.), *Organization of memory* (pp. 93–134). Orlando, FL: Academic Press.

Bransford, J. D., & Johnson, M. K. (1972). Contextual prerequisites for understanding: Some investigations of comprehension and recall. *Journal of Verbal Learning and Verbal Behavior, 11*, 717–721.

Bransford, J. D., & Stein, B. S. (1984). *The IDEAL problem solver.* New York: W. H. Freeman.

Briggs, L. J. (1968). Learner variables and educational media. *Review of Educational Research, 38*, 160–176.

Briggs, L. J. (1970). Handbook of procedures for the design of instruction. *American Institute for Research Monograph, 4.*

Broadbent, D. E. (1958). *Perception and communication.* Elmsford, NY: Pergamon Press.

Brown, J. S., & Burton, R. R. (1978). Diagnostic models for procedural bugs in basic mathematical skills. *Cognitive Science, 2*, 155–192.

Brown, J. S., Burton, R. R., & de Kleer, J. (1982). Pedagogical, natural language and knowledge engineering techniques in SOPHIE I, II, and III. In D. Sleeman & J. S. Brown (Eds.), *Intelligent tutoring systems.* Orlando, FL: Academic Press.

Burton, R. R. (1982). Diagnosing bugs in a simple procedural skill. In D. Sleeman & J. S. Brown (Eds.), *Intelligent tutoring systems* (pp. 157–183). Orlando, FL: Academic Press.

Butler, K. A., & Corter, J. E. (1986). The use of psychometric tools for knowledge acquisition: A case study. In W. Gale (Ed.), *Artificial intelligence and statistics* (pp. 295–319). Reading, MA: Addison-Wesley.

Campbell, J. P. (1971). Personnel training and development. *Annual Review of Psychology, 22*, 565–602.

Caramazza, A., Hersh, H., & Torgerson, W. (1976). Subjective structures and operations in semantic memory. *Journal of Verbal Learning and Verbal Behavior, 15*, 103–117.

Card, S. K., Moran, T. P., & Newell, A. (1983). *The psychology of human-computer interaction.* Hillsdale, NJ: Erlbaum.

Carroll, J. M., & Mack, R. L. (1982). Metaphor, computing systems, and active learning [Summary]. *IEEE Proceedings of the International Conference on Cybernetics and Society,* 72–74.

Chase, W. G., & Simon, H. A. (1973). Perception in chess. *Cognitive Psychology, 5,* 55–81.

Chi, M. T. H., Feltovich, P. J., & Glaser, R. (1981). Categorization and representation of physics problems by experts and novices. *Cognitive Science, 5,* 121–152.

Christensen, J. M. (1987). The human factors profession. In G. Salvendy (Ed.), *Handbook of human factors* (pp. 3–16). New York: Wiley-Interscience.

Clark, H. H. (1974). Semantics and comprehension. In T. A. Sebeok (Ed.), *Current trends in linguistics: Vol. 12. Linguistics and adjacent arts and sciences.* The Hague: Mouton.

Collins, A. M., & Loftus, E. F. (1975). A spreading activation theory of semantic processing. *Psychological Review, 82,* 407–428.

Collins, A. M., & Quillian, M. R. (1969). Retrieval time from semantic memory. *Journal of Verbal Learning and Verbal Behavior, 8,* 240–247.

Cooke, N. M., & McDonald, J. E. (1986). A formal methodology for acquiring and representing expert knowledge. *IEEE Special Issue on Knowledge Representation, 74,* 1422–1430.

Cooke, N. M., & McDonald, J. E. (1987). The application of psychological scaling techniques to knowledge elicitation for knowledge-based systems. *International Journal of Man-Machine Studies, 26,* 533–550.

Cooke, N. M., & Schvaneveldt, R. W. (1988). Effects of computer programming experience on network representations of abstract programming concepts. *International Journal of Man-Machine Studies, 29,* 407–427.

Craik, F. I. M., & Lockhart, R. S. (1972). Levels of processing: A framework for memory research. *Journal of Verbal Learning and Verbal Behavior, 11,* 671–684.

Davis, R. (1977). Interactive transfer of expertise: Acquisition of new inference rules. *International Joint Conference on Artificial Intelligence, 5*, 321–328.

Davis, R. (1987). Robustness and transparency in intelligent systems. In T. B. Sheridan, D. S. Kruser, & S. Deutsch (Eds.), *Human factors in automated and robotic space systems: Proceedings of a symposium* (pp. 211–233). Washington, DC: National Research Council.

Dodd, D. H., & White, R. M., Jr. (1980). *Cognition: Mental structures and processes*. Newton, MA: Allyn & Bacon.

Eberts, R. E., & Brock, J. F. (1987). Computer-assisted and computer-managed instruction. In G. Salvendy (Ed.), *Handbook of Human Factors* (pp. 976–1011). New York: Wiley-Interscience.

Einhorn, H. J. (1982). *Theory of diagnostic interference I: Imagination and the psychophysics of evidence* (*Technical Report No. 2*). Chicago: School of Business, University of Chicago.

Einhorn, H. J., & Hogarth, R. M. (1981). Behavioral decision theory. *Annual Review of Psychology, 32*, 53–88.

Ericsson, K. A., & Simon, H. A. (1984). *Protocol analysis: Verbal reports as data*. Cambridge, MA: MIT Press.

Fischhoff, B. (1982). Debiasing. In D. Kahneman, P. Slovic, & A. Tversky (Eds.), *Judgment under uncertainty: Heuristics and biases* (pp. 422–444). New York: Cambridge University Press.

Fischhoff, B. (1987). Decision making—aided and unaided. In T. B. Sheridan, D. S. Kruser, & S. Deutsch (Eds.), *Human factors in automated and robotic space systems: Proceedings of a symposium* (pp. 234–262). Washington, DC: National Research Council.

Fisk, A. D., & Schneider, W. (1981). Controlled and automatic processing during tasks requiring sustained attention: A new approach to vigilance. *Human Factors, 23*, 737–750.

Flexman, R. E., & Stark, E. A. (1987). Training simulators. In G. Salvendy (Ed.), *Handbook of human factors* (pp. 1012–1038). New York: Wiley-Interscience.

Fotta, M. E. (1987). Artificial intelligence: An introduction and applications to the human-computer interface. In L. S. Mark, J. S. Warm, & R. L. Huston (Eds.), *Ergonomics and human factors* (pp. 266–275). New York: Springer-Verlag.

Gagné, R. M. (1962). Factors in acquiring knowledge of a mathematical task. *Psychological Monographs, 76*(7).

Gagné, R. M. (1970). *The conditions of learning*. New York: Holt, Rinehart & Winston.

Gagné, R. M. (1984). Learning outcomes and their effects: Useful categories of human performance. *American Psychologist, 39*, 377–385.

Gagné, R. M., & Briggs, L. J. (1979). *Principles of instructional design*. New York: Holt, Rinehart & Winston.

Gagné, R. M., & Dick, W. (1983). Instructional psychology. *Annual Review of Psychology, 34*, 261–295.

Gagné, R. M., & Driscoll, M. P. (1988). *Essentials of learning from instruction*. Englewood Cliffs, NJ: Prentice-Hall.

Gagné, R. M., & Glaser, R. (1987). Foundations in learning research. In R. Glaser (Ed.), *Instructional techniques: Foundations* (pp. 49–83). Hillsdale, NJ: Erlbaum.

Gammack, J. G., & Young, R. M. (1985). Psychological techniques for eliciting expert knowledge. In M. A. Bramer (Ed.), *Research and development in expert systems* (pp. 105–112). London: Cambridge University Press.

Gentner, D., & Stevens, A. (1983). *Mental models*. Hillsdale, NJ: Erlbaum.

Gitomer, D. H. (1988). Individual differences in technical troubleshooting. *Human Performance, 1*, 111–131.

Glaser, R. (1964). Implications of training research for education. In E. R. Hilgard (Ed.), *Theories of learning and instruction* (pp. 118–152). Chicago: University of Chicago Press.

Glaser, R. (1966). Psychological bases for instructional design. *AV Communication Review, 14*, 433–449.

Glaser, R. (1972). Individuals and learning: The new aptitudes. *Educational Researcher, 1*, 5–12.

Glaser, R. (1984). Education and thinking. *American Psychologist, 39*, 93–104.

Glaser, R. (1986). Training expert apprentices. In I. Goldstein (Ed.), *Learning research laboratory: Proposed research issues* (Technical Report No. AFHRL-TP-85-54) (pp. 20–28). Brooks Air Force Base, TX: Manpower and Personnel Division, Air Force Human Resources Laboratory.

Goldsmith, T. E., & Schvaneveldt, R. W. (1985). ACES: Air Combat Expert Simulation. In *Memoranda in Computer and Cognitive*

Science (Report No. NCCS-85-34). Las Cruces: New Mexico State University, Computing Research Laboratory.

Goldstein, I. L. (1974). *Training: Program development and evaluation.* Monterey, CA: Brooks/Cole.

Goldstein, I. L. (1986). *Training in organizations: Needs assessment, development, and evaluation* (2nd ed.). Monterey, CA: Brooks/Cole.

Greeno, J. G. (1978). Natures of problem-solving abilities. In W. K. Estes (Ed.), *Handbook of learning and cognitive processes: Vol. 5. Human information processing* (pp. 239–270). Hillsdale, NJ: Erlbaum.

Greeno, J. G. (1983). Forms of understanding in mathematical problem solving. In S. G. Paris, G. M. Olson, & H. W. Stevenson (Eds.), *Learning and motivation in the classroom* (pp. 83–111). Hillsdale, NJ: Erlbaum.

Hamm, R. M. (1985). *Moment-by-moment variation in the cognitive activity of experts* (Report No. 257). Boulder, CO: Center for Research on Judgment and Policy, University of Colorado.

Hammond, K. R. (1986). *A theoretically based review of theory and research in judgment and decision making* (Report No. 260). Boulder, CO: Center for Research on Judgment and Policy, University of Colorado.

Hayes, J. R., & Simon, H. A. (1977). Psychological differences among problem isomorphs. In N. J. Castellan, D. B. Pisoni, & G. R. Potts (Eds.), *Cognitive theory: Vol. 2.* Hillsdale, NJ: Erlbaum.

Hintzman, D. L., & Ludlam, G. (1980). Differential forgetting of prototypes and old instances: Simulation by an exemplar-based classification model. *Memory and Cognition, 8,* 378–382.

Hoffman, P. J., Earle, T. C., & Slovic, P. (1981). Multidimensional functional learning (MFL) and some new conceptions of feedback. *Organizational Behavior and Human Performance, 27,* 75–102.

Hogarth, R. M. (1981). Beyond discrete biases: functional and dysfunctional aspects of judgmental heuristics. *Psychological Bulletin, 90,* 197–217.

Howell, W. C., & Goldstein, I. L. (1971). *Engineering psychology:*

Current perspectives in research. East Norwalk, CT: Appleton-Century-Crofts.

Hyde, T. S., & Jenkins, J. J. (1973). Recall for words as a function of semantic, graphic, and syntactic orienting tasks. *Journal of Verbal Learning and Verbal Behavior, 12,* 471–480.

Kahneman, D. (1973). *Attention and effort.* Englewood Cliffs, NJ: Prentice-Hall.

Kahneman, D., Slovic, P., & Tversky, A. (Eds.). (1982). *Judgment under uncertainty: Heuristics and biases.* New York: Cambridge University Press.

Kahneman, D., & Tversky, A. (1973). On the psychology of prediction. *Psychological Review, 80,* 237–251.

Kramer, A. F., & Schumacher, R. M. (1987). Human-computer interaction: A brief glimpse of an emerging field. In L. S. Mark, J. S. Warm, & R. L. Huston (Eds.), *Ergonomics and human factors* (pp. 213–224). New York: Springer-Verlag.

Lachman, R., Lachman, J. L., & Butterfield, E. C. (1979). *Cognitive psychology and information processing: An introduction.* Hillsdale, NJ: Erlbaum.

Larkin, J. H., McDermott, J., Simon, D. P., & Simon, H. A. (1980). Expert and novice performance in solving physics problems. *Science, 80,* 1335–1342.

Lopes, L. L. (1982). *Procedural debiasing* (Technical Report WHIPP 15). Madison: Wisconsin Human Information Processing Program.

Lorayne, H., & Lucas, J. (1974). *The memory book.* New York: Ballantine.

McKeithen, K. B., Reitman, J. S., Rueter, H. H., & Hirtle, S. C. (1981). Knowledge organization and skill differences in computer programmers. *Cognitive Psychology, 13,* 307–325.

Mackie, R. R. (1987). Vigilance research: Are we ready for countermeasures? *Human Factors, 29,* 707–723.

Mark, L. S., Warm, J. S., & Huston, R. L. (1987). An overview of ergonomics and human factors. In L. S. Mark, J. S. Warm, & R. L. Huston (Eds.), *Ergonomics and human factors* (pp. 1–7). New York: Springer-Verlag.

Mayer, R. E. (1975). Different problem-solving competencies

established in learning computer programming with and without meaningful models. *Journal of Educational Psychology, 65,* 725–734.

Mayer, R. E. (1983). *Thinking, problem solving, cognition.* New York: W. H. Freeman.

Mayer, R. E., & Bromage, B. K. (1980). Differential recall protocols for technical texts due to advance organizers. *Journal of Educational Psychology, 72,* 209–225.

Medin, D., & Schaffer, M. M. (1978). Context theory of classification learning. *Psychological Review, 85,* 207–238.

Meister, D. (1985). *Behavioral analysis and measurement methods.* New York: Wiley.

Miller, G. A. (1956). The magical number seven, plus or minus two: Some limits on our capacity for processing information. *Psychological Review, 63,* 81–97.

Miller, R. B. (1953). *A method for man-machine task analysis.* Wright Patterson Air Force Base, OH: Wright Air Development Center, Air Research Development Command. (DTIC No. AD–15721)

Minsky, M. L. (1975). A framework for representing knowledge. In P. Winston (Ed.), *The psychology of computer vision.* New York: McGraw-Hill.

Montague, W. (1986). In V. E. Holt (Ed.), *Issues in psychological research and application in transfer of training* (pp. 25–30). Alexandria, VA: U.S. Army Research Institute for the Behavioral and Social Sciences.

Morris, C. D., Bransford, J. D., & Franks, J. J. (1977). Levels of processing versus transfer-appropriate processing. *Journal of Verbal Learning and Verbal Behavior, 16,* 519–534.

Navon, D., & Gopher, D. (1979). On the economy of the human-processing system. *Psychological Review, 86,* 214–256.

Neisser, U. (1976). *Cognition and reality.* New York: W. H. Freeman.

Newell, A., & Simon, H. A. (1972). *Human problem solving.* Englewood Cliffs, NJ: Prentice-Hall.

Nickerson, R. S., Perkins, D. N., & Smith, E. E. (1985). *The teaching of thinking.* Hillsdale, NJ: Erlbaum.

Nisbett, R. E., Krantz, D. H., Jepson, C., & Kunda, Z. (1983). The use of statistical heuristics in everyday inductive reasoning. *Psychological Review, 90*, 339–363.

Nisbett, R. E., & Wilson, T. D. (1977). Telling more than we can know: Verbal reports on mental processes. *Psychological Review, 8*, 231–259.

Norman, D. A. (1984). Stages and levels in human-machine interaction. *International Journal of Man-Machine Studies, 21*, 365–375.

Norman, D. A., & Bobrow, D. G. (1975). On data-limited and resource-limited processes. *Cognitive Psychology, 7*, 44–64.

Paivio, A. (1971). *Imagery and verbal processes.* New York: Holt, Rinehart & Winston.

Parasuraman, R. (1987). Human-computer monitoring. *Human Factors, 20*, 695–706.

Pintrich, P. R., Cross, D. R., Kozma, R. B., & McKeachie, W. J. (1986). Instructional psychology. *Annual Review of Psychology, 37*, 611–651.

Posner, M. I., & Keele, S. W. (1968). On the genesis of abstract ideas. *Journal of Experimental Psychology, 77*, 353–363.

Posner, M. I., & Keele, S. W. (1970). Retention of abstract ideas. *Journal of Experimental Psychology, 83*, 304–308.

Posner, M. I., & McLeod, P. (1982). Information processing models—in search of elementary operations. *Annual Review of Psychology, 33*, 477–514.

Posner, M. I., & Snyder, C. R. R. (1975). Attention and cognitive control. In R. L. Solso (Ed.), *Information processing and cognition: The Loyola symposium* (pp. 55–85). Hillsdale, NJ: Erlbaum.

Rasmussen, J. (1980). The human as a system component. In H. T. Smith & R. G. Green (Eds.), *Human interaction with computers* (pp. 67–96). Orlando, FL: Academic Press.

Reed, S. K. (1988). *Cognition.* Monterey, CA: Brooks/Cole.

Reed, S. K., Ernst, G. W., & Banerji, R. (1974). The role of analogy in transfer between similar problem states. *Cognitive Psychology, 6*, 436–450.

Resnick, L. B. (1983). Toward a cognitive theory of instruction. In S. G. Paris, G. M. Olson, & H. W. Stevenson (Eds.), *Learning and motivation in the classroom* (pp. 5–38). Hillsdale, NJ: Erlbaum.

Rips, L. J., Shoben, E. J., & Smith, E. E. (1974). Semantic distance and the verification of semantic relations. *Journal of Verbal Learning and Verbal Behavior, 12*, 1–20.

Rouse, W. B. (1978). A model of human decision making in a fault-diagnosis task. In *IEEE Transactions on Systems, Man and Cybernetics* (Report No. SMC-8) (pp. 357–361).

Rouse, W. B., & Hunt, R. M. (1984). Human problem solving in fault diagnosis tasks. In W. B. Rouse (Ed.), *Advances in man-machine systems research* (pp. 195–222). Greenwich, CT: JAI Press.

Royer, J. M. (1986). Approaches to the acquisition of understanding. In I. Goldstein (Ed.), *Learning research laboratory: Proposed research issues* (Technical Report No. AFHRL-TP-85-54) (pp. 45–65). Brooks Air Force Base, TX: Manpower and Personnel Division, Air Force Human Resources Laboratory.

Rumelhart, D. E., & Norman, D. A. (1981). Analogical processes in learning. In J. R. Anderson (Ed.), *Cognitive skills and their acquisition* (pp. 335–359). Hillsdale, NJ: Erlbaum.

Ryder, J. M., Redding, R. E., & Beckschi, P. F. (1987). Training development for complex cognitive tasks. *Proceedings for the Thirty-first Annual Meeting of the Human Factors Society, 2*, 1261–1265.

Schank, R. C., & Abelson, R. (1977). *Scripts, plans, goals, and understanding.* Hillsdale, NJ: Erlbaum.

Schoenfeld, A. H. (1979). Explicit heuristic training as a variable in problem solving performance. *Journal for Research in Mathematics Education, 10*, 173–187.

Schoenfeld, A. H. (1980). Teaching problem-solving skills. *American Mathematical Monthly, 87*, 794–805.

Schvaneveldt, R. W., Durso, F. T., Goldsmith, T. E., Breen, T. J., Cooke, N. M., Tucker, R. G., & DeMaio, J. C. (1985). Measuring the structure of expertise. *International Journal of Man-Machine Studies, 23*, 699–728.

Schvaneveldt, R. W., & McDonald, J. E. (1981). Semantic context and the encoding of words: Evidence for two modes of stimulus analysis. *Journal of Experimental Psychology: Human Perception and Performance, 7*, 673–687.

Schwartz, R. M., & Humphreys, M. S. (1973). Similarity judgments and free recall of unrelated words. *Journal of Experimental Psychology, 101,* 10–15.

Sheridan, T. B., Charney, L., Mendel, M. B., & Roseborough, J. B. (1986). *Supervisory control, mental models, and decision aids* (Report No. 169-179). Cambridge: Man-Machine Systems Laboratory, Massachusetts Institute of Technology.

Sheridan, T. B., Kruser, D. S., & Deutsch, S. (Eds.). (1987). *Human factors in automated and robotic space systems: Proceedings of a symposium.* Washington, DC: National Research Council.

Shiffrin, R. M., & Atkinson, R. C. (1969). Storage and retrieval processes in long-term memory. *Psychological Review, 76,* 179–193.

Shiffrin, R. M., & Schneider, W. (1977). Controlled and automatic human information processing: II. Perceptual learning, automatic attending, and a general theory. *Psychological Review, 84,* 127–190.

Shuell, T. J. (1986). Contributions of cognitive psychology to learning from instruction in Air Force training. In *Learning research laboratory: Proposed research issues* (Technical Report No. AFHRL-TP-85-54) (pp. 29–44). Brooks Air Force Base, TX: Manpower and Personnel Division, Air Force Human Resources Laboratory.

Simon, H. A. (1980). Problem solving and education. In D. T. Tuma & F. Reif (Eds.), *Problem solving and education: Issues in teaching and learning* (pp. 81–96). Hillsdale, NJ: Erlbaum.

Simon, H. A. (1981). Cognitive science: The newest science of the artificial. In D. A. Norman (Ed.), *Perspectives on Cognitive Science.* Norwood, NJ: Ablex.

Simon, H. A., & Hayes, J. R. (1976). The understanding process: Problem isomorphs. *Cognitive Psychology, 8,* 165–190.

Sleeman, D., & Brown, J. S. (1982). *Intelligent tutoring systems.* Orlando, FL: Academic Press.

Smith, E. E., Shoben, E. J., & Rips, L. J. (1974). Structure and process in semantic memory: A featural model for semantic decision. *Psychological Review, 81,* 214–241.

Stern, L. (1985). *The structures and strategies of human memory.* Homewood, IL: Dorsey Press.

Treisman, A. M. (1964). Selective attention in man. *British Medical Bulletin, 20,* 12–16.

Tullis, T. S. (1983). The formatting of alphanumeric displays: A review and analysis. *Human Factors, 25,* 657–682.

Tulving, E. (1962). Subjective organization in free recall of "unrelated" words. *Psychological Review, 69,* 344–354.

Tversky, A. (1977). Features of similarity. *Psychological Review, 84,* 327–352.

Tversky, A., & Kahneman, D. (1974). Judgment under uncertainty: Heuristics and biases. *Science, 185,* 1124–1131.

Van Cott, H. P. (1984). From control systems to knowledge systems. *Human Factors, 26,* 115–122.

Waterman, D. A. (1986). *A guide to expert systems.* Reading, MA: Addison-Wesley.

Wexley, K. N. (1984). Personnel training. *Annual Review of Psychology, 35,* 519–551.

White, R. H., Jr., & Zsambok, C. (1987). An overview of cognitive psychology. In L. S. Mark, J. S. Warm, & R. L. Huston (Eds.), *Ergonomics and human factors* (pp. 71–78). New York: Springer-Verlag.

Wickens, C. D. (1984). *Engineering psychology and human performance.* Westerville, OH: Merrill.

Wickens, C. D. (1987). Information processing, decision making, and cognition. In G. Salvendy (Ed.), *Handbook of human factors.* New York: Wiley-Interscience.

Wiener, E. L. (1987). Application of vigilance research: Rare, medium, or well done? *Human Factors, 29,* 725–736.

Wulfeck, W. H., II, Ellis, J. A., Richards, R. E., Wood, N. D., & Merrill, M. D. (1978). *The instructional quality inventory: I. Introduction and overview* (NPRC Tech. Report 79-3).

6

Individual Attributes
and Training Performance

Edwin A. Fleishman
Michael D. Mumford

People differ from one another in the abilities, skills, and knowledges they bring to the training situation. These individual characteristics of the trainees are mong the most important determiners of training outcomes. Although trainers have long been aware of the need to consider individual characteristics as well as situational influences on performance (Goldstein & Buxton, 1982; Snow, 1986), principles of learning and instructional systems design have focused, for the most part, on the development of a common learning environment for all trainees. Emphasis is on the construction of training environments with respect to general principles of learning, such as practice (McGehee & Thayer, 1961), reinforcement (Pedalino & Gamboa, 1974), feedback (Salmoni, Schmidt, & Walter, 1984), and instructor expertise (Eden & Shani, 1982), which are assumed to have relatively constant effects on skills acquisition. The primary issue emphasized in instructional systems design is finding an optimal application of these principles with respect to performance on a defined set of tasks that must be performed by all trainees (Mitchell, Ruck, & Driskill, 1988).

Educators and trainers have, for many years, been forced to struggle with the fact that, although training interventions derived from these postulates clearly have value, they are not always successful. Even when exposed to a common training environment, some individuals seem to acquire skilled task performance far more rapidly than others. Sometimes carefully designed training programs, which expressly consider the application of these principles to well-defined task domains, fail altogether, apparently because none of the trainees is able to profit from the instruction. In still other cases, it is found that a training program that benefits one group of workers fails completely with another group.

Such observations have led many trainers and researchers to wonder whether some key elements may be missing from our strategies for linking learning principles to task requirements. Of course, when one considers the fact that performance in training has been shown to be a joint function of certain individual and situational attributes (Mumford, Weeks, Harding, & Fleishman, 1988), the answer to this question becomes more obvious. Specifically, we need to consider the characteristics that people bring to the training environment as essential ingredients of instructional systems design (Cronbach & Snow, 1977).

In recent years, we have learned a great deal about the nature of human abilities and their relationship to the effective performance of human tasks. This chapter discusses some of the implications of research on these human attributes for issues of learning and training. In particular, we will emphasize a program of research that has attempted to link task characteristics to the abilities required for learning to perform effectively on these tasks. What does this information tell us about the design of training or about factors related to training outcomes?

We will describe how the development of a taxonomy of human abilities has led to some insights, concepts, and methods for identifying abilities relevant to the learning and performance of job tasks. We will then discuss how this information about human abilities can be used in particular areas of training design, including strategies for determining the abilities involved in various kinds of learning activities and task performance. Other applications that we will consider include the selection of training interventions, the allocation of individuals to alternative training interventions, the specification and sequencing of training activities, and the ongoing development and retraining of employees. To accomplish these goals, we have attempted to integrate information from a number of research areas, including psychometric research, cognitive psychology, and instructional technology.

The Importance of the Learners' Characteristics

First, we need to establish if the learner's characteristics really represent an important class of variables related to learning and training. The potential significance of learners' characteristics has been demonstrated in numerous studies. For instance, work by Christal (1974) and Gettinger and White (1979) indicates that the rate of skill acquisition is strongly influenced by preexisting ability levels in a common learning environment. Similarly, Ghiselli (1973) and Tyler (1965) have summarized a number of studies indicating that differences among trainees in aptitudes, motivation, interest, and prior history will influence performance and attrition in training.

Along somewhat different lines, Cronbach and Snow (1977), Snow and Yallow (1982), and Lohman and Snow (1984) have reviewed a host of studies concerned with potential aptitude-treatment interactions. Although the results obtained in these studies are not unambiguous, they do suggest that certain types of instructional environments are more likely to facilitate learning among certain classes of individuals. For instance, Snow and Yallow (1982) and Lohman and Snow (1984) conclude that a training environment emphasizing the independent exercise of principles is more likely to promote learning for high-ability individuals than for low-ability individuals, for whom a directed rather than a concrete instructional orientation seems more appropriate. What is lacking in these studies is specific information on the kinds of human abilities related to the effectiveness of particular training treatments.

A variety of laboratory studies have clearly demonstrated the relations between the learner's status on particular abilities and his or her subsequent progress in learning a number of complex tasks (Fleishman, 1966, 1972a; Fox, Taylor, & Caylor, 1969). Figure 6.1 provides some examples of learning curves for subjects who are acquiring a complex signal discrimination and reaction skill (Fleishman & Hempel, 1955). The curves illustrate clearly that performance levels and learning rates differed for subjects who scored at different levels on different generic ability tests. The curves show that some abilities made more of a difference than others, that some abilities were more important than others in early learning, and other abilities were more important at later stages of learning. (We will return to how such information can be used in training.)

In one of the most comprehensive investigations of the role of individual and situational attributes in ongoing training settings, Mumford, Weeks, Harding, and Fleishman (1988) obtained evidence of the fundamental importance of learner characteristics. This investigation began with an extensive series of structured interviews intended to identify the student characteristics and course-content variables that U.S. Air Force trainers thought most likely to influence the outcomes of training. Measures of six student characteristics and sixteen course-content variables, which trainers believed to be of some general significance in describing the technical training process (apart from specific course content), were later obtained in thirty-nine U.S. Air Force training programs involving 5,078 students. The relationships among these variables, as well as their causal impacts on seven training outcome measures, were then assessed in a structural modeling effort, and the stability of this model was assessed in a cross-validation sample containing 890 people drawn from nine additional U.S. Air Force training programs.

Figure 6.2 presents the model constructed and cross-validated in this study. The model indicates that such student characteristics as aptitude, reading, and motivation levels are among the most powerful determinants of human performance in training, as indexed by measured training outcomes. Further, comparison of the total effects of the student-characteristic variables with the effects of the course-content variables showed that the student-characteristic variables had a stronger impact on performance in training than the course-content variables did.

**Figure 6.1. Comparison of Learning Curves for Groups Scoring
High and Low on Different Ability Test Measures.**

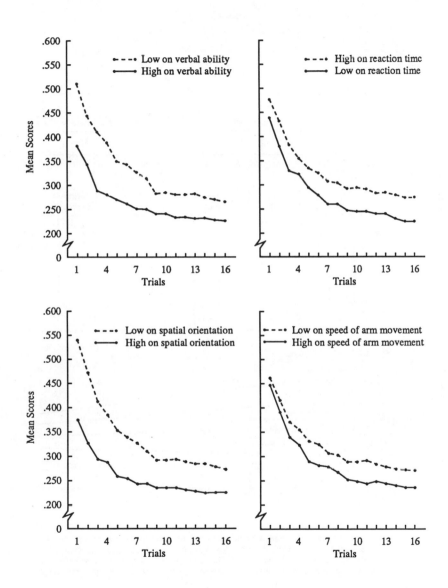

Source: Fleishman & Hempel, 1955. Reprinted with permission.

Figure 6.2. Model of the Relationships Among Student Characteristics and Course-Content Variables for Determining Training Performance.

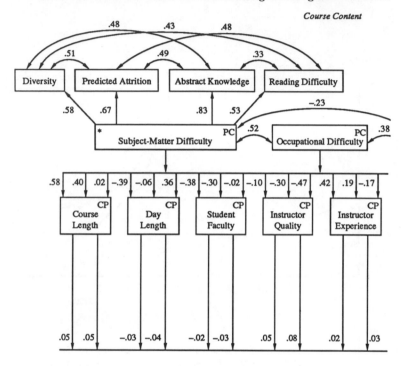

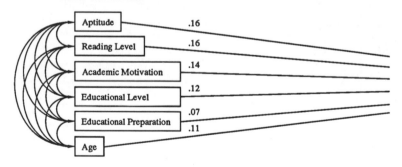

Note: Model with standardized path coefficients. PC indicates primal course-content variable, and CP indicates course parameter. * indicates multiple indicator latent. All other variables were treated as single indicator latents. The three values flowing into the seven course parameters reflect the path coefficients obtained for subject-matter difficulty, occupational

Source: Adapted from Mumford, Weeks, Harding, & Fleishman, 1988, with permission.

Figure 6.2, Cont'd.

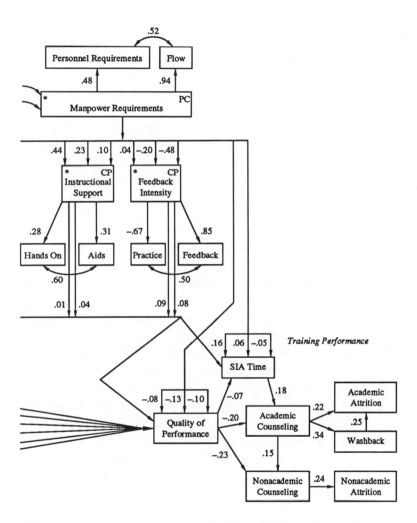

difficulty, and manpower requirements, respectively, for determining the status of course parameters. The two values flowing from the seven course parameters reflect the path coefficients indicative of each parameter's impact on the assessed quality of performance and special individualized assistance time, respectively.

Finally, it was found that the type of course content that was most effective depended on certain student characteristics.

Recognizing the potential significance of learners' characteristics, Goldstein (1986) and Goldstein and Buxton (1982) argue that effective instructional systems design requires careful examination of trainees' attributes in relation to task demands. Nevertheless, only a few instructional design efforts have explicitly considered the characteristics of the learner (Prien, Goldstein, & Macey, 1985), and even some of the most advanced training system designs constructed to date ignore the potential significance of learners' characteristics (Mitchell, Ruck, & Driskill, 1988). This state of affairs is surprising, in view of the recognized importance of learners' characteristics. Individuals differ from one another in a wide variety of ways, however, and at first glance it is not clear exactly what characteristics of the learner should be considered in the design of a training program.

One potential solution to this problem is to formulate a taxonomic system capable of describing and summarizing the characteristics of the individuals which are most likely to influence skill acquisition on particular kinds of tasks. Certainly, the success of taxonomic efforts intended to simplify the domain of instructional objectives (Bloom, 1967; Stahl, 1979; Cox & Unks, 1967) indicates that this approach has value. Thus, it seems reasonable to expect that a taxonomy of learners' characteristics would also be usefully applied to the training environment.

A number of investigators (Annett & Duncan, 1967; Gagné, 1962; Melton, 1964; Miller, 1966; Cotterman, 1959; Stolurow, 1964) have called for taxonomic systems intended to permit the classification of tasks into categories that would be relatively homogeneous with respect to applicable principles of learning and training techniques. Their suggestions, however, do not include categories that take into account our present knowledge about human abilities, nor do they advance taxonomic development to the point of including measurement systems. A taxonomy of human abilities developed by Fleishman and his colleagues (e.g., Fleishman, 1967, 1972a; Fleishman & Quaintance, 1984) meets some of these requirements, and we will review these developments in the discussion that follows. Specifically, we will attempt to present a general taxonomic system for the description of learner abilities, strategies for applying this system to defining learners' characteristics that operate in a particular situation, and some potential applications of this information to instructional systems design.

Some Taxonomic Issues

When one considers the role of classification in the sciences, there is every reason to expect that a well-defined taxonomic system could do much to encourage the examination of learners' characteristics. Because individuals differ from one another in such a large number of ways, is the domain of human differences simply too complex to permit all this information to be considered in training program designs? This simplification problem is by no means unique; it has confronted investigators working in many areas of the natural sciences. In fields ranging from biology to astronomy, a valuable tool for solving this simplification problem has been provided by classification systems that yield viable summary descriptions of the relevant observational domains.

Fleishman and Quaintance (1984) reviewed the evolution of taxonomies in scientific development, with a view to the relevance of this experience to developing taxonomies of human performance. A classification can be defined as a set of specified rules for describing the structure and relationships among a set of objects or units, drawn from some domain, which permits statements to be made about relative similarity, so that it is possible to assign similar units to a smaller number of categories or classes (Simpson, 1961; Sokal, 1974; Sokal & Sneath, 1963). By assigning similar objects or units to a common category, it becomes possible, within the limits set by the rules of the classification system, to treat these objects or units as functionally equivalent entities. Thus, the search for scientific principles need not consider each object as an entity unto itself; instead, laws can be constructed with reference to all members of a category, seen or unseen, on the basis of a limited number of observations within a category.

While the definition of principles within classes or categories of similar objects often provides a viable simplification strategy, the construction of classification systems can serve a number of other purposes. According to Fleishman and Quaintance (1984), classification systems can also be used to define the essential characteristics of the domain at hand, generate hypotheses pertaining to the nature of this domain, delimit and organize inferences concerning the properties of objects within this domain, and facilitate communication and understanding. When these varied applications are considered in light of the fundamental need for simplification, it is not surprising that the construction of particularly effective taxonomies has provided a basis for many fundamental advances in the sciences (Crowson, 1970).

Broadly speaking, the construction of a classification system involves four basic steps (Fleishman & Quaintance, 1984). First, the domain of objects to be classified must be operationally defined. Second, measures of the properties of these objects are specified, and some index is obtained for appraising the overall similarity of the objects with respect to these measures. Third, a set of decision rules is specified for determining when two or more objects display sufficient similarity to permit assignment to a common category. Fourth, the object relationships actually specified in category assignments, as well as the relationships with other relevant objects not examined in the initial classification effort, are established and used in drawing an inference of construct validity (Cronbach, 1971; Fleishman & Quaintance, 1984). These four basic steps occur in the development of any taxonomic system, but a variety of different decisions can be made at each point, and different decisions may result in a number of alternative classification schemes. In making such decisions, investigators commonly attend to the intent or purpose of the taxonomic system, to maximize the meaningfulness of the resulting inferences with respect to the practical goals at hand. This observation led Fleishman and Quaintance (1984) to conclude that the intended application of

the classification is perhaps the single most powerful determinant of the nature of the resulting system.

The Ability Requirements Taxonomy

Defining Abilities. Because the purpose or intent of a
classification effort provides an underlying framework for the
development, evaluation, and application of the resulting descriptive system, it is clear that any system intended to classify
human attributes with respect to potential training applications
must begin with the goals. As Fitts (1962) pointed out, "A taxonomy of human performance should identify important corre-
lates of learning, performance levels, and individual differences" (p. 178).

Not so long ago, a favorite distinction in psychology textbooks was between mental and motor tasks, or between cognitive and noncognitive tasks. Such broad distinctions are
clearly too all-inclusive to have training implications. Job analysts, in contrast, have developed highly detailed task-analysis
systems, but these are probably too specific to particular jobs to
help us arrive at the general task dimensions that would be
applicable across many different tasks and jobs. Other psychologists (Miller, 1962; Gagné, 1962; Alluisi, 1967; Sternberg, 1979)
have proposed categories of tasks in terms of the broad human
functions required to perform them (for example, such categories as identification, discrimination, sequence learning, information processing, motor skills, scanning, and problem solving
have been used in the literature). Nevertheless, everything we
know about actual correlations among human performances
indicates a considerable diversity of functions within each of
these broad areas.

The most developed human performance taxonomy,
which meets a number of taxonomic criteria, is called the *ability
requirements approach* (Fleishman, 1972a; Fleishman & Quaintance, 1984), wherein tasks are described, contrasted, and compared in terms of the abilities required of the individuals
performing the tasks. It is assumed that specific tasks require
certain abilities, if performance is to be maximized. Tasks that

require similar abilities are placed in the same category or said to be similar.

Abilities are defined as general capacities related to the performance of some set of tasks (Fleishman, 1972a). These abilities are held to be relatively enduring (although not necessarily unmalleable) attributes of the individual. Such attributes develop over time through the interplay between genetic influences and the cumulative effects of prior developmental experiences (Fleishman, 1972a; Lohman & Snow, 1984). It is assumed that tasks differ in the extent to which they require various abilities, and that tasks requiring similar abilities may have similar performance demands.

Much of what we know today about the categorization of human abilities, at least so far as it is based on empirical research, comes from correlational and factor-analysis studies. Such studies are typically carried out in the psychometric tradition. Until recently, few attempts have been made to integrate the ability concepts developed there into the more general body of psychological theory. Here, the fact of individual differences is exploited to gain insights about the common processes required for performing different groups of tasks. Abilities are defined by the empirically determined relations among observed separate performances.

The logic underlying the implementation of this approach is relatively straightforward: The activities that people perform on their jobs differ in the extent to which certain abilities are required for timely, efficient, or appropriate action. Thus, such abilities as verbal comprehension and spatial visualization can be utilized to summarize the requirements for individuals to perform various tasks. The fact that spatial visualization is demonstrably related to performance on the diverse tasks involved in aerial navigation, blueprint reading, and dentistry makes this ability somehow more basic. The assumption is that the skills involved in such complex activities as flying an airplane, operating an industrial machine, or playing baseball can be described in terms of the more basic abilities.

The basic implication for training is that training should improve people's performance on certain sets of tasks. Thus, if the attributes that condition performance in certain task domains can be identified, then the resulting categories should provide a basis for defining and summarizing the characteristics of people that are related to performance and learning.

Procedures for Identifying Ability Categories. In defining these categories, an attempt has been made to identify the fewest and most useful independent ability categories for describing performance on the widest variety of tasks. The methodology for identifying human abilities is illustrated in the research of Fleishman and associates on developing a taxonomy of perceptual-motor and physical abilities, summarized by Fleishman (1964; 1972b). This program involved a series of interlocking, experimental factor-analytical studies, in which tasks were explicitly designed or selected to test certain hypotheses about the organization of abilities over a wide range of tasks. The experimental battery of tasks was administered to several hundred subjects, and the correlation patterns were examined. Studies were then designed to introduce task variations aimed at sharpening, limiting, or broadening factor definitions.

Even without reviewing the list of ability categories developed or their operational definitions, we can say that a limited number of categories (nine or ten in the psychomotor area and nine in the physical proficiency area) seemed to account for most of the variance in several hundred tasks investigated over many years. It became apparent that, in defining these ability factors, the investigators were really linking up a great deal of information about task characteristics and ability requirements. It was possible to state a number of principles relating task characteristics and abilities; for example, *multilimb coordination ability* was common to tasks involving two hands, hands and feet, and so on, in operating equipment, but it did not extend to tasks in which the body was in motion (as in athletic skills). It was also possible to say that there was an ability common to simple reaction tasks (auditory and visual), but complicating the response or stimulus brought in another ability, termed *response orientation*. A *rate-control ability* appears common to compensatory and following pursuit tasks, but the essential task requirement is the timing of a movement, not the judging of a stimulus rate. It is important to note that it is not too useful to talk about *strength*, for example, as a single physical ability. In terms of what tasks the same people can do well, it is more useful to talk in terms of at least three general strength categories—*static*, *dynamic*, and *explosive*—which may be involved in different ways in a variety of physical tasks.

These investigations, along with a variety of other factor-analysis studies, have provided well-documented evidence indicating the ability categories that could be used to provide a meaningful description of human task performance. Specification of the relevant categories in this system, and the implied classification of learners' characteristics, began with a comprehensive literature review intended to identify abilities that had been empirically established in earlier research and that had construct validity as descriptors of task performance (Theologus & Fleishman, 1973; Theologus, Romashko, & Fleishman, 1973). The primary sources of evidence for the utility of potential cognitive constructs was Guilford and Hopfner's (1966) work on the structure of intellect, along with the work of French, Ekstrom, and Price (1963). From these sources, ability categories were selected according to the criterion that each ability had been identified in ten separate factor-analysis investigations. In the psychomotor and physical ability areas, the categories of concern were specified on the basis of Fleishman's (1964, 1966, 1972b) prior research.

The initial literature review and the available research base provided substantial convergent evidence for the meaningfulness of the thirty-seven ability constructs, but a number of additional steps were taken to ensure the adequacy of this classification structure. One striking finding in this review of the factor-analysis literature was the difficulty of moving from the factor analysts' definitions to more operational definitions that could be reliably used by observers who wished to estimate the ability requirements of a new task. A large effort in this program involved the successive refinement of such definitions, to improve the utility of these concepts for describing tasks and developing measurement systems.

Initially, the consolidated list of ability constructs and their associated definitions was reviewed by panels of subject-matter experts and psychologists. Subsequent interview data indicated the need for a more comprehensive listing of abilities, more precise definitions of each ability, and examples of the task performances indicative of each ability construct. As a result, attempts were made to generate specific task examples and formulate more precise definitions concerning the nature and the extent of each ability construct. An extended review of the experimental and measurement literatures was also conducted, to determine whether any significant categories might have been overlooked. This extended review, as well as subsequent reviews of more recent work (Carroll, 1976; Ekstrom, French, & Harmon, 1979; Horn, 1976; Peterson & Bownas, 1982), indicated that the initial descriptor set was not yet complete. That observation led to the inclusion of a group of abilities that had not been intensively studied but nevertheless appeared to be of some general importance in the description of human task performance; for example, sensory abilities (Schemmer, 1982) and other cognitive capacities, such as time sharing and attention (Imhoff & Levine, 1980), were added to the descriptor set. This activity resulted in the list of ability constructs presented in Exhibit 6.1. Based on expert reviews, the list seems to be a well-established and reasonably comprehensive set of descriptor constructs for appraising the ability characteristics that influence task performance (Fleishman & Mumford, 1988). Certain generic dimensions of job-relevant knowledge and skills were also identified, such as driving skills and electronics skills (Fleishman, 1975b), which appeared to influence performance on social-interactional tasks. The discussion that follows will emphasize the training applications of the ability taxonomy, but we will also point out some implications for imparting generic knowledge structures and broadly based skills.

Measuring Ability Requirements. Once a viable set of ability categories had been identified, it was necessary to develop

Exhibit 6.1. Updated Definitions for the Ability Categories in Recent
Forms of the *Manual for the Ability Requirement Scales (MARS).*

1. *Oral comprehension:* This is the ability to understand spoken English words
   and sentences.
2. *Written comprehension:* This is the ability to understand written sentences
   and paragraphs.
3. *Oral expression:* This is the ability to use English words or sentences in
   speaking, so that others will understand.
4. *Written expression:* This is the ability to use English words or sentences in
   writing, so that others will understand.
5. *Fluency of ideas:* This is the ability to produce a number of ideas about a
   given topic.
6. *Originality:* This is the ability to produce unusual or clever ideas about a
   given topic or situation. It is the ability to come up with creative solutions
   to problems or to develop new procedures to situations where standard
   operating procedures do not apply.
7. *Memorization:* This is the ability to remember information, such as words,
   numbers, pictures, and procedures. Pieces of information can be remembered by themselves or with other pieces of information.
8. *Problem sensitivity:* This is the ability to tell when something is wrong or is
   likely to go wrong. It includes being able to identify the whole problem,
   as well as the elements of the problem.
9. *Mathematical reasoning:* This is the ability to understand and organize a
   problem and then to select a mathematical method or formula to solve
   the problem. It encompasses reasoning through mathematical problems, in order to determine appropriate operations that can be performed to solve problems. It also includes the understanding or structuring of mathematical problems. The actual manipulation of numbers is
   not included in this ability.
10. *Number facility:* This ability involves the degree to which adding, subtract-
    ing, multiplying, and dividing can be done quickly and correctly. These
    can be steps in such other operations as finding percentages and taking
    square roots.
11. *Deductive reasoning:* This is the ability to apply general rules to specific
    problems, to come up with logical answers. It involves deciding whether
    an answer makes sense.
12. *Inductive reasoning:* This is the ability to combine separate pieces of
    information, or specific answers to problems, to form general rules or
    conclusions. This involves the ability to think of possible reasons why
    things go together.
13. *Information ordering:* This is the ability to correctly follow a rule or set of
    rules and arrange things or actions in a certain order. The rule or set of
    rules to be used must already be given. The things or actions to be put in
    order can include numbers, letters, words, pictures, procedures, sen-
    tences, and mathematical or logical operations.
14. *Category flexibility:* This is the ability to produce many rules, so that each
    rule tells how to group a set of things in a different way. Each different
    group must contain at least two things from the original set of things.

15. *Speed of closure:* This ability involves the degree to which different pieces of information can be quickly combined and organized into one meaningful pattern. It is not known beforehand what the pattern will be. The material may be visual or auditory.
16. *Flexibility of closure:* This is the ability to identify or detect a known pattern (like a figure, word, or object) hidden in other material. The task is to distinguish the pattern one is looking for from the background material.
17. *Spatial orientation:* This is the ability to tell where you are in relation to some object or to tell where the object is in relation to you.
18. *Visualization:* This is the ability to imagine how something will look when it is moved around or when its parts are moved or rearranged. It requires the forming of mental images of how patterns or objects would look after certain changes, such as unfolding or rotation. One has to predict what an object, set of objects, or pattern would look like after the changes are carried out.
19. *Perceptual speed:* This ability involves the degree to which one can compare letters, numbers, objects, pictures, or patterns quickly and accurately. The things to be compared may be presented all at once or one after another. This ability also includes comparison of a presented object with a remembered object.
20. *Control precision:* This is the ability to make highly controlled, precise arm-hand or foot-leg movements in positioning the controls of a machine or a vehicle. It involves the degree to which these controls can be quickly and repeatedly moved to exact positions.
21. *Multilimb coordination:* This is the ability to coordinate the movements of two or more limbs (for example, two arms, two legs, or one leg and one arm), such as in moving equipment controls. Two or more limbs are in motion while the individual is sitting, standing, or lying down.
22. *Response orientation:* This is the ability to choose between two or more movements quickly and accurately when two or more different signals (lights, sounds, pictures, and so on) are given. This ability is concerned with the speed with which the right response can be started with the hand, foot, and so on.
23. *Rate control:* This is the ability to adjust an equipment control in response to changes in the speed and/or direction of a continuously moving object or scene. The ability involves timing these adjustments in anticipation of these changes. This ability does not extend to situations in which both the speed and the direction of an object are perfectly predictable.
24. *Reaction time:* This is the ability to give one fast response to one signal (sound, light, picture, and so on) when it appears. This ability is concerned with the speed with which the movement can be started with the hand, foot, and so on.
25. *Arm-hand steadiness:* This is the ability to keep the hand and arm steady. It includes steadiness while making an arm movement as well as while holding the arm and hand in one position. This ability does not involve strength or speed.
26. *Manual dexterity:* This is the ability to make skillful, coordinated move-

ments of one hand, a hand together with its arm, or two hands to grasp, place, move, or assemble objects like hand tools or blocks. This ability involves the degree to which these arm-hand movements can be carried out quickly. It does not involve moving such equipment controls as levers.

27. *Finger dexterity:* This is the ability to make skillful, coordinated movements of the fingers of one or both hands and to grasp, place, or move small objects. This ability involves the degree to which these finger movements can be carried out quickly.

28. *Wrist-finger speed:* This is the ability to make fast, simple, repeated movements of the fingers, hands, and wrists. It involves little if any accuracy or eye-hand coordination.

29. *Speed of limb movement:* This ability involves the speed with which a single movement of the arms or legs can be made. This ability does not include accuracy, careful control, or coordination of movement.

30. *Selective attention:* This is the ability to concentrate on a task one is doing and not be distracted; any distraction presented is not part of the task being done. This ability also involves concentrating while performing a boring task.

31. *Time sharing:* This is the ability to shift back and forth between two or more sources of information.

32. *Static strength:* This is the ability to use muscle force to lift, push, pull, or carry objects. It is the maximum force that one can exert for a brief period of time.

33. *Explosive strength:* This is the ability to use short bursts of muscle force to propel oneself or an object. It requires gathering energy for bursts of muscle effort over a very short time.

34. *Dynamic strength:* This is the ability of the muscles to exert force repeatedly or continuously over a long time. This is the ability to support, hold up, or move the body's own weight and/or objects repeatedly. It represents muscular endurance and emphasizes the resistance of the muscles to fatigue.

35. *Trunk strength:* This ability involves the degree to which one's stomach and lower back muscles can support part of the body repeatedly or continuously over time. The ability involves the degree to which these trunk muscles do not give out, or become fatigued, when they are put under repeated or continuous strain.

36. *Extent flexibility:* This is the extent to which one can bend, stretch, twist, or reach out with the body, arms, or legs. This involves the suppleness of the muscles.

37. *Dynamic flexibility:* This is the ability to repeatedly and quickly bend, stretch, twist, or reach out with the body, arms, and/or legs, both quickly and repeatedly. This involves the resilience of the muscles in recovering from strain and distortion.

38. *Gross body coordination:* This is the ability to coordinate the movement of the arms, legs, and torso in activities *where the whole body is in motion.*

39. *Gross body equilibrium:* This is the ability to keep or regain one's balance or to stay upright when in an unstable position. This ability includes being

able to maintain one's balance when changing direction, while moving or when standing motionless.

40. *Stamina:* This is the ability of the respiratory and cardiovascular body systems to perform efficiently over extended periods. It is the ability to exert oneself in prolonged physical tasks without getting out of breath.
41. *Near vision:* This is the capacity to see close environmental surroundings.
42. *Far vision:* This is the capacity to see distant environmental surroundings.
43. *Visual color discrimination:* This is the capacity to match or discriminate among colors. This capacity also includes detecting differences in color purity (saturation) and brightness (brilliance).
44. *Night vision:* This is the ability to see under low light conditions.
45. *Peripheral vision:* This is the ability to perceive objects or movement near the edges of the visual field.
46. *Depth perception:* This is the ability to distinguish which of several objects is more distant from or nearer to oneself, or to judge the distance of an object from oneself.
47. *Glare sensitivity:* This is the ability to see objects in the presence of glare or bright ambient lighting.
48. *General hearing:* This is the ability to detect and discriminate among sounds that vary over broad ranges of pitch and/or loudness.
49. *Auditory attention:* This is the ability to focus on a single source of auditory information in the presence of other (distracting and irrelevant) auditory stimuli.
50. *Sound localization:* This is the ability to identify the direction from which an auditory stimulus has originated, relative to oneself.

Source: Adapted from Fleishman, 1975a; Fleishman and Mumford, 1988.

the measurement system for appraising the extent to which task performance could be described and summarized by each ability construct. Although a number of strategies could have been used to generate these relational statements, the most straightforward and flexible approach involved applying scaling techniques that used ratings of the extent to which each ability was required for performing various task activities. A series of studies was initiated to determine whether a rating format could be used to identify the ability constructs that contribute to task performance. The result of these efforts was a set of scales incorporated into a *Manual for the Ability Requirement Scales* (MARS) (Fleishman, 1975a; Fleishman & Mumford, 1988) by means of which a profile of a job's ability requirements could be determined.

We will now describe how this measurement system was developed, how it was evaluated, and how the procedures can be used in instructional system design. A host of different reliability studies were conducted, in which task descriptions were examined by individuals who rated them in terms of different cognitive, perceptual, and motor abilities (Fleishman & Hogan, 1978; Theologus & Fleishman, 1973). These descriptions have included descriptions of laboratory apparatus, training tasks, and jobs. The attempt was to use the same ability concepts to bridge the gap in describing laboratory, training, and job tasks within the same conceptual framework. A number of studies have shown that high interjudge reliabilities were obtained when these scales were used to describe the ability requirements of a wide range of jobs and tasks (Hogan, Ogden, & Fleishman, 1978; Myers, Gebhardt, Price, & Fleishman, 1981).

In earlier investigations, Theologus, Romashko, and Fleishman (1973) and Theologus and Fleishman (1973) had presented descriptions of laboratory and job tasks (activities performed by computer programmers, firefighters, and metalworkers), along with definitions and rating scales for the abilities identified in the initial taxonomic effort, to a panel of eighteen psychologists. The judges were asked to evaluate these tasks in terms of the importance of each ability to overall performance. An examination of interrater agreement coefficients indicated that it was possible to obtain reliable ratings, although follow-up interviews indicated that clearer instructions and more precise definitions might improve reliability. One important finding was the high correlation between the ratings and the factor loadings of the laboratory tasks that had been obtained in earlier studies.

After the requisite revisions had been made, thirty-two subject-matter experts (psychometricians) and twenty-five other psychologists (drawn from diverse specialties) were presented with the material just described. Judges were asked to rate each task with regard to the thirty-seven ability dimensions. To obtain an index of reliability, interclass correlation coefficients were obtained with twenty-five, fifteen, and five judges and one judge across abilities. It was found that fifteen judges were sufficient to produce a reliable evaluation of ability requirements. Further, when judges' profiles of task evaluations were examined, it was found that psychometric specialists and other psychologists produced nearly identical appraisals of ability requirements (although again, the judges' comments indicated that more behaviorally oriented definitions of the abilities and rating scales were needed).

While these observations provided some support for the feasibility of this rating strategy, they also suggested that evaluation of the ability requirements of tasks should be obtained with behaviorally anchored rating scales. Development of such scales was carried out in accordance with the following format (Fleishman, 1975a; Fleishman & Quaintance, 1984). First, psychologists familiar with the abilities were asked to generate definitional anchors for the high and low end of each scale. Second, these anchors and ability definitions were presented to panels of individuals, who were asked to generate examples of everyday tasks that would reflect high, moderate, and low levels of each ability. Third, more than one thousand task examples resulting from this operation were presented to a group that was asked to rate, on a seven-point scale, the extent to which each task required the pertinent ability. Fourth, the means and standard deviations of these task ratings were obtained. Fifth, tasks were selected as anchors for the high, middle, and low points on each scale, on the basis of their average ratings and the degree of dispersion around these averages. Examples of the rating scales developed for written comprehension and static strength are presented in Figures 6.3 and 6.4.

Evaluating the Ability Descriptive System

Reliability. A number of studies have been concerned with establishing the meaningfulness of the descriptive information, as used in Fleishman's (1975a) manual for the ability requirement scales (MARS). In an attempt to establish the reliability of the task evaluations generated through the revised rating format, Theologus, Romashko, and Fleishman (1973) obtained task descriptions for metalworkers, air traffic controllers, astronauts,

Figure 6.3. Definition and Ability Rating Scale for Written Comprehension.

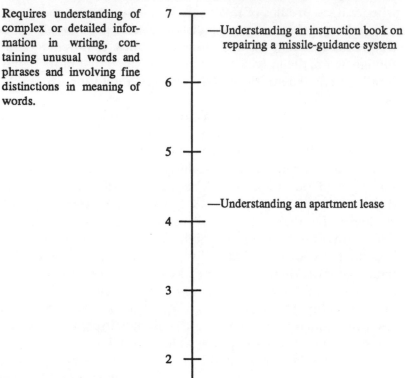

Requires understanding of complex or detailed information in writing, containing unusual words and phrases and involving fine distinctions in meaning of words.

7

—Understanding an instruction book on repairing a missile-guidance system

6

5

—Understanding an apartment lease

4

3

2

Requires understanding of short, simple, written information containing common words and phrases.

—Reading a road map

1

Note: Written comprehension is the ability to understand written language. This ability involves reading and understanding the meanings of words, phrases, sentences, and paragraphs. This involves reading, not writing.

Source: Adapted from Fleishman, 1975a.

helicopter pilots, automobile drivers, and basketball players. One group of nineteen judges was asked to rate the tasks with unanchored, seven-point scales. A second group of twenty-two judges was asked to rate the tasks with the behaviorally anchored scales. The data obtained from these judges indicated that the

Figure 6.4. Definition and Ability Rating Scale for Static Strength.

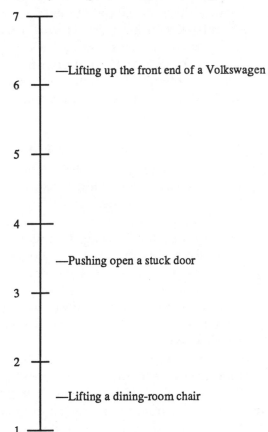

Requires use of all the muscle force possible to lift, carry, push, or pull a very heavy object.

7

—Lifting up the front end of a Volkswagen

6

5

4

—Pushing open a stuck door

3

2

Requires use of a little muscle force to lift, carry, push, or pull a light object.

—Lifting a dining-room chair

1

Note: Static strength is the ability to exert muscular force in pushing, pulling, lifting, or holding heavy objects. The ability does not involve continuous or prolonged exertion of the muscles.

Source: Adapted from Fleishman, 1975a.

behaviorally anchored scales yielded better reliability, particularly in small samples of ten judges, where reliability coefficients in excess of .80 were obtained.

Other studies have been conducted to determine the conditions that influence the consistency of ability evaluations.

For the most part, these studies have focused on agreement among alternative types of raters. In one such study, Romashko, Brumback, Fleishman, and Hahn (1974) contrasted supervisors' and job incumbents' evaluations of the abilities required by sanitation workers, firefighters, and police officers in New York City and obtained a median correlation of .67. Assessing the abilities required by Philadelphia police officers, Romashko, Hahn, and Brumback (1976) obtained a correlation of .75 between incumbents and supervisors, a correlation of .66 between incumbents and job analysts, and a correlation of .81 between supervisors and job analysts. In a somewhat wider-ranging study, Hogan, Ogden, and Fleishman (1978) asked 864 incumbents, 360 supervisors, and 79 job analysts to appraise the abilities required in nineteen civil service jobs in San Bernardino County (California). In this study, it was found that the scales for ability requirements yielded a reliable description of job tasks, in the sense that interrater agreement coefficients within rater types were most typically in the .90s. More central, however, is the fact that substantial agreement ($>.80$) was observed between the evaluations by incumbents, supervisors, and job analysts.

Similar results have been obtained in studies examining interrater agreement on twenty jobs at a large public utility (Inn, Schulman, Ogden, & Sample, 1982), as well as in studies of military occupational specialties (Myers, Gebhardt, Price, & Fleishman, 1981), lineman and maintenance jobs in the electric power industry (Cooper, Schemmer, Gebhardt, Marshall-Mies, & Fleishman, 1982), and U.S. Navy shipboard jobs (Gebhardt, Jennings, & Fleishman, 1981). Further, a study by Fogli (1988) has shown that the degree of agreement observed in these other studies is not affected much by such potential biasing factors as time in a company, educational level, age, and sex. Taken as a whole, then, these studies suggest that the MARS classification allows a relatively clear and unambiguous assessment of tasks in terms of their associated requirements for human performance.

Construct Validity. Over the years, a variety of other evidence has been collected on the construct validity, or meaningfulness, of the descriptive information derived with the MARS classification system. Studies by Landy (1988), Hogan, Ogden, and Fleishman (1978, 1979), Cooper, Schemmer, Jennings, and Korotkin (1983), and Mumford, Yarkin-Levin, Korotkin, Wallis, and Marshall-Mies (1985) indicated that more than 80 percent of the tasks performed on jobs ranging from pipeline repair to criminal investigation can be accounted for by assignment to one of these ability categories. Moreover, the findings obtained in these studies indicate that most of the remaining tasks can be accounted for by the addition of a limited number of job-specific categories for knowledge, skills, and personal characteristics. Additional evidence of the MARS system's internal validity has been found by Hogan, Ogden, and Fleishman (1978), Cooper et al. (1987), and Inn, Schulman, Ogden, and Sample (1982), who found that subject-matter experts' assignments of tasks to the ability dimension yielded categories of homogeneous content that were readily interpretable, given the proposed ability definitions.

External Validity. This evidence for the internal validity of the MARS taxonomy provides a crucial basis for an initial evaluation of the system. Nevertheless, it is important to recognize that a strong inference of meaningfulness requires evidence for the verifiability of the relationships implied (but not expressly considered) in the initial development of the system. Consequently, a number of studies have been undertaken in an attempt to obtain some evidence of the external validity of the ability requirements taxonomy. Because abilities are held to be related to task performance, the nature of this system leads to the expectation that, in jobs that incorporate tasks calling for substantial amounts of a certain ability, marker tests designed to appraise individual differences in the expression of this ability would be effective predictors of performance. To test this hypothesis, various forms of MARS were used by job incumbents to identify the abilities likely to be related to performance among warehouse workers (Hogan, Ogden, & Fleishman, 1978), correctional officers (Gebhardt & Weldon, 1982), pipeline workers (Gebhardt, Cooper, Jennings, Crump, & Sample, 1983), electrical utility workers (Cooper, Schemmer, Gebhardt, Marshall-Mies, & Fleishman, 1982), and U.S. Army enlistees (Myers, Gebhardt, Price, & Fleishman, 1981). In each study, this information was then used to draw inferences concerning the marker tests most likely to predict performance. These tests were then administered to a sample of incumbents and correlated with measures of job performance. It was found that these marker tests were highly correlated with job performance, and that a linear combination of these measures yielded highly effective performance prediction (often with R's of .60 +). Similar results were obtained in studies by Cooper, Schemmer, Jennings, and Korotkin (1983), Gebhardt, Cooper, Jennings, Crump, and Sample (1983), and Hogan, Ogden, and Fleishman (1978). It seems reasonable to conclude that the ability requirements taxonomy displays some external validity.

Other Evidence of the Taxonomy's Utility. The studies just mentioned provide important evidence that justifies the application of the MARS approach to the assessment and control of learners' characteristics. It should be noted, however, that a number of other studies, although they are somewhat less directly relevant to instructional system design, provide additional evidence for the external validity of the MARS systems. For instance, studies of civil service jobs in Pittsburgh (Weldon, 1983) and San Bernardino County (Hogan, Ogden, & Fleishman, 1978) indicate that the appraisal of ability requirements yields stable and substantively interpretable job "families." In another set of studies, Hogan, Ogden, Gebhardt, and Fleishman (1979, 1980) found that ratings of ability requirements were closely related to the ergonomic demands made by various tasks. In still another set of investigations, the ability requirements taxonomy was used to improve generalizations and predictions about the types of vigilance tasks that were the least likely to show performance decrements (Levine, Romashko, & Fleishman, 1973; Parasuraman, 1976). These studies invite additional confidence in the construct validity and utility of the ability concepts.

Other Applications. The MARS methodology has concentrated on the specification of ability requirements, but some parallel developmental work has proceeded on the identification of the kinds of generic knowledges, high-level skills, and interpersonal characteristics that may be required in particular classes of jobs. The procedures already described for task generation, task scaling, and task anchoring have been used to provide scales for such requirements as driving and typing skills, mechanical knowledge (Fleishman, 1975b), persuasion, and social sensitivity (Fleishman, Cobb, & Spendolini, 1976). These scales can be used to determine the level at which such a broader range of knowledges, skills, abilities, and other characteristics are required in particular jobs. Although their development, application, and evaluation is less than that of the ability requirement scales, there is considerable potential for their use in identifying additional learner characteristics that are required for success in particular training situations and jobs.

Linking Abilities and Task Requirements

In our discussion of the ability requirements approach, we indicated how the identification of abilities, through combinations of experimental and correlational research, has integrated a great deal of information regarding commonalities in task characteristics. For example, the characteristics of tasks with requirements of written comprehension, spatial orientation, inductive reasoning, response orientation, and multilimb coordination are now well understood. We can make fairly good estimates of the ability requirements of tasks from specifications of task characteristics. Fleishman and Quaintance (1984) also describe another conceptual approach to task classification, called the *task characteristic approach.* This taxonomic approach (Farina & Wheaton, 1973) is an attempt to develop a language to describe tasks, independent of the human operator (for example, complexity of displays, display-control relations, precision of controls), and to quantify the degree to which tasks possess these characteristics. A long-range objective of this program is to develop more systematic relations between abilities and task characteristics (Fleishman, 1975b). One of the conclusions drawn from the Fleishman and Quaintance (1984) review of alternative classificatory approaches is that a system linking task characteristics and ability requirements may be particularly fruitful in achieving a fuller understanding of human task performance.

Other psychologists, notably Dunnette (1976) and Peterson and Bownas (1982), have called for similar links. Peterson and Bownas propose that jobs be analyzed in terms of a job requirements matrix. Such a matrix contains rows defined by the categories of tasks, as well as columns containing the categories for human attributes. Each cell of the matrix represents the degree to which the ability is required for performing the particular task. Peterson and Bownas suggest that the linking of the task and ability taxonomies is "necessary in order to produce an operationally useful job-requirements matrix" (p. 86). They believe that such a matrix, prepared for a wide assortment of task and ability categories, can make substantial contributions to personnel management activities, including training.

Encouraging results from a series of studies indicate that it is possible to build up a body of principles about interactions between task characteristics and ability requirements, through experimental-correlational studies in the laboratory (see Fleishman, 1975b). In this research paradigm, tasks that can be varied along specified task dimensions are developed. The tasks are administered to groups of subjects, who also receive a series of ability reference tasks known to sample certain more general abilities, such as spatial orientation and control precision. Correlations between the ability reference tasks and scores on variations of the criterion tasks specify the ability requirements (and changes in these requirements) as a function of task variations. Such studies were carried out in several domains of human performance.

Psychomotor Performance. In an earlier study of psychomotor performance (see Fleishman, 1957), the task characteristic varied was the degree of display-control compatibility.

Subjects were required to press a button within a circular arrangement of buttons on a control panel, in response to particular lights that appeared in a circular arrangement of lights on a display panel. The correct choice of the button depended on the relative position of the light. Subjects performed under seven different conditions, in which the display panel was rotated from the standard position of 0° to displacements of 45°, 90°, 135°, 180°, 225°, and 270°. The same subjects also performed on a series of spatial, perceptual, and psychomotor reference tests.

The results showed systematic changes in the ability factors sampled by the criterion task, as a function of degree of rotation of the display panel from the fully compatible (0°) condition. Progressive rotation of the display panel shifted the ability requirements from perceptual speed to two other factors, response orientation and spatial orientation. Perceptual speed was measured in the upright and slight-displacement conditions. The other abilities were measured at larger display rotations. Here, individual differences along known ability dimensions were used to explore the relations between changes in task dimensions and the characteristics of people who could perform the tasks most effectively.

Performance on Perceptual Tasks. A later study in this program (Wheaton, Eisner, Mirabella, & Fleishman, 1976) took another step toward applying this paradigm to a particular job. The task, which is involved in the job of a U.S. Navy sonar operator, consisted of auditory signal identification. Subjects were to determine the identity of a variety of complex sounds representing various types of ships. Each time a signal was presented, subjects had to determine whether it belonged to a cargo ship, a warship, a submarine, or a light craft.

Two task characteristics were selected for manipulation—signal duration and signal-to-noise ratio. Nine different task conditions were generated according to a factorial arrangement of these two variables. Stimuli were presented for nine, six, or three seconds, and under one of three signal-to-noise ratios. Background noise was set at − 5 dB, 0 dB, or + 5 dB, referenced to the intensity of the signal to be identified. Each of the nine different task conditions generated in this manner was represented by a tape containing one hundred signals, twenty-five for each ship category. A battery of twenty-four specifically selected tests was administered to all subjects before their involvement in the criterion task. The battery contained tests representing a variety of well-established factors in perceptual and cognitive ability.

Upon completion of the battery, and after extensive training in identifying the ship sounds, subjects performed under the nine different task conditions. Variations in the two characteristics resulted in highly significant differences in performance; as signal duration and signal-noise ratio increased, signal detection decreased. What of the relation of the ability factors to these changes in task characteristics?

Of the five separate ability factors that were identified in the total battery, an auditory perceptual ability was found to be most related to performance of the criterion task. Within each signal duration, the loadings on this factor increased as background noise grew louder. The same was generally true, within each level of background noise, when loadings on the auditory perceptual factor increased in magnitude as signal durations grew shorter. In other words, the contribution of this ability to individual differences in performance increased as the criterion task became more difficult. There appeared to be two critical levels for each task dimension. Thus, signal duration could be decreased from nine to six seconds, without much change in the auditory perceptual ability requirement, but a further decrease, to three seconds, increased this ability requirement substantially. Furthermore, at the three-second signal duration, an equivalent increase in background noise produced a further requirement for this ability, beyond which an additional increase in sound level produced little effect on the ability requirement. Thus, knowledge of these task conditions allowed much more precision in specifying the ability requirements for effective performance.

Performance on Reasoning Tasks. Another study in this program involved the extension of this paradigm to cognitive, or higher-order, reasoning tasks (Rose, Fingerman, Wheaton, Eisner, & Kramer, 1974). Specifically, representative tasks faced by electronic trouble shooters and maintenance personnel were examined. The criterion task was an analogue of a fault-finding or trouble-shooting situation. Working with wiring diagrams, the subjects were to determine which of a number of possible breakpoints actually was faulty. Each wiring diagram contained a number of logic gates, switches, and probe points. The subjects tested the points by placing a light bulb at various points in the circuit and pressing a switch or a combination of switches.

The basic task was varied along two dimensions—formal difficulty, and perceptual complexity of the wiring diagram. Variations in formal difficulty involved increasing the number of possible breakpoints and the number of logic gates. Variations in perceptual complexity involved changing the perceptual organization of the circuits. For example, the first level of difficulty was a left-to-right circuit with no crossed wires; the second level rearranged the locations of the switches on the same circuit, creating several crossed wires; the third level changed the locations of both the switches and the logic gates. Subjects were given training in the mechanics of using the diagrams to test for breakpoints.

The task was analyzed according to the abilities hypothesized as contributing to task performance. A comprehensive battery of twenty-one ability tests was selected and administered to all subjects, who then performed on the eighteen trouble-shooting problems in a replicated 3×3 design. The order of presentation was counterbalanced.

Flexibility of closure ability was found to be related to task performance, and it increased in importance as difficulty increased on both dimensions. Syllogistic reasoning ability remained stable across conditions, whereas the associative memory and induction abilities dropped out, but at different levels of perceptual complexity.

Performance on Concept-Identification Tasks. The final study in this series (Fingerman, Eisner, Rose, Wheaton, & Cohen, 1975) extended this work to changes in the characteristics of concept-identification tasks. Such tasks (for example, aircraft or ship identification) are prototypical problem-solving tasks, in which a large number of targets must be classified on the basis of such attributes as tracks on a radar display, visual silhouettes, and sounds. The study involved the formation and testing of hypotheses, to identify a classification rule. As in the previous work, all subjects performed on the criterion task under varying conditions and received a battery of selected reference ability measures as well.

Performance was found to be markedly affected by increases in the two task dimensions—perceptual complexity and formal difficulty. Most of the performance variance on the criterion task, however, could be accounted for by four abilities—associative memory, flexibility of closure, syllogistic reasoning, and induction. The involvement of the different abilities varied as a function of the task manipulation. For example, prediction of performance from the subjects' associative memory scores increased as task difficulty increased, but it remained constant for different levels of perceptual complexity. Perceptual speed and speed of closure had insignificant relations with task performance under any condition.

These studies have demonstrated empirically that the patterns of abilities related to criterion-task performance may undergo changes as specific characteristics of a task are systematically manipulated. The results of the research on the cognitive tasks confirmed earlier findings with psychomotor and perceptual tasks and extended the principles to more realistic, job-related tasks. If one were to predict from these abilities which individuals would do well on these tasks, the choices would depend on task characteristics.

Two general types of training or selection decisions are implied by these studies. One type of decision occurs when a change in a task characteristic results in a change in the importance of particular abilities but does not require different abilities. Here, a change in the cutoff value on the relevant selection test is appropriate. The second type of decision occurs when changes in task demands also change the combinations of abilities involved. In such situations, the implication is that different individuals would be selected for training if the nature of the task changed, or that the training would need modification, or that the task would have to be redesigned in accordance with the characteristics of the trainee population (see Fiedler & Garcia, 1987). The information provided can be seen as relevant to the *needs assessment* component of training design.

The ability taxonomy and the MARS system can assist the task analyst who must estimate the ability requirements for a given task configuration. Generally, such judgments are called for when a job is analyzed to determine what abilities can serve as a basis for the selection of personnel (or, if personnel will not be preselected, to determine what abilities can serve as a basis for formulating training programs). In special cases, these same kinds of selection and training decisions are required when a new task bears some specifiable resemblance to an old task for which selection and training programs have been developed. In either a special or a more general case, task analysts need a method for predicting ability requirements, one that shortcuts the process of studying each situation empirically, with little generalization across cases. This need, of course, was anticipated by Lawshe (1985) and Guion (1965) in their work on synthetic validity and by Primoff (1959) at the Civil Service Commission. To be of real utility, such a method must also permit assessment of the impact that systematic changes in the nature of a task have on ability requirements. The methods described here should help.

Validity-Generalization Issues. Recent research by validity-generalization theorists (for example, Schmidt, Hunter, & Pearlman, 1981) indicates that relations between cognitive abilities and performance variables can be generalized across jobs to a greater extent than was previously believed possible. The underlying assumption of validity generalization is that task requirements do not moderate test validities. How can the apparently conflicting results of the validity-generalization research be reconciled with the research described here, which indicates the strong moderating effects of particular task characteristics on the relations between ability measures and performance?

One possible resolution is suggested by Tenopyr and Oeltjen (1982). They state, "While there is sufficient reason to conclude that validities generalize across a variety of jobs, there is insufficient evidence to reject the possibility of situational effects on the size of the validity coefficients" (p. 598). Specifically, they suggest that such criteria as supervisors' ratings, which are used in many of the validity-generalization studies, are subject to a large general factor, and this may give the impression of more extensive generalizability. Criteria that are more focused on specific aspects of job behavior may result in different relations with different abilities. It appears that when the researcher has better control over the measurement of the criterion performance, as in the studies by Fleishman and his associates described above, it is possible to show that different task requirements can moderate test validities. Tenopyr and Oeltjen (1982) consider this a plausible explanation that reconciles the data.

Describing Ability Requirements in Training

Granted that the ability requirements approach provides a meaningful system for describing and summarizing the human characteristics that influence task performance; the next question concerns the strategies for using this system to obtain a summary description of ability requirements in training. Broadly speaking, three kinds of useful descriptive information can be obtained through the ability requirements taxonomy. The first is description of the abilities associated with performance on the jobs targeted for training. The second is assessment of the abilities required for adequate performance on the associated training materials. The third involves the assessment of trainees with respect to those abilities found to be relevant to job performance and training activities.

Abilities in Targeted Job Performance

Application of the ability requirements taxonomy to training program design typically begins with an appraisal of the abilities that contribute to adequate job performance. The results obtained in the studies described earlier indicate a general framework for generating this descriptive information in practical, day-to-day settings. The MARS would be completed by a group of fifteen to twenty subject-matter experts (SMEs), who might be job incumbents, job analysts, supervisors, or trainers. After orientation to the rating task and a detailed review of the ability definitions and rating scales, the SMEs would be presented with job descriptions or lists of tasks describing the job or jobs in question. The SMEs would then be asked to rate the extent to which each of these abilities was required for adequate task performance or overall job performance.

Job-Level Use. In job-level applications, a respondent familiar with the job generally reviews the job description or a set of critical core-task statements and makes an overall evaluation of the relevance of a given ability to performance. This job-level approach has proved useful in the development of selection tests and job families (Hogan, Ogden, & Fleishman, 1978), but its value for training design may be more limited. This conclusion derives partly from the fact that most training programs focus on the development of specific kinds of task performance and partly from the fact that this approach is not especially amenable to remediation of the taxonomic system, to incorporate certain kinds of job-specific knowledge and skills that might be relevant to performance.

Performance Dimensions–Level Use. An alternative procedure employed to reduce rating demands involves formulating a separate taxonomy for summarizing the task statements. A variety of different procedures have been used in formulating taxonomic summaries of job tasks, to simplify administration of the ability requirement ratings. Such summaries have generally been accomplished through definition of performance dimensions that incorporate tasks of similar content (Reilly & Zink, 1980, 1981; Israelski & Reilly, 1988). These dimensions can be established through some type of cluster or factor analysis of the intercorrelations among task frequencies or importance ratings, or they can be developed on the basis of literature reviews and inspection and evaluation of task content by job analysts for SMEs, with respect to the nature of the most appropriate catego-

ries. The SMEs are asked to rate the ability requirements associated with each performance dimension. These ratings can also
be weighted — to incorporate the variable importance, frequency, or criticality of performance on these job dimensions —
by obtaining ratings of these indices for each performance
dimension or by cumulating task ratings on these indexes
within a given dimension, when these task-level data are
available.

Task-Level Use. Recent applications have stressed ability
profiling at the task level (Cooper et al., 1987; Inn, Schulman,
Ogden, & Sample, 1982; Myers, Jennings, & Fleishman, 1981;
Myers, Gebhardt, Price, & Fleishman, 1981). First, all available
descriptive materials are obtained and used to construct an
initial task inventory. Second, a panel of ten to twenty SMEs is
asked to review the inventory, specify any additional task statements required to describe the job, specify the percentage of job
tasks covered by this list, and make any indicated changes in or
additions to the task list necessary to enhance clarity and coverage. Review and revision are repeated until 90 percent coverage
has been attained. Third, this final task list is presented to ten to
twenty experienced incumbents, who are asked to rate on a
seven-point scale the frequency, importance, and criticality of
task performance. Although these indexes have been found to
be of the greatest general value, it may also prove useful to
obtain indexes of task-learning difficulty (Mumford, Weeks,
Harding, & Fleishman, 1987) or level of skill required at the end
of training (Weeks, 1984). Tasks that fall below some critical level
on these indexes can be eliminated from further analysis.

Once these initial task-descriptive data have been obtained, a panel of fifteen to twenty SMEs is presented with the
revised task list and the ability definitions. The SMEs are then
asked to allocate tasks to the ability dimensions. After they
complete this operation, they are asked to specify any additional
job-specific abilities necessary to account for performance on
the remaining tasks (Mumford, Yarkin-Levin, Korotkin, Wallis,
& Marshall-Mies, 1985). This fourth step is carried out to incorporate important but highly specific abilities — for example,

acting ability for Federal Bureau of Investigation special agents (Cooper, Schemmer, Jennings, & Korotkin, 1983). In the fifth step, a panel of SMEs is asked to rate the abilities required for performing each task (or some subset of the more critical, important, frequent, or difficult tasks) with the general paradigm just sketched out.

Once tasks have been rated with respect to ability requirements, an overall description of ability requirements can be obtained through summing task ratings or weighting this sum for certain task characteristics, such as the importance and frequency of task performance. One advantage of this approach is that it allows for a particularly flexible application of the ability requirements data. For instance, ability profiles can be formed for task modules on only the tasks that are to be taught. Alternatively, ability requirements can be weighted for task criticality. This high degree of flexibility is especially likely to prove useful when ability requirements data will be used to address a number of different issues in training design.

Abilities Required for Training Tasks and Materials

When the application of ability requirements data for training is under examination, it is commonly assumed that description of task-relevant ability requirements will provide the basis for the definition of required characteristics of learners. To the extent that the activities performed in training fully replicate the job tasks that are the basis of the training objectives, this would be true. Nevertheless, the work of Mumford, Weeks, Harding, and Fleishman (1988) indicates that even in the most carefully constructed training program, there is not a one-to-one correspondence between job tasks and training activities. Moreover, although careful instructional systems design ensures some overlap between training activities and job tasks, this overlap is almost always incomplete, because of the need to adjust these activities so as to ensure the effective application of more basic learning principles.

The foregoing observations indicate that a more germane and complete definition of learner characteristics requires an examination of the training environment per se. Assessment of abilities (and of other generic knowledge and skill requirements) with regard to actual learning activities can be accomplished through an extension of the paradigm already presented. Here, the activities performed by individuals in training would be identified through a review of relevant documentary materials, and standard inventory construction procedures would be used to specify a set of learning tasks. These learning tasks should describe each of the activities to be performed, or required, of the individual in the early, middle, and later stages of skills acquisition for a given task.

For instance, a common learning task statement may be "Read basic instructional texts in microelectronics." Trainers or incumbents can be asked to rate the frequency, importance, and criticality of each activity for overall performance in training. After the general taxonomy is adjusted, to capture additional required knowledge and skills, another sample of trainers or incumbents can be asked to evaluate each of these learning tasks in terms of their associated ability requirements. The learning-environment profile of ability requirements can be obtained through the summing of weighted or unweighted ability ratings across learning tasks. More specific aggregations can also be formulated, such as an ability requirements profile applicable to the most important learning tasks that occur during the first month of training.

These specific profiles may display certain unique characteristics, but the aggregate learning-characteristics profile that is generated should overlap substantially with the profile developed for job tasks, if the course has been designed appropriately. Differences observed in this analysis should identify the unique demands of the learning environment.

Assessing the Trainees' Characteristics

The information obtained in the preceding analyses will have specified the abilities required for task performance and the completion of learning tasks. Having identified the abilities required for performance or performance acquisition on the basis of this task analysis, one must now assess the extent to which trainees possess these abilities. This information may be of great interest in its own right, since many applications of the ability requirements taxonomy to program design also require information about the characteristics of trainees as they enter the learning environment. Even though trainees exhibit a variety of different characteristics, the foregoing analysis of the job and learning environments, in terms of ability requirements, will have served to specify the abilities most likely to be required for adequate job performance and performance acquisition. Thus, the assessment of learners' characteristics can focus on those abilities held to be of more than moderate importance to performance and performance acquisition. Such information can also be used to select individuals for training or assign them to training where the ability requirements match their ability profiles.

Assessment of trainees can be accomplished through application of marker tests explicitly designed to tap each of the abilities. The taxonomy provides for links among abilities, job tasks, and tests that tap the ability constructs. One advantage of the ability requirements taxonomy is that many of the requisite tests are already available (Fleishman & Quaintance, 1984). The detailed descriptions of the abilities in the taxonomy, as well as of their associated task characteristics, also provide guidance for the development of new assessment procedures.

Relating Abilities to Skill Acquisition

In the design of training programs to enhance employees' performance, the concern is to structure training activities in such a way that practice will result in more highly skilled performance of job tasks. One relevant question with respect to using the ability requirements taxonomy in training design concerns how these abilities influence the nature and rate of skill acquisition during practice. We will briefly review some of the research on these questions and examine what this research tells us about training design.

Abilities at Different Stages of Learning. It is a fairly common observation that people differ considerably in the skills they achieve for complex tasks, even after extensive training. Moreover, prolonged practice or experience with such tasks may actually increase individual differences. A frequent assumption is that the variability among people that is observed early in learning is highly related to the variability observed later. It turns out that this is not necessarily so. More typically, one observes decreasing correlations between performance at early and later stages of learning (Woodrow, 1946; Reynolds, 1952; Fleishman & Hempel, 1954; Humphreys, 1960; Jones, 1962).

Figure 6.1, presented earlier, displays performance curves for learning a complex signal discrimination and reaction task. The subjects differed in previously measured abilities (Fleishman & Hempel, 1955). The abilities of verbal comprehension, spatial orientation, reaction time, and speed of arm movement were each related to skill acquisition on the complex task. Furthermore, subjects whose assessed characteristics indicated high amounts of these task-relevant abilities displayed better initial performance, reached higher levels of final performance, and reached performance asymptotes more rapidly.

An extensive program of research has been concerned with the use of ability constructs for describing proficiency at different stages of learning more complex skills (Fleishman, 1972a). What is the relative contribution of these more general ability components, which people bring with them to new tasks, as proficiency in those skills is increased? Ability patterns at the early and the advanced stages of practice can be compared, with a view to establishing what kinds of abilities are most accurately predictive of higher proficiency levels in such skills.

The studies have used (but have not been confined to) combinations of experimental and factor-analysis designs. As confidence in the constructs has increased, later studies have relied more on multiple regression and a variety of experimental approaches. One design involved giving samples of two hundred to three hundred subjects extended practice on a criterion task (Fleishman & Hempel, 1954). The same subjects also received a carefully selected, comprehensive battery of tests on generic reference abilities. (The tests had been identified as diagnostic of different abilities in earlier research.) Correlations among scores, taken from different segments of the practice period on the criterion task and from the reference tests, were then subjected to factor-analysis study. The loadings of the various stages of practice on the criterion-task on the factors defined by the reference tests specified the changes in the factor pattern of this task as practice continued. Figure 6.5 provides an illustration of results from an early study, which involved a complex perceptual-motor task requiring coordinated stick and pedal responses to different patterns of visual signals. The *size* of the labeled area reflects the percentage of variance in task performance accounted for by each ability at each stage of learning. The figure illustrates the importance of spatial orientation, visualization, and perceptual speed early in learning. The status of individual trainees on these three abilities accounts for approximately 40 percent of the variance in performance during early stages of practice. However, the contribution of these abilities declines to insignificant levels in later stages. One psychomotor ability is important at all stages of learning, and a second psychomotor ability (speed of arm movement) increases in importance through the practice period. At advanced levels of proficiency, the two psychomotor abilities are the main abilities contributing to performance. The figure also shows the increasing importance of a factor specific to the practice task. Individual differences at advanced levels depend on both generic abilities and a task-specific factor.

These studies, using a variety of practice tasks, generally indicate that the particular combinations of abilities that contribute to performance on such tasks may change as practice continues and proficiency increases. It has also been shown that these changes are progressive and systematic throughout the practice period, until a point later in practice, when they become stabilized. (See Figure 6.5, for example.) Beyond this point, the pattern of abilities contributing to performance does not vary much. There is also an increase in a factor specific to the task itself, but the contribution of this factor, with respect to generic basic abilities, also stabilizes. In other words, the com-

Figure 6.5. Percentage of Variance Represented by Loadings on Each Factor
at Different Stages of Practice on a Complex Perceptual-Motor
Coordination Task.

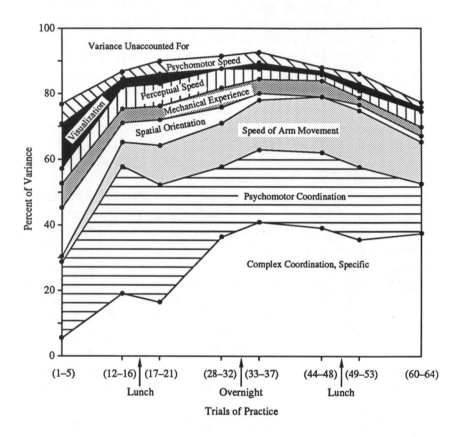

Note: Shaded areas show percentage of variance for each factor at different stages of practice on the Complex Coordination Task.
Source: Adapted from Fleishman & Hempel, 1954, with permission.

bination of abilities contributing to individual differences later in training may be different from those involved early in training. The fact that most of these changes occur earlier in skills acquisition is important, as is the finding of more stability of these patterns once higher levels of proficiency are attained. The latter finding has not been stressed enough (Fleishman & Mumford, 1989).

Although earlier studies factor-analyzed matrices that contained both reference and learning-trial variables, a variety of different approaches have since been used, all confirming these basic findings. Additional designs have used separate cross-sectional analyses of skilled and unskilled psychomotor performances (Fleishman, 1957), regression techniques for predicting practice-trial loadings on reference factors (Parker & Fleishman, 1960; Fleishman & Fruchter, 1960), and analyses of interrelations among component and total-task measures at different practice stages (Fleishman, 1965; Fleishman & Fruchter, 1965). Still later work has used straight experimental procedures (Fleishman & Rich, 1963).

The repeated finding of an increase in specificity of the learned tasks indicates that performance becomes increasingly a function of habits and skills acquired in the task itself. However, pretask abilities also play a role at later stages of learning, and their interactions with learning phenomena are important sources of variance to be studied.

Other work has been concerned with identifying the variance that is defined as specific to the late stages of learning. Hypotheses have been that late-stage measures of different practiced tasks have abilities in common that are not found in early stages of the same tasks (Fleishman, 1957), that the ability to integrate component abilities represents a separate individual-difference variable that is not found in early-stage learning but is critical in late-stage learning and that kinesthetic ability plays an increasing role in psychomotor learning relative to spatial-visual abilities. To further test the latter hypothesis, Fleishman and Rich (1963) developed a measure of kinesthetic sensitivity, on which subjects differed reliably. Performance on this measure was found to be a good predictor of late learning in a two-hand coordination task, but not of early learning, where spatial ability contributed to performance. More research is needed to identify those abilities especially predictive of proficiency in advanced learning. Attempts to identify abilities unique to the late stages of learning have not been successful (for example, Jones, Dunlap, & Bilodeau, 1984).

These findings and methods have been extended to more complex tasks studied over long periods and in real training environments. Thus, Parker and Fleishman (1960) developed a simulation of an air-intercept mission, on which subjects learned a highly complex tracking task over a seven-week period. The same subjects received one of the most extensive batteries of perceptual-motor and cognitive tests ever assembled. The design allowed for the identification of fifteen ability factors and the specification of their contribution to performance at different stages of learning over this period. It was found that spatial ability was important earlier in skills acquisition, and that multilimb coordination was important at later stages of proficiency.

Fleishman and Fruchter (1960) identified abilities underlying the acquisition of skills at different stages of Morse Code learning in a U.S. Air Force radio-telegraphy school. Specifically, early learning depended on two abilities (auditory perceptual speed and auditory rhythm discrimination), and later learning was increasingly a function of speed of closure, representing the ability to unify or organize an apparently disparate field into meaningful units. This study extended findings on learning and individual differences to the area of perceptual learning.

Fleishman (1966) provides an initial explanation for this pattern of results, suggesting that general abilities may play an especially important role in the initial stages of skills acquisition because they represent capacities that guide the definition and generation of responses, which become more integrated over time. Fleishman and Rich (1963) had already introduced the notion that abilities can be conceived of as representing the capacities of individuals for processing different kinds of information. The results from this program are consistent with more recent formulations from cognitive psychology. Anderson (1982), for example, has suggested that skills acquisition can be segmented into three phases. The early, "declarative knowledge" phase involves requisite memory and reasoning processes. This phase involves the understanding of instructions and goals, and the learner may encode and store task rules and devise strategies. The "knowledge compilation" phase involves integration of the cognitive and motor processes required for performing a task. The final phase, which involves "procedural knowledge," occurs when the individual has automatized the skill, so that the task can be performed without the learner's conscious mediation.

Ackerman (1986, 1987) has extended the research of Fleishman's program, using newer methodologies and concepts from cognitive psychology. He has proposed that three major ability classes are important to individual differences at the three phases of learning described by Anderson (1982). During phase 1, "general intelligence" (reasoning, verbal, numerical, and spatial ability) is critical. These abilities encompass the individual's repertoire of knowledge and facility with "acquiring, storing, retrieving, [and] comparing," all related to the information-processing construct of declarative knowledge. When learners already have basic understanding but seek more efficient methods, abilities shift to those that require efficient "proceduralizing" of information. The final stage represents processing speed, mostly independent of information processing.

All these developments are consistent with the notion that skills acquisition may proceed in three distinct stages: a "novice" phase, in which basic abilities are used to gain an understanding of the task and generate initial responses; a "journeyman" phase, in which the individual must master the controlled application of these abilities in the pursuit of task performance; and a "master" phase, in which the application of these abilities becomes virtually automatic and highly attuned to particular tasks.

There has been some interest in whether changes in the relation of abilities to performance, as practice continues, are due to changes in the underlying abilities or to changes in the tasks (Alveres & Hulin, 1972, 1973; Jones, Dunlap, & Bilodeau, 1984). These pretask abilities have already been practiced and "overlearned," before the learner's exposure to the criterion task, which may involve a number of different abilities. It is difficult to see how these underlying abilities could change with the brief amounts of practice involved in the early stages of task performance, when most of the changing factor structure occurs. We prefer the interpretation that different abilities (capacities) of the learner are required as practice proceeds, to the point at which these relations become stabilized (Fleishman & Mumford, 1989). The abilities identified at these later stages are the ones required for high levels of proficiency.

Individual Differences and Part-Whole Task Relationships. Other studies have investigated the relations between individual differences in performance on task components and subsequent performance on a total task. In Fleishman (1965), 204 subjects practiced the components of a complex multidimensional compensatory pursuit task, singly and in combination. These components involved discrete display-control relationships. The total task, which was practiced last, required an integration of these components—that is, the subjects had to operate the multiple controls to minimize error indications on all displays simultaneously. The problems investigated were the extent to which performance on task components, individually practiced, is predictive of total task performance; the extent to which practice on combinations of components is predictive of total task performance; the interrelationships among component performances; and the relative contribution of various component performances to total and subtask performances. The analysis provides some tentative principles of part-whole task relationships relevant to the understanding of skilled performance. The results point up the oversimplification of explanations that are based on simple stimulus-response concepts. Thus, prior performance with the individual controls or the individual display-control relationships found in the total task mattered less than whether coordinated control movements were practiced, regardless of whether these particular coordinated movements were involved in the final task. The level of description that provides the best explanation of the observed relations among the components, and with the total task, involves "common ability" requirements.

Individual Differences in Retention. Very little is known about how an individual trainee's characteristics are related to the long-term retention of skills. In one of the most extensive experimental studies of long-term skills retention, Fleishman and Parker (1962) gave 203 individuals extended (seven weeks) practice on a highly complex perceptual-motor skill and obtained matched groups of subjects after periods of no practice for one, four, nine, fourteen, and twenty-four months. Thus, retention intervals, as well as types of initial guidance and levels of original learning, were varied. The main points of interest in the results of this study are that there was virtually no loss in skills, regardless of the length of the retention interval, and that the most powerful variable was individual difference in the final level of original learning. The prediction of retention from original learning was independent of the length of the retention interval. Thus, for all retention intervals, even those up to two years, individual differences at the end of learning correlated in the .80s and .90s with subsequent performance after various periods of no practice (up to two years). The design also allowed the investigators to say that this prediction could not be accounted for by the subjects' original pretask abilities but was instead explainable in terms of individual differences among subjects in the specific habits acquired while practicing the original task. This study underscores the importance of initial training for achieving high levels of proficiency among all trainees, especially in skills where practice may not be possible for long periods. Final level of proficiency was more important for retention than was type of initial training used to attain this proficiency.

Individual Differences and Other Learning Phenomena. Relations between individual differences in learner attributes and a variety of learning phenomena, including associative interference and transfer and performance during massed versus distributed trials, have been examined (Fleishman & Ellison,

1969). Space does not permit even a summary of this work. It must suffice to say that knowledge about subjects' previously developed abilities helped predict these phenomena. Personality measures were unsuccessful in predicting associative interference, but certain of these measures did predict the performance decrement that occurred during massed-practice periods. Such results point up the need for more research on learners' attributes other than abilities (see Peterson & Bownas, 1982).

Implications for Training Design

We have shown the importance of human abilities as characteristics of learners, related to the characteristics of the tasks that people perform. We have examined how abilities are defined, and we have described a taxonomic system for identifying the ability requirements of jobs and their associated tasks. We have shown how information about ability requirements can be developed for training programs, and we have reviewed research that shows how abilities operate during the acquisition of skills. We turn now to some further implications for training and training research.

Developing Generic Abilities. We have already discussed the implications of assessing the abilities of trainees before assignments to training are made. These observations imply that selection systems should ensure requisite levels of those general abilities required by the training and job tasks. Of course, many research questions are raised by the earlier discussion: Should one select trainees on the basis of the abilities that will ultimately be required at high levels of proficiency? Is it better or necessary to select trainees for abilities that are likely to facilitate more rapid progress during early practice? It does seem reasonable that failing to consider the abilities that ultimately will be needed limits the level of attainment ultimately achieved. It appears that the abilities needed at all stages of training, as well as those required in the job situation, should be taken into account. The research already cited provides some guidance, but there is a lot of research still to be done on how to optimize the use of this information in matching trainees' characteristics to training requirements.

Of special relevance is the possibility that training programs can develop the basic abilities required for a variety of jobs and tasks. Can general abilities be improved in the adult? Since abilities underlie performance in a wide variety of tasks, the answer to this question has significant implications. If, for example, an ability could be improved, would it be transferred to the wide variety of tasks, in various job contexts, that involve this ability?

Other chapters in this volume (for example, Chapter Five) have examined specific attempts to impart broad human capacities, such as information processing and problem solving, and we will not review these developments here. We can say, however, that empirical data on the organization of human abilities suggest that these categories may be too broad for definitive conclusions about effective training regimens and principles. Categories like "motor-skills training" do not help us much in relating individual differences to specific task requirements. Subsumed under "motor skills" are such abilities as multilimb coordination, response orientation, arm-hand steadiness, manual dexterity, and rate control. Consequently, the category "motor skills" comprises too broad a range of different tasks for us to expect generalizations regarding procedures and training design.

At present, the limited research on whether abilities can be trained has had only modest success, but there are encouraging signs. Certainly, the emphasis on process variables is an important development. Perhaps the research on human abilities can help delimit and focus attention on the whole range of activities that must be addressed within the domains to be examined by cognitive and instructional psychologists.

A number of studies have examined whether training interventions can be formulated for enhancing intelligence. Studies conducted by Jacobs and White (1971), Kennedy (1978), and Feuerstein (1979, 1980) have found that well-designed training interventions that are intended to improve relevant problem-solving processes may lead to gains in measured intellectual ability. Stanton (1986) and Jensen (1980), however, have noted that the gains brought about by these interventions are not large (typically lying between three and eight points). This finding might have been expected on the basis of the complex, multifaceted nature of general intellectual ability, since any single intervention is unlikely to fully compensate for years of prior intellectual development in a variety of task domains. In fact, evidence compiled by Snow and Yallow (1982), Siegler and Richards (1982), Bjorklund and Weiss (1985), and Perkins (1985) suggests that although schooling may lead to gains in general intellectual ability, these gains occur relatively slowly, over a long time, and in an integrated fashion consistent with the problem-solving demands placed on the individual.

These observations suggest that training interventions targeted on lower-order group factors (such as spatial ability, inductive reasoning, and spatial visualization) may prove somewhat more effective. Studies conducted by Willis, Bliesner, and Baltes (1980), White and Alexander (1986), and Alexander, White, Hanesly, and Jeaner (1986) have shown that training on analogy tasks—intended to improve the application of encoding, inferring, and mapping processes by describing rules and procedures, demonstrating process application, and providing practice and systematic feedback—will improve performance. Whitley and Dawis (1974) found that performance on verbal analogy tasks could not be improved simply through provision of feedback and practice, but when semantic categorization strategies were provided along with feedback and practice, performance improvements were observed. Similarly, Holzman, Glaser, and Pellegrino (1976) obtained performance improvements when training and practice were provided in basic problem-solving processes, such as the recognition of relations and cycles.

There is additional evidence for the feasibility of designing training interventions capable of improving performance on generic abilities. For instance, Fitzgerald and Teasley (1986) have shown that written comprehension can be improved by training interventions that discuss the structure and main parts of narrative prose, provide models for the analysis of narrative prose, and encourage active practice. In a study of writing ability, Day (1986) found that performance improvements could be brought about by training procedures that emphasized the understanding of rules and strategies, coupled with active independent practice. In underscoring the role of active practice, these studies point to another consideration that appears relevant: The development of abilities may depend on the application of deep or elaborative processing strategies (Schmeck & Grove, 1979). For example, Davey and McBride (1986) found that training in question-generation techniques may improve reading comprehension; Wollin, Case, Bruchter, and Mindemir (1985) have found that, because it focuses attention, underlining may improve reading comprehension. Other studies, conducted by Gagné, Widerman, Bell, and Ander (1984), Eisenstein, Morner, and Smith (1985), Withers (1984), and Wilding, Raskind, Gilmore, and Valentine (1986), have also underscored the importance of active elaborative processing in the development of abilities.

A number of studies concerned with the development of spatial abilities have also been undertaken. As McGee (1979) points out, these investigations have produced mixed results. Studies conducted by Faubian, Cleveland, and Hassell (1942), Ranucci (1952), Brown (1954), Myers (1958), and Levine, Schulman, Brahlek, and Fleishman (1980) all failed to obtain improvements in spatial ability after practice on relevant tasks. In contrast, studies conducted by Brinkman (1966), Dailey and Neyman (1967), Levine, Brahlek, Eisner, and Fleishman (1979), and Kyllonen, Lohman, and Snow (1984) have provided evidence for the trainability and transferability of certain spatial abilities. These inconsistent results can probably be attributed to a number of factors. For instance, studies that provide practice and feedback on a variety of relevant tasks, where general rules, principles, and procedures are delineated, are more likely to yield improvements in performance than studies that simply provide practice in a limited task domain. Furthermore, differences appear between the more successful and more unsuccessful interventions in the extent to which deep or elaborative processing is called for, rather than superficial task performance. Finally, on the basis of Kyllonen, Lohman, and Snow's (1984) findings, it is possible to say that these inconsistent results may be attributable to the failure to control for other significant differential influences.

Taken as a whole, the studies reviewed here do paint a rather consistent picture of the training interventions that are likely to facilitate ability development. First, the more successful interventions appear to be those that systematically identify component processes or strategies and provide training in their application to a variety of task domains. Second, training programs are more likely to prove effective when their strategy and process application is explained and modeled and when systematic feedback concerning the application of these strategies and processes is provided during practice (Brown, Bransford, Ferrara, & Campione, 1983; Brown, Campione, & Day, 1981; Brown & Campione, 1984). Third, effective training for ability development appears to depend on the construction of training interventions that will encourage active practice and facilitate deep or elaborative processing strategies during practice. Fourth, it appears that the success of these interventions will vary inversely with the breadth of the ability under consideration.

Abilities and Sequencing of Training. Earlier, we discussed research on abilities related to performance at different stages of learning. This information is certainly related to issues in instructional design. We can illustrate this with a study by Parker and Fleishman (1961). We described an earlier study by Parker and Fleishman (1960) in which the abilities contributing to performance on a complex piloting-target intercept simulation were identified as practice continued over a six-week period. In a follow-up study, these investigators examined the impact of ability-relevant training on the learning of this skill. To accomplish this, three groups were given practice on the task. Group one received no formal training, group two received common-sense training reflecting standard task-oriented training practices, and group three received this training but was also given guidance at certain points on the basis of prior analyses of ability requirements. The guidance given to this third group consisted of strategies for applying a certain ability just before and during the point when it became an especially important determinant of performance. Thus, a focus on spatial requirements was given early, and a focus on the multilimb requirements was given later. When performance, as measured by time on target, was assessed over fifty trials, it was found that both training groups performed better than the untrained control group, but the ability-targeted training group showed a 39 percent increase in performance over the more traditionally trained group.

The work of Parker and Fleishman (1961) is consistent with more recent studies examining optimal procedures for training in complex skills, such as composition writing (Hayes & Flower, 1986). Broadly speaking, it appears that early performance in training is influenced by general abilities relating to task performance. Thus, it is not surprising that training interventions that describe the nature and the significance of a given ability to task performance, and that later illustrate strategies for applying this ability to the task at hand, using its component processes, have proved successful in enhancing performance on analogy and writing tasks (Alexander, White, Hanesly, & Jeaner, 1986; Hayes & Flower, 1986; Holzman, Glaser, & Pellegrino, 1976; White & Alexander, 1986; Whitley & Dawis, 1974). The notion that the later stages of task learning will involve more discrete abilities, requiring the integration and organization of responses, suggests that interventions illustrating the systematic integration and application of these skills, abilities, and knowledges may enhance task performance during this stage of skill acquisition.

Some support for this proposition has been provided in a study of writing skills conducted by Day (1986), where it was found that training interventions that illustrate how various performance components are to be structured and combined may lead to improved performance, if practice and feedback concerning the success of these efforts is provided. To the extent that performance in the later stages of practice is largely a function of task-specific factors, one could expect that interventions that encourage the development of such capacities would prove useful. Correspondingly, the varied findings indicating that active, involved, independent practice will facilitate the development of performance are not especially surprising (Eisenstein, Morner, & Smith, 1985; Gagné, Widerman, Bell, & Ander, 1984; Wilding, Raskind, Gilmore, & Valentine, 1986).

When the nature of these interventions is considered in relation to the various stages of skills acquisition, a paradigm is suggested for the application of ability data to course design. Initially, ability ratings should be obtained for each task that will be trained. These data should then be reviewed, to identify those broad, general abilities and knowledges that are likely to play an important role in initial skill acquisition, as it is reflected in the initial generation of adaptive responses to a task. Once these have been identified, it is necessary to specify a set of training interventions or learning activities intended to facilitate the application of these capacities to task performance. Although the specific content of these activities will necessarily vary, as a function of the abilities and generic knowledge that condition response generation, several steps seem likely to be required at this stage. First, the content and the nature of the task should be described. Second, the manner in which each of these capacities influences task performance should be delineated, along with the nature of each ability and kind of knowledge. Third, effective strategies for applying each kind of ability and knowledge to task performance should be specified and illustrated. Fourth, trainees should be given practice in applying each strategy. Fifth, trainees should be required to apply these strategies to task performance over a sufficient number of practice sessions to ensure adequate retention.

This general framework is a limiting case, where training is targeted on a single task occurring in a single job setting. In the design of operational training programs, it is generally necessary to consider multiple tasks to be trained (Goldstein, 1986). While it is true that this general paradigm could be used to devise learning activities for each task, this would represent an inefficient and time-consuming approach. Many tasks display substantial similarity in overt behavioral content, as well as in the abilities that contribute to effective task performance. If tasks that share a common set of abilities can be identified, then it should prove possible to train these tasks as a set and thereby increase the efficiency of the training program and maximize potential transfer effects (Fleishman, 1987).

One illustration of the utility of this general approach can be found in Mitchell, Ruck, and Driskill (1988), who describe the efficiency gains obtained in U.S. Air Force technical training programs through institution of an electronics-principles course intended to facilitate the application of general underlying abilities and knowledges to electronic repair and maintenance tasks. Later, there was a branching out from this base into occupationally specific task clusters relevant to the "journeyman" stage.

A further comment seems in order concerning the specification of learning activities. Typically, learning activities should be specified in such a way that they reflect the abilities and knowledge requirements relevant to task performance at a given stage of skill acquisition (Goldstein, 1986). Thus, these requirements for potential learning activities should be evaluated with respect to assessments of task ability and knowledge requirements. Complete overlap in task and learning-activity requirements cannot be expected, because of the unique demands made by the training environment, particularly in the early stages of skill acquisition. If, however, substantial overlap is not observed with regard to the abilities and knowledge that influence learning activity, then the learning activity is suspect and should be revised. For instance, initial readings in an electronics-principles course, which do not receive high scores on inductive reasoning and electronics knowledge, are unlikely to represent appropriate training activities. While this comparative analysis is likely to prove useful for screening potential training activities, it should also be recognized that documenting the relevance of the abilities and knowledges to task performance on the job will provide substantial evidence for the content and construct validity of the proposed course design. Information of this sort may prove especially valuable, since it will permit some evaluation of the course's utility before its implementation, while guiding course revision to maximize its relevance to job performance.

Individual Differences and Training Design. One may expect that the effectiveness of alternative training interventions will to some extent be conditioned by the nature of trainees' abilities. For instance, a shorter course may be possible if trainees manifest high levels of task-relevant abilities. Alternatively, for relatively inexperienced populations, a training program focusing on ability and knowledge-structure development, as well as on basic fact acquisition, may prove useful, although the value of this training strategy may be limited in populations with high abilities and well-developed knowledge structures. These observations indicate that interactions may emerge between characteristic trainees' abilities and optimal training procedures. For example, recent reviews by Lohman and Snow (1984), Snow and Yallow (1982), and Snow (1986) suggest that training strategies that emphasize the independent acquisition of information will improve learning in high-ability samples, while more detailed, concrete training strategies that focus on basic principles will facilitate learning in low-ability samples. These findings are readily understood when it is recognized that high-ability individuals possess the underlying capacities required for rapid skills development and the generation of accurate and elaborate cognitive schema, while low-ability individuals require trainers to carefully build up this structure over time. Kyllonen, Lohman, and Snow (1984) indicate that the design of learning activities intended to offset deficiencies in certain abilities, such as spatial visualization, may also lead to improved performance.

It can also be expected that in the early stages of skills acquisition, trainees will be more likely to profit from learning activities that are consistent with their extant patterns of broad, general abilities. Thus, alternative learning activities can be screened, and activities consistent with students' ability patterns could be eliminated, in preference to activities more in line with students' existing capacities. In many cases, different individuals entering training may display very different patterns of abilities.

While it is possible to tailor training programs for each individual's pattern, such techniques may prove unduly expensive in the industrial context (Corno & Snow, 1986). In contrast, prior selection and development in the occupational environment may result in systematic differences in the ability patterns manifested by certain clusters of individuals. For instance, Hogan, Ogden, and Fleishman (1978) have shown that different occupations are associated with very different patterns of ability requirements, and Weldon (1983) has shown that these profile differences are replicated in samples of occupational incumbents. Where groups of trainees can be grouped according to such common profiles, the construction of group-specific training programs may prove cost-effective.

   Skills Selection and Remediation. Traditionally, "basic skills" have been conceived of as the "three R's." A basic skill has been defined as some capacity of the individual that is required for the successful completion of learning activities (Hooke & Sticht, 1981). Thus, in a lecture class, listening skills or attentional capacities can be viewed as preconditions for learning and as representing basic skills. The potential significance of these basic skills for instructional system design has been examined in a number of studies. For instance, Mumford, Weeks, Harding, and Fleishman (1988) found that reading grade level and skills, which contributed to adaptation to the training environment, had a substantial causal impact on measured achievement and attrition in U.S. Air Force training programs. Studies by Huff, Sticht, Joyner, Groff, and Burkett (1977), Sticht (1977), and Vineberg and Joyner (1983) indicate that training intended to enhance basic reading and listening skills leads to enhanced performance in military training programs. Other work by Sticht (1982), Mikulecky and Diehl (1982), and Lave (1980) indicates that training intended to build numerical and mathematical reasoning abilities may yield enhanced performance in a number of technical training programs.

   While reading, writing, arithmetic, and listening may represent abilities required for many learning activities, it should be recognized that exactly what constitutes a basic skill will be dictated by the nature of learning activities required in the training program. Consider the impact of inductive reasoning on electronic trouble-shooting learning activities (Mumford, Dyer, & Costa, 1981), or the impact of information ordering on the planning of learning activities (Nutt, 1984). The question arises of how the basic skills that operate in a particular learning environment can be identified.

Given the availability of descriptive information concerning the abilities and generic knowledge required for the various learning activities embedded in a training program, a relatively straightforward strategy could be used to specify basic skills. Initially, the learning activities embedded in a training program, or some subset of the more important or frequently performed learning activities, would be identified. Next, the ability ratings generated for each activity would be obtained, in accordance with the format described earlier. A weighted sum of these ratings across activities would be generated. *Basic skills* could be defined as abilities and knowledges of more than moderate importance to performance on a large percentage (70 percent) of the learning activities on all tasks, of more than moderate importance to performance on a large percentage (70 percent) of the learning activities occurring in the early phases of training on all tasks, or of more than moderate importance to performance across all activities or on the activities that occur in the earlier stages of training, for all tasks. Although the application of a particular definition should be guided by the intent of the training program, it can be expected that, in most situations, investigators will prefer to define basic skills with respect to the learning activities occurring in the earlier phases of training. The obvious concern in attaining this information is to ensure that trainees possess the capacities required to profit from learning experiences.

Two strategies could be used to reach this goal. First, an attempt could be made to determine whether potential trainees possessed these basic skills. If they did not, they would be excluded from training. Second, individuals who did not possess these basic skills might be assigned to remedial skills-development programs before being admitted to training. The choice between these alternatives is likely to be conditioned by a variety of factors, including the number of potential trainees, manpower requirements, and available funds. In most situations, however, both strategies should be employed, according to whether it appears possible to develop the requisite basic abilities in a timely and cost-efficient manner.

Conclusion

This chapter has presented evidence that the individual capacities that people bring to the training environment constitute a critical determinant of the success of training efforts. Human individuality represents a phenomenon of nearly incomprehensible complexity. Nevertheless, we have shown that, by identifying salient domains of task performance, the systematic analysis of the factors giving rise to performance differences in each domain can be used to formulate a classification system for the summary description of human attributes relevant to task performance and skill acquisition. Further, we have provided evidence bearing on the construct validity of this classification of human attributes, while demonstrating its relevance to skill acquisition. We have also discussed how this taxonomic system can be used to address a number of practical concerns likely to arise in the design of training programs.

We have provided some illustrations of how this system could be used to uncover the general processes by which, with practice, underlying human capacities are translated into skilled performance. This information is of substantial interest in its own right. When coupled with an analysis of the human capacities required for various kinds of task performance, however, it allows us to address a number of issues relevant to training. These include the selection and assignment of individuals to training, the training of requisite abilities, the use of optimal learning activities for individuals at different stages of skills acquisition, the specification of training content relevant to trainees' abilities, and the design of training.

Many of the issues discussed in this chapter raise new research questions, and some of our suggestions for training applications may go beyond available data. We hope that this effort will stimulate some experimental applications. For the present, it underscores how the capacities of people, and the operation of these capacities in skill acquisition, can combine information about tasks, training content, the basic properties that influence learning, and the uniqueness of the learner in an integrated framework.

References

Ackerman, P. L. (1986). Individual differences in information processing: An investigation of intellectual abilities and task performance during practice. *Intelligence, 10*, 101–139.

Ackerman, P. L. (1987). Individual differences in skill learning: An integration of psychometric and information processing perspectives. *Psychological Bulletin, 102*, 3–37.

Alexander, P. D., White, C. S., Hanesly, P. A., & Jeaner, M. (1986). Analogy training: A developmental study of the effects of verbal reasoning. *Journal of Educational Research, 80*, 77–88.

Alluisi, E. A. (1967). Methodology in the use of synthetic task to assess complex performance. *Human Factors, 9*, 375–384.

Alveres, K., & Hulin, C. (1972). Two explanations of temporal changes in ability-skill relationships: A literature review and theoretical analysis. *Human Factors, 14*, 295–308.

Alveres, K., & Hulin, C. (1973). An experimental evaluation of a temporal decay in the prediction of performance. *Organizational Behavior and Human Performance, 9*, 169–185.

Anderson, J. R. (1982). Acquisition of cognitive skill. *Psychological Review, 89*, 369–406.

Annett, J., & Duncan, K. D. (1967). Task analysis and training design. *Occupational Psychology, 41*, 211–221.

Bjorklund, D. F., & Weiss, S. C. (1985). Influence of socioeconomic status on children's classification and free recall. *Journal of Educational Psychology, 77*, 119–128.

Bloom, B. S. (1967). *A taxonomy of educational objectives: The classification of educational goals: Handbook I. Cognitive domain.* New York: McKay.

Brinkman, E. H. (1966). Programmed instruction as a technique for improving spatial visualization. *Journal of Applied Psychology, 50*, 179–184.

Brown, A. L., Bransford, J. D., Ferrara, R. A., & Campione, J. C. (1983). Learning, remembering, and understanding. In J. H. Flavell & E. M. Markman (Eds.), *Handbook of child psychology: Volume 3. Cognitive development*. New York: Wiley.

Brown, A. L., & Campione, J. C. (1984). Three faces of transfer: Implications for early competence, individual differences, and instruction. In M. Lamb, A. Brown, & B. Ragoff (Eds.), *Advances in developmental psychology*. Hillsdale, NJ: Erlbaum.

Brown, A. L., Campione, J. C., & Day, J. D. (1981). Learning to learn: On training students to learn from text. *Educational Researcher, 10*, 14–21.

Brown, F. R. (1954). *The effect of an experimental course in geometry on ability to visualize in three dimensions*. Unpublished doctoral dissertation, Columbia University.

Carroll, J. B. (1976). Psychometric tests as cognitive tasks: A new "structure of intellect." In L. Resnick (Ed.), *The nature of intelligence*. Hillsdale, NJ: Erlbaum.

Christal, R. E. (1974). *The United States Air Force occupational research project* (AFHRL-TR-73-75). Lackland Air Force Base, TX: Air Force Human Resources Laboratory.

Cooper, M. A., Schemmer, F. M., Fleishman, E. A., Yarkin-Levin, K., Harding, F. D., & McNelis, J. (1987). *Task analysis of navy and marine corps occupations: A taxonomic basis for evaluating CW antidote/pretreatment drugs* (ARRO Report No. R87-1). Bethesda, MD: Advanced Research Resources Organization.

Cooper, M., Schemmer, F. M., Gebhardt, D. L., Marshall-Mies, J., & Fleishman, E. A. (1982). *Development and validation of physical ability tests for jobs in the electric power industry* (ARRO Final Report No. R82-2). Bethesda, MD: Advanced Research Resources Organization.

Cooper, M., Schemmer, F. M., Jennings, M. C., & Korotkin, A. (1983). *Development of measures for the selection of FBI special agents* (ARRO Report No. R83-20). Bethesda, MD: Advanced Research Resources Organization.

Corno, L., & Snow, R. E. (1986). Adapting teaching to individual differences among students. In M. Wittrock (Ed.), *Third hand-book of research on teaching*. New York: Macmillan.

Cotterman, T. E. (1959). *Task classification: An approach to partially ordering information on human learning* (WADC TN 58-374). Wright-Patterson Air Force Base, OH: Wright-Patterson Air Development Center.

Cox, R. C.., & Unks, N. J. (1967). *A selected and annotated bibliography of studies concerning the taxonomy of educational objectives: Cognitive domain*. Pittsburgh: University of Pittsburgh, Learning Research and Development Center.

Cronbach, L. J. (1971). Test validation. In R. L. Thorndike (Ed.), *Educational measurement*. Washington, DC: American Council on Education.

Cronbach, L. J., & Snow, R. E. (1977). *Aptitude and instructional methods*. New York: Wiley.

Crowson, R. A. (1970). *Classification and biology*. New York: Atherton.

Dailey, J. T., & Neyman, C. A. (1967). *Development of a curriculum and material for teaching basic vocational talents*. Washington, DC: George Washington University, Education Research Project.

Davey, B., & McBride, S. (1986). Effects of question-generation training on reading comprehension. *Journal of Educational Psychology, 75*, 256–262.

Day, J. (1986). Teaching summarization skills: Influences of student ability level and strategy difficulty. *Cognition and Instruction, 3*, 193–210.

Dunnette, M. D. (1976). Aptitudes, abilities, and skills. In M. D. Dunnette (Ed.), *Handbook of industrial and organizational psychology*. Skokie, IL: Rand McNally.

Eden, D., & Shani, A. B. (1982). Pygmalion goes to boot camp: Expectancy, leadership, and trainee performance. *Journal of Applied Psychology, 67*, 194–199.

Eisenstein, G. O., Morner, J., & Smith, S. (1985). Note taking, individual differences, and memory. *Journal of Educational Psychology, 77*, 522–537.

Ekstrom, R. B., French, J. W., & Harmon, H. H. (1979). Cognitive factors: Their identification and replication. *Multivariate Behavioral Research Monographs 79-2*, 1–84.

Farina, A. J., Jr., & Wheaton, G. R. (1973). Development of a taxonomy of human performance: The task-characteristics approach to performance prediction. *JSAS Catalog of Selected Documents in Psychology, 3*, 26–27 (Ms. No. 323).

Faubian, R. W., Cleveland, E. A., & Hassell, T. W. (1942). The influence of training on mechanical aptitude test scores. *Educational Psychological Measurement, 2*, 91–94.

Feuerstein, R. (1979). *The dynamic assessment of retarded performers: The learning potential assessment device, theory, instruments, and techniques.* Baltimore, MD: University Park Press.

Feuerstein, R. (1980). *Instrumental enrichment: An intervention program for cognitive modifiability.* Baltimore, MD: University Park Press.

Fiedler, F. E., & Garcia, J. E. (1987). *New approaches to effective leadership, cognitive resources, and organizational performance.* New York: Wiley.

Fingerman, P., Eisner, E., Rose, A., Wheaton, G., & Cohen, F. (1975). *Methods for predicting job ability requirements: III. Ability requirements as a function of changes in the characteristics of a concept identification task* (AIR Technical Report No. 75-4). Washington, DC: American Institutes for Research.

Fitts, P. M. (1962). Factors in complex skill training. In R. Glaser (Ed.), *Training research and education.* Pittsburgh: University of Pittsburgh Press.

Fitzgerald, J., & Teasley, A. B. (1986). Effects of instruction in narrative structure on children's writing. *Journal of Educational Psychology, 78*, 424–432.

Fleishman, E. A. (1957). Factor structure in relation to task difficulty in psychomotor performance. *Educational and Psychological Measurement, 17*, 522–532.

Fleishman, E. A. (1964). *The structure and measurement of physical fitness.* Englewood Cliffs, NJ: Prentice-Hall.

Fleishman, E. A. (1965). The prediction of total task performance from prior practice on task components. *Human Factors, 7*, 18–27.

Fleishman, E. A. (1966). Human abilities and the acquisition of skill. In E. A. Bilodeau (Ed.), *Acquisition of skill.* Orlando, FL: Academic Press.

Fleishman, E. A. (1967). Development of a behavior taxonomy for describing human tasks: A correlational-experimental approach. *Journal of Applied Psychology, 51*, 1–10.

Fleishman, E. A. (1972a). On the relation between abilities, learning, and human performance. *American Psychologist, 27*, 1017–1032.

Fleishman, E. A. (1972b). Structure and measurement of psychomotor abilities. In R. N. Singer (Ed.), *The psychomotor domain: Movement behavior*. Philadelphia: Lea and Febiger.

Fleishman, E. A. (1975a). *Manual for the ability requirement scales*. Bethesda, MD: Management Research Institute.

Fleishman, E. A. (1975b). Toward a taxonomy of human performance. *American Psychologist, 30*, 1127–1149.

Fleishman, E. A. (1975c). *Development of ability requirement scales for the analysis of Bell System jobs*. Bethesda, MD: Management Research Institute.

Fleishman, E. A. (1987). Foreword. In S. M. Cormier & J. D. Hagman (Eds.), *Transfer of learning: Contemporary research and applications*. Orlando, FL: Academic Press.

Fleishman, E. A., Cobb, A. T., & Spendolini, M. J. *Development of ability requirement scales for the analysis of yellow page sales jobs in the Bell System*. Bethesda, MD: Management Research Institute.

Fleishman, E. A., & Ellison, G. D. (1969). Prediction of transfer and other learning phenomena from ability and personality measures. *Journal of Educational Psychology, 60*, 300–314.

Fleishman, E. A., & Fruchter, B. (1960). Factor structure and predictability of successive stages of learning Morse Code. *Journal of Applied Psychology, 44*, 96–101.

Fleishman, E. A., & Fruchter, B. (1965). Component and total task relations at different stages of learning a complex tracking task. *Perceptual and Motor Skills, 20*, 1305–1311.

Fleishman, E. A., & Hempel, W. E., Jr. (1954). Changes in factor structure of a complex psychomotor test as a function of practice. *Psychometrika, 18*, 239–252.

Fleishman, E. A., & Hempel, W. E., Jr. (1955). The relation between abilities and improvement with practice in a visual discrimination reaction task. *Journal of Experimental Psychology, 49*, 301–312.

Fleishman, E. A., & Hogan, J. C. (1978). *A taxonomic method for assessing the physical requirements of jobs: The physical abilities analysis approach* (ARRO Technical Report No. R78-6). Bethesda, MD: Advanced Research Resources Organization.

Fleishman, E. A., & Mumford, M. D. (1988). The ability requirements scales. In S. Gael (Ed.), *The job-analysis handbook for business, government, and industry*. New York: Wiley.

Fleishman, E. A., & Mumford, M. D. (1989). Abilities as causes of individual differences at different stages of learning. *Human Performances, 2*, 201–222.

Fleishman, E. A., & Parker, J. R. (1962). Factors in the retention and relearning of perceptual-motor skill. *Journal of Experimental Psychology, 64*, 215–226.

Fleishman, E. A., & Quaintance, M. K. (1984). *Taxonomies of human performance: The description of human tasks*. Orlando, FL: Academic Press.

Fleishman, E. A., & Rich, S. (1963). Role of kinesthetic and spatial-visual abilities in perceptual-motor learning. *Journal of Experimental Psychology, 66*, 6–11.

Fogli, L. (1988). Supermarket cashier. In S. Gael (Ed.), *The job-analysis handbook for business, government, and industry*. New York: Wiley.

Fox, W. L., Taylor, J. E., & Caylor, J. S. (1969). *Aptitude level and the acquisition of skills and knowledges in a variety of military training tasks* (Technical Report No. 69-6). Monterey, CA: The George Washington University Human Resources Research Office, HumRRO Division No. 3 (Recruit Training).

French, J. W., Ekstrom, R. B., & Price, L. A. (1963). *Kit of reference tests for cognitive factors*. Princeton, NJ: Educational Testing Service.

Gagné, E. D., Widerman, C., Bell, M. S., & Ander, T. D. (1984). Training thirteen-year-olds to elaborate while studying text. *Human Learning, 3*, 281–294.

Gagné, R. M. (1962). Factors in acquiring knowledge of a mathematical task. *Psychological Monographs, 76* (entire issue 7).

Gebhardt, D. L., Cooper, M., Jennings, M. C., Crump, C., & Sample, R. A. (1983). *Development and validation of selection tests for a natural gas company* (ARRO Final Report No. R83-17). Bethesda, MD: Advanced Research Resources Organization.

Gebhardt, D. L., Jennings, M. C., & Fleishman, E. A. (1981). *Factors affecting the reliability of physical ability and effort ratings of navy tasks* (ARRO Technical Report No. R81-1). Bethesda, MD: Advanced Research Resources Organization.

Gebhardt, D. L., & Weldon, L. J. (1982). *Development and Validation of Physical Performance Tests for Correctional Officers* (ARRO Final Report No. 3080). Bethesda, MD: Advanced Research Resources Organization.

Gettinger, M., & White, M. A. (1979). Which is the stronger correlate of school learning, time to learn or measured intelligence? *Journal of Educational Psychology, 71,* 405–412.

Ghiselli, E. E. (1973). The validity of aptitude tests in personnel selection. *Personnel Psychology, 26,* 461–477.

Goldstein, I. L. (1986). *Training in organizations: Needs assessment, development, and evaluation* (2nd ed.). Monterey, CA: Brooks/ Cole.

Goldstein, I. L., & Buxton, V. M. (1982). Training and human performance. In M. D. Dunnette & E. A. Fleishman (Eds.), *Human performance and productivity: Human capability assessment.* Hillsdale, NJ: Erlbaum.

Guilford, J. P., & Hopfner, R. (1966). *Structure of intellect factors and their tests.* Los Angeles: University of Southern California, Psychological Laboratory.

Guion, R. M. (1965). *Personnel testing.* New York: McGraw-Hill.

Hayes, J. R., & Flower, L. S. (1986). Writing research and the writer. *American Psychologist, 41,* 1106–1113.

Hogan, J. C., Ogden, G. D., & Fleishman, E. A. (1978). *Assessing the physical requirements for establishing medical standards in selected benchmark jobs* (ARRO Final Report No. R78-8). Bethesda, MD: Advanced Research Resources Organization.

Hogan, J. C., Ogden, G. D., & Fleishman, E. A. (1979). *The development and validation of tests for the order selector job at Certified Grocers of California, Ltd.* (ARRO Technical Report No. 3029). Bethesda, MD: Advanced Research Resources Organization.

Hogan, J. C., Ogden, G. D., Gebhardt, D. L., & Fleishman, E. A.

(1979). An index of physical effort required in human task performance. *Journal of Applied Psychology, 65,* 672–679.

Hogan, J. C., Ogden, G. D., Gebhardt, D. L, & Fleishman, E. A. (1980). Reliability and validity of methods for evaluating perceived physical effort. *Journal of Applied Psychology, 65,* 672–679.

Holzman, T. G., Glaser, R., & Pellegrino, J. W. (1976). Process training derived from computer simulation theory. *Memory and Cognition, 4,* 349–356.

Hooke, L. R., & Sticht, T. G. (1981). *Instructional systems design for the army's on-duty educational program: Development of technical objectives.* Alexandria, VA: Human Resources Research Organization.

Horn, J. L. (1976). Human abilities: A review of research and theory in the early 1970s. *Annual Review of Psychology 27,* 437–485.

Huff, K. H., Sticht, T. G., Joyner, J. N., Groff, S. D., & Burkett, J. R. (1977). *A job-oriented reading program for the Air Force: Development and field evaluation.* Alexandria, VA: Human Resources Research Organization.

Humphreys, L. G. (1960). Investigations of simplex. *Psychometrika, 25,* 313–323.

Imhoff, D. L., & Levine, J. M. (1980). *Development of a perceptual-motor and cognitive performance task battery for pilot selection* (ARRO Report No. R80-4). Bethesda, MD: Advanced Research Resources Organization.

Inn, A., Schulman, D. R., Ogden, G. D., & Sample, R. A. (1982). *Physical ability requirements of Bell System jobs* (ARRO Final Report No. 3057/R82-1). Bethesda, MD: Advanced Research Resources Organization.

Israelski, E. W., & Reilly, R. R. (1988). Telecommunications craftworkers. In S. Gael (Ed.), *The job-analysis handbook for business, industry, and government.* New York: Wiley.

Jacobs, P. I., & White, M. N. (1971). *Transfer of training in double classification skills across operations in Guilford's Structure of Intellect Model.* Princeton, NJ: Educational Testing Service.

Jensen, A. R. (1980). *Bias in mental testing.* New York: Basic Books.

Jones, M. B. (1962). Practice as a process of simplification. *Psychological Review, 69*, 274–294.

Jones, M., Dunlap, W., & Bilodeau, I. (1984). Factors appearing late in practice. *Organizational Behavior and Human Performance, 33*, 153–173.

Kennedy, M. M. (1978). Findings from the follow-through planned variation study. *Educational Researcher, 7*, 3–11.

Kyllonen, P. C., Lohman, D. F., & Snow, R. E. (1984). Effects of aptitude strategy training and task facets on spatial task performance. *Journal of Educational Psychology, 71*, 130–145.

Landy, F. J. (1988). Selection procedure development and usage. In S. Gael (Ed.), *The job-analysis handbook for business, government, and industry*. New York: Wiley.

Lave, J. (1980). *Observation of math skills at work*. Paper presented at the Conference on Basic Skills for Productivity and Participation, Washington, DC.

Lawshe, C. H. (1985). Inferences from personnel tests and their validity. *Journal of Applied Psychology, 70*, 237–241.

Levine, J. M., Brahlek, R. E., Eisner, E. J., & Fleishman, E. A. (1979). *Trainability of abilities: Training and transfer of abilities related to electronic fault-finding* (ARRO Report No. R79-2). Bethesda, MD: Advanced Research Resources Organization.

Levine, J. M., Romashko, T., & Fleishman, E. A. (1973). Evaluation of an abilities classification system for integrating and generalizing findings about human performance: The vigilance area. *Journal of Applied Psychology, 58*, 149–157.

Levine, J. M., Schulman, D., Brahlek, R. E., & Fleishman, E. A. (1980). *Trainability of abilities: Training and transfer of spatial visualization* (ARRO Report No. 80-3). Bethesda, MD: Advanced Research Resources Organization.

Lohman, D. F., & Snow, R. E. (1984). Toward a theory of cognitive aptitude for learning from instruction. *Journal of Educational Psychology, 76*, 347–376.

McGee, M. G. (1979). Human spatial abilities: Psychometric studies and environmental, genetic, hormonal, and neurological influences. *Psychological Bulletin, 86*, 889–918.

McGehee, W., and Thayer, P. W. (1961). *Training in business and industry*. New York: Wiley.

Melton, A. W. (1964). The taxonomy of human learning: Overview. In A. W. Melton (Ed.), *Categories of human learning*. Orlando, FL: Academic Press.

Mikulecky, L., & Diehl, W. (1982). *Job literacy: A study of literacy demands, attitudes, and strategies in a cross-section of occupations*. Bloomington, IN: University of Indiana, Reading Research Center.

Miller, R. B. (1962). Analysis and specification of behavior for training. In R. Glaser (Ed.), *Training Research and Education*. Pittsburgh: University of Pittsburgh Press.

Miller, R. B. (1966). *Task taxonomy: Science or technology?* Armonk, NY: International Business Machines.

Mitchell, J. L., Ruck, H. W., & Driskill, W. E. (1988). Task-based training program development. In S. Gael (Ed.), *The job-analysis handbook for business, government, and industry*. New York: Wiley.

Mumford, M. D., Dyer, P., & Costa, M. M. (1981). *On the development of a training sample test for the selection of technical trainees*. Armonk, NY: International Business Machines.

Mumford, M. D., Weeks, J. L., Harding, F. D., & Fleishman, E. A. (1987). Measuring occupational difficulty: A construct validation against training criteria. *Journal of Applied Psychology, 72*, 578–587.

Mumford, M. D., Weeks, J. L., Harding, F. D., & Fleishman, E. A. (1988). Relations between student characteristics, course content, and training outcomes: An integrative modeling effort. *Journal of Applied Psychology, 73*, 443–456.

Mumford, M. D., Yarkin-Levin, K., Korotkin, A., Wallis, M. R., & Marshall-Mies, (1985). *Characteristics relevant to performance as an Army leader: Knowledges, skills, abilities, other characteristics, and generic skills*. Alexandria, VA: U.S. Army Research Institute for the Behavioral and Social Sciences.

Myers, C. T. (1958). *The effects of training in mechanical drawing on spatial relations: Test scores as predictors of engineering drawing grades* (ETS RM 58-4). Princeton, NJ: Educational Testing Service.

Myers, D. C., Gebhardt, D. L., Price, S. J., & Fleishman, E. A. (1981). *Development of physical performance standards for Army jobs: Validation of the physical abilities analysis methodology* (ARRO Final Report No. R81-2). Bethesda, MD: Advanced Research Resources Organization.

Myers, D. C., Jennings, M. C., & Fleishman, E. A. (1981). *Development of job-related medical standards and physical tests for court security officer jobs* (ARRO Final Report No. 3062/R81-3). Bethesda, MD: Advanced Research Resources Organization.

Nutt, P. C. (1984). Types of organization decision processes. *Administrative Science Quarterly, 24,* 415–450.

Parasuraman, R. (1976). Consistency of individual differences in human vigilance performance: An abilities classification approach. *Journal of Applied Psychology, 61,* 486–492.

Parker, J. R., Jr., & Fleishman, E. A. (1960). Ability factors and component performance measures as predictors of complex tracking behavior. *Psychological Monographs 74* (entire issue 503).

Parker, J. R., Jr., & Fleishman, E. A. (1961). Use of analytical information concerning task requirements to increase the effectiveness of skill training. *Journal of Applied Psychology, 45,* 295–302.

Pedalino, E., & Gamboa, V. V. (1974). Behavior modification and absenteeism: Intervention in one industrial setting. *Journal of Applied Psychology, 59,* 694–698.

Perkins, D. N. (1985). Postprimary education has little impact on informal reasoning. *Journal of Educational Psychology, 77,* 562–571.

Peterson, N. G., & Bownas, D. A. (1982). Skill, task structure, and performance acquisition. In M. D. Dunnette & E. A. Fleishman (Eds.), *Human performance and productivity: Human capability assessment.* Hillsdale, NJ: Erlbaum.

Prien, E. P., Goldstein, I. L., & Macey, W. H. (1985). *Needs assessment: Program and individual development.* Paper presented at the meeting of the American Psychological Association, Los Angeles.

Primoff, E. S. (1959). The development of processes for indirect or synthetic validity: IV. Empirical validations of the J-coefficient: A symposium. *Personnel Psychology, 12,* 413–418.

Ranucci, E. R. (1952). *The effect of the study of solid geometry on certain aspects of space perception abilities.* Unpublished doctoral dissertation, Columbia University.

Reilly, R. R., & Zink, D. L. (1980). *Analysis of three outside craft jobs.* New York: American Telephone & Telegraph Company.

Reilly, R. R., & Zink, D. L. (1981). *Analysis of four inside craft jobs.* New York: American Telephone & Telegraph Company.

Reynolds, B. (1952). The effect of learning on the predictability of psychomotor performance. *Journal of Experimental Psychology, 44*, 189–198.

Romashko, T., Brumback, G. B., Fleishman, E. A., & Hahn, C. P. (1974). *The development of a procedure to validate physical tests: Physical requirements of the parking enforcement agent's job* (Technical Report No. 2). Washington, DC: American Institutes for Research.

Romashko, T., Hahn, C. P., & Brumback, G. B. (1976). *The prototype development of job-related physical testing for Philadelphia policeman selection.* Washington, DC: American Institutes for Research.

Rose, A., Fingerman, P., Wheaton, G., Eisner, E., & Kramer, G. (1974). *Methods for predicting job ability requirements: II. Ability requirements as a function of changes in the characteristics of an electronic fault-finding task* (AIR Technical Report No. 74-6). Washington, DC: American Institutes for Research.

Salmoni, A. W., Schmidt, R. A., & Walter, C. B. (1984). Knowledge of results and motor learning: A review and critical reappraisal. *Psychological Bulletin, 95*, 355–386.

Schemmer, F. M. (1982). *Development of rating scales for selected visual, auditory, and speech abilities* (ARRO Final Report No. 3064). Bethesda, MD: Advanced Research Resources Organization.

Schmeck, R. R., & Grove, E. (1979). Academic achievement and individual differences in the learning process. *Applied Psychological Measurement, 3*, 43–50.

Schmidt, F. L., Hunter, J. E., & Pearlman, K. (1981). Task differences as moderators of aptitude test validity. *Journal of Applied Psychology, 66*, 166–185.

Siegler, R. S., & Richards, D. (1982). The development of intelligence. In R. J. Sternberg (Ed.), *Handbook of human intelligence.* New York: Cambridge University Press.

Simpson, G. G. (1961). *Principles of animal taxonomy.* New York: Columbia University Press.

Snow, R. E. (1986). Individual differences and the design of educational programs. *American Psychologist, 41,* 1029–1039.

Snow, R. E., & Yallow, E. (1982). Education and intelligence. In R. J. Sternberg (Ed.), *Handbook of human intelligence.* New York: Cambridge University Press.

Sokal, R. R. (1974). Classification: Purposes, principles, progress, prospects. *Science, 185,* 1115–1123.

Sokal, R. R., & Sneath, P. H. (1963). *Principles of numerical taxonomy.* San Francisco: Freeman.

Stahl, R. J. (1979). *The domain of cognition: A useful model for looking at thinking and instructional outcomes.* Tempe: Arizona State University.

Stanton, L. (1986). Kashch's experiment: Can we boost intelligence? *Intelligence, 10,* 209–230.

Sternberg, R. J. (1979). The nature of mental abilities. *American Psychologist, 34* (3), 214–230.

Sticht, T. G. (1977). Comprehending reading at work. In M. A. Just & P. A. Carpenter (Eds.), *Cognitive processes in comprehension.* Hillsdale, NJ: Erlbaum.

Sticht, T. G. (1982). *Basic skills in defense.* Alexandria, VA: Human Resources Research Organization.

Stolurow, L. A. (1964). *A taxonomy of learning task characteristics* (AMRL-TD 12-74-Z). Wright-Patterson Air Force Base, OH: Aerospace Medical Research Laboratories.

Tenopyr, M. L., & Oeltjen, P. D. (1982). Personnel selection and classification. *Annual Review of Psychology, 33,* 581–618.

Theologus, G. C., & Fleishman, E. A. (1973). Development of a taxonomy of human performance: Validation study of ability scales for classifying human tasks. *JSAS Catalog of Selected Documents in Psychology, 3,* 29 (Ms. No. 326).

Theologus, G. C., Romashko, T., & Fleishman, E. A. (1973). Development of a taxonomy of human performance: A feasibility study of ability dimensions for classifying human tasks. *JSAS Catalog of Selected Documents in Psychology, 3,* 25–26 (Ms. No. 321).

Tyler, L. E. (1965). *The psychology of human differences*. Englewood Cliffs, NJ: Prentice-Hall.

Vineberg, R., & Joyner, J. N. (1983). *Task-related job reading inventory: Development and field trial of a prototype*. Lowry Air Force Base, CO: Air Force Human Resources Laboratory.

Weeks, J. L. (1984). *Occupational learning difficulty: A standard for determining the order of aptitude requirement minimums* (AFHRL-SR-84-26). Brooks Air Force Base, TX: Air Force Human Resources Laboratory.

Weldon, L. (1983). *Recommendations for physical ability testing and medical guidelines for the City of Pittsburgh* (ARRO Final Report No. R83-18). Bethesda, MD: Advanced Research Resources Organization.

Wheaton, G., Eisner, E., Mirabella, G., & Fleishman, E. (1976). Ability requirements as a function of changes in the characteristics of an auditory signal identification task. *Journal of Applied Psychology, 61*, 663–676.

White, S. C., & Alexander, P. A. (1986). Effects of training on four-year-olds' ability to solve geometric analogy problems. *Cognition and Instruction, 3*, 261–268.

Whitley, S. E., & Dawis, R. (1974). The effects of cognitive intervention on latent ability measured from analogy items. *Journal of Educational Psychology, 66*, 710–717.

Wilding, J., Raskind, W., Gilmore, D., & Valentine, E. (1986). A comparison of two mnemonic methods in learning medical information. *Human Learning, 5*, 201–216.

Willis, S. L., Bliesner, R, & Baltes, P. B. (1980). *Training research and aging: Modification of intellectual performance on a fluid ability component*. University Park: Pennsylvania State University.

Withers, D. (1984). Student learning processes: An exploratory study in the Philippines. *Human Learning, 3*, 33–42.

Wollin, K. A., Case, R. S., Bruchter, J. C., & Mindemir, K. M. (1985). The effects of instructional sets upon the appointment of study time to individual lines of text. *Human Learning, 4*, 89–103.

Woodrow, H. (1946). The ability to learn. *Psychology Review, 53*, 147–158.

7

Behavioral Approaches to the Training and Learning Process

Gary P. Latham

In the 1988 *Annual Review of Psychology*, a theme of despair in the scientific literature on training and development was discussed (Latham, 1988). This theme can be traced at least as far back as the seminal book by McGehee and Thayer (1961). In the preface, the authors pointed to the problems with accepting on faith the effectiveness of training programs when little or no effort is made to evaluate them in a rigorous fashion: "Until training is submitted to systematic and carefully controlled research and evaluation, management will continue to use (or discard) a tool of unknown worth, or, worse yet, jump from bandwagon to bandwagon as training fads skip from case method, to role playing, to brainstorming, and back again" (McGehee and Thayer, 1961, p. ix).

This dissatisfaction with the training literature has also been voiced by Goldstein (1980), Wexley (1984), and Rowland and Ferris (1986). It is noticeably absent, however, from the

Note: The author is grateful to his colleagues Marilyn Gist, Vandra Huber, Edwin Locke, and Terence Mitchell for their constructive comments on this chapter. The author is especially grateful to Dawn Winters, who identified studies for and edited this manuscript.

behaviorally based training literature. The reasons for this absence are at least three-fold. First, behaviorally based training has strong philosophical and theoretical roots. Historically, these roots have been in behaviorism. In the past ten years, these roots have led to the growth and development of social learning theory. Second, its methodology, emanating from operant techniques, makes explicit the operations that must be followed to increase the probability that the intervention will bring about a relatively permanent change in behavior. This level of specificity has been labeled a milestone in industrial-organizational (I/O) psychology (Dunnette, 1976). Third, its application has been subjected to systematic and carefully controlled research and evaluation. This is because the theory, the underlying philosophy, and the methodology make explicit the types of data that should be collected and the operations that should be followed in collecting those data. This has made measurement a relatively straightforward process, in terms of evaluating the effectiveness of a training intervention.

The purpose of this chapter is to provide a brief overview of two theories that underlie behaviorally based training—namely, behaviorism and social learning theory. Second, the accompanying methodologies and resulting applications of these theories to training are described. Third, the contribution of these approaches to the measurement and evaluation of training is shown. The chapter concludes with speculations on future directions for behaviorally based training programs.

Theoretical Roots

Behaviorism. As the name might imply, behaviorally based training programs have their roots in the philosophy of behaviorism. The term *behaviorism* was coined by John B. Watson (1913). It was the predominant scientific paradigm in North American psychology for the first half of the twentieth century.

In their review of behaviorism, Marx and Hillix (1963) credited Watson with showing how the principles and techniques of animal psychology, on which he had been working, could be applied to human beings. Specifically, Watson showed how Pavlov's conditioning principles explain the acquisition of phobias, and how phobias can be extinguished. His radical position on the importance (or the lack thereof) of mental processes to scientific inquiry, however, partially obscured this contribution and has remained to this day at the center of much of the controversy surrounding behaviorism.

In brief, Watson adopted the philosophy of positivism — namely, the belief that only social, objectively observable knowledge is valid. Thus, scientific data are restricted to the objective report of muscular movements or glandular secretions in time and space. At least in principle, these must be analyzed quantitatively. Thus, from the outset, systematic measurement was a cornerstone of behaviorism.

Watson argued, "The time seems to have come when psychology must discard all reference to consciousness; when it need no longer delude itself into thinking that it is making mental states the object of observation" (1913, p. 158). Instead, he advocated a focus on two specific objectives: to predict the response, knowing the stimulus; and to predict the stimulus, knowing the response. One postulate of behaviorism is that there is an immediate response of some sort to every effective stimulus. Thus, there is strict cause-and-effect determinism in behavior.

Watson's work had a profound effect on the early work of B. F. Skinner, a man who was to become one of the dominant influences on North American psychology (Heyduk & Fenigstein, 1984). Skinner (1938, 1953) showed how voluntary or instrumental behavior is affected by environmental events that immediately follow a given behavior. Such spontaneous behavior, which voluntarily operates on the environment, he called *operants*. Environmental events that increase the frequency with which an operant behavior occurs is called *reinforcers*; those that decrease the frequency he called *punishers*. The frequency of an operant response can be changed, he showed, by alteration of the schedule on which a reinforcer is presented. These systematic changes, which altered the frequency of the response, were called *operant conditioning* or *behavior modification*. As with

Watson, neither internal drive states nor cognitive processes were given any explanatory status in Skinner's research.

Influence of Behaviorism on I/O Psychology. The behaviorists were primarily experimental or clinical psychologists. Little or no mention of their work was given in I/O psychology textbooks (for example, Harrell, 1949; Tiffin, 1952; Blum & Naylor, 1968). Ryan and Smith (1954) devoted only a page of their textbook to behaviorism and concluded that a useful theory of motivation must include the wants, wishes, and desires of the worker: "To attempt to translate such facts into terms of 'stimulus and response' seems not only useless, but actually misleading, since it implies that the laws which govern these stimuli and responses are the same as those which hold for all other stimuli and responses." (pp. 356–357).

The influence of behaviorism on I/O psychology was not directly evident until the late 1960s. Nord (1969) was among the first to argue the need for applying its concepts to organizational settings. The thrust of his argument was threefold. First, he downplayed the metaphysical differences between humanistic psychologists, such as Maslow and McGregor, and behaviorists. Instead, he emphasized similarities by showing how McGregor, like the behaviorists, gave primary importance to the environment as the determinant of individual behavior. Differences, Nord said, were largely metaphorical. Second, he showed that when McGregor's writings are stripped of Maslow's model of man, McGregor's conclusions, at both the descriptive and the prescriptive level, remain congruent with those of the behaviorists. Third, he cited Maslow himself for evidence of the lack of empirical data that could support McGregor's metaphysical assumptions.

> After all, if we take the whole thing from McGregor's point of view of contrast between a Theory X view of human nature, a good deal of the evidence upon which he bases his conclusions comes from my researches and my papers on motivations, self-

actualization, et cetera. But I of all people should
know just how shaky this foundation is as a final
foundation. My work on motivations came from
the clinic, from a study of neurotic people. The
carry-over of this theory to the industrial situation
has some support from industrial studies, but certainly I would like to see a lot more studies of this
kind before feeling finally convinced that this
carry-over from the study of neurosis to the study of
labor in factories is legitimate. The same thing is
true of my studies of self-actualizing people — there
is only this one study of mine available. There were
many things wrong with the sampling, so many in
fact that it must be considered to be, in the classical
sense anyway, a bad or poor or inadequate experiment. I am quite willing to concede this—as a
matter of fact, I am eager to concede it—because
I'm a little worried about this stuff which I consider
to be tentative being swallowed whole by all sorts of
enthusiastic people, who really should be a little
more tentative in the way that I am [Maslow, 1965,
pp. 55–56].

In contrast, the work of the behaviorists, Nord pointed out, is
supported by millions of observations made of animals at all
levels of the phylogenetic scale, including human beings. Nord
concluded that, since managers are concerned primarily with
employees' behavior, management texts should include material
on behaviorism.

Drucker (1973) perhaps unwittingly reinforced this view:
"An employer has no business with a man's personality. Employment is a specific contract calling for specific performance, and
for nothing else. Any attempt of an employer to go beyond this is
usurpation. It is immoral as well as illegal intrusion of privacy. It
is abuse of power. An employee owes no 'loyalty,' he owes no
'love,' and no 'attitudes'—he owes performance and nothing
else. . . . Management and manager development should concern themselves with changes in *behavior* [emphasis added] likely

to make a man more effective" (pp. 424–425). The North American judicial system, undoubtedly ignorant of behaviorism, has nevertheless reinforced one of behaviorism's tenets by favoring performance appraisals that focus on observable behaviors rather than personal traits (Feild & Holley, 1982; Latham, 1986).

Of direct relevance to this chapter is Nord's (1969) suggestion that training programs be based on operant principles. Although Nord did not conduct empirical research to support his view, Campbell (1971), in the first *Annual Review of Psychology* chapter on training and development, endorsed Nord's arguments: "The operant conditioning model, in truth, has a great deal of structured similarity to the motivational theories of McGregor, Maslow, and Herzberg. It simply gets to the heart of the matter much more quickly" (p. 571). Campbell argued that it is the behavior that is at issue, not underlying causes or internal mediators. Campbell, as will be discussed later, was prescient in the importance he attached to Bandura's work, especially the work on behavior modeling.

In the following year, Jablonsky and DeVries (1972) developed a predictive model of individual behavior, based on principles of behaviorism. By this time, empirical experiments were beginning to appear in the I/O literature, showing the efficacy of behavioristic approaches with respect to cognitively based models (Cherrington, Reitz, & Scott, 1971; Yukl, Wexley, & Seymore, 1972). Writers began to reinterpret the I/O literature within a behavioristic framework. For example, Parsons (1974) argued that the so-called Hawthorne effect could be explained in terms of response-consequence (operant) contingencies. He showed how piecework wages and information feedback were immediate consequences of employees' performance at Hawthorne.

Many I/O studies that contained knowledge of results or feedback began to be interpreted within a behavioristic framework (for example, entire issues of the *Journal of Organizational Behavior Management*). One of the most publicized accounts was the work conducted by a vice-president at Emery Air Freight (Feeney, 1973). Performance during a baseline period was compared with performance after the introduction of feedback, which included praise and recognition. The result was said to be a savings to the company of approximately $3 million over a three-year period.

Nevertheless, the overall reaction to behaviorism among I/O scholars was largely hostile. Mitchell (1975) argued that while radical behaviorism increases the ability to predict behavior, it does not permit an adequate explanation of why the behavior occurs, because it fails to take account of interactions between environmental and cognitive influences as causes of behavior. That one cannot see or directly measure these cognitions is irrelevant; numerous disciplines (for example, physics and astronomy) refer to unobservables as causal variables. "These unobservables can be indirectly measured through their effects on other variables and eventually on observables. Through what is called a 'logic of theoretical networks' (Cronbach & Meehl, 1955), we can ascribe meaning to these constructs and through a process of empirical confirmation provide support for this meaning. Thus. . . a logical positivist position is both an unnecessary limitation on scientific inquiry and a poor representation of current thought in the philosophy of science (Kaplan, 1964)" [Mitchell, 1975, p. 65].

Locke (1977) attacked the behavioristic model for being neither valid nor useful to managers who want to improve employees' abilities and motivation. Specifically, he attacked two basic premises of behaviorism: determinism (people are devoid of volition, because behavior is solely a function of the environment) and epiphenomenalism (the mind has no causal efficacy, and cognitive processes are irrelevant to the understanding of behavior). He also showed how the behaviorists contradict in practice the principles of behaviorism by taking cognitive processes into account. For example, Feeney's (1973) work at Emery Air Freight emphasized the use of setting goals and giving feedback in relation to the goals. Locke (1980) later argued that an empirically based study which showed that feedback affects performance, should not and logically cannot be interpreted as supporting behaviorism, because cognitive factors (namely, goal setting) were an integral part of the procedures used. Locke's own research shows that feedback affects behavior only to the extent that it leads to the setting of and commitment to specific hard goals (Locke, Cartledge, & Koeppel, 1968). That the converse is also true (Locke, Shaw, Saari, & Latham, 1981) — namely, that feedback is a necessary condition for goal setting to affect behavior — neither supports behaviorism nor refutes the importance of taking cognitive variables into account.

It is perplexing that at the very time when behaviorism was finding proponents in I/O psychology (for example, Nord, 1969), empirical evidence was accumulating in experimental psychology that behaviorism should be rejected. For example, Dulany (1968) showed that even the simplest forms of learning may not occur unless people are conscious of what is required of them, while Kaufman, Baron, and Kopp (1966) showed that cognitive influences can weaken, distort, or nullify the effects of reinforcement schedules. In the latter study, everyone was rewarded on the same schedule. Nevertheless, those who were informed that they were being reinforced once every minute (a fixed-interval schedule) produced a very low response rate (mean = 6); those who were informed that they were reinforced on a variable-ratio schedule maintained an exceedingly high response rate (mean = 259); and those who were correctly informed that their behavior would be rewarded every minute, on the average (a variable-interval schedule), displayed an intermediate level of response. Thus, identical environmental consequences can have different behavioral effects that depend on the subject's cognitions.

To show conclusively that behavior is determined solely by cognitions, one would have to find a control group consisting of individuals who cannot think. Similarly, to provide empirical support for the argument that behavior is due to environmental consequences alone, one would have the impossible task of forming a control group for which there is no environment (Latham & Saari, 1979). Clearly, a rapprochement between the cognitivists and the behaviorists was needed, and it occurred in clinical psychology, with the work of Albert Bandura on social learning theory (which Bandura later renamed *social cognitive theory*, to minimize confusion between his theory and others' — for example, Rotter, 1954).

Social Learning Theory. In the first *Annual Review of Psychology* chapter on training and development, Campbell (1971) cited Bandura's (1969) book on behavior modification as a source for extrapolating the principles of behaviorism to organizational psychology. In 1974, however, Bandura repudiated behaviorism, holding that it embodies an erroneously "mechanistic" view of behavior; specifically, he argued that reinforcing events change behavior through the intervening influence of thought (Bandura, 1974). Bandura (1977a, 1977b) summarized his theory and research in the *Psychological Review* and in a book, *Social Learning Theory.*

Social learning theory is a social cognitive theory (Bandura, 1986). The theory states that behavior is a continuous reciprocal interaction among cognitive, behavioral, and environmental variables. Explicit in this view is the idea that behavior is both determined by and affects environmental consequences, which in turn affect the person's conscious intentions or goals, and vice versa. Thus, this social cognitive theory provides a theoretical framework that encompasses the primary variables in both the cognitive and the behavioristic approaches — namely, expectations, anticipated outcomes, goal setting, and reinforcers.

Social learning theory emphasizes vicarious, symbolic, and self-regulating processes in acquiring and maintaining behavior. Behavioristic doctrine states that learning can occur only through performing responses and experiencing their effects. Bandura (1977a, 1986) enlarged this view, showing that people can learn on a vicarious basis by observing the behavior of others and its consequences for them. Through the use of symbols, people are able to foresee probable consequences, set goals, and act accordingly. Consequently, as a result of self-regulatory processes, people can learn to function as agents in their own self-motivation, through rewards for progress toward goal attainment.

Influence of Social Learning Theory on I/O Psychology. The influence of social learning theory on I/O psychology in general, and on training and development programs in particular, was immediate and positive. The basis for this positive reaction is at least twofold.

First, industrial psychology, from the outset, has been concerned with the study of individual differences, especially in cognitive abilities (Hull, 1928; Munsterberg, 1913). The behaviorists, however, advocated a "black box" approach to psychology. The sole focus on observable stimuli, responses, and consequences of responses removed the necessity of peering inside an organism (the "black box"); individual differences were dismissed as merely differences among organisms in their histories of reinforcement and thus were not of any particular scientific interest. This is why Skinner advocated the intensive study of a single organism, as well as the use of within-group designs (this topic is discussed in a subsequent section of this chapter). Social learning theory, however, led to research (Bandura, 1982; Bandura & Adams, 1977; Bandura, Adams, & Beyer, 1977) that identified two individual-difference variables that play a critical mediating role among the stimulus, the response, the consequence, and the subsequent behavior. These two cognitive variables are self-efficacy (one's belief that one can execute a given behavior in a given setting) and outcome expectancies (one's belief that the given outcome will occur if one engages in the behavior).

Psychology is concerned with the prediction, understanding, and control of behavior. The principles of behaviorism allowed prediction and control; social learning theory provided what was missing: understanding. It opened the "black box" to explain why behavior did or did not occur, by examining the reciprocal interactions among the environment, cognition, and behavior.

A second reason for social learning theory's immediate influence on I/O psychology is that the theory, by positing a reciprocal interaction among these three variables, freed itself of the philosophical objections of I/O psychologists to behaviorism. In doing so, it freed I/O psychologists to use the operant methodology on which much of social learning theory is based. As noted earlier, operant methodology is considered one of seven milestones in I/O psychology (Dunnette, 1976).

Initial support for social learning theory was signaled in

an article by Johnson and Sorcher (1976) on the application of behavior-modeling principles (to be discussed later) to training programs at the General Electric Company. (In 1979, Sorcher became the first person to receive the Professional Practice Award from Division 14—Society of Industrial/Organizational Psychology—of the American Psychological Association.) Locke, one of I/O psychology's most vocal critics of the philosophy of behaviorism, began empirical research on self-efficacy (one of the main tenets of social learning theory) and obtained supportive results (Locke, Frederick, Lee, & Bobko, 1984). Mitchell, another early critic of behaviorism, has used operant methodology to evaluate the effects of employee behavior in an organizational setting (Evans, Kienast, & Mitchell, 1988).

As of 1989, to this writer's knowledge, no one in I/O psychology has criticized social learning theory. This is not to imply that there are no critics; for example, Wolpe (1978), a behaviorist and a clinician, argued that cognitive behavior is a biological function and belongs, like any other behavior, to the lawful universe of science. Therefore, to believe that people manifest some degree of independence from their biology, so that they are in some respects free agents, is at best naïve. If Wolpe were aware of Ryan and Smith's (1954) comment (cited earlier in this chapter) that not all stimuli and responses are governed by the same laws, he would disagree vehemently. Thus, in the field of psychology, the debate on the appropriateness of one theoretical position versus the other continues unabated (see Skinner, 1987).

Methodology and Application

Behaviorism

Programmed Instruction. The best-known applications of behavioristic principles to training are the teaching machine and programmed-learning textbooks. First developed by Pressey (1926), this approach received little attention until Skinner (1954, 1958) provided empirical support for its use, on the basis of operant principles.

Skinner showed that performance is enhanced if information is presented in small increments, which require a response followed immediately by feedback. This has been done through a variety of devices, including electronic machines that display material and whose buttons, when pressed, indicate the correctness of a response, as well as textbooks that provide spaces for responses to questions (the correct answer is usually shown on the next page) (see Fiedler, Chemers, & Mahar, 1984).

Research in this area is no longer going on in industrial settings. Goldberg, Dawson, and Barrett (1964) found that the use of programmed-learning textbooks resulted in higher scores on examinations that were similar in format and language to the programmed-learning materials. Slow learners (defined in terms of their low mental-ability test scores) did perform better, however, if they received programmed instruction.

Welsh, Antoinetti, and Thayer (1965) also failed to find evidence demonstrating the superiority of programmed learning. In a review of 213 studies comparing programmed instruction, Nash, Muczyk, and Vettori (1971) found that while programmed instruction consistently reduced training time by about one-third, most well-controlled studies were unable to show significant differences in learning between programmed instruction and conventional learning methods. They concluded that the studies that did obtain differences usually compared well-thought-out programmed instruction with a company's less organized training programs. This conclusion, however, misses a fundamental point—namely, the precision of operant methodology. The trainer is required to specify the stimulus, the desired response, and the immediate outcome that will be presented to reinforce this response, as well as the schedule and method for administering it. This level of specification not only lends itself to measurement and evaluation but also increases the probability that a well-thought-out plan will be effective. Measurement provides objective feedback to the trainer about whether the training intervention should be continued, modified, or discontinued. Objective feedback is far superior to the subjective reactions of trainees and upper-level managers; subjective reactions often result in the elimination of effective training programs and the adoption of new fads.

Training Through Reinforcement. In addition to the principle of providing feedback, three other fundamental operant principles have influenced the practice of many I/O psychologists: making an outcome immediately contingent on a specific behavior, in order to increase (reinforce) or decrease (punish) its frequency; altering the schedule by which the outcome is administered; and adhering to the principle of shaping, or successive approximation (the latter term refers to reinforcing successive approximations of a behavior until the desired behavior occurs). The simplicity and effectiveness of these basic operant principles prompted Porter (1973) to advocate their use in training marginal workers, those whose performance in general is considered well below industry standards. Consequently, two field studies by the present author and his colleagues (Yukl & Latham, 1975; Yukl, Latham, & Pursell, 1976) were conducted with women employed to plant trees in a rural area of South Carolina. Research on animals (Honig, 1966) and an organizational simulation (Yukl, Wexley, & Seymore, 1972) led to the hypothesis that high response rates would occur with a variable-ratio schedule, but cognitive factors explain why the resulting data did not support this hypothesis. Money administered on the variable-ratio schedule was interpreted by the women as a form of gambling; thus, the women did not approve of the program. The continuous schedule, however, was interpreted by the employees as piecework pay, rather than as a form of gambling; thus, it was perceived as morally acceptable.

In a subsequent study in the state of Washington, Latham and Dossett (1978) repeated the study with high school– and college-educated, unionized workers. Consistent with laboratory research, employees who were learning the job performed better on a continuous than on a variable-ratio schedule; employees who had already learned the job performed better on a variable-ratio schedule than on a continuous one.

Today, I/O psychology books on training (e.g. Goldstein, 1986; Wexley & Latham, 1981) acknowledge the importance of taking into account operant methodology in training programs. Its effectiveness is explained in terms of the social foundations of thought and action (Bandura, 1986).

Social Learning Theory

Behavior-Modeling Techniques. Bandura (1977b) showed that inhibitions can be extinguished in a relatively short time with behavior-modeling techniques. The phobic individual watches a model perform fear-provoking behavior and experience no adverse consequences. The effectiveness of this approach in eliminating dysfunctional fears (of heights, public speaking, making "cold calls") in the workplace has not been investigated by I/O psychologists, but behavior modeling techniques have been rigorously studied in the workplace for increasing leadership skills.

Typically, this training involves developing a set of learning points and presenting a model, usually on film or videotape, who demonstrates these learning points. This presentation is followed by a discussion among the trainees about the rationale underlying each learning point, and about what the model did behaviorally to demonstrate each point. Finally, each trainee, through role playing, demonstrates the learning point and receives feedback from fellow trainees and from the trainer on what was done well and what should be done differently. The trainee's homework assignment is to practice these behaviors on the job. The perceived effectiveness, based on self-report, is discussed in a subsequent training session. Feedback from fellow trainees and from the trainer is provided on what the trainee needs to continue doing, start doing, or stop doing.

Moses and Ritchie (1976) evaluated the effectiveness of behavior modeling in teaching AT&T supervisors interpersonal skills for dealing with employees. The data showed that people who had been trained through the use of filmed models were rated by judges as more effective in role-playing simulations than people who had not received such training. Burnaska (1976) reported that supervisors at General Electric who participated in behavior-modeling training also received higher ratings on role-playing simulations than untrained supervisors. Similarly, Byham, Adams, and Kiggins (1976), as well as Smith (1976), found that subordinates' perceptions of trained supervisors, in interactions with them, were more favorable than their perceptions of the untrained supervisors.

McGehee and Tuller (1978) criticized these studies with regard to their internal validity. They also pointed to the possibility of criterion bias, which may have occurred from the use of role-playing exercises during training and again in the collection of the evaluating data. Finally, the use of role playing as a dependent variable raised questions regarding the external validity of two of these studies.

Latham and Saari (1976) overcame these problems in a field experiment involving first-line supervisors at Weyerhaeuser Company. Multiple criteria (reaction, learning, and behavioral measures) for evaluating behavior modeling were established before training, a control group was used, and a follow-up measure of performance on the job was assessed. Subsequent training of the individuals in the control group raised their performance to the level of the initially trained group's. This study strongly supports the use of behavior-modeling training programs in industry for bringing about a relatively permanent change in supervisory behavior (Goldstein, 1980; Wexley, 1984).

Fundamental to the effectiveness of behavior modeling are learning points for the trainee, which are stated in concrete behavioral terms (for example, make the praise specific; give the praise immediately after the behavior occurs; focus on the issue, rather than on the employee; focus on the future, rather than on the past).

One job analysis that lends itself to the formulation of these learning points is the critical-incident technique (Flanagan, 1954). This technique is also one of the seven milestones in I/O psychology cited by Dunnette (1976), because it results in the articulation of exactly what behaviors have led to success or to failure in different job settings.

The importance of learning points for behavior-modeling training in organizational settings has been investigated by Mann and Decker (1984). They found that attaching learning points to the key behaviors performed by a filmed model (especially key behaviors that are not naturally distinctive) enhances both the recall and the acquisition of those behaviors. Subjects were unable to identify key behaviors simply from observing the model. Like Latham and Saari (1979), they also found that giving the learning points in the absence of the model did not bring about a behavior change.

Hogan, Hakel, and Decker (1986) found that trainees should not be restricted to the use of learning points generated by trainers, even when trainer-generated learning points are assessed by subject-matter experts to be of higher quality than trainee-generated learning points. Their experiment showed that when trainees developed their own rule mnemonics in organizing the material presented via modeling and displays, better performance occurred on a generalization test administered one week later, than when the trainees were restricted to learning trainer-generated rules.

Manz and Sims (1986) discovered serendipitously that the absence of learning points can have unintended and undesirable effects on trainees. The exposure to a reprimanding model inadvertently led to a decrease in both goal setting and positively reinforcing behavior.

That behavior-modeling training is not always effective was found by Russel, Wexley, and Hunter (1984). The reasons remain unclear. One hypothesis the authors offered is that the posttraining environment did not allow for adequate reinforcement of the modeled behaviors. Regardless of the reason, a meta-analysis of seventy studies on the effectiveness of management training showed that behavior modeling is among the most effective training methods (Burke & Day, 1986). One reason for this superiority is that modeling affects self-efficacy as a mediating variable affecting performance (Bandura, 1986). In a study involving the use of computer software, Gist, Schwoerer, and Rosen (in press) found that modeling increased performance for people regardless of their initial level of self-efficacy.

Self-Management. A second area of social learning theory that is only now beginning to be studied empirically in organizational settings is training in self-management, or self-regulation. This training has proved especially effective in increasing self-efficacy. The core of the training is goal setting.

Goal setting, too, has been labeled a milestone in I/O psychology, because of its specificity and simplicity in making clear to the employee-trainee what is to be attained (Dunnette, 1976). The theory (Locke, 1968; Locke & Latham, 1984, 1990) on which it is based is among the most scientifically valid and useful motivational theories in organizational science (Miner, 1980; Pinder, 1984).

Perhaps the most rigorously developed self-management program is that of Kanfer, a clinical psychologist. Kanfer's (1974, 1975, 1980) training program was designed for obtaining commitment to and attainment of self-generated goals. In brief, the training teaches people to assess problems, set specific hard goals in relation to those problems, monitor ways in which the environment facilitates or hinders goal attainment, and identify and administer reinforcers for working toward (and punishers for failing to work toward) goal attainment. In essence, this training teaches people skills in self-observation, to compare their behavior with the goals that they set and to administer reinforcers and punishers that will bring about and sustain goal commitment (Karoly & Kanfer, 1982). The reinforcer or punisher is made contingent on the degree to which the behavior approximates the goal. Reinforcers and punishers are viewed in terms of informational and emotional feedback, in order to take account of cognitive as well as motoric and autonomic effects. (This training has proved especially effective in teaching people coping skills for overcoming alcoholism and substance abuse; see Kanfer, 1974.)

Brief & Hollenbeck (1985) surveyed salespersons to identify the extent to which self-regulatory activities take place in the absence of training. Self-regulation was operationalized in terms of three components: goal setting, self-monitoring, and self-rewarding or self-punishing contingent on the magnitude of the discrepancy between one's behavior and one's goal. The data revealed that the salespeople did not regulate their own job performance. The benefit of such self-management training in an organizational setting has been shown in two field experiments.

Using Kanfer's (1980) methodology, Frayne and Latham (1987) trained unionized state government employees to increase their work attendance. The training consisted of goal setting, the writing of a behavioral contract, self-monitoring, and the selection and self-administration of rewards and punishments. Compared to a controlled condition, training in self-management gave employees the skills to manage personal and social obstacles to job attendance, and it increased their perceived self-efficacy. As a result, employee attendance was significantly higher in the training group than in the control group. The higher the perceived self-efficacy, the better the subsequent job attendance. A follow-up study (Latham & Frayne, 1989) showed that this increase in job attendance continued over twelve months. The control group was then given the same training. Both self-efficacy and job attendance increased, relative to that of the original experimental group.

Today, many industries are reducing the number of managers (Latham, 1988). Concomitant with this deemphasis on formal supervision is an emphasis on employee self-management. Thus, finding research sites and measuring the effects of training in self-management should prove relatively easy.

Measurement and Evaluation

As noted earlier in this chapter, Watson (1913) made systematic evaluation a cornerstone of behaviorial interventions. No behaviorist or social learning theorist, to this writer's knowledge, has taken issue with this emphasis. The only controversy with regard to evaluation has, once again, been generated by Skinner.

Skinner (1957) criticized the use of inferential statistics. Specifically, he charged that statistical techniques are often used as a surrogate for good experimental controls. As a result, he advocated the sole use of experimental controls in the study of a single subject. When large numbers of data from a single organism are collected under stringent controls, he argued, the results should be both clearly observable and replicable.

One positive outcome of Skinner's advocacy for studying a single subject has been the development of within-group designs. This approach to measurement has been embraced by many I/O psychologists because of the difficulty of obtaining control groups in organizational settings. The advantage of within-group designs for I/O psychologists has been championed repeatedly by Komaki (1977, 1982). The two most widely known single-group designs are the *reversal* and the *multiple baseline*.

Reversal Designs. The reversal is sometimes referred to as the *ABAB design*, wherein baseline data (A) are collected before the intervention (B). Data continue to be collected while the intervention (B) is ongoing, and then data are collected when the intervention is deliberately discontinued (A), before it is reintroduced (B). If the behavior increases only when the intervention is in effect and decreases during the reversal phases, one can conclude that the intervention, rather than any extraneous event(s), has affected performance.

A major disadvantage of the reversal design is that training programs are designed to bring about a relatively permanent change in an employee's behavior. Thus, the acquisition of new skills should lead to a behavior change after the training has been discontinued. Consequently, the reversal design would lead to a Type II error—namely, the erroneous conclusion that the training has not been effective. Thus, a multiple-baseline design is usually preferable to a reversal design for evaluating training effectiveness.

Multiple-Baseline Designs. As its name implies, the multiple-baseline design involves the collection of data on two or more baselines. Equally important is that the training intervention is staggered, so that the training is done first with only one person or group. When a change in behavior is observed, training is conducted with a second person or group.

The use of two or more baselines at different times allows

one to rule out alternative rival hypotheses of why behavior has changed. If performance improves each time the intervention is presented, causality can be ascribed to the training program. This is because it is unlikely that one or more variables would coincide with each introduction of the intervention in exactly the same way at exactly the same time in exactly the same order (Komaki, 1982).

The multiple-baseline design can be used across behaviors, groups, and settings. For the multiple-baseline design across behaviors, two or more behaviors are selected. For example, Komaki, Waddell, and Pearce (1977) collected data on store clerks daily for twelve weeks, on three different behaviors: remaining in the grocery store, assisting customers, and stocking merchandise. After eighteen baseline observations, reinforcing consequences were administered for remaining in the grocery store. When this behavior increased (demonstrated over twenty-four observations), an intervention was made with regard to the second behavior (asking customers if they would like assistance). After the clerks were consistently in the store and consistently helping customers (demonstrated over thirty observations), an intervention was made with regard to the third behavior (stocking merchandise). Through this use of the multiple-baseline design, the researchers were able to conclude that changes in the three behaviors were a function of the training interventions. The clerks' performance improved only after, and not before, the introduction of each intervention.

The advantage of using the multiple-baseline design across groups is that it makes use of preexisting administrative units. Because comparisons are made within rather than between groups, it is not necessary to ensure, through random assignment, that the groups are equivalent. Moreover, as Komaki (1982) has pointed out, the more the groups differ from one another on such variables as age, educational background, job description, job task, and so on, the more that can be said about the generalizability of the training intervention. For example, Panyon, Boozer, and Morris (1970) collected baseline data on the percentage of training sessions conducted by staff in eleven very different hospital units. In some units, feedback was posted immediately; in others, feedback was provided four, eight, and thirty-eight weeks after an administrative request for training. Only when feedback was in effect did the percentage of conducted training sessions increase, and this increase occurred regardless of the type of hospital unit.

With regard to settings, Kirchner and colleagues (1980) evaluated the residential burglary–deterrent efforts of a helicopter patrol in four separate areas of the Nashville metropolitan area. Through the use of the multiple-baseline design, it became evident that the intervention was effective in areas with high (but not low) population density.

In summary, multiple-baseline designs are ideally suited to the evaluation of training effectiveness, because they do not require behavior to return to baseline conditions before causal inferences can be made. With the multiple-baseline design, it is necessary only to select behaviors, settings, persons, or groups that are sufficiently independent of one another so that an intervention with regard to one does not affect the other (Komaki, 1982).

Future Directions

In this section, the three preceding topics—theory, application, and measurement—are reviewed in terms of speculation on future directions. This attempt to peer into the future is in keeping with the "frontier" theme of this book. Frontier, as a North American metaphor, connotes at least three different images: barrenness, arrows, and riches or rewards.

Theory

I/O psychologists have a long heritage of "dust bowl empiricism." Behaviorally, this heritage has manifested itself in an emphasis on the careful collection of data and in the philosophy "If it works, use it." The result of this heritage, in the first sixty years of I/O practice, has been an emphasis on collecting data, as opposed to developing theory. This heritage encourages the rather safe prediction that I/O psychology is likely to continue using behavioral methodology, because it works; it generally leads to the attainment of the objectives for which it has been designed. The philosophy of behaviorism will be rejected, simply because the empirical data do not support it. Cognition, behavior, and the environment have been shown to have a reciprocal effect. Further debate on the philosophy of behaviorism is likely to be barren; there are no riches to be gained from it.

Similarly, empirical research conducted in favor of one position versus the other is also likely to prove barren. At best, the research will be ignored by people in the opposing camp; at worst, it will stimulate rejoinder arguments or research, which in turn will only let fly more arrows. Thus, Campbell (1982) concluded that little will be gained from further attempts to tease apart the relative effects of goal setting, feedback, and reinforcers. What is required is true bridging theory (Staats, 1983). Social cognitive theory (Bandura, 1977a, 1977b, 1986) constructs this bridge by taking into account two bodies of knowledge and examining what each body is, how its knowledge has been acquired, what its purposes are, how its knowledge is used, what functions the knowledge serves, and so on. Thus, two schismatic bodies of knowledge, from cognitive psychology and behaviorism, are brought into meaningful, useful conjunction.

I/O psychology has a long history of studying cognition (for example, aptitudes), affect (for example, job satisfaction), and economic constructs, commonly referred to as *hard criterion measures* (for example, number of units produced). This historical emphasis on cognition will further contribute to the ignoring of behaviorism as a philosophy of science. It will, however, predispose acceptance of social learning theory.

It is hoped that the speed with which I/O psychologists remember that psychology is the science of behavior, rather than of economic constructs, will be among the riches of social cognitive theory. Hard criterion measures are too often contaminated, both positively and adversely, by factors beyond the control of the individual (Campbell, Dunnette, Lawler, & Weick, 1970; Latham & Wexley, 1981). Thus, such measures are prone to both Type I errors (that is, the erroneous conclusion that costs have been reduced because of training) and Type II errors (that is, the erroneous conclusion that because costs remain unchanged, training has been ineffective).

Self-Efficacy. The greatest potential reward, from a theoretical perspective, is likely to come from an increased understanding of the intervening role of self-efficacy and outcome expectancies, as well as from an understanding of the importance of symbols. At least two issues await further research, with regard to self-efficacy. The first has to do with how it should be measured (Eastman & Marzillier, 1984; Marzillier & Eastman, 1984). The second has to do with its relationship (discriminant validity) to other constructs, such as Vroom's (1964) measures of expectancy and instrumentality. Once these two issues are resolved, this construct will probably become an important dependent variable in its own right.

Outcome Expectancy. Psychologists, in evaluating the effectiveness of training, will probably focus on outcome expectancies, since these constitute a parsimonious explanation of why transfer of training does or does not occur. This prediction is based on Napier and Latham's (1986) finding that managers who have high self-efficacy with regard to the belief that they can conduct accurate performance appraisals, but who have low outcome expectancies that anything consequential will occur for subordinates who receive high or low appraisals, rarely conduct them. Frayne and Latham (1987), however, found that high outcome expectancies alone do not affect a trainee's behavior in the absence of high self-efficacy. Thus, both variables need to be studied together.

Outcome expectancy is usually measured in terms of perceived external rewards and punishers. In future research, it would be informative to measure self-evaluative outcomes as well as anticipated external ones. The rewards are there for trainers who continue to explore the linkages among behavior, self-efficacy, and outcome expectancies.

Symbolic Processes. Currently, only two of the three aspects of social cognitive theory have been investigated by I/O psychologists — namely, vicarious learning through behavior modeling, and self-regulation processes through training in self-management. Symbolic processes, the third aspect of social learning theory, remain in the discussion stage. In a heuristic article, Gioia and Manz (1985) argued for the study of schematic information processing, especially script processing, for understanding the link between cognitive processes and behavior. They hypothesized that a primary basis of vicarious learning is the process of acquiring, developing, or altering cognitively held scripts on the part of the trainee of the target behaviors.

Scripts are developed through experience, vicarious observation, and verbal mechanisms. They allow an individual to respond to situations and engage in relatively little active information processing. They originate through three evolutionary levels: the episodic, the categorical, and the generalized.

An episodic script is retained as a memory of a specific, context-related set of behaviors. Repetitions of similar experiences, however, allow the trainee to derive a categorical script, which is a set of responses to a relatively narrow class of situations. A generalized script is developed after the trainee has experiences across situations to develop rules for behavior over a wide range of situations.

The implication for behavior-modeling training is that the type of script through which the trainee learns can influence the nature of the script enacted. Precise models that use descriptive codes will lead to the development of episodic scripts; general models that use rule codes will probably lead to the development of generalized scripts, which can be enacted across situations.

Empirical research on this aspect of social cognitive theory remains to be done. In the further development and exploration of this theory, however, one must remember the admonitions (arrows) of Dunnette (1976). The emphasis must remain on simplicity. The predilection to use unnecessarily complicated models, whether models of motivation (such as expectancy) or models of statistical prediction strategies, has contributed to the major disappointments in I/O psychology. "These efforts to deal with great complexity just have not worked out, and we should take the hint and become more single-minded and less mush-headed" (Dunnette, 1976, p. 98).

Application

Dysfunctional Fears. In the future, research will be done on training programs designed to eliminate dysfunctional fears in the workplace. This prediction is based on the fact that Ph.D. programs are increasingly turning out graduates who are trained in both clinical and industrial psychology. Dysfunctional fears abound in maintenance departments alone (fear of heights, equipment, electricity); among white-collar workers are fear of speaking before large groups, preparing and defending budgets, and accepting additional responsiblity. The "impostor effect" (Clance, 1985)—namely, the fear that one truly is not as effective or proficient as others believe—may be especially worthy of study among executives.

Programmed Instruction and Computer-Managed Instruction. Programmed textbooks are currently used to teach leadership principles (Fiedler, Chemers, & Mahar, 1984). In the future, the teaching machine, too, will once again present an exciting area for study, in the form of research on computer-managed instruction (CMI), because of the interaction that is now becoming possible between the trainee and the machine. For example, a training system developed to teach cardiopulmonary resuscitation exemplifies the capabilities of CMI. The system uses a videodisc player, video monitors, a random-access videotape player, and a mannequin, all of which are controlled by a microcomputer. The system will "answer questions upon request, instantaneously gather information about each student's hands-on performance, respond with appropriate spoken or video demonstration, gather data on the student's next attempt, respond with appropriate instruction or demonstration, provide performance feedback, give repeated drill and practice, and be cost-effective" (Huber & Gay, 1984, p. 102). Evaluation of this system indicates that training time is reduced from several hours to twenty minutes. The system allows precise coaching, providing for exact feedback and individualized responses.

In another experimental program, Rabin, Blechman, and Milton (1984) codified what effective families do well. They then developed a program to guide a couple through the process of solving problems. A couple identifies a problem, describes how the situation would look if the problem were solved, conjures up a solution, and talks about how to reach it. Finally, the couple negotiates a behavioral contract. This training in negotiating solutions would probably be especially applicable to the teaching of team-building skills among employees in industry, not to mention quality-of-worklife skills among union officers and managers, who could learn how to make and implement decisions in the best interests of employees, without resorting to an adversarial process.

Punishment. Where operant principles of reinforcement are concerned, attention in the future will shift from a sole focus on reinforcers and will include punishers. This prediction is based on the heuristic article by Arvey and Ivancevich (1980). As they noted, the question is not whether punishment is good or bad; it exists in virtually every organization and is a frequent and naturally occurring event in our lives. Therefore, it is more ethical to study the punishment process, so that it can be applied correctly and humanely, than it is to ignore it.

The generally accepted conclusion regarding punishment is that its effects are not only temporary but can also produce undesirable side effects. This conclusion is not supported by data from either experimental or clinical psychology (Azrin & Holz, 1966; Kazdin, 1975). Among the intriguing hypotheses advanced by Arvey and Ivancevich (1980), on the basis of these data, are that punishment is more effective when the supervisor who administers it has a relatively close and friendly relationship with the employee than when the relationship is distant and unfriendly; that punishment is more effective when administered on a continuous, rather than an intermittent, schedule; and that the effect of punishment is enhanced if the employee is made aware of alternative acceptable responses. Suggested dependent variables include job attendance, behavior consistent with safety rules, and reduction in thefts. Regression analyses could be used to measure the relationship between the dependent variable and such independent variables as training and the magnitude and scheduling of the punishment. The results of such research, combined with the rediscovered need by industry for an emphasis on ethics courses (Keogh, 1988; Hoffman, 1984; Hosmer, 1985), should lead to highly beneficial training programs.

Behavior Modeling. Behavior modeling will probably be applicable to training programs designed to teach operant principles of punishment. Behavior-modeling training may also benefit from the prospective research on scripts that was described earlier. What may prove especially beneficial are training programs that combine behavior modeling with self-management. In a sense, the homework assignments that are part of most behavior-modeling training are a form of self-management. The additive effects of these two approaches, behavior modeling and self-management, should be assessed. Their combination may prove especially effective in controlling sexist behavior in the workplace, including sexual harassment.

Self-Management. Empirical evaluations of self-management training in organizational settings will increase in frequency. This prediction is based on the fact that self-management is not only a substitute for leadership from others (Kerr & Jerimier, 1978) but also lends itself to training courses on ethical behavior.

In addition to ethical behavior, a primary concern of organizations will be corporate wellness programs. The overall health of employees will become an issue for organizations, with the advancing age of the post–World War II generation. Training in self-management is ideally suited to the maintenance of one's own health. This training may also benefit from computer-aided instruction.

For example, Schneider (1984), a clinician, has developed a computer program, supported by the National Heart, Lung, and Blood Institute, to stop smoking. The program is on

CompuServe, a collection of computerized information available to 360,000 people, each of whom uses a computer and a modem. The smoker answers questions about the nuances of the habit, and the computer responds accordingly. One light smoker, after responding to eighteen questions, received the following advice: "Your answers on the questionnaire suggest that you smoke to accentuate pleasure. Soon, you'll see you don't really need to smoke." Schneider's program employs mental restructuring, now a traditional tool of behavior modification, to advise smokers who call in to CompuServe when they feel an overwhelming urge for a cigarette: "Now, imagine a giant neon sign brightly lit up, saying, DON'T SMOKE!!! Do that now. This technique is called *thought stopping*, because it makes you focus on an image that counteracts the thought that smoking is desirable. Once you stop the thought that you should smoke, the urge will pass away." Smokers record their progress in diaries and get feedback on their screens, in the form of a graph of their tobacco consumption. Some of Schneider's subscribers can even log in and leave messages, to share their experiences.

Mental restructuring is sometimes referred to as *self-statement modification* (SSM). The assumption underlying this technique is that covert self-verbalizations, or private monologues, can influence behavior on a wide variety of tasks. The training is a form of cognitive behavior modification, because it is based on the proposition that an excess of maladaptive self-statements or deficits of adaptive self-statements can be measured and modified in a manner parallel to the way behavior is measured and modified in the laboratory. The typical treatment consists of about five sessions over four weeks. A meta-analysis has revealed that SSM is indeed effective, relative to placebo and control groups (Dush, Hirt, & Schroeder, 1983). Nevertheless, this work was based on a disproportionate number of studies that dealt with simple fears (fear of animals, speaking, assertion; test anxiety), as well as on a disproportionate number of college-student volunteers.

Another application of training in self-management likely to prove effective will be to the area of executive self-development. The problems in this area are described by Kaplan, Drath, and Kofodimos (1987). Their hypothesis was that executives avoid coming to terms with their limitations and that the people who work with them are reluctant, because of the executives' power, to give them constructive feedback. Further, executives are often unable to accept criticism, because of their need to appear highly competent. Thus, there is often adamant refusal to admit weakness or acknowledge any need for improvement. The best use of self-analysis, these researchers concluded, is in response to a specific need: a setback at work, repeated difficulties in one's job, a career impasse, a buildup of health-threatening stress, and so on. Systematic experiments are needed to test these conclusions.

Finally, training in self-management should improve transfer of training to the job. Through such techniques as goal setting, self-monitoring, and self-rewarding, trainees should increase the effectiveness with which they implement newly learned skills.

Measurement

Again and again, reviewers of the training literature have bemoaned the embarrassing lack of solid evaluation research (Campbell, 1971; Dunnette, 1962, 1976; Goldstein, 1980; McGehee & Thayer, 1961; Wexley, 1984). This situation has not been, is not, and, it is predicted, will not become true of behaviorally based training programs. As noted earlier in this chapter, systematic research and measurement have always been the cornerstone of behaviorally based interventions. The emphasis has been and will continue to be on operationalizing both the independent and the dependent variables. The power of the behavioral model will remain in this descriptive analysis, especially with regard to the dependent variable. This emphasis on careful description, in concrete terms, of the behaviors that a trainee should demonstrate after training is what has made the effectiveness of behaviorally based programs so susceptible to measurement. Measurement has been and will continue to be a richly rewarding activity for trainers in this area.

Reciprocal Effects. The big riches or payoffs in measurement will be in simultaneously studying the reciprocal effects among three variables; environment, behavior, and cognition. The problems in doing so will be formidable; hence, the rewards for those who meet the challenge. For example, James and Brett (1984) described the problems of using mediation models that imply additivity but take on a distinctly nonadditive flavor in empirical operationalizations, tests, and explanations of results. How does one deal with the assumption of recursiveness (unidirectionality) that underlies most statistical tests, when social cognitive theory explicitly rejects this assumption? James and Brett (1984) concluded that current procedures for testing mediating variables need to be updated, because these procedures usually involve a dubious interplay between exploratory (correlational) statistical tests and causal inference.

Treatment Utility. Less daunting but equally rewarding will be the exploration of the treatment utility of procedures embedded in modeling and self-management (for example, self-monitoring and writing behavioral contracts) to bring about intended outcomes. From the training perspective, the question of utility can be phrased as follows: In what way and to what extent does this technique or component aid the trainer in helping the trainee? Meehl (1959) called this type of question "ultimately the practically significant one by which the contributions of our techniques must be judged" (p. 116).

As a start, one can again look to clinical psychology, particularly the approach described by Hayes, Nelson, and Jarrett (1987). They presented a taxonomy of treatment utility methods appropriate for treatment utility questions. The immediate reward of this approach is that it may move the I/O field beyond cost-benefit analyses. Using this approach will no doubt draw arrows from those committed to treating utility only in monetary terms, but the reward will be in the demonstration of a particular type of behavioral benefit, in terms of fostering or bringing about a treatment outcome: "Treatment utility research sets the stage for important theoretical developments in part because it points out differences that are functionally important and thus in need of theoretical explanation" (Hayes, Nelson, & Jarrett, 1987, p. 971).

    Idiographic Research. The arrows that have flown from those who are interested in lawfulness or nomothetic research toward those who are interested in uniqueness or idiographic research will cease flying over the next decade. The basis of this prediction involves five observations. First, idiographic research is inductive and therefore reinforcing to people who enjoy the excitement of discovery. It allows one to generalize beyond one's data and develop interesting hypotheses. Second, there is no logical basis for objecting to idiographic research. Through the development of hypotheses, deductive research becomes possible. Third, idiographic research allows I/O psychologists to study, through within-group designs, what before they have studied primarily through correlational designs—namely, individual differences. Behavioral laws may be nomothetic in their form for a given group, but they are idiographic in their parameters, and they are strongly idiographic in their end terms (Meehl, 1959). Fourth, a leading group of organizational theory scholars, who are not behaviorists, has joined in the call for idiographic research (Van Maanen, 1983). Fifth, payoffs of idiographic research are already appearing in research on leaders (Mintzberg, 1983).

    In closing this chapter, I am reminded of Campbell's (1971) conclusion that the training literature was voluminous and dull. Campbell set the stage for the behaviorally based training programs that have been conducted in organizational settings over the past two decades. Today, the word *dull* cannot be applied to the literature on behaviorally based training. To the extent that its methodology remains grounded in theory and subjected to rigorous measurement, the word *dull* will not be applied to this literature in the future.

References

Arvey, R. D., & Ivanevich, J. M. (1980). Punishment in organizations: A review, propositions, and research suggestions. *Academy of Management Review, 5,* 123–132.

Azrin, N. H., & Holz, W. C. (1966). Punishment. In W. K. Honig (Ed.), *Operant behavior* (pp. 380–447). East Norwalk, CT: Appleton-Century-Crofts.

Bandura, A. (1969). *Principles of behavior modification.* New York: Holt, Rinehart & Winston.

Bandura, A. (1974). Behavior theory and models of man. *American Psychologist, 29,* 859–869.

Bandura, A. (1977a). Self-efficacy: Toward a unifying theory of behavioral change. *Psychology Review, 84,* 191–215.

Bandura, A. (1977b). *Social learning theory.* Englewood Cliffs, NJ: Prentice-Hall.

Bandura, A. (1982). The assessment and predictive generality of self-percepts of efficacy. *Journal of Behavior Therapy and Experimental Psychiatry, 13, 195*–199.

Bandura, A. (1986). *Social foundations of thought and action.* Englewood Cliffs, NJ: Prentice-Hall.

Bandura, A., & Adams, N. E. (1977). Analysis of self-efficacy theory of behavioral change. *Cognitive Therapy and Research, 1,* 287–310.

Bandura, A., Adams, N. E., & Beyer, J. (1977). Cognitive processes mediating behavioral change. *Journal of Personality and Social Psychology, 35,* 125–139.

Blum, M. L., & Naylor, J. C. (1968). *Industrial psychology: Its theoretical and social foundations.* New York: Harper & Row.

Brief, A. P., & Hollenbeck, J. R. (1985). An exploratory study of self-regulating activities and their effects on job performance. *Journal of Occupational Behavior, 6,* 197–208.

Burke, M. J., & Day, R. R. (1986). A cumulative study of the effectiveness of managerial training. *Journal of Applied Psychology, 71,* 232–246.

Burnaska, R. F. (1976). The effect of behavior-modeling training upon managers' behaviors and employees' perceptions. *Personnel Psychology, 29,* 329–335.

Byham, W. C., Adams, D., & Kiggins, A. (1976). Transfer of modeling training to the job. *Personnel Psychology, 29,* 345–349.

Campbell, D. J. (1982). Determinants of choice of goal difficulty level: A review of situational and personality influences. *Journal of Occupational Psychology, 55,* 79–95.

Campbell, J. P. (1971). Personnel training and development. *Annual Review of Psychology, 22,* 565–602.

Campbell, J. P., Dunnette, M. D., Lawler, E. E., & Weick, K. E. (1970). *Managerial behavior, performance, and effectiveness.* New York: McGraw-Hill.

Cherrington, D. J., Reitz, H. J., & Scott, W. E. (1971). Effects of contingent and noncontingent reward on the relationship between satisfaction and task performance. *Journal of Applied Psychology, 55,* 531–536.

Clance, P. R. (1985). *The impostor phenomemon: Overcoming the fear that haunts your success.* Atlanta, GA: Peachtree Press.

Cronbach, L. J., & Meehl, P. E. (1955). Construct validity in psychological tests. *Psychological Bulletin, 52,* 581–602.

Drucker, P. (1973). *Management: Tasks, responsibilities, and practices.* New York: Harper & Row.

Dulany, D. E. (1968). Awareness, rules, and propositional control: A confrontation with S-R behavior theory. In T. R. Dixon & D. L. Horton (Eds.), Verbal behavior and general behavior theory (pp. 340–387). Englewood Cliffs, NJ: Prentice-Hall.

Dunnette, M. D. (1962). Personnel management. In P. R. Farnsworth, O. McNemar, & Q. McNemar (Eds.), *Annual Review of Psychology.* Palo Alto, CA: Annual Reviews.

Dunnette, M. D. (1976). Mishmash, mush, and milestones in organizational psychology. In H. Meltzer & F. R. Wiskert (Eds.), *Humanizing organizational behavior* (pp. 86–102). Springfield, IL: Charles C. Thomas.

Dush, D. M., Hirt, M. L., & Schroeder, H. (1983). Self-statements modification with adults: A meta-analysis. *Psychological Bulletin, 94,* 408–422.

Eastman, C., & Marzillier, J. S. (1984). Theoretical and methodological difficulties in Bandura's self-efficacy theory. *Cognitive Therapy and Research, 8,* 218–229.

Evans, K. M., Kienast, P., & Mitchell, T. R. (1988). The effects of lottery incentive programs on performance. *Journal of Organizational Behavior Management, 19,* 113–135.

Feeney, E. J. (1973). *Behavioral engineering systems training*. Redding, CT: Edward J. Feeney & Associates.

Feild, H. S., & Holley, W. H. (1982). The relationship of performance appraisal system characteristics to verdicts in selected employment discrimination cases. *Academy of Management Journal, 25,* 392–406.

Fiedler, F. E., Chemers, M. M., & Mahar, L. (1984). *Improving leadership effectiveness: The leader match concept*. New York: Wiley.

Flanagan, J. C. (1954). The critical incident technique. *Psychological Bulletin, 51,* 327–358.

Frayne, C. A., & Latham, G. P. (1987). The application of social learning theory to employee self-management of attendance. *Journal of Applied Psychology, 72,* 387–392.

Gioia, D. A., & Manz, C. C. (1985). Linking cognition and behavior: A script-processing interpretation of vicarious learning. *Academy of Management Review, 10,* 527–539.

Gist, M. E., Schwoerer, C., & Rosen, B. (in press). Effects of alternative training methods on self-efficacy and performance in computer software training. *Journal of Applied Psychology*.

Goldberg, M. H., Dawson, R. I., & Barrett, R. S. (1964). Comparison of programmed and conventional instruction methods. *Journal of Applied Psychology, 64,* 110–114.

Goldstein, I. L. (1980). Training in work organizations. *Annual Review of Psychology, 31,* 229–272.

Goldstein, I. L. (1986). *Training in organizations: Needs assessment, development, and evaluation* (2nd ed.). Monterey, CA: Brooks/Cole.

Harrell, T. W. (1949). *Industrial psychology*. New York: Holt, Rinehart & Winston.

Hayes, S. C., Nelson, F. O., & Jarrett, R. B. (1987). The treatment utility of assessment: A functional approach to evaluating assessment quality. *American Psychologist, 42,* 963–974.

Heyduk, R. G., & Fenigstein, A. (1984). Influential works and authors in psychology: A survey of eminent psychologists. *American Psychologist, 39,* 556–559.

Hoffman, W. M. (1984). Ethics in business education: Working toward a meaningful reciprocity. *Journal of Business Ethics, 3,* 259–268.

Hogan, P. M., Hakel, M. D., & Decker, P. J. (1986). Effects of trainee-generated versus trainer-provided rule codes on generalization in behavior-modeling training. *Journal of Applied Psychology, 71,* 469–473.

Honig, W. K. (1966). *Operant behavior.* East Norwalk, CT: Appleton-Century-Crofts.

Hosmer, L. T. (1985). The other 338: Why a majority of our schools of business administration do not offer a course in business ethics. *Journal of Business Ethics, 4,* 17–22.

Huber, V. L., & Gay, G. (1984). Uses of educational technology for formative evaluation. *Education for Program Improvement, 24,* 55–64.

Hull, C. L. (1928). *Aptitude testing.* New York: World.

Jablonsky, S. F., & DeVries, D. L. (1972). Operant conditioning principles extrapolated to the theory of management. *Organizational Behavior and Human Performance, 7,* 340–358.

James, L. R., & Brett, J. M. (1984). Mediators, moderators, and tests for mediation. *Journal of Applied Psychology, 69,* 307–321.

Johnson, P. D., & Sorcher, M. (1976). Behavior-modeling training: Why, how, and what results. *Journal of European Training, 5,* 62–72.

Kanfer, F. H. (1974). Self-regulation: Research, issues, and speculations. In C. Neuringer & J. Michael (Eds.), *Behavior modification in clinical psychology* (pp. 397–409). East Norwalk, CT: Appleton-Century-Crofts.

Kanfer, F. H. (1975). Self-management methods. In F. H. Kanfer (Ed.), *Helping people change* (pp. 309–355). Elmsford, NY: Pergamon Press.

Kanfer, F. H. (1980). Self-management methods. In F. H. Kanfer & A. P. Goldstein (Eds.), *Helping people change: A textbook of methods* (pp. 334–389). Elmsford, NY: Pergamon Press.

Kaplan, A. (1964). *The Conduct of Inquiry.* Scranton, PA: Chandler.

Kaplan, R. E., Drath, W. H., & Kofodimos, J. R. (1987). High hurdles: The challenge of executive self-development. *The Academy of Management Executive, 1,* 195–206.

Karoly, P., & Kanfer, F. H. (Eds.) (1982). *Self-management and behavior change: From theory to practice.* Elmsford, NY: Pergamon Press.

Kaufman, A., Baron, A., & Kopp, R. E. (1966). Some effects of instructions on human operant behavior. *Psychonomic Monograph Supplements, 1,* 243–250.

Kazdin, A. E. (1975). Covert modeling, imagery, assessment, and assertive behavior. *Journal of Consulting and Clinical Psychology, 43,* 716–724.

Keogh, J. (Ed.). (1988). *Corporate ethics: A prime business asset.* New York: The Business Roundtable.

Kerr, S., & Jerimier, J. (1978). Substitutes for leadership: Their meaning and measurement. *Organizational Behavior and Human Performance, 22,* 375–403.

Kirchner, R. E., Schnelle, J. F., Domash, M., Larson, L., Carr, A., & McNees, M. P. (1980). The applicability of a helicopter control procedure to diverse areas: A cost-benefit evaluation. *Journal of Applied Behavior Analysis, 13,* 143–148.

Komaki, J. L. (1977). Alternative evaluation strategies in work settings: Reversal and multiple-baseline designs. *Journal of Organizational Behavior Management, 1,* 53–77.

Komaki, J. L. (1982). The case for the single case: Making judicious decisions about alternatives. In L. W. Frederiksen (Ed.), *Handbook of organizational behavior management* (pp. 145–176). New York: Wiley.

Komaki, J. L., Waddell, W. M., & Pearce, M. G. (1977). The applied behavior analysis approach and individual employees: Improving performance in two small businesses. *Organizational Behavior and Human Performance, 19,* 337–352.

Latham, G. P. (1986). Job performance and appraisal. In C. L. Cooper & I. T. Robertson (Eds.), *International Review of Industrial and Organizational Psychology.* New York: Wiley.

Latham, G. P. (1988). Human resource training and development. *Annual Review of Psychology, 39,* 545–582.

Latham, G. P., & Dossett, D. L. (1978). Designing incentive plans for unionized employees: A comparison of continuous and variable-ratio reinforcement schedules. *Personnel Psychology, 31,* 47–61.

Latham, G. P., & Frayne, C. A. (1989). Increasing job attendance through training in self-management: A review of two studies. *Journal of Applied Psychology, 74,* 411–416.

Latham, G. P., & Saari, L. M. (1979). The application of social learning theory to training supervisors through behavior modeling. *Journal of Applied Psychology, 64,* 239–246.

Latham, G. P., & Wexley, K. N. (1981). *Increasing productivity through performance appraisal.* Reading, MA: Addison-Wesley.

Locke, E. A. (1968). Toward a theory of task motivation and incentives. *Organizational Behavior and Human Performance, 3,* 157–189.

Locke, E. A. (1977). The myths of behavior modification in organizations. *The Academy of Management Review, 2,* 543–553.

Locke, E. A. (1980). Latham versus Komaki: A tale of two paradigms. *Journal of Applied Psychology, 65,* 16–23.

Locke, E. A., Cartledge, N., & Koeppel, J. (1968). Motivational effects of knowledge of results. *Psychological Bulletin, 70,* 474–485.

Locke, E. A., Frederick, E., Lee, C., & Bobko, P. (1984). Effect of self-efficacy, goals, and task strategies on task performance. *Journal of Applied Psychology, 69,* 242–251.

Locke, E. A., & Latham, G. P. (1984). *Goal setting: A motivational technique that works!* Englewood Cliffs, NJ: Prentice-Hall.

Locke, E. A., & Latham, G. P. (1990). *A theory of goal setting and task performance.* Englewood Cliffs, NJ: Prentice-Hall.

Locke, E. A., Shaw, K. N., Saari, L. M., & Latham, G. P. (1981). Goal setting and task performance: 1969–1980. *Psychological Bulletin, 90,* 125–152.

McGehee, W., & Thayer, P. W. (1961). *Training in business and industry.* New York: Wiley.

McGehee, W., & Tuller, W. (1978). A note on evaluating behavior modification and behavior modeling as industrial training techniques. *Personnel Psychology, 31,* 477–484.

Mann, R. B., & Decker, P. J. (1984). The effect of key behavior distinctiveness on generalization and recall in behavior-modeling training. *Academy of Management Journal, 27,* 900–909.

Manz, C. C., & Sims, H. P., Jr. (1986). Beyond imitation: Complex behavioral and affective linkages resulting from exposure to leadership training models. *Journal of Applied Psychology, 71*, 571–578.

Marx, M. H., & Hillix, W. A. (1963). *Systems and theories in psychology*. New York: McGraw-Hill.

Marzillier, J. S., & Eastman, C. (1984). Continuing problems with self-efficacy theory: A reply to Bandura. *Cognitive Therapy and Research, 8*, 257–262.

Maslow, A. (1965). *Eupsychian Management*. Homewood, IL: Dorsey.

Meehl, P. E. (1959). Some ruminations on the validation of clinical procedures. *Canadian Journal of Psychology, 13*, 102–128.

Miner, J. B. (1980). *Theories of organizational behavior*. Hinsdale, IL: Dryden.

Mintzberg, H. (1983). An emerging strategy of "direct" research. In J. Van Maanen (Ed.), *Qualitative methodology*. Newbury Park, CA: Sage.

Mitchell, T. R. (1975). Cognitions and Skinner: Some questions about behavioral determinism. *Organization and Administrative Sciences, 6*, 63–72.

Moses, J. I., & Ritchie, R. J. (1976). Supervisory relationship training: A behavioral evaluation of a behavior-modeling program. *Personnel Psychology, 29*, 351–359.

Munsterberg, H. (1913). *Psychology and industrial efficiency*. Boston: Houghton Mifflin.

Napier, N. K., & Latham, G. P. (1986). Outcome expectancies of people who conduct performance appraisals. *Personnel Psychology, 39*, 827–837.

Nash, A. N., Muczyk, J. P., & Vettori, F. L. (1971). The relative practical effectiveness of programmed instruction. *Personnel Psychology, 24*, 397–418.

Nord, W. R. (1969). Beyond the teaching machine: The neglected area of operant conditioning in the theory and practice of management. *Organizational Behavior and Human Performance, 4*, 375–401.

Panyon, M., Boozer, H., & Morris, N. (1970). Feedback to attendants as a reinforcer for applying operant techniques. *Journal of Applied Behavior Analysis, 3*, 1–4.

Parsons, H. M. (1974). What happened at Hawthorne? *Science, 183*, 922–932.

Pinder, C. C. (1984). *Work motivation*. Glenview, IL: Scott, Foresman.

Porter, L. W. (1973). Turning work into nonwork: The rewarding environment. In M. D. Dunnette (Ed.), *Work and nonwork in the year 2001* (pp. 113–133). Monterey, CA: Brooks/Cole.

Pressey, S. L. (1926). A simple device which gives tests and scores — and teaches. *School and Society, 23*, 373–376.

Rabin, C., Blechman, E. A., & Milton, M. C. (1984). A multiple-baseline study of the Marriage Contract Game's effect on problem solving and affective behavior. *Child and Family Behavior Therapy, 6*, 45–60.

Rotter, J. B. (1954). *Social learning and clinical psychology*. Englewood Cliffs, NJ: Prentice-Hall.

Rowland, K. M., & Ferris, G. R. (1986). *Current issues in personnel management*. Newton, MA: Allyn & Bacon.

Russel, J. S., Wexley, K. N., & Hunter, J. E. (1984). Questioning the effectiveness of behavior-modeling training in an industrial setting. *Personnel Psychology, 37*, 465–482.

Ryan, T. A., & Smith, P. C. (1954). *Principles of industrial psychology*. New York: Ronald Press.

Schneider, S. J. (1984). Who quits smoking in a behavioral treatment program? *Addictive Behaviors, 9*, 373–381.

Skinner, B. F. (1938). *The behavior of organisms*. East Norwalk, CT: Appleton-Century-Crofts.

Skinner, B. F. (1953). *Science and human behavior*. New York: Macmillan.

Skinner, B. F. (1954). The science of learning and the art of teaching. *Harvard Educational Review, 24*, 86–97.

Skinner, B. F. (1957). Are theories of learning necessary? *Psychological Review, 19*, 193–216.

Skinner, B. F. (1958). Teaching machines. *Science, 128*, 969–977.

Skinner, B. F. (1987). What ever happened to psychology as the science of behavior? *American Psychologist, 42*, 780–786.

Smith, P. C. (1976). Behaviors, results, and organizational effectiveness: The problem and the criteria. In M. P. Dunnette

(Ed.), *Handbook of industrial and organizational psychology.* Skokie, IL: Rand McNally.

Staats, A. W. (1983). *Psychology's crisis of disunity: Philosophy and method for a unified science.* New York: Praeger.

Taylor, M. S., Locke, E., Lee, C., & Gist, M. (1985). Type A behavior and faculty research productivity: What are the mechanisms? *Organizational Behavior and Human Performance, 34,* 402–418.

Tiffin, J. (1952). *Industrial psychology.* Englewood Cliffs, NJ: Prentice-Hall.

Van Maanen, J. (1983). *Qualitative methodology.* Newbury Park, CA: Sage.

Vroom, V. H. (1964). *Work and motivation.* New York: Wiley.

Watson, J. B. (1913). Psychology as the behaviorist views it. *Psychology Review, 20,* 158–177.

Welsh, P., Antoinetti, J. A., & Thayer, P. W. (1965). An industry-wide study of programmed instruction. *Journal of Applied Psychology, 49,* 61–73.

Wexley, K. N. (1984). Personnel training. *Annual Review of Psychology, 35,* 519–551.

Wexley, K. N., & Latham, G. P. (1981). *Developing and training human resources in organizations.* Glenview, IL; Scott, Foresman.

Wolpe, J. (1978). Cognition and causation in human behavior and its therapy. *American Psychologist, 66,* 437–446.

Yukl, G. A., & Latham, G. P. (1975). Consequences of reinforcement schedules and incentive magnitudes for employee performance: Problems encountered in an industrial setting. *Journal of Applied Psychology, 60,* 294–298.

Yukl, G. A., Latham, G. P., & Pursell, E. D. (1976). The effectiveness of performance incentives under continuous and variable-ratio schedules of reinforcement. *Personnel Psychology, 29,* 221–231.

Yukl, G. A., Wexley, K. N., & Seymore, J. E. (1972). Effectiveness of pay incentives under variable-ratio and continuous reinforcement schedules. *Journal of Applied Psychology, 56,* 19–23.

PART THREE

Social Systems Issues
in Training Research

8

Aging and the Training and Learning Process

Harvey L. Sterns
Dennis Doverspike

The growing presence of middle-aged and older workers in the national labor force is recognized as a potential influence on our national economy and the health of individual organizations. Simultaneously, technological innovation is having both positive and negative effects on the workplace. Technological innovation may affect the workplace in several ways, some of which render skills and knowledge obsolete, require the development of new knowledge and skills, change employees' attitudes and satisfaction regarding the workplace (positively and negatively), create new job openings and potential for career mobility, and create unemployment (Sterns & Patchett, 1984). Regardless of the direction of its effects, technological innovation creates needs for training and retraining of workers.

Industrial gerontology is the study of aging and work, focusing on the employment and retirement issues of middle-aged and older workers. A common theme in this area for over four decades has been the training and retraining of adult and older adult workers. Older adults can be trained and retrained in both laboratory and industrial settings. This has led to the development of training principles and methods that recognize the unique attributes of the older adult worker (Sterns, 1986; Sterns & Alexander, 1987; Sterns & Doverspike, 1988).

The purpose of this chapter is to examine issues, research, and theory relevant to the topic of training and retraining of the older worker. It is also the purpose of this chapter to suggest future avenues or frontiers for research, theory, and application to organizational settings. We have approached the task by providing a fairly wide review of the field. We begin by reviewing different approaches to defining the older worker. The more traditional, and older, research on retraining and training is then reviewed. This is followed by a discussion of what we find to be the most promising avenue for future research and application to adult and older adult workers. We conclude by offering specific applied suggestions.

The Older Worker: Problems of Definition

The foundation of logical argument and scientific study rests on the adequate definition of terms. Unfortunately, much of the research and theory on the older worker has avoided the problem of defining the older worker. The result has been that a chronological definition is usually put forward, by default. The age limits of the chronological definition are often arbitrary and the rationale is unstated, although a reliance has emerged recently in the United States on the use of legal definitions. We prefer to view the question of defining the older worker in a multidimensional manner. We identify here, and briefly review, five general approaches to the classification and definition of the older worker. The five approaches are the chronological/ legal, the functional, the psychosocial, the organizational, and the life-span orientation.

Chronological/Legal Approach. The distinction between older and younger workers rests most frequently on a definition based on chronological age. Although little theoretical justification is offered for the age ranges, there appears to be an implicit justification based on a legal definition of age, as found in the Age Discrimination in Employment Act (ADEA) of 1967. This act protects workers who are forty through sixty-five years old from age discrimination. Hence, it separates older workers — those covered by the ADEA — from uncovered, younger workers. In 1978, the ADEA was amended, to extend its coverage to age seventy and to abolish mandatory retirement for federal employees. The most recent amendment, in 1986, removed the maximum age restriction, with certain exceptions. In terms of this act, an older worker is currently defined as any individual forty and above who is still an active worker.

It is a violation of the ADEA to fail or refuse to hire, to discharge, or in other ways to discriminate against any individual who is forty or older. Thus, workers cannot be limited, segregated, or classified so as to deprive them of employment opportunities on account of their age. This implies that failure to train or retrain because of age is discriminatory. Snyder and Barrett (in press) provide a comprehensive review of cases filed under the ADEA. Until now, few cases have dealt with the issue of age-related access to training.

The Comprehensive Employment and Training Act (CETA) provided some employment assistance to older adults. This was the first major training legislation, and its programs used classroom and on-the-job training. The focus of these efforts for older workers was on people over the age of fifty-five who had incomes below the poverty level. The Senior Community Service Employment Program, which is part of Title V of the Older Americans Act, creates part-time public-sector work placements for chronically unemployed workers who are over the age of fifty-five and below federal poverty levels. In 1984, CETA was replaced by the Job Training Partnership Act. This program has had special allocations for economically disadvantaged older workers. Its focus has been on training for private-sector employment. For federal programs, people fifty-five and older have been considered older workers (Bornstein, 1986).

Functional Approach. Given individual variability in biological and psychological aging, researchers have turned to a performance-based definition of age, commonly referred to as *functional age.* As chronological age increases, individuals go through various biological and psychological changes, including declines as well as increased experience, wisdom, and judgment. There is substantial variation, however. Psychological changes take place at different times for different individuals. The concept of functional age has been criticized from a number of perspectives, including the definitional, research design, and statistical points of view (Avolio, Barrett, & Sterns, 1984; Salthouse, 1986); major problems are the use of a single index and the assumption of a decline model. Despite these criticisms of the concept, different approaches and definitions of functional age continue to exert their influence on the field. Currently, attempts are being made to refine the measurement of functional age through techniques such as LISREL (Birren & Stafford, 1986). Avolio, Barrett, and Sterns (1984) have also proposed an alternative approach, based on more traditional methods drawn from industrial psychology. They suggest that a greater emphasis needs to be placed on appropriate assessment strategies—designing of measures that assess intrinsic attributes directly related to job performance.

Psychosocial Approach. Psychosocial definitions of the older worker include those based on social perceptions of the older worker, the age typing of occupations, and the aging of knowledge, skill, and ability sets. In terms of perceptions of the older worker, the psychosocial definitions have focused on three issues: the age at which society perceives an individual to be older; the social attitudes that are held toward older workers; and the implications for personnel decisions (especially training) of labeling a worker *older*. Relatively little research has addressed the quite basic question of how we know when workers will perceive themselves, or be perceived by others, as old or older. Despite the importance of this question, it has attracted scant attention. Recent prototype and other social-categorization theories of stereotyping appear to suggest possible answers and will no doubt be studied in the future. Like the researchers, many individuals may rely simply on chronological age for definitions of old age.

A significant amount of research has investigated the

perceived attributes of older workers. Although the research is equivocal, older workers are perceived as harder to train, less able to keep up with technological changes, more accident-prone, less promotable, and less motivated (Avolio & Barrett, 1987; Bird & Fisher, 1986; Rosen & Jerdee, 1976, 1978; Schwab & Heneman, 1978; Slater & Kingsley, 1976; Stagner, 1985). Older workers are also perceived as having positive traits: They are seen as dependable, cooperative, conscientious, consistent, and knowledgeable (Rosen & Jerdee, 1976, 1978; Schwab & Heneman, 1978; Slater & Kingsley, 1976). In a study of performance evaluation in a large organization, Cleveland and Landy (1981) found very small but significant effects of age on some rating dimensions. These results were consistent with those found in earlier studies (Rosen & Jerdee, 1976; Schwab & Heneman, 1978), which suggests that if age effects are present in real performance evaluations, the size of the effect is relatively small.

In addition to individuals' being perceived as older workers, jobs can be considered as more or less appropriate for older workers. While the study of age typing in occupations is a fairly new area, several preliminary studies have begun to map the age typing of occupations. Gordon and Arvey (1986) found that both college students and the general public held age stereotypes of occupations, and their estimates corresponded to actual census data. Cleveland and Landy (1981, 1983) have completed a series of studies on age typing. Their results document the importance of investigating the age type of the occupation, as well as the age of the incumbent. A definitive theory of the age typing of occupations does not yet exist, and a significant amount of research remains to be completed on the topic.

For managerial and technical workers, one problem that often accompanies age is obsolescence. There have been a number of different theoretical and operational approaches to defining obsolescence.

Fossum, Arvey, Paradise, and Robbins (1986) propose a combined psychological and economics-based approach, rooted in expectancy theory and human capital theory, for understanding obsolescence and the motivational factors that contribute to an individual's decision to pursue training in the face of obsolescence. On the basis of expectancy theory, individuals can be expected to pursue updating and retraining opportunities when they believe that training will lead to the development of relevant knowledge, skills, and abilities, and that these will lead to valued outcomes. Fossum, Arvey, Paradise, and Robbins (1986) suggest that obsolescence may increase with age: Importance of outcomes changes with age, and there is decreased expectancy of obtaining valued outcomes through the updating of knowledge, skills, and abilities. Human capital theory shares a common foundation in rational decision making with expectancy theory and leads to similar predictions. With age, individuals should be less willing to invest in training. This will be true not only for chronological age, but also for job and occupational tenure (Fossum, Avery, Paradise, & Robbins, 1986).

Organizational Approach. Individuals age, both in jobs and in organizations. An older worker has often spent a substantial amount of time in a job, and substantially more time in an organization. A definition of *older worker* based on the aging of individuals in organizational roles is more commonly discussed under the topics of seniority and tenure, or organizational and job tenure. The effects of aging may often be confounded by the effects of tenure, and vice versa. For example, Gordon, Cofer, and McCullough (1986) found a correlation of .72 between age and organizational tenure. They also found that seniority was unrelated to trainability, both before and after they controlled for age.

Organizations, too, may age (Schrank & Waring, 1981). The aging of organizations can be defined either at the aggregate (individual) level or at the macro (organizational) level. At the micro level, an organization may be perceived as old because of the average age of its members. As the average age of the members increases, new demands are placed on the organizational subsystems, including the human resource subsystem. At the macro level, organizational age can be defined in terms of organizational life cycles. Organizational old age is a fairly new topic of study in the literature. The decline of organizations leads to pressures on suprasystems for legislative and regulatory changes (such as plant-closing legislation) and to pressures on organizations for new types of training, including retraining, outplacement services, and early-retirement counseling (Hansen, 1984). Regardless of how we define organizational age, individual and organizational age can often be correlated, and their effects may be cumulative on older employees.

The way an organization is perceived may be different among older versus younger workers. Pond and Geyer (1987) found that the negative correlation between perceived work alternatives and job satisfaction was weaker for older than for younger employees. It has been suggested that some other aspects of employees' age, other than organizational tenure and educational level, were responsible for this moderating effect. Values, needs, and expectations of employees change as they go through different developmental stages in their lives and careers (Rhodes, 1983).

Life-Span Approach. The life-span orientation to a definition of the older worker borrows from a number of the previous approaches but adds its own unique emphasis. The life-span approach emphasizes that behavioral change can occur at any point in the life cycle. There is no special year or date where we can differentiate young from old; rather, there are substantial individual differences in aging (Baltes, Reese, & Lipsitt, 1980).

Three sets of factors are seen as affecting behavioral change during the life cycle. The first set includes normative, age-graded biological and/or environmental determinants. These bear a strong relationship to chronological age. The second set of factors is normative, history-graded influences, which affect most members of a cohort (generation) in similar ways. The third set of events is nonnormative and includes unique career and life changes, as well as individual health and stress-inducing events. The unique status of the individual is the result of the joint impact of age-graded biological and/or environmental factors, history-graded factors, and nonnormative life events. These interactive dimensions are responsible for individual differences and similarities, depending on the influence. In general, according to this approach, there are probably more individual differences as people grow older.

The life-span approach emphasizes the individual differences found in career patterns or processes. As such, it is compatible with many process models of careers. Patchett and Sterns (1984) and Sterns and Patchett (1984) have developed a model that assumes the possibility of changes at any point in a life span. The model treats career planning from the goal-setting perspective. Career planning itself is a result of attitudes toward career development and such system pressures as technology. Attitudes toward career development are influenced by external support, system changes, mobility, and attitudes toward market reentry.

A strong emphasis on the developmental potentials of adulthood may transform work organizations. Transforming work organizations will offer opportunities for realizing the developmental potentials of adult and older adult workers (Basseches, 1986).

The challenge presented by new, increasingly complex work roles may be seen as playing a crucial role in stimulating the development of cognitive structures in adult workers. Effective organizational functioning is seen as a dialectical process that comprises both individual and organizational development. For many individuals, the workplace is an important mechanism for continued learning, either vicariously on the job or through formal training programs (Cross, 1981).

Research on the training of older workers has avoided the question of defining *older*. Recent research on psychological approaches has expanded our need to understand how workers, jobs, and organizations may come to be perceived as old. For training purposes, we find the life-span approach particularly useful. The life-span approach emphasizes individual differences in aging and is compatible with the recent emphasis on process models of career development.

Age and Training Interactions: Past Research Trends

Both industrial gerontology and research on training the older worker have their roots in the 1940s and the 1950s. This period represents a peak in retraining efforts, when retraining was defined, and differentiated from training, as "arranged in response to a need shown to be present at a particular time and in a particular place. [Retraining and training] are discontinued automatically, unless special authorization is given to repeat them, [and are] designed primarily to equip experienced adult workers with new job skills and to increase the competence of those workers in skills they already possess" (Hardin & Borus, 1971, p. 3).

In the 1940s and the 1950s, the aftermath of World War II had left England and Germany with a shortage of younger male employees and with an accompanying need to rebuild industry during a time of technological change. One solution was to retrain older workers. In 1946, the Nuffield Foundation awarded a grant to the Cambridge Psychological Laboratory, which created the Nuffield Research Unit. The main goal of the grant was to apply findings to industry on the changes in skills and trainability that occurred with aging (Welford, 1976). The work of the Nuffield Research Unit was to shape much of the early history and thinking on training older workers.

The early studies tended to be of two types. In Great Britain, the primary search was for aptitude-treatment interactions, or training interactions. The bulk of work in this area can be traced to the influence of E. Belbin, R. M. Belbin, and S. M. Downs. Most of this work was based on the assumption that traditional methods of training do not work well with older adults, because older adults do not function well in school-type environments. Thus, a search was started for alternative methods under which older employees could perform more effectively. In the United States there was a similar emphasis, accompanied by case studies and economic-based approaches (for example, Jakubauskus and Taylor, 1969).

One of the early methods (Belbin, Belbin, & Hill, 1957; Belbin & Downs, 1966) was activity learning. Activity learning was based on the assumptions that learning among older workers should involve activity, reduce descriptions and memorization, be error-free, and involve tasks of graded difficulty. This resulted in a training program whose instructions and tasks were as directly related as possible; opportunities for ambiguity were kept to a minimum, and training was structured to avoid errors (Belbin & Shimmin, 1964; McFarland, 1973). Although a number of research studies were performed on this technique, the results were not consistent, and the assumptions and methodology were partially subsumed into the discovery method.

On the basis of research and assumptions similar to those underlying the activity method, the Belbins developed the discovery method (Belbin, 1969, 1970; Belbin & Belbin, 1972). This theory, or set of assumptions, held that older trainees need to understand the essentials of a task, to have clear written instructions, to have the pace of training slowed or under their control, to avoid early errors, and to avoid demands on short-term memory. It also held that older trainees require longer and uninterrupted learning sessions, a greater consolidation of learning before attempting new skills, and rapid feedback (Belbin & Belbin, 1968). The essential idea of discovery training was that trainees discover for themselves how things work and eventually discover why things work. Thus, discovery training emphasized learning through doing, rather than through verbal or physical instruction. Once a problem was solved, understanding was reinforced through group discussion of principles. The discovery method required substantial preparation, to ensure that material was organized into sets of graded tasks. Thus, tasks were simplified enough for trainees to discover the right responses. The discovery method was found to improve older workers' performance, as compared to both traditional learning and activity learning (Belbin & Shimmin, 1964), and was used in a number of field studies (Barkin, 1970; Belbin & Downs, 1964; Belbin, 1969). The theoretical basis and assumptions of the discovery method continue to influence the training of older adults today.

A recent expansion and revision of the discovery method is found in a comprehensive technique known as the CRAMP method (Downs & Roberts, 1977). The CRAMP method divides learning into five distinct areas: comprehension, reflex, attitude, memory, and procedure. Through a task analysis, tasks are identified and then matched to appropriate learning methods, through the learning types. The CRAMP technique incorporates elements of discovery learning, discrimination learning, role playing, and self-paced learning. In a study with train guards, the CRAMP technique, as compared to a traditional method, produced a greater pass rate for older men and fewer resignations.

In addition to techniques specifically developed for the older worker, other nontraditional techniques, such as programmed instruction, have been investigated as methods for improving the training of older employees. Programmed instruction is closely tied to Skinner's behavior-modification theories. Programmed instruction involves the presentation of material in frames, or small segments. The frames are organized to allow for immediate feedback and positive reinforcement. Positive reinforcement is encouraged through the organization of frames in terms of difficulty. Neale, Toye, and Belbin (1968) examined the effectiveness of programmed instruction for bus conductors and found no difference in the effectiveness of programmed and more standard classroom techniques. In a second study, session length was found to be a crucial variable. Sieman (1976) reported positive results for programmed instruction used to teach basic concepts in anatomy and physiology, but his study did not involve any comparison to other training methods, and older trainees took more than twice as long to master the material.

Before we end our discussion of past research trends, the issue of methodology needs to be addressed. Early studies, especially those performed in England, often relied on designs in which age was crossed with type of training. The hope was to find training programs that would result in advantages for older workers; today, we would speak of looking for an aptitude-treatment interaction. Given the problem under investigation, many of the designs were relatively weak, with numerous threats to internal validity. In the research performed in the United States, there was often a feeling of advocacy, and a number of studies could be regarded as case studies, at best. (Of course, this criticism could be leveled at the field of training in general.)

Recent research has tended to investigate a slightly different question: To what degree can older workers' performance be brought up to the level of younger workers' performance, and under what conditions, or in what training situations, will older and younger workers perform similarly?

Studies of training with older employees continue to present numerous methodological challenges. Research in this area poses not only problems unique to aging research (such as increasing variation with age, progressive selection, selective survival, and cohort or life-experience differences) but also problems related to the evaluation of training, the use of quasi-experimental designs, appropriateness of criteria, and the transfer and duration of training effects.

Not all barriers to training participation involve the methods used. Objective tests, used as selection devices for entry into training, may also serve as barriers to the participation of older workers. Relatively little empirical research exists on the extent to which tests do restrict access, but the possibility has generated a search for nontraditional alternatives.

One method that has attracted substantial attention in England is trainability testing (Robertson & Downs, 1979). Trainability testing is based on the not uncommon principle that one of the best predictors of training success is performance in a shortened version of training. It began in England as an attempt to improve the selection of older workers and increase their acceptance rates into training. The approach involved three major steps: The instructor taught the applicant a task, using standardized instructions and demonstration techniques; the applicant performed the task unaided; and the instructor graded the applicant's performance through the recording of errors on a standardized checklist and through an overall trainability rating. This technique has been supported by research specific to its methodology, as well as by other research on the feasibility of using a short training program to predict training success. Robertson and Downs (1979) reviewed a number of studies where trainability testing predicted well for older workers.

Much of the early research consisted of a search for age-by-training-method interactions. As with other searches in the training area for aptitude-by-treatment interactions, this research was beset with methodological and design problems, but it greatly increased our knowledge of the problems and led to much greater sophistication in research design. Many of the findings, methods, and assumptions of the early research continue to have a strong influence today. For example, many of the assumptions of the Belbins' methods can be found in the rapidly expanding field of adult education. As with much of the aptitude-by-treatment interaction, the research was largely unsuccessful. We now know that older workers can be trained, and we know how to train them, but it is still difficult to point to methods that operate differently for older and younger workers.

Practical Principles for Training the Older Worker

We are left with questions that have haunted the training field: Does the research have applied relevance? Will practitioners use it (Latham, 1988)? We cannot know whether practitioners will avail themselves of our research conclusions, but the research does suggest seven factors that should be considered in actually developing training programs with the older worker in mind (Sterns, 1986; Sterns & Doverspike, 1988): motivation, structure, familiarity, organization, time, active participation, and learning strategies.

Consideration of motivation is critical, regardless of trainees' ages. Older workers present a special situation. While they do want to participate, special effort may be required to create the circumstances conducive to initial entry. This effort may include organizational interventions to change supervisors' and managers' attitudes. Once in training, older employees may fear failure or inability to compete. This fear may be conquered through adequate design and structuring of the training program.

The training program should be based on job or task analysis. Reliance on task analysis has proved to be a strong predictor of a training program's success. To build trainees' self-confidence, failure experiences should be minimized by having trainees proceed from simple to complex tasks and demonstrate mastery of each task before going on to the next one.

Adequate time should be allowed for mastery (Goldstein, 1986; Wexley & Latham, 1981).

On the average, older workers require longer to reach proficiency than younger workers do. Thus, they may need slower presentation rates, longer periods to complete diagnostic tests, and longer periods for study (Belbin & Belbin, 1972). They may also require strategy training on the effective use of time. Longer training times will allow for organization and strategy training.

Older employees may have developed alternative methods of organizing information, and these methods may clash with the requirements of the training program. Strategy training in organizational and memory processes can lead to improved performance (Schmidt, Murphy, & Sanders, 1981). The training program should also ensure adequate retention and comprehension. This can be achieved through the appropriate use of tests before and after training modules. The training of learning strategies is a fairly new and evolving concept. The rationale behind training in learning strategies is that if we expect people to learn, we should first show them how to learn. Training in learning strategies may be especially effective with older employees, who have been removed from the tasks required in educational settings (Weinstein & Mayer, 1982).

While older employees have extensive experience, they may feel alienated from the environment inherent in many training programs. As a result, they feel stressed, and they lack confidence to complete the tasks often required in standard lecture training. Active participation in the learning process has proved effective with older employees (McGehee & Thayer, 1961; Mullen & Gorman, 1972).

In addition to encouraging active participation, it is critical to ensure the recall of prerequisites to further training. Training should build on the extensive skills of older workers. To do this, training must be based on familiar elements—that is, training should build on past skills, knowledge, and abilities, using relevant material from the perspective of the trainees. The future transferability and generalization of the training experience should be emphasized (Mullen & Gorman, 1972). The keen observer may have noted that the principles articulated here are similar to the guidelines for training found in a number of textbooks (Goldstein, 1986; McGehee & Thayer, 1961; Wexley & Latham, 1981). The principles of training are similar, regardless of the adult population that is targeted. While the points of emphasis may vary, a trainer who is well schooled in the principles of effective program development is already quite knowledgeable about the techniques appropriate for training adults.

Improved Training Methods: The Cognitive Aging Tradition

In the last fifteen or so years, cognitive training research on older adults has focused on the question of cognitive potential in adulthood. The emphasis has been on the potential for adults and older adults to profit from educational and training experiences. There has been new information to support continuing abilities to learn in adults and older adults and continuing growth or stability of many dimensions of intelligence (Sterns & Sanders, 1980; Willis, 1985, 1987). This section briefly looks at examples of past work and new research. We explore how the new approaches can influence our work in training and education.

In summarizing much current work on differences in learning, memory, and problem solving, Poon (1985, 1987) sees a positive picture for healthy, community-dwelling older adults. Older adults tend to be slower and to have more problems with learning new information. This appears to be true with respect to their own performance when they were younger as well as with respect to the performance of younger adults. Some of the decline may be related to learning and individual-difference variables, rather than to chronological age. A number of findings indicate that being old may not be the reason for one's being a poor learner.

Environmental, biomedical, cognitive, and psychological factors can influence learning and memory. Intelligence, educational level, motivation, familiarity with materials, cognitive and learning styles, demands of the learning task, rate of information presentation, and inter- and intratask interference can all affect learning efficiency. The health of the learner can also influence these processes. Taking account of the variables associated with learning, Poon, Krauss, and Bowles (1984) indicate that the chronological age of the learner may have no significant influence on performance.

Older adults may not have been involved in learning new information on a regular basis, and they may not have been involved in education or training experiences. Thus, learning strategies are not well practiced. When older adults are given the opportunity to engage in continuous activity in a particular area, however, age may be irrelevant. The emerging research literature on expertise (Charness, 1985; Rybash, Hoyer, & Roodin, 1986; Salthouse, 1987) advances the idea that practicing experts in a field probably maintain their learning efficiency in that field over their life spans (Poon, 1987).

Expertise is defined as the extremely high level of skill that occurs as a consequence of experience in a given domain. Practice and training are seen as systematic ways of providing experience. Training is distinguished from practice in that an attempt is made to control the nature of experience acquisition, while there is little direction and/or control in practice situations. Training and practice are similar in that both attempt to change the quality and quantity of an individual's experience (Salthouse, 1987). When we conceptualize experience in this task-specific or domain-restricted manner, we have the opportunity to separate the effects of age and the effects of experience. It becomes possible to examine the outcome on cognition of experience with a specific activity.

Research has indicated that expertise in a given domain is associated with more extensive declarative (factual) knowledge and procedural ("how to") knowledge. This knowledge is better organized in experts than in novices. There appear to be more automatic connections between the perceptual (or pattern-recognizing) processes and the procedural (or response) processes among the more skilled individuals (Salthouse, 1987). Effects of practice or expertise are found at all levels of cognitive activities. The benefits of experience seem to be so pervasive that they can be found in nearly all stages or components of information processing (Salthouse, 1987).

Salthouse also emphasizes that it is extremely difficult to provide quantities of experience that come close to approaching what is encountered in daily life, or in most occupational situations: "Very few experimental studies have been reported in which age differences have been examined after five hours of practice—which might be considered to be equivalent to a single day on a new job. Furthermore, there have apparently been no studies in which performance of young or old adults was contrasted after the equivalent of one month's experience, approximately one hundred hours; and yet in many occupations, people would be still considered rank novices after only a month on the job" (Salthouse, 1987, p. 142).

Recent reviews of the effects of age and experience on job performance (Davies & Sparrow, 1985) suggest that there is little overall consistency in outcomes. Type of job, specific performance measures, and level of experience all seem relevant. Murrell, Powesland, and Forsaith (1962) compared inexperienced adults in their twenties with inexperienced workers in their fifties. The task was aiming an industrial drill. Age-related deficits in speed of performance were evident among the inexperienced adults. Experienced workers in their fifties were just as fast as experienced workers in their twenties. Murrell and Humphries (1978) examined simultaneous translation as a task. They found that young novices were superior to old novices, while older professional translators performed at the same level as young professional translators. Such studies indicate that experience may compensate for age-related changes. There may be selective survival, however—"survival of the fittest." An older worker who remains on the job may be more competent than a contemporary who has left the same occupation. This confound presents a problem for age-by-experience interaction, but it does show that there are older workers who continue to be good performers. The relationship between experience and age-related changes does not specify the mechanisms or processes that are used to achieve compensation (Salthouse, 1987).

Salthouse (1984, 1987) has developed what he calls the Motor Equivalence–Motor Decomposition Strategy. This approach involves selecting a sample of adults from a wide range of ages who demonstrate a wide range of proficiency on some motor activity. The motor activity is decomposed into molecular processes (such as reaction time), and age trends are examined for each process. Adults of different ages who are equal on a motor proficiency are then studied. It becomes possible to determine how people of different ages, and different degrees of competence in molecular processes, are able to perform at the same level on the motor activity. The investigator can determine what compensatory mechanisms are used by older adults to overcome deficits that may accompany aging. In a groundbreaking experiment, Salthouse (1984) reported that typing speed did not decline with age, even though tapping rates and reaction time did. He proposed the idea of an adaptive mechanism on the part of older typists to plan ahead by using larger eye-hand spans. This adaptation allowed older typists to anticipate characters earlier than younger typists did.

Expertise research will provide new opportunities to understand underlying processes and will provide new sources for the design of effective training programs. What is becoming even more apparent is that expertise gained over years of experience can no longer be valued, given the change to new computer-controlled production approaches. At the same time, new technologies demand new kinds of expertise, and there is great concern about how the new expertise will be achieved (Zuboff, 1988). We also need to develop a better understanding of the relationship between people's work experience and their cognitive functioning. Strategies used by successful older managers have been studied, and the studies indicate that older managers continue to perform well even while they show age-related cognitive change (Rebok, Offerman, Wirtz, & Montaglione, 1986).

The use of cognitive approaches, such as crystallized and fluid intelligence, have led us to understand the differential changes that may be taking place in individuals (Willis, 1985). Some older workers may be showing gains in crystallized ability—gaining information, knowledge, job-relevant skills, and expertise. They may be simultaneously sharing a stabilization or decline in fluid abilities—the more basic perceptual performance aspects of intellectual behavior. Whether changes in fluid or crystallized intelligence are relevant to a particular job must be assessed. One of the biggest issues for future research is the need to tie specific cognitive attributes to actual work performance. We now realize that many developmental changes may be irrelevant to work situations. The critical factor seems to be understanding what is required in a particular job situation and then finding out whether an individual possesses the necessary skills or can learn them. Research on intelligence and aging has shown not only that there are minimal declines but also that some individuals may actually show gains into their sixties and seventies. Most individuals remain stable, but some do decline. We need to be able to identify the individuals who show important cognitive changes. If cognitive decline is relevant to job performance, then individuals in decline should not be selected for particular situations.

One thing that has characterized our changing thinking in the 1970s and the 1980s is research that demonstrates continued cognitive growth and development well into late older adulthood. The idea that there is an optimal point in the life span for acquiring information is really no longer acceptable.

Another important area of research deals with learning and memory. There are individuals who, with increasing age, may show different speeds of learning and information acquisition. Very often, differences within age groups are greater than differences between age groups, in terms of ability levels. It is now inappropriate to believe that we are unable to provide training situations for older people, but it may take older people longer to learn. The evidence is quite clear that older adults may require longer training and may make more errors. Once they have reached proficiency, however, they may be able to perform at the same level as younger individuals.

Current Research on Training Adults and Older Adults

The need for studies of training methods appropriate to older adult learners has been apparent. We need such studies, if we are to stimulate training and retraining efforts. Computer training represents one of the major areas of concern. Although it is clear that older adults can be retrained, specific research in training approaches should emphasize task analysis and use paradigms shown to be successful with older adults. There is a need to understand component processes, as well as the nature of any difficulty experienced by older workers that may be different from difficulty among younger trainees. Until recently, few studies have been designed with this emphasis in mind.

One of the best recent examples of well-done applied research is Elias, Elias, Robbins, and Gage (1987). This study intended to determine whether there were age differences in the speed and performance levels achieved with a basic word-processing training program. A major focus of the study was identifying sources of difficulty encountered by older persons during training and at completion. The study was designed specifically to evaluate the performance of older (fifty-five to sixty-seven), middle-aged (thirty-seven to forty-eight), and younger (eighteen to twenty-eight) female subjects under training conditions that have been shown to be optimal for older workers. Task analysis was used to identify areas of training (Egan & Gomez, 1985). Self-pacing and the availability of a trainer who could answer questions were incorporated into the design. The study used a widely available commercial word-processing program representative of the type of software available to computer customers. The program included both an audiotape and a training manual. Training consisted of sessions of approximately three and one-half hours each. Subjects had to meet screening requirements for typing speed, a personnel test, and a reading and spelling test. A learning efficiency test was also given. In sessions 2, 3, and 4, subjects went through the formal training program. Session 5 provided the opportunity to bring all of the subjects up to a standard level of word-processing proficiency and to obtain measures of the number of times necessary to reach this level. Subjects were trained to process a two-page document until all word-processing commands had been executed correctly and all errors were eliminated. Sessions 6 and 7 provided subjects with an evaluation of their skills.

Subjects were then required to input, edit, and (as necessary) reedit and print a seven-page document that used a large variety of commands and procedures learned during training. In the final task, assigned after seven sessions, subjects were given hard copies and standard disk versions of the document and asked to make all editorial changes on the disk and to output corrected versions. Trainers evaluated the subjects and documented number and content of assists required and time to complete each segment of training and testing.

With one exception, all time measurements revealed that the older group took significantly longer to complete training and evaluation than the younger and middle-aged groups, which did not differ from each other.

Printouts from training and evaluation sessions were scored for errors of omission (for example, transpositions, insertions of inappropriate letters or words) and word-processing command errors (for example, improper tabs and block movements). Overall error rate was found to be low for all subjects. The total number of errors for evaluation-session printouts was used to produce a score for each type of error. There were no significant age effects for omission, commission, or command errors.

During training, there were significant age effects for commission errors in lessons 2 and 3. Middle-aged and older groups had significantly more commission errors than the younger group did, but they did not differ between themselves for lesson 2. The older group had significantly more commission errors than the younger and middle-aged groups, who did not differ from each other in lesson 3.

The older group's performance was significantly poorer than that of the younger and middle-aged groups on a review examination that tested their knowledge of word-processing commands and techniques. There was an item analysis of outcomes that allowed for specific targeting of problem areas and future training design. Older subjects required more help from the trainer than either the middle-aged or younger groups did; those groups did not differ from each other.

The most important outcome of this study was that all

participants, regardless of age, did learn the fundamentals of word processing, as was indicated by the final outputs of the evaluation documents. Error rates for evaluation documents were found to be low, and all of the necessary commands had been executed. Age differences were found for time to complete the subunits of training and evaluation sessions: Older subjects took longer.

The study used a training approach that involved self-paced, trainer-assisted methods to promote older adults' success and provide a supportive learning environment. Even under these conditions, older subjects required many more interventions, and this contributed to the longer times for older adults to complete the program. Assistance to the older adults was often initiated by the trainer. When older subjects were perseverating on erroneous commands or procedures or did not understand the material, assistance would be given. Training could well have taken longer without such assistance. The information retained by older persons for the review examination was not equivalent to that retained by younger or middle-aged persons.

Hartley, Hartley, and Johnson (1984) also investigated word-processing training with older (sixty-five to seventy-five) and younger (eighteen to thirty) subjects. A word-processing program (EDITOR) was written that made it possible to record user action and the time taken to select and execute word-processing commands. Computer-assisted instruction was used to present concepts, functions, examples, practice exercises, and editing problems. Results of an initial study showed that older adults were able to carry out word-processing commands and solve related problems. After twelve hours of instruction (six two-hour sessions), there were no differences between older and younger learners in recall of information. No differences were found in the correctness and efficiency with which computer operations were carried out. Older adults took longer to select and carry out the appropriate procedures. Older adults also required more assistance while carrying out editing tasks. The major conclusion of this research is that older adults' use of word-processing information is somewhat slower and somewhat less effective than that of younger adults. Access to assistance during learning facilitates performance in older adults, especially during the early phases. The study suggests that, with appropriate training, older adults will be successful.

Valasek (1988) developed a program of instruction on the use of a computer terminal. The program was based on task analysis, rather than on the standard, commercially available program for microcomputers. A self-paced program provided practice on each component and gradually added new tasks as old ones were mastered. An enhanced-training condition was developed. Enhancement modules encouraged older workers to deal with fears about the computer, fears about learning, and methods of memorization. The enhanced modules were designed to increase self-efficacy expectations and promote a positive attitude toward the computer.

The subjects were 124 adults recruited from the community. They had no previous experience with computers. Each subject participated in one training session, conducted in small groups. Age groups were twenty-five to thirty-nine and fifty to sixty-five. For each age bracket, an enhanced-training group and a control group were tested. The control group read an article on the history of the microchip and answered questions. If subjects performed correctly on three items in a row, the training program went on to the next task. There were nineteen training tasks grouped into four training categories. The task-analysis training program designed for this research appeared beneficial for older as well as younger adults. It eliminated almost all need on the part of younger adults to question the trainer. An unexpected outcome of this research was that the enhanced training condition did not produce a significant difference from the control condition, either for young or for older subjects. Total training-time measures indicated that the young group's mean was significantly different from the mean of the older group. Total posttest time indicated that the older subjects were significantly slower than younger subjects. An extensive analysis was possible for all training responses. Younger adults demonstrated significantly shorter training-item response times. Older adults had longer training times, partially due to their using more items to reach the criterion. Younger adults got significantly more items correct on the posttest. Use of keys, sign-on procedures, and generalized items were more difficult for older subjects. There was no age difference on the posttest for fixing common errors or making insertions and deletions. A major finding was that even in a training situation designed to maximize older adults' performance, age differences still existed. It is possible to identify problem areas and to focus revised training on these areas, although we will not discuss this process here. Real value is trial-by-trial data with the potential to help develop a new training design.

The training approach worked well for younger adults. We now need to develop additional training, to further assist older adults. One important result was that there were 15 percent more correct responses from younger than from older adults. Sample and post-training speed for the younger group was 33 percent better. A major question is whether, if there were additional training time for a valued older employee, these differences would be meaningful in a practical sense.

Another recent study focused on the most effective training method for imparting computer skills (Gist, Schwoerer, & Rosen, 1988). In this study, 146 adults volunteered to participate in one of four conditions: under forty-five years old, behavior-modeling condition; under forty-five years old, computer-tutorial condition; over forty-five years old, behavior-modeling condition; and over forty-five years old, computer-tutorial condition. This was a three-hour training program. The researchers' hypothesis was that, by watching a model handle each step of the computer task, trainees might develop confidence in their ability to master it. It was predicted that the behavior-modeling format would be particularly helpful to older trainees.

The computer-tutorial condition had subjects complete exercises and solve problems on the computer. Each exercise required trainees to perform various software functions and provided immediate feedback on performance. Trainees set their own pace. The behavior-modeling condition had subjects observe a videotape that showed a middle-aged male demonstrating the use of a spreadsheet software program. The model sat before a computer, described each step, and enacted the appropriate procedure. The results of his actions were shown on his computer terminal. After each demonstration, the tape was stopped, and participants practiced the procedure and received immediate feedback. On a posttest, younger subjects performed at a higher level than older subjects. Under both conditions, the behavior-modeling approach was found to be in the predicted direction for both the older and the younger group; the age and training interaction was not significant, however. It was clear that older adults did not do so well in a training situation designed to improve their performance. The use of a model to demonstrate the proper execution of each task enhanced learning for both groups. This study was self-paced, but all subjects worked under a three-hour time constraint, which may have limited the performance of the older group.

Thus, it has been shown that an important issue related to aging and training is the difference in training time needed by different individuals. Given knowledgeable employees who have performed well in many other areas, would we not want to take extra time to provide them training in word processing? What is the magnitude of that training difference — an extra day? an extra week? an extra two weeks? What is the trade-off, given the person's commitment and other knowledge? In reality, we have not yet fully explored the effectiveness of training procedures, nor have we determined whether time is critical. So far, the research on training older adults to use computers shows that older adults do have greater difficulty. Part of the explanation may be that the training programs were not well designed and that the environment was not supportive. As we have seen in the recent studies just reviewed, however, there continue to be age-related differences in skills acquisition, even with well-developed training approaches. The question is how to improve training still more. (In the past, such training efforts would not have been tried at all.)

To understand the training process better, we need to have a better understanding of the motivations of older learners. What is the attitude of the individual going into the training program? Is this a positive program? Is this a positive situation for the trainees? Do they feel good about engaging in new training activities, or are they afraid of failure?

In our writing, we have drawn on self-concept, self-efficiency, and growth-needs strength as relevant dimensions. These factors are probably important in determining the level of functioning and success of a training program. Our analysis of these training situations agrees with many of the earlier conclusions discussed by the Belbins in their industrial training situations. Sensitivity on the part of corporate trainers to middle-aged and older individuals continues to need further development.

Government programs, such as CETA, have often used on-the-job training. How well has this approach worked with middle-aged and older workers? Is there the opportunity for instruction and reinforcement of behavior, or are these training situations highly discouraging? Very often, individuals who have been assigned to train or supervise new people use their position to foment a power relationship. As a result, an on-the-job trainer may consciously or unconsciously withhold information that is directly relevant to the success or failure of the trainee. We have seen this happen in offices that have brought in new word-processing equipment, and the individual who has the first and highest level of mastery is very often in a controlling situation; how much of the information he or she is willing to share with other individuals becomes a factor. Often the success or failure of another person coming into that office is directly related to how much sharing of information that particular individual is willing to do. Some of the power relationships and dynamics in the work situation may include not sharing information and not training; at best, the results of the on-the-job training situation are difficult to document, and they depend on the people involved. It has already been established that older workers may have greater difficulty, even under optimal conditions. We have no research on older adults under adverse learning conditions; such conditions may not allow older workers to be successful.

There is another issue that is not often discussed in the training literature: the importance of individual, self-determined, self-paced training. Many individuals take on major learning tasks relevant to their job of their own volition. This striking out by employees to learn things on their own may be a very important dimension that has been underrepresented in our discussions of industrial training.

Conclusions

A small number (10 to 20 percent) of people of retirement age, and a growing number of people now in middle age, want to work into their seventies and beyond. This group of older adult workers represents a talented group of people who will be able to continue functioning, do a good job, and be very competitive with younger workers. A select group of today's retirement-age older adults will be excellent models for the emerging middle-aged work force. This group will continue to be competitive and is characterized by its continual updating of skills, excellent work habits, and sophistication in working with other people. These people will be strong contributors as long as they choose to work. They are the survivors with expertise.

Since new skills often become obsolete after five years, because of technological changes, updating the skills of a fifty-five-year-old, who has ten or fifteen more years of employment, represents a benefit to the company that is equal to updating the skills of a twenty-year-old. Both employees' skills will continue to need updating every five years. Whether someone is twenty, thirty, forty, fifty, or sixty is irrelevant; everyone can benefit from training to stay productive and use new skills. We need to determine how middle-aged and older workers themselves view the educational situation and their potential within it. Some middle-aged and older workers continue to work in law, medicine, engineering, and other areas; they are skilled professionals, with high levels of expertise, who continue to learn and remain sources of information for people of all ages. Other middle-aged and older professionals carry out their jobs in a very acceptable fashion but perhaps need to have newer perspectives or updated skills before they can function at a higher level. What is their attitude about training and retraining? Because of social conditioning, many older people do not feel so able to carry out or participate in training and retraining activities as they once may have. It is important to sensitize managers to workers' potential and to be aware that managers may be discriminating against middle-aged and older workers by not providing adequate and well-designed training and retraining programs.

References

Avolio, B. J., & Barrett, G. V. (1987). Effects of age stereotyping in a simulated interview. *Psychology and Aging, 2,* 56–115.

Avolio, B. J., Barrett, G. V., & Sterns, H. L. (1984). Alternative to age for assessing occupational performance capacity. *Experimental Aging Research, 10,* 101–105.

Baltes, P. B., Reese, H. W., & Lipsitt, L. P. (1980). Life-span developmental psychology. *Annual Review of Psychology, 31,* 65–110.

Barkin, S. (1970). Retraining and job redesign: Positive approaches to the continued employment of older persons. In H. L. Sheppard (Ed.), *Toward an industrial gerontology.* Cambridge, MA: Schenkman.

Basseches, M. (1986). Cognitive structural development and the conditions of employment. *Human Development, 29,* 101–112.

Belbin, E., & Belbin, R. M. (1968). New careers in middle age. In B. Newgarten (Ed.), *Middle age and aging: A reader in social psychology* (pp. 341–350). Chicago: University of Chicago Press.

Belbin, E., & Belbin, R. M. (1972). *Problems in adult retraining.* London, England: Heineman.

Belbin, E., Belbin, R. M., & Hill, F. (1957). A comparison between the results of three different methods of operator training. *Ergonomics, 1,* 39–50.

Belbin, E., & Downs, S. M. (1964). Activity learning and the older worker. *Ergonomics, 7,* 429–437.

Belbin, E., & Downs, S. M. (1966). Teaching paired associates: The problem of age. *Occupational Psychology, 40,* 67–74.

Belbin, E., & Shimmin, S. (1964). Training the middle-aged for inspection work. *Occupational Psychology, 38,* 49–57.

Belbin, R. M. (1969). Industrial gerontology: Origins, issues, and applications in Europe. *Industrial Gerontology, 1,* 12–25.

Belbin, R. M. (1970). The discovery method in training older workers. In H. L. Sheppard (Ed.), *Toward an industrial gerontology* (pp. 56–60). Cambridge, MA: Schenkman.

Bird, C. P., & Fisher, T. D. (1986). Thirty years later: Attitudes toward the employment of older workers. *Journal of Applied Psychology, 71,* 515–517.

Birren, J. E., & Stafford, J. I. (1986). Changes in the organization of behavior with age. In J. E. Birren, P. K. Robinson, & S. E. Livingston (Eds.), *Age, health, and employment* (pp. 1–26). Englewood Cliffs, NJ: Prentice-Hall.

Bornstein, J. M. (1986). Retraining the older worker: Michigan experience with senior employment service. *Journal of Career Development, 13,* 14–22.

Charness, N. (1985). Aging and problem-solving performance. In N. Charness (Ed.), *Aging and human performance* (pp. 225–259). New York: Wiley.

Cleveland, J. N., & Landy, F. J. (1981). The influence of rater and ratee age on two performance judgments. *Personnel Psychology, 34,* 19–34.

Cleveland, J. N., & Landy, F. J. (1983). The effect of person and job stereotypes on two personnel decisions. *Journal of Applied Psychology, 68,* 609–619.

Cross, K. P. (1981). *Adults as learners: Increasing participation and facilitating learning.* San Francisco: Jossey-Bass.

Davies, D. R., & Sparrow, P. R. (1985). Age and work behavior. In N. Charness (Ed.), *Aging and human performance* (pp. 293–332). New York: Wiley.

Downs, S., & Roberts, A. (1977). The training of underground train guards: A case study with a field experiment. *Journal of Occupational Psychology, 50,* 111–120.

Egan, D. E., & Gomez, L. M. (1985). Assaying, isolating, and accommodating individual differences in learning a complex skill. In R. F. Dillon (Ed.), *Individual differences in cognition* (pp. 173–217). San Diego, CA: Academy Press.

Elias, P. K., Elias, M. F., Robbins, M. A., & Gage, P. (1987). Acquisition of word-processing skills by younger, middle-aged, and older adults. *Psychology and Aging, 2,* 340–348.

Fossum, J. A., Arvey, R. D., Paradise, C. A., & Robbins, N. E. (1986). Modeling the skills obsolescence process: A psychological/economic integration. *Academy of Management Review, 11,* 362–374.

Gist, M., Schwoerer, C., & Rosen, B. (1988). The influence of training methods and trainee age on the acquisition of computer skills. *Personnel Psychology, 41,* 255–266.

Goldstein, I. L. (1986). *Training in organizations: Needs assessment, development, and evaluation* (2nd ed.). Monterey, CA: Brooks/Cole.

Gordon, R. A., & Arvey, R. D. (1986). Perceived and actual ages of workers. *Journal of Vocational Behavior, 28,* 21–28.

Gordon, M. E., Cofer, J. L., & McCullough, P. M. (1986). Relationships among seniority, past performance, interjob similarity, and trainability. *Journal of Applied Psychology, 71,* 518–521.

Hansen, G. B. (1984). Ford and the UAW have a better idea: A joint labor-management approach to plant closings and worker retraining. *Annals of the American Academy of Political and Social Science, 475,* 158–174.

Hardin, E., & Borus, M. (1971). *The economic benefits and costs of retraining.* Lexington, MA: Heath.

Hartley, A. A., Hartley, J. T., & Johnson, S. A. (1984). The older adult as computer user. In P. K. Robinson, J. Livingston, & J. E. Birren (Eds.), *Aging and technological advances* (pp. 347–348). New York: Plenum.

Jakubauskas, E. B., & Taylor, V. (1969). On-the-job training and reemployment of the older worker. *Industrial Gerontology, 2,* 10–18.

Latham, G. P. (1988). Human resource training and development. *Annual Review of Psychology, 39,* 545–582.

McFarland, R. A. (1973). The need for functional age measurements in industrial gerontology. *Industrial Gerontology, 19*, 1–19.

McGehee, W., & Thayer, P. W. (1961). *Training in business and industry*. New York: Wiley.

Mullen, C., & Gorman, L. (1972). Facilitating adaptation to change: A case study in retraining middle-aged and older workers at Aer Lingus. *Industrial Psychology, 15*, 23–29.

Murrell, K. F. H., & Humphries, S. (1978). Age, experience, and short-term memory. In M. M. Gruneberg, P. E. Morris, & R. N. Sykes (Eds.), *Practical aspects of memory* (pp. 363–365). Orlando, FL: Academic Press.

Murrell, K. F. H., Powesland, P. F., & Forsaith, B. (1962). A study of pillar-drilling in relation to age. *Occupational Psychology, 36*, 45–52.

Neale, J. G., Toye, M. H., & Belbin, E. (1968). Adult training: The use of programmed instruction. *Occupational Psychology, 42*, 23–31.

Patchett, M. B., & Sterns, H. L. (1984, February). *Career progression in middle and later adulthood*. Paper presented at tenth annual meeting of the Association for Gerontology in Higher Education, Indianapolis.

Pond, S. B., & Geyer, P. D. (1987). Employee age as a moderator of the relations between perceived work alternatives and job satisfaction. *Journal of Applied Psychology, 72*, 552–557.

Poon, L. W. (1985). Differences in human memory with aging: Nature, causes, and clinical implications. In J. E. Birren & K. W. Schaie (Eds.), *Handbook of the psychology of aging* (pp. 427–455). New York: Van Nostrand Reinhold.

Poon, L. W. (1987). Learning. In G. L. Maddox (Ed.), *The encyclopedia of aging* (pp. 380–381). New York: Springer.

Poon, L. W., Krauss, I., & Bowles, N. L. (1984). On subject selection in cognitive aging research. *Experimental Aging Research, 10*, 43–49.

Rebok, G. W., Offerman, L. R., Wirtz, P. W., & Montaglione, C. J. (1986). Work and intellectual aging: The psychological concomitants of social-organizational conditions. *Educational Gerontology, 12*, 359–374.

Rhodes, S. R. (1983). Age-related differences in work attitudes and behaviors: A review and conceptual analysis. *Psychological Bulletin, 93*, 328–367.

Robertson, I., & Downs, S. (1979). Learning and prediction of performance: Development of trainability testing in the United Kingdom. *Journal of Applied Psychology, 64*, 42–50.

Rosen, B., & Jerdee, T. H. (1976). The nature of job-related stereotypes. *Journal of Applied Psychology, 61*, 180–183.

Rosen, B., & Jerdee, T. H. (1978). The influence of age stereotypes on managerial decisions. *Journal of Applied Psychology, 63*, 573–578.

Rybash, J. M., Hoyer, W. J., & Roodin, P. A. (1986). *Adult cognition in aging*. Elmsford, NY: Pergamon Press.

Salthouse, T. A. (1984). Effects of age and skill in typing. *Journal of Experimental Psychology: General, 113*, 345–371.

Salthouse, T. A. (1986). Functional age. In J. E. Birren, P. K. Robinson, & J. E. Livingston (Eds.), *Age, health and employment* (pp. 78–92). Englewood Cliffs, NJ: Prentice-Hall.

Salthouse, T. A. (1987). The role of experience in cognitive aging. *Annual Review of Gerontology and Geriatrics, 7*, 135–158.

Schmidt, F. A., Murphy, M. D., & Sanders, R. (1981). Training older adults' free-recall rehearsal strategies. *Journal of Gerontology, 36*, 329–337.

Schrank, H. T., & Waring, J. M. (1981). Aging and work organizations. In B. B. Hess & K. Bond (Eds.), *Leading edges: Recent research on psychosocial aging* (pp. 91–118). Washington, DC: U.S. Department of Health and Human Services, National Institute on Aging.

Schwab, D. P., & Heneman, H. G., III (1978). Age stereotyping in performance appraisal. *Journal of Applied Psychology, 63*, 573–578.

Sieman, J. R. (1976). Programmed materials as a training tool for older persons. *Industrial Gerontology, 3*, 183–190.

Slater, R., & Kingsley, S. (1976). Predicting age-prejudiced employers: A British pilot study. *Industrial Gerontology, 3*, 121–128.

Snyder, C. J., & Barrett, G. V. (in press). The Age Discrimination in Employment Act: A review of court decisions. *Experimental Aging Research.*

Stagner, R. (1985). Aging in industry. In J. E. Birren & K. W. Schaie (Eds.), *Handbook of the psychology of aging* (pp. 789–817). New York: Van Nostrand Reinhold.

Sterns, H. L. (1986). Training and retraining adult and older adult workers. In J. E. Birren, P. K. Robinson, & J. E. Livingston (Eds.), *Age, health and employment* (pp. 93–113). Englewood Cliffs, NJ: Prentice-Hall.

Sterns, H. L., & Alexander, R. A. (1987). Industrial gerontology: The aging individual and work. *Annual Review of Gerontology and Geriatrics, 7*, 243–264.

Sterns, H., & Doverspike, D. (1988). Training and developing the older worker: Implications for human resource management. In H. Dennis (Ed.), *Fourteen steps to managing an aging workforce* (pp. 97–110). New York: Lexington.

Sterns, H. L., & Patchett, M. (1984). Technology and the aging adult: Career development and training. In P. K. Robinson & J. E. Birren (Eds.), *Aging and Technology* (pp. 261–277). New York: Plenum.

Sterns, H. L., & Sanders, R. (1980). Training and education of the elderly. In R. R. Turner & H. W. Reese (Eds.), *Life-span developmental psychology: Intervention* (pp. 307–331). Orlando, FL: Academic Press.

Valasek, D. C. (1988). *Young/old differences in training and self efficacy on computer skills and computer attitudes.* Unpublished doctoral dissertation, University of Akron, Akron, Ohio.

Weinstein, E., & Mayer, R. E. (1982). The teaching of learning strategies. In M. C. Wittrock (Ed.), *Handbook of research on teaching* (pp. 315–327). New York: Macmillan.

Welford, A. T. (1976). Thirty years of psychological research on age and work. *Journal of Occupational Psychology, 49*, 129–138.

Wexley, K. N., & Latham, G. P. (1981). Developing and training human resources in organizations. Glenview, IL: Scott, Foresman.

Willis, S. L. (1985). Toward an educational psychology of the older adult learner: Intellectual and cognitive bases. In J. E.

Birren & K. W. Schaie (Eds.), *Handbook of the psychology of aging* (pp. 818–847). New York: Van Nostrand Reinhold.

Willis, S. L. (1987). Cognitive training and everyday competence. *Annual Review of Gerontology and Geriatrics, 7,* 159–188.

Zuboff, S. (1988). *In the age of the smart machine.* New York: Basic Books.

9

Retraining Midcareer Workers
for the Future Workplace

Manuel London
Emily Bassman

This chapter examines training and retraining of midcareer employees. The focus is on individual career motivation, career change, and development, as well as on organizational change and human resource requirements. *Training* refers to developing one's current knowledge and skills base. *Retraining* refers to learning new skills and knowledge that prepare an individual for a new career direction. Training and retraining are growing issues for individuals and organizations, because of organizational change (workforce reductions), technological obsolescence and advancements, and individuals' feelings of midlife crisis, career plateauing, and related desires for midcareer change. These reasons for career change are examined in relation to career motivation and directions for continuous learning, personal growth, and development. Adult learning principles are discussed, and alternative training programs are reviewed. Organizational policies for investing in training are examined. The chapter concludes with recommendations for organizational and individual planning for career development and education.

Figure 9.1 outlines components of and relationships between individual and organizational processes affecting training and retraining. These processes are described throughout this chapter. The figure suggests that organizational changes influence midcareer experiences. Individual and organizational changes alike influence such individual characteristics as career motivation. Moreover, career motivation affects how individuals react to organizational events (for example, the extent to which lack of opportunity for advancement is felt to be negative). The organization supports career motivation through supervisory behavior and human resource policies and programs providing rewards, opportunities, performance feedback, and organizational information. Adult learning processes are influenced by both career motivation and organizational support factors. A changing work environment requires continuous learning, the success of which depends on adult learning processes. Also, a continuous learning environment affects opportunities for adult learning. Training provides support for organizational change strategies, which in turn provide the context and encouragement for continuous learning.

Midcareer Change

Midcareer is usually ten to twenty years after the time an individual starts his or her first job. It is often the point at which career development levels off—after the individual has been in the same job for a number of years, in a single functional area, or with the same employer. Midcareer is generally a time when individuals reassess the extent to which their needs and aspirations have been met. It is also a time when they forecast their career potential over the next fifteen to twenty years (Work in America Institute, 1978).

Several social trends are at the heart of the phenomenon of midcareer change. One is the increasing rate of change, making commitment to a lifelong career difficult. Health and economic factors beyond the individual's control may influence career directions and opportunities. Also, as people are living longer, a forty-year work life is a long time to devote to one career. Finally, many people have high expectations for low-level

Figure 9.1. Individual and Organizational Change Processes Affecting Training and Retraining.

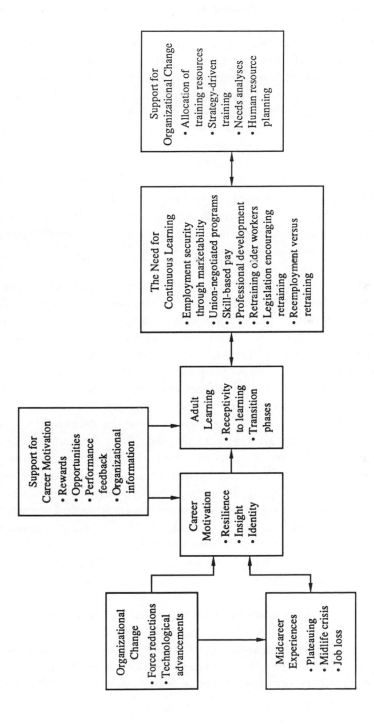

jobs, and for these people, a career change can be an avenue to mobility, self-actualization, and job satisfaction (Leider, 1974).

A recent study suggests that staying with a single company throughout one's career tends to bring less happiness and success than switching jobs ("Switch Rather Than Stew," 1985). The report indicates that five of every six people between the ages of thirty and forty contemplate a career change. Nevertheless, the odds against a successful midcareer shift are high. "To throw away credentials, confidence, and contacts in the hope of finding the equivalent to the Fountain of Youth can harm a person's mental health and destroy financial standings. It is better to be a self-starter, to realize how much latitude there is to explore and to act on worthwhile ideas" (Blotnick, 1985, pp. 140–141).

London and Mone (1987) provide examples of several people who changed careers in midstream: a merchant turned artist, a housewife turned music conservatory director, a college administrator turned corporate manager, an engineer turned cabinetmaker, and a college professor turned market researcher. While in some cases there is transfer of the skills and knowledge of the previous position to the new occupation, the change is still fraught with personal risk. Reeducation can pave the way for the transition by providing the individual with the knowledge and self-confidence to make the change.

Some retraining programs sensitize people to new opportunities and career paths to which skills are transferable and where job and advancement opportunities are better. For example, several university business schools offer one- to two-month programs for Ph.D.s in the humanities and social sciences, to provide them with overviews of finance, marketing, economics, organizational behavior, and other business topics. The programs also offer job placement and counseling services, which give the participants access to job interviews with major corporations. The contacts made with fellow students and professors also form a valuable network for future job openings.

Career Plateauing. Career plateauing is defined as "the point in a career when the likelihood of additional hierarchical promotion is very low" (Ference, Stoner, & Warren, 1977, p. 602).

Personal plateauing occurs when an employee's abilities do not match the needs of the associated career path in the company, and the employee decides not to seek further advancement.

Hall (1985) investigated the attitudes and coping skills of professionals who reached their career plateaus in a corporate engineering department of a large manufacturing organization. He found that plateaued individuals feel a loss of opportunity, flexibility, and job satisfaction, particularly as management becomes top-heavy and engages in more restricted and centralized decision making, and as the workload for professionals begins to decrease. Reactions to plateauing depend on the perceived possibilities for alternative employment outside the company. Attitudes are likely to be more positive when alternatives are available.

Career plateauing does not necessarily affect job performance adversely (Bardwick, 1986). Indeed, the organization's success may depend on the performance of plateaued people who are "solid citizens"—consistently good performers who know how to get things done in the organization. Career plateauing is likely to lead to less organizational commitment, however. Stout, Slocum, and Cron (1987) studied salespeople in an industrial products firm. Employees who *remained plateaued* during the three-year study showed declining commitment to the organization and a greater propensity to leave, and they were less concerned about career issues. Employees who *became plateaued* during the study indicated that they were less marketable and had lower promotional aspirations since they had become plateaued. Employees who *remained nonplateaued* improved their levels of performance, indicated a desire to get promoted, and believed that they had become more marketable.

Plateauing is likely to decrease one's receptivity to training. The employee's attitude may be "What's the point?" If the employee looks forward to career opportunities resulting from retraining, however, plateauing may be viewed as a transition step, and the individual may be highly receptive to learning. Technical career ladders can provide new advancement opportunities for scientists and engineers who want to move into managerial positions (Hall, 1985). Enhanced technical knowledge and professional affiliations are needed to maintain currency in one's field and improve one's expertise. Other ways to alleviate the feelings of being plateaued include rotating among different technical specialties and working on a variety of assignments. Learning opportunities, coupled with new rewards (more money, more responsibility, professional recognition), can renew an individual's career motivation and enhance personal growth and contributions to the organization.

Midlife Crisis. Decision-making power and responsibility peak in importance in the late thirties (Hill & Miller, 1981). Absence of these factors may generate feelings of crisis, which precipitate job change, Noncareer-oriented variables reflecting immediate job, career, and life concerns are at their maximum in the forties. One perspective is that everyone experiences one or more personal crises at some point during a career (Levinson, Darrow, Klein, Levinson, & McKee, 1978; Levinson, 1986). Another perspective is that many people avoid personal crises. They cope with life all along and are able to reevaluate their positions in midlife constructively and accept reality. People who have difficulty committing themselves to major life decisions early in life experience feelings of acute distress or crisis when confronting midlife issues (DuBois, 1981; Vaillant, 1977).

Korman (1988) and Korman and Korman (1980) describe the negative emotions and feelings of personal failure among successful people in mid- to late-career stages. These people experience a sense of alienation and do not use their interests and needs to make choices. This happens to individuals when their expectations are not met, when they are around strong people who control their lives, and when they do not have close friendships.

Organizations can contribute to midlife crisis (London, 1985). For instance, frequent geographical relocation can destroy a marriage. Lack of feedback from the boss may make it difficult to set realistic career goals and evaluate the extent to which they are accomplished. Little reinforcement for tasks well done makes it hard to have a positive self-image. Lack of opportunity for advancement discourages advancement motivation.

Lack of job challenge discourages work involvement. Not providing employees with the knowledge, skills, or experiences to handle organizational change or new technology is another potential cause of crisis.

Job Loss. A major reason for retraining and subsequent career change is losing one's position. Whether precipitated by the individual's actions (low performance, high absenteeism) or corporate cutbacks (often accomplished by laying off poor performers first), the experience is a blow to one's self-confidence.

Indeed, many people have described job loss as the most devastating experience of their lives (Leana & Feldman, 1988). People lose not only their paychecks but also their social contacts, a regular structure for the day, and a connection with goals and a sense of larger purpose (Latack & Kaufman, 1988). Unless the individual finds new work, he or she is likely to withdraw from activities, including the search for work. Outplacement activities sponsored by the employer are aimed at rebuilding the employee's self-confidence, providing information and structure for setting goals in line with career interests and capabilities, and developing career identity through action plans.

Career Motivation and Midcareer Change

The concept of career motivation may help explain midcareer feelings and reactions and receptivity to training and retraining. London (1983, 1985, 1988), London and Bray (1984), and London and Mone (1987) define career motivation as a multidimensional concept with three principal domains: career resilience, career insight, and career identity.

> *Career resilience* is the extent to which people resist career barriers or disruptions affecting their work. People who are high in career resilience see themselves as competent individuals able to control what happens to them. They get a sense of accomplishment from what they do. They are able to take risks. They also know when and how to cooperate

with others and when to act independently. Career resilience determines a person's persistence in obtaining career goals.

Career insight is how realistic people are about themselves and their careers and how accurately they relate these perceptions to their career goals. People who are high in career insight try to understand themselves and their environment. They look for feedback about how well they are doing, and they set specific career goals and formulate plans to achieve them. Their career insight is thus likely to affect the degree to which they pursue career goals.

Career identity is the extent to which people define themselves by their work. People who are high in career identity are involved in their jobs, their careers, and their professions, and they are likely to feel loyal to their employers. Career identity reflects the direction of career goals — whether a person wants to advance in the company, to be in a position of leadership, to have high status, to make money, and to accomplish these goals as soon as possible (London & Mone, 1987, p. 54).

Developing Career Motivation. Career resilience is probably fairly well established for most people by the time they start their careers. It stems from reinforcements received from early childhood and adolescence. For instance, our self-confidence, an element of career resilience, is likely to rise when we are positively rewarded for our decisions and actions. Because career resilience starts early in life does not mean that it cannot change; work experiences support or discourage career resilience. For instance, supervisors reinforce their subordinates' career resilience by giving them feedback on their performance, praising them for what they do well, providing opportunities for achievement, and rewarding innovative behavior, without undue punishment for failure.

Training may also support career resilience. Enhancing an individual's skills and knowledge is likely to build self-confidence and the desire to achieve. Conversely, level of re-silience is likely to influence receptivity to training. Midcareer individuals who have low self-confidence and a low desire to achieve and take risks are likely to doubt their abilities to learn and apply the new knowledge to improving their career opportunities.

Career insight and identity stem from the information people receive about themselves and the environment, what they see others doing, and what they are likely to be rewarded for doing. Insight develops as people experiment with different career goals. They explore the environment, make some tentative choices, and see how others react. This exploration continues into adulthood when people actually try different careers by taking courses in various fields and trying different jobs or assignments. Career identity develops as people receive feedback about themselves, the political and social environment, and job opportunities.

The accuracy of information people receive about career opportunities is important to their career choices. People who receive more accurate, complete, and useful information about a job choice are likely to have lower turnover than those who receive inaccurate, irrelevant, or incomplete information (Caldwell & O'Reilly, 1985; Wanous, 1981). Training is a major source of career insight, in terms of both self-understanding and subject-matter knowledge.

Career identity develops over time, as people commit themselves to career directions. The longer one stays in a job, or the longer one works for a company, the more likely one is to identify with work in the organization. One element of career identity is how much a person wants success. Organizations enhance a success-oriented identity by the opportunities made available and the rewards offered and received. For instance, placing a new employee in a manager development program for high-potential individuals is likely to increase the employee's identification with the organization and enhance the importance of work in his or her life.

Patterns of Career Motivation. Career resilience sets the foundation for developing career insight, which in turn contributes to establishing a meaningful and successful career identity—that is, self-confident, achievement-oriented people who are willing to take some risks are likely to obtain and accept information about themselves and the environment. Moreover, they are likely to place themselves in situations that test their abilities and provide them with feedback on their performance.

Redirection is a pattern that signifies career adjustments. People may become bored or feel that they could accomplish more. They may lose a job or work in a company that has few advancement opportunities. They may feel like runners-up. A solid foundation of resilience is likely to prompt exploration of alternatives in midcareer. Alternatively, resilience may lead an individual to adjust his or her career expectations to match reality and ultimately be content with modest goals.

Intervening self-doubt is a pattern that occurs when people experience failure, and the negative feedback is so severe that they question their abilities. Their resilience is shaken; they feel like misfits. Some people who experience self-doubt may make a major career change, such as switching jobs or quitting work to return to school. Such a change may restore their belief in themselves. Others become mired in self-doubt and depression—a likely response to job loss and being out of work for a long time (Leana & Feldman, 1988).

Individuals break away from ineffective patterns as they experience small successes. Over time, they begin to feel better about themselves, and they establish new, realistic goals. Training for such people, especially those who have experienced such a major setback as job loss, must provide the positive reinforcement to build resilience and must offer the information and opportunities to generate realistic career insight and, ultimately, a renewed sense of career identity.

Training That Supports Career Resilience, Insight, and Identity. Classroom training, on-the-job training, special training assignments, and other forums for learning can reinforce and support the domains of career motivation. For instance, career resilience may be promoted by such experiences as chairing a special task force or committee or attending an executive development program. The training demonstrates to the individual that he or she can succeed in a challenging situation. It also demonstrates to the individual that the organization and the supervisor have confidence in him or her.

Training contributes to career insight by allowing individuals to test their abilities and develop better understanding of their strengths, weaknesses, and interests. In addition, self-assessment programs and assessment centers help people analyze present career satisfaction, understand career changes they may face, evaluate their skills and interests, gather information about career opportunities, and identify realistic goals and action plans that increase the likelihood of success.

Training programs support career identity by demonstrating the rewards from alternative career pursuits and helping the individual to envision the future and obtain a sense of self-renewal. Some companies have experimented with programs to foster new insights and new identities. Polaroid, Xerox, and IBM offer employees time off, with pay, to participate in community action projects, research, special scientific endeavors, and government programs. Of course, the risk of such sabbaticals is that a person may not want to return to work. The potential benefit, however, is a renewed sense of purpose and direction in one's life.

Adult Learning Processes

Training in the mid- and late-career stages requires a consideration of adult learning processes. People learn throughout their lifetimes. Unlike children in school, adults have had time to develop intellectually and emotionally. They have formed bad habits, as well as good ones. They have had the time to practice what they learned. Adults learn the knowledge and skills for which they perceive a need (Fisher, 1985). Adults learn best by doing. They need to know what they are doing and how well they are doing it. Adults also need to be able to integrate new ideas and skills with what they already know, if they are to retain and use the new learning.

The key to successful adult learning may be appropriate

activities, materials, procedures, and environmental conditions. Job training is especially effective if the trainee's financial concerns are removed, via continuation of salary and benefits and the guarantee of a job at the end of training. Adults seem to learn better when discovering for themselves the answers to problems, as opposed to following traditional classroom methods that emphasize oral communication. They also learn better when they have an opportunity to design and structure the learning experiences for themselves (Belbin, 1958; Belbin, 1970; Fisher, 1985).

While training must be planned, the structure can be flexible. The learners can be asked to describe their objectives for the training (for example, the requirements of the tasks they are about to learn). They can be asked to state the purpose of the material they will learn, in terms of the benefits to themselves, their customers, their co-workers, or the company. Using self-assessment, students can articulate their present abilities in terms of what they need to know.

Overall, then, the midcareer learning environment should encourage trial-and-error experimentation, allow students to restructure the process, impose change and challenge, and offer support for learning through feedback and rewards for success. Training methods that accomplish this include learning on the job, analyzing business cases in a classroom setting, and simulations (London, 1988).

Change Stimulates Learning Receptivity. A career change stimulates a person's motivation to learn, because a real or perceived gap is likely to exist between the individual's skills, tools, and confidence and the demands of a new job (Van Velsor & Musselwhite, 1986). Many firms take advantage of such career transitions—for instance, at the time of hiring and promotion—to socialize employees to the values of the organization and to educate them on behavior the organization deems critical for people at that level (for example, the importance of spending time developing subordinates). Supervisory training may become a mandatory initiation rite after a promotion.

Periods of self-doubt and personal examination are also

times for learning. Feelings of crisis may accompany such events as marriage and family problems, job loss, doubts about career progress, and organizational stress (such as corporate re-organization). Leadership development training often includes time and resources for self-reflection, counseling, and career planning, and corporate-sponsored career-planning programs usually offer these tools before steering an individual into training or retraining.

While change stimulates learning, other conditions are necessary to sustain learning. A study that followed the learning of forty-three managers over two years found that managers in changing situations were likely to learn if the change resulted in ambiguity in their goals and if their supervisors pressured them to excel (Lowy, Kelleher, & Finestone, 1986). This also led to feelings of stress, but managers who responded to change by learning were most likely to be promoted.

Transition Phases. A theoretical approach to the impact of change on learning can be developed through consideration of the training process. Training can be thought of as a series of transition phases, and individuals progress at different rates through these phases. Taylor (1986) developed a transition model that focuses on the adult learner's self-awareness and redirection. The model consists of a sequence of events, forming a cycle from one state of equilibrium to another. *Equilibrium* is the steady state at the time people enter the learning process.

The initial transition phase is *disorientation*. This is a period of intense confusion, accompanied by a crisis of confidence or withdrawal from other people associated with the confusion (one's boss or one's family in a career-change situation). This arises from the recognition of a major discrepancy between expectations and experience.

Exploration is the phase that follows disorientation. It begins with relaxation with an unresolved issue. It entails gathering insights and evidence of self-effectiveness. It is intuitively guided, collaborative, and open-ended. It can take different directions, depending on the sources of input and the results.

The next phase, *reorientation*, occurs when there is major

insight into a new approach to the learning. This occurs as one examines one's abilities, needs, interests, and opportunities for rewards.

Reorientation results in the final phase, *reequilibrium*. During this phase, the individual tests the new understanding with others. This leads to a new perspective, which is elaborated, refined, and applied to form a revised self-concept and a new sense of contentedness.

Transition Phases and the Learner's Career Motivation. Change is likely to stimulate learning when disorientation is resolved rapidly and the individual moves forward to exploration and reorientation. The extent to which this occurs is likely to depend on the individual's career motivation. Learners' career resilience, insight, and identity are likely to influence how quickly they move through the transition phases. The disorientation stage is likely to be extended for the individual who starts with a strong career identity. The individual will need to find a way to rationalize a change in commitment, from his or her current career identity to a new one. This new identity will take time to emerge as the individual learns, applies the new learning, and begins to experience success. A strong foundation of high resilience and insight will facilitate understanding of the discrepancy between current expectations and the need for retraining. Disorientation will not last long. The individual will recognize the problem and begin to develop new insights and evidence of self-effectiveness in the new endeavor. The individual will actively explore newfound abilities, needs, interests, and opportunities for reward (reorientation) and will begin to develop a renewed career identity (reequilibrium).

When resilience and insight are low, disorientation is likely to be long and accompanied by defensive coping responses, such as denial of change. The individual is likely to distort reality and try to overadapt to current conditions and preestablished habits, especially if career identity is initially high (although identity is less likely to be high when resilience and insight are low). Distortion will be difficult to maintain for any length of time, however, because of the salience of the change. The individual will move on to an extended exploration stage. If the individual begins to experience success, resilience and insight may increase, and the reorientation and reequilibrium stages may emerge. If the individual does not experience success, and if resilience and insight remain low, the individual may never successfully complete the transition process. The result may be that the person flounders and is never able to adapt to or be successful in the new environment or new career direction.

Support for Career Motivation During Transition. In addition to the influence of individuals' career motivation on training, situational factors may also influence the effects of the change. Earlier, we considered environmental conditions that support career motivation. The consequences of behavior (rewards and punishments) are likely to affect resilience. Information about the individual or about the organization is likely to affect career insight. Information about career opportunities (anticipated rewards) and the specific goals one sets are likely to affect career identity. During transition, environmental support influences disorientation by encouraging attention to reality and by requiring or rewarding active responses and punishing (or at least not rewarding) passivity. Approaches to training that force a realistic viewpoint (for example, through strong performance feedback from peers) and encourage proaction are likely to enhance training success.

Relapse Prevention. The intention of adult learning experiences is to bring about long-term behavioral change. After retraining, however, the learning must be generalized to on-the-job behavior and continue over time. The new behaviors are likely to continue when they are rewarded. In addition, behaviors are likely to be enhanced through anticipation and monitoring of past and present failures (Marlatt & Gordon, 1980). Employees also need to be equipped with appropriate skills for coping with difficult situations. There are several self-control techniques for relapse prevention (Marx, 1982). These include thinking about the conditions that surround failure to use the learned behavior, sensitizing the individual to conditions that are most likely to result in failure (for example, time pressure and lack of support from bosses), and providing additional training in such areas as time management, assertiveness, and planning.

In summary, adult learning can be enhanced by support for career resilience, insight, and identity, especially during early phases of the transition process. Long-term behavioral change requires continued monitoring and reinforcement. These theoretical positions set an agenda for research on adult learning. As the next section shows, organizations need to support adult learning, to ensure that employees have the skills they need to maintain the organization's competitiveness.

The Need for Continuous Learning

Corporate-sponsored training has shifted from preparing entry-level workers to ensuring that all employees have the skills they need to maintain the company's competitiveness. Thus, investment in employees' education becomes a strategic tool (Mandel, 1987; Work in America Institute, 1985). Corporations are also recognizing that management training must extend beyond a select high-potential group to all managers, enhancing their abilities and their preparedness for change, uncertainty, and risk.

Technological Change. Rapid advancements in technology have led to substantial organizational changes in many industries, affecting how work is done, as well as the output of work. As new technology has spread across the globe, competition has increased, with a renewed focus on using technology to enhance product quality and to increase a firm's competitive advantage. There has been a shift in management, from concern solely about the end product (sales, inventory, and productivity) to concern about the source of quality and service (design of the product and the processes that turn out the product and service) (Deming, 1987).

Computer-aided design and "just in time" manufacturing

have integrated automation and customization to meet customers' needs more flexibly (Piore & Sabel, 1984). Such advances have changed job descriptions and skill requirements. Computerized, remote monitoring centers of operating systems, such as telephone networks, have lowered the skill requirements for onsite technicians and changed reporting relationships, with maintenance employees taking instructions from machines, rather than from supervisors (London & MacDuffie, 1987). Electronic mail has changed the way people communicate, by increasing the speed of communications and the number of possible contacts. The selling of electronic components, such as transistors, once focused on the component as an interchangeable commodity sold to manufacturers' purchasing agents; this has changed to selling as developing partnership relationships with systems designers, to demonstrate how a computer chip can be customized for use in a customer's high-technology products. Branch sales managers who know their product lines and how to sell must learn sophisticated techniques of financial control and human resource management in order to manage their branches as entrepreneur-executives. Technicians who know product installation and repair must now develop skills in project management, to be part of sales teams and to work in partnership with customers. In addition, technicians often have to switch from trouble shooting on electromechanical equipment, which allowed hands-on repair, to the software diagnosis and systems analysis that are required to maintain computer-driven solid-state machines. Moreover, self-managing work teams demand that workers and supervisors develop new skills in problem solving and team development (Manz & Sims, 1987).

Ten years ago, technological change could be accomplished by selecting people who had the required educational background and retiring longtime workers, or moving them into less-skilled employment. Retraining programs were thought to be expensive, with little chance for success because of the degree of new knowledge and different skills required. Now the focus is moving toward ensuring that employees are constantly kept abreast of new developments in their fields or are retrained for new positions (Cyert & Mowery, 1987).

Retraining is becoming mandatory, because technology is continually evolving. Engineers must keep pace with their fields. They must be up to date on innovations in product design, and they must be able to educate technicians and operators about new production processes. The quality-circle movement for involving employees in improving productivity requires educating the employees in group-process skills, such as conflict resolution and negotiation. Team manufacturing approaches require workers to increase their skills, so that team members can interchange jobs, thereby allowing flexible work schedules and maximum group efficiencies. As we will discuss later, some companies compensate workers not only for their performance but also for learning new skills that enhance their value to the firm.

Employment Security. Job security is increasingly tied to retraining, or continual learning. While learning new skills is not a guarantee of continued employment, it becomes necessary in order for continued employment to be a viable option.

At Motorola, retraining is considered part of the job; in fact, it is related to job security. While Motorola does not have a full-employment policy, there is an unspoken agreement that a long and productive work history contributes to job security. In return, the company expects that employees will keep their skills current and remain productive (Lee, 1986). In this context, *job security* becomes an outdated term, replaced by *employment security.* Job security implies the ability to retain one's current job; employment security implies that an employee may remain at the same company, but retraining and movement into a different job may be necessary.

The difference between job security and employment security can also be understood in the context of the *psychological contract.* This term refers to the implicit understanding between the company and the individual about what each can expect of the other. In the past, especially in large organizations, the unstated psychological contract was that one could count on having a job as long as one showed up for work, performed satisfactorily, and did not do anything dishonest. The new psychological contract that has evolved in American companies in recent years is one in which the employee, in return for giving top performance, can expect continued opportunities for challenge, growth, and development.

Offering retraining, instead of laying workers off, is an investment in the future, both for the company and for the workers. Advantages to the employee include enhanced probability of continued employment with the same employer or, if that is not possible over the long term, a better chance of finding suitable employment elsewhere with a new skills repertoire. Advantages to the company include lower hiring costs and the possibility of keeping employees who have proven track records and strong dedication to the company.

The Work in America Institute has been carrying on a long-term study on training for new technology (see Rosow & Zager, 1988; Casner-Lotto & Associates, 1988). The fourth of five reports (Work in America Institute, 1987) articulates how training and retraining benefit both employer and employees. The report suggests the following conclusions:

- A stable, motivated, well-trained work force is critical to the long-term prosperity of an enterprise.
- Long-term prosperity enables the enterprise to fulfill its commitment to employment security.
- Employment security motivates employees to identify with the goals of the enterprise and to learn continuously.
- Continuous learning appeals to one of the most powerful drives among employees: the desire for self-development, growth, and career advancement.
- Continuous learning is feasible, because employees have unexplored capacities for education, and educated employees are capable of a surprising amount of adaptation to the changing needs of the enterprise.

Thus, continuous learning, in its connection with employment security, binds individual and corporate goals into a strong, resilient web.

Tuition Assistance. One traditional method that corporations use to encourage continuing education among their employees is tuition assistance. These firms pay for employees' tuition and other course-related expenses. There are usually some restrictions on tuition assistance (being a full-time employee, having at least six months with the company, or limiting the funding or number of credits per year). Large companies fund more tuition costs than medium-sized companies do. Companies described by their training executives as "innovative" tend to provide greater tuition aid (75 percent of tuition costs) than companies described as equally or less innovative than others (67 percent of tuition costs) (American Society for Training and Development, 1986).

In a recent study of tuition assistance costs, the amount funded per employee varied from a low of approximately $300 to $400 per year to a high of $1,000 per year (Bureau of National Affairs, 1987). The percentage of employees in an organization participating in the program ranged from 3 percent to a high of 15 percent to 18 percent. Many companies require supervisors' approval before enrollment, to ensure that courses are in line with business needs. Most companies pay only for job-related courses. For instance, in one of the companies surveyed, an example was given of an employee who wanted to take a photography course. In this case, the skill was not related to the employee's job or to any current job opening in the company; therefore, the request for tuition reimbursement was denied. Johnson and Johnson, however, offers employees who are close to retirement tuition assistance for retraining in new career areas. The goal is to prepare people for second careers after early retirement from Johnson and Johnson. This increases promotion opportunities for younger people in the firm.

Negotiated Learning and Retraining Programs. In corporations in which there is a union presence, continuous educational efforts are most likely to succeed when the union is involved. In fact, a policy of continuous learning can be carried out in a unionized workplace only if the union is involved, because collective bargaining issues (job descriptions, work rules) are always involved.

The Ford Motor Company was one of the first major corporations to enter into a negotiated agreement to offer continuous learning and retraining. This agreement was part of a major initiative undertaken to retool Ford's entire approach to the human dimension, along with its technology, and it was the successful beginning of redesigning the management-union relationship at Ford. In return for agreeing to allow management to restructure the company's outdated and rigid job-classification scheme, the United Auto Workers won a commitment to a significant educational agenda, which has since become a $20 million retraining fund in very active use throughout the company. This agreement is now viewed as a watershed in Ford's amazing turnaround. It has since been expanded to include a parallel educational fund for Ford's managers.

Another example of a negotiated agreement for retraining occurred at one of Ford's competitors, General Motors (GM). The Packard Electric Division of GM is engaged in a long-term transition to move most of its traditional high-labor, low-technology assembly-line work out of Warren, Ohio, to plants in Mexico. At the same time, the company is moving into high-technology, low-labor wiring-component manufacturing, which involves introducing less equipment and machinery into its former assembly facilities, but the remaining jobs are more technologically sophisticated. A landmark union-management agreement called for employees' participation in the transition and training process. Despite a commitment to training, GM encountered start-up problems in some of its sites, because the company failed to allow enough time for the complex training that integrates multiple technologies (Mandel, 1987).

In Chrysler's new plant in Sterling Heights, Michigan, the company allowed one year to develop and implement its training program. Some of this training is remedial, in basic math and reading skills, to prepare employees for the more complex training on new technologies. At the Sterling Heights plant, professional trainers first trained groups of supervisors, who were then charged with training others in the plant. All employees in the plant became used to learning from one another, a practice that promotes continuous learning as future changes are made in the manufacturing process.

There is substantial motivation to achieve such union-management agreements in industries that have undergone significant trauma in recent years. The automotive industry in this country has suffered from foreign competition, to the point where it became clear that something had to change. Another industry that has undergone dramatic changes is the communications industry. AT&T negotiates with three major unions every three years. In 1983, the year preceding the divestiture of the Bell System, an agreement was reached between the Communications Workers of America and the management of AT&T to develop a training and retraining program designed to encourage individual initiative in learning new skills among the work force.

At AT&T, the program offered textbooks and other course materials on administrative, managerial, and technical subjects relevant to the company. More than ten thousand occupational employees and first-level managers enrolled by telephone. A self-administered test was given when the employees completed the material. As a result of the 1986 bargaining, this correspondence program was discontinued, and a new program was established to focus more closely on surplus employees. An independent union-management–sponsored organization was formed, the Alliance for Employee Growth and Development. When employees become surplus, because of an impending plant closing or technological change, the alliance provides funding for retraining at local colleges and vocational schools.

Changes in the types of industries dominating the American workplace (from manufacturing to service) may stimulate changes in union membership (from blue-collar to white-collar); 38 percent of union members in 1985 were white-collar workers (Work in America Institute, 1987). The basic principles underlying the continuous learning–employment security connection will remain, however. In fact, given the rapid advances in technology and information management that characterize service industries, we expect that such changes will only reinforce this connection.

Skill-Based Pay. A concept that has become increasingly popular and that supports continuous learning in a practical way in organizations is skill-based, or knowledge-based, pay. Instead of being paid according to the job, in a skill-based pay system the worker is paid according to the skills that he or she has learned. Typically, when such a system is designed, the first step is to identify the tasks that need to be done and then identify the skills that are needed to perform those tasks. Measures of competence must also be developed, to assess when a particular skill has been mastered. As a worker masters an increasing number of skills that the organization needs, his or her pay also increases.

This concept is highly compatible with continuous learning and self-managing work teams, since workers can coach and train one another for the good of the individuals, the team, and the organization. It is also compatible with (and, in fact, reinforces) a participative management style (Lawler & Ledford, 1987). From the organizational perspective, it is an approach that is consistent with the need for the organization to be flexible, responsive, and adaptive in an increasingly competitive environment. In this kind of work design, different workers can fill in for one another when particular skills are needed or when there is a temporary increase in demand for one type of skill. The organization gains enormous flexibility when using a work force of multiskilled people.

Skill-based pay is ideally suited to new plant start-ups, which try to implement a high-involvement, participative style (Lawler & Ledford, 1987). Start-ups, after all, require new learning, and they are not limited by entrenched norms against training. Converting a traditional, job-based pay system to a skill-based one is not impossible, but the problems that inevitably arise must be anticipated. Even in situations where the conversion is done in a highly participative manner, with employees involved in the design of the work, there will probably be some mismatches. Employees may resent the new demands for learning new skills. There may be entrenched "turf" issues and unwillingness to give up the most desirable jobs. For these reasons, skill-based pay is easier to implement in a start-up setting, when the expectations can be made clear at the beginning. Workers who want to participate in such a scheme can be selected or can self-select for the new positions.

Skill-based pay is also more directly applicable to production work than to managerial work, because of greater ease in identifying skills and measuring competence required in production processes. Nevertheless, systems used to compensate technical specialists and professionals are similar to skill-based pay systems in some respects. Technical ladders and maturity-curve approaches traditionally have been used for these types of employees (Lawler & Ledford, 1987; Tosi & Tosi, 1986). These approaches tie increased pay to increased depth of skill in a chosen field. The difference is that they usually base increased rewards either on educational credentials or on experience in the field, and not necessarily on demonstrated competence in performing particular tasks, as in a skill-based system.

A skill-based pay system reinforces continuous learning. Tosi and Tosi (1986) analyzed skill-based pay in two different settings and came to the following conclusions:

- Workers in skill-based pay systems have strong incentives to increase knowledge and skills.
- Training costs are high in skill-based organizations.
- Workers with high self-esteem will be more satisfied with skill-based pay.
- Workers with low motivation, low ability, and low tolerance for work ambiguity will not be satisfied with skill-based pay.

Professional Development. The concept of professionalism is spreading from law, science, and engineering to other fields that require increased specialization, such as marketing, production, personnel, and management. Being the best in any field today requires keeping abreast of developments, continually fine-tuning one's skills, and being prepared to learn about and implement new technologies. Unlike recognized, well-defined disciplines, these other fields are likely to be highly organization-specific, with skill and output requirements dependent on the organization's business and the philosophy of its leaders.

One way to foster professionalism is to develop mastery paths (London & Mone, 1987). Mastery paths outline job sequences within job families. The mastery path makes explicit the requirements for moving into a job and the training and performance expectations of the job. The paths specify the criteria on which employees are to be evaluated as they become more expert in their positions. The paths may also specify the style of management the department wishes to reinforce (for example, rewarding supervisors who develop and facilitate self-directed work teams more than supervisors who monitor and make decisions for subordinates).

The Xerox Reprographic Business Group developed a dual-thrust effort to promote state-of-the-art professional knowledge and development among its employees, to ensure competitiveness in the high-technology office equipment industry. An important aspect of this effort included a performance feedback and development system, to allow effective performance evaluation and develop employees' strengths in specific directions, according to corporate needs. It also included establishing an employee training organization to offer specialized courses unavailable in most universities, refresher courses to review material originally studied in college for updated knowledge of the field, and special courses designed to broaden employees' perspectives and avoid the tunnel vision often associated with overspecialization. This organization also offers a one-hundred-hour, forty-week professional engineering review course, to help engineers review and update their skills and pass the New York State Professional Engineering Examination (Plous, 1985).

As another example, the marketing department of a large firm wanted to enhance the professionalism of its managers. Representatives from each job family were appointed to develop mastery paths. A mastery path designated the skills and knowledge needed for proficiency in each job, the training needed along the way, supervisory evaluations at critical points of development, and criteria for supervisors to use for judging when employees had attained mastery. An engineering department, concerned that its employees were not keeping up with new technology and with the latest management skills, developed a program allowing employees to evaluate themselves on dimensions of knowledge and to agree with their supervisors on programs of training and job experiences to enhance their skills.

Retraining Older Workers. Today, more than 49 million Americans are fifty-five and older, and this number will jump to 91 million in three years, according to the American Association of Retired Persons (cited in Bové, 1987). Nevertheless, the work participation rate for older workers has been declining, with more people retiring earlier. Many organizations do not view older workers as able to learn or accept new technologies and function in an increasingly competitive environment. Older workers in the position of needing to find reemployment often face age discrimination. One study found that, of skilled workers who were displaced, the younger workers were all able to find new jobs, while 38 percent of the older workers (those who were over age thirty-eight) remained unemployed (Sheppard, 1970).

Recently, however, the tight supply of new entrants to the labor force suggests that businesses will become increasingly reliant on the skills and abilities of older workers. Some companies have initiated programs to attract older workers who may be interested in second careers, often as part-time employees. Other corporate efforts provide financial incentives to older workers not to retire—for example, by continuing to contribute to the pension plan beyond age sixty-five. Moreover, some firms offer courses that upgrade older workers' skills. Job counseling and retraining for older displaced employees allow the organization to keep loyal, motivated people who know the organization.

Unfortunately, such efforts are few and far between. Perhaps one reason for limited corporate retraining efforts for older employees has been organizational retrenchment and restructuring, which uses financial incentives to pressure older workers to take early retirement. These individuals could have productive employment if they and their employers were willing to invest in retraining. In addition, older workers may be reluctant to try retraining because they lack confidence in their learning ability (Rosen, Williams, & Foltman, 1965) or because they are afraid to fail (Mintz, 1986). Their career resilience may be lower than younger workers'. Their career identity may be more directed toward complacency than achievement. Their insight, while sharp for understanding themselves and the environment, may not allow them to appreciate their ability for redevelopment.

Thus, organizations and older individuals are likely to need advice and counseling to appreciate the potential value of retraining. In particular, since methods stressing activity rather than conscious memorization or rote learning seem to work better for older learners (Mumford, 1987), such advice and counseling should stress that retraining will be based on practical experiences, and not on the traditional classroom activities that older workers may remember from their formal schooling.

One policy report recognized that corporations often exclude workers who are fifty and older from training and redevelopment opportunities (Work in America Institute, 1980). The report's recommendations still hold. The report advised that more consideration be given to lateral assignments, job redesign, ease of shifting between functional specialties, and freer movement of employees out of companies (to gain experience or training, perhaps in different fields) and then back into the companies. The report recommended that employers, before hiring a work force for a new plant or office, should first seek to train current employees, including older workers, who wish to seek new skills, careers, or assignments. In addition, the report recommended that top management make it known that the training of older workers must not be sacrificed to current pressures, and that more concrete benefits and incentives be offered to older workers for training, self-development, and self-renewal. Training programs should recognize that older workers have different learning patterns than younger workers do. Training and retraining should be adjusted to the needs of adult learners and take advantage of older workers' prior experience.

Legislation and Government Regulations. The turmoil that the American workplace has experienced in recent years, due to increasing foreign competition, has resulted in lowered profits for many industries and corresponding loss of employment for scores of workers. This situation has prompted government concern, in the form of proposed legislation to remedy the negative effects of job loss. Although legislative efforts have taken many directions, we will concentrate here on retraining and related issues.

Many legislative attempts have met with mixed reviews. Training professionals have charged that employment and retraining legislation in this country does not seriously address the problems of displaced workers caused by unemployment, recession, and new technologies. Government tends to create public employment to give unskilled workers jobs but does not train them for higher-skilled jobs in the private sector (Lee, 1983). The Job Training Partnership Act (JTPA) of 1982 was designed to offer training and retraining to displaced workers and to unemployed youths and disadvantaged adults. One assessment of its success, as of 1986, was that it has been effective in training and placing the best of the unemployed in jobs in the private sector (Lee, 1986). Nevertheless, only 48 percent of the dislocated workers placed under JTPA received some form of training (U.S. General Accounting Office, 1987). In 1988, Congress replaced Title III of the JTPA—the dislocated worker program—with the Economic Dislocation and Workers Adjustment Act. This increases the funding for training and placing dislocated workers. Some experts feel that retraining is more effective when it is provided to active workers in order to maintain their employability, and that retraining for displaced workers is not a viable solution (Condon, 1984).

One innovative state program, the California Employment Training Panel, was established in 1983 to provide funds for schools and employers to retrain the unemployed and workers likely to be displaced. The panel was set up with funds previously designated for unemployment insurance. The idea is that unemployment insurance payouts will ultimately be lowered if fewer people are unemployed. The goal is to move people into careers, not dead-end, high-turnover jobs. Research through December 1987 found a significant increase in earnings and a substantial reduction in unemployment for panel trainees (California Employment Training Panel, 1987).

In general, there does not appear to be a comprehensive and future-directed approach to retraining as a national need. Proposals coming before our legislative bodies still deal with the issue in a reactive way, providing federal and state funds to cope with displacement when it occurs. A more proactive, comprehensive approach, based on analysis and projections of the future course of technological developments, could effectively unite the government and private industry in an effort to ensure continuous learning and skills development in the American work force.

The U.S. Army recently began an investigation of the possibility of creating an expanded retraining program for its dislocated or excess civilian employees, recognizing organizational changes and the need to retrain its civilian work force to keep pace with modern technology. Regulatory and legal procedures, such as those detailed in the *Federal Personnel Manual* (U.S. Office of Personnel Management, 1981), allow government agencies to provide retraining to employees who may be affected by changes in organizational mission, new work methods, or increased contracting out for services. Government agencies must plan for retraining, request funds, design programs to benefit employees, and identify who would be retrained, in what skills, and for which positions. This must be done well in advance of employees' receiving notice of proposed separation, since by that time there is little opportunity for retraining.

Reemployment Programs. Many companies have begun to fulfill their commitment to employment security, not only by retraining employees for new jobs within the company but also by helping employees find good jobs elsewhere. Indeed, some workers are not interested in training and may prefer vocational counseling or help in finding a job. Major union-management agreements have, in effect, extended their practice of "outplacement" of managers to bargained-for employees as well. For instance, at Pacific Bell, a training advisory board developed a system that keeps workers informed about job growth and decline and provides opportunities for retraining. Employees who express interest in jobs outside the company are entitled to, and provided with, outplacement services (Work in America Institute, 1987).

General Electric (GE) implemented a program at its site in Columbia, Maryland, to retrain displaced workers for alternative employment in the area, because opportunities are not available within the company. The program is managed by a reemployment center funded jointly by GE, the State of Maryland, and the federal government (Hickey, 1987).

The development of such programs is necessary and unavoidable, given the rapid growth of technology. As a company adapts to and develops new technology, there will be a flux in its need for skilled workers. Such programs may be considered innovations today, but in the future they may become just another part of doing business in an increasingly competitive environment.

Training in Support of Organizational Change

Many organizations have changed their internal systems and structures to match changes in the environment. Increased competition and uncertain economic conditions have led many firms to reduce fixed costs, often by reducing the number of both management and nonmanagement employees. The surviving managers are left with broader spans of control and increased responsibility. Work demands and pressures are greater, and opportunities for advancement are fewer. As a result, top managers need to learn how to support employees' career and work motivation under these conditions. Training can help supervisors learn how to develop subordinates in retrenched environments. For example, supervisors can learn about the resources available in the organization for development (for example, retraining programs). Supervisors can learn how to give meaningful feedback and help subordinates formulate development plans. The organization can also reward supervisors for successfully developing people.

The move in some organizations to participative management, employee involvement programs, and self-managing work teams has also been a response to the need to maximize productivity with fewer resources. Decisions can no longer be escalated through layers of middle management, and employees must be trusted to make decisions and take actions that are in the best interests of the organization. Quality circles and quality-of-work-life programs will not succeed unless they are supported by training on such topics as conflict resolution, problem solving, negotiation, and leadership.

Organizational changes like force reductions and moves to increased employee involvement require comprehensive training programs. It is not enough to send a few people through training, unless they are equipped to educate others when they return. Broad-based learning systems, with integrated curricula, are required to prevent a learning gap in the organization (Rosow, 1987).

One attempt at such a comprehensive approach to education in an organization was the development of a management model based on the company's business plans. The model specified general outputs that were important, given the goals of the organization. For example, a major business goal was to provide integrated solutions to customers' data-communication and data-transmission needs. This required employees from different functions to work together, and so building networks and alliances was one of the major outputs expected of all managers, and they would be appraised on it. Training courses were developed to teach the skills associated with developing effective cross-functional links, such as problem-solving skills. Other outputs in the model included setting performance goals, developing effective working relationships in the work group, and designing meaningful task and organizational structures. A special publication distributed to all managers in the company explained the model, described the policies and procedures for performance appraisal, and outlined the comprehensive training curriculum.

Temporary Employees. One problem that many organizations in retrenchment are facing is that some of their good people have left, but their skills are still needed. Temporary employees are often hired to solve this problem. Some organizations, such as Delta Airlines and American Transtech, use temporary workers as a buffer, so that they can maximize the job security of permanent employees. (At Delta, about 13 percent of the employees are temporary, and the company would like to increase that proportion to 20 percent; Parker, 1987). Temporary workers do not have the commitment to the company that permanent workers do. Another problem is that temporary workers may not be given company-supported training to make their behavior consistent with the requirements of the organization. Firms that rely on temporary employees may find that they must invest in training to make them productive. Some temporary employees may be rewarded with permanent status or with monetary bonuses in addition to the training that makes them more marketable outside the firm, as well as inside it.

Corporate Allocation of Training Resources. There are many ways for corporations to conduct the activities involved in allocating training resources. These activities include setting budgets, designing curricula and courses, selecting course participants, and even designing the structure of training departments or staffs. Methods for accomplishing these tasks range from centralized corporate decision making to decentralized control among business units. Training may be driven by business strategies, tradition, chance, or politics. We will concentrate on firms that make strategically driven decisions about training and education. A recent study found that corporations that surpassed their financial goals were more likely to agree strongly with the statement "Training is an integral part of corporate strategic planning" than were corporations that fell short of their goals

(American Society for Training and Development, 1986). Another study found data supporting a relationship between profitability and amount of top managers' formal training per year, in a sample of small, medium, and large businesses (Organization and Strategy Information Service,1986).

Strategy-Directed Training. Companies that use strategic processes in planning and executing their investments in training and education frequently demonstrate their commitment by involving senior officers in the process. This involvement of top management goes beyond verbal statements of support for training and education; it includes actual behavior that employees can observe. For example, at Corning Glass Works, employee training is the basis of a program to enhance product quality. A committee of six top corporate managers sets training policy, authorizes resources, reviews results, and gives the entire effort strong, visible support and leadership. At Motorola, the chief executive officer personally selected the director of the Motorola Training and Education Center. The chairman and nine top officers form an executive advisory board that meets twice yearly to determine the training budget and set program priorities. All training must support corporate strategic goals, as identified and communicated by this board. The directory of services for the training center describes each course and its objectives and specifies the strategic business issue that each one addresses (Lee, 1986).

General Electric places similar emphasis on training. Its corporate training facility in Crotonville, New York, is the center for communicating GE's values to its managers as they experience major career transitions. Going to the training center becomes a rite of passage for people when they are promoted. When GE acquired RCA, key middle managers and upper managers from RCA went to Crotonville to learn GE's philosophy of management.

Just as career transitions cause individuals to be more receptive to learning, changes in corporate financial performance and other environmental changes can make organizations more likely to allocate additional resources to training and education. Top managers use training and education as tools to bring about change, combat competition, and deal with operational priorities. Corporate commitment to training and retraining is growing deeper as it becomes a strategic effort to improve competitiveness. For example, Ford Motor Company analyzed its failure to stay competitive and committed substantial resources not just to retrain its employees but also to get them involved in a continuous learning process. An endeavor of this magnitude clearly requires commitment, cooperation, and support from the unions, as well as from management.

Analyzing Training Needs. Another way to identify and respond to needs for training is to analyze the skills and knowledge of the work force in relation to the needs of the business and the training required to perform needed functions (London, 1989). In one such study, work-group managers and training consultants examined current employees' training records in relation to work demands. This identified the need for training, to bring the current work force up to speed. The degree of turnover expected during the next three years was also analyzed, to estimate the amount and type of training needed for new employees. In addition, projections were made of training needs, given new products and services that were likely to be introduced by the firm during the next three years. The data were combined to form an estimate of the training gap, expressed in approximate numbers of student days of training required in different curriculum areas. This indicated the training resources the corporation needed to include in its business plans and suggested the desirability of exploring more cost-effective ways to meet the training requirements. A "training gap solution-implementation team" was appointed to identify and try alternative training methods, as opposed to standard, instructor-led training. The team, consisting of representatives from the training department and field organizations served by the department, explored such alternatives as computer-based training (self-paced training modules on personal computer discs); printed job aids and inexpensively produced videos, to explain technical procedures; a hotline with subject-matter experts to answer technicians' questions. Other alternatives included setting up temporary training centers in field locations where new technology was being implemented, improving supervisors' skills for counseling subordinates and enhancing their career development, developing better control over work-force movement within the company, offering financial incentives to discourage trained technicians from leaving the company, and intensifying recruitment of already qualified technicians into the organization. (The latter three alternatives indicate that training is not always the answer to a training gap.)

Human Resource Planning. In an environment where competition and technological advances are the norm, employers need to develop sophisticated human resource planning systems to forecast accurately which skills will be needed, which skills will become obsolete, which new jobs will be created, which existing jobs will change in nature or even disappear, and how geographical deployment of facilities will change over time. Employees also need to have this information, to effectively plan for their own development and growth. Motorola's human resource strategies are an extension of its business plans in that the company requires that all plans for major capital investment and new plant facilities include detailed training plans. These plans must specify how the company will ensure that employees will be fully trained when the new facility opens (Mandel, 1987). In general, a firm's business plans should include goals for human resource development and training, as well as goals for evaluating and rewarding employees, to enhance business objectives.

Conclusions and Recommendations

Environmental forces, including changing demographics, economics, and technology, are altering career paths and creating the need for employee training and retraining. Midcareer is becoming a time of change for many people, and retraining is a means of avoiding the stagnation of a career plateau or the anxiety of job loss or midlife crisis. Individuals' resilience, insight, and identity affect their receptivity to new knowledge and skills. In addition, successful learning can reinforce resilience and increase insight and identity. Midcareer training must take into account adults' motivation and abilities. Adults are especially responsive to active learning that uses job assignments, cases, and simulations. Adults are also particularly responsive to learning during periods of change, such as promotion.

Organizations facilitate midcareer change through educational and developmental opportunities. Organizations can encourage continuous learning through skill-based pay programs, union-management agreements to offer training and retraining, and professional development programs. These efforts enhance employment security and increase the organization's competitiveness. Prompted by legislative initiatives, organizations are increasingly anticipating work-force adjustments and offering retraining to meet new skill needs.

Organizations increasingly view training and retraining as a way to implement corporate strategies and accomplish business goals—for example, by using training to explain and demonstrate corporate values and prepare employees to achieve desired outputs. Training to meet an organization's human resource needs requires planning, and information about job opportunities helps individuals recognize their own needs for learning, to ensure their career stability.

Here are fifteen recommendations for individuals and organizations:

1. Individuals and organizations should view training as a way to prepare for future contingencies. Updates in technological advancements, management development courses, and programs to help people learn how to learn provide individuals with the abilities and confidence (resilience) to meet unforeseen changes in the midcareer and late-career stages. Continuous learning should be the central policy of an organization, supported by rewards for self- and subordinate development.

2. Managers and organizational policy setters should understand career motivation and help supervisors understand

employees' reactions to change and acceptance of new directions. Training and appropriate support mechanisms (counseling, goal setting, and feedback) can build career resilience, insight, and identity.

3. Training can be used to help individuals break away from ineffective patterns of behavior, renew self-confidence, provide information for accurate career insight, and reward career identity.

4. A career plateau is a difficult pattern to break away from, because the pattern does not stimulate receptivity to learning. Job changes should be planned so that employees avoid the feeling of stagnation accompanying a career plateau and so that they not only continue to learn but also find new opportunities for advancement.

5. Training and retraining can be constructive responses to crisis and change. As organizational changes occur, training should be used to communicate the changes, give people confidence that they can deal with the changes successfully, and prepare them for the future.

6. Successful retraining requires financial and social support. When individuals seek retraining, the organization should provide support through tuition assistance or through early-retirement education bonuses, to facilitate the transition.

7. The need for training should be anticipated by the individual and the organization. For instance, in designs for organizational change, training is often the last item considered, when it should be the first. Are people capable of learning a new technology? How long is the learning curve to bring them up to speed? On the individual level, what can I do to prepare for a second career ten years from now? Organizations should provide individuals with support, such as counseling sessions leading to action plans and financial assistance to accomplish those plans. In addition, organizations should demonstrate planning through human resource forecasts and actions to meet tomorrow's human resource needs.

8. An organization needs a comprehensive learning system as a critical support for organizational change. Courses must be designed to communicate and enhance the outputs

required by the organization. Mechanisms should be established to spread the learning throughout the organization, either through widely available courses or through the training of key people who can train others.

9. Training should be part of a comprehensive human resource program aimed at meeting the organization's need for human resources today and in the future. Human resource planning should identify future skills requirements. This should be input for hiring and developing individuals, to ensure that the right people are available at the right time.

10. Planning for training and retraining in the organization should be part of human resource planning, which in turn should be an extension of the organization's overall strategy. Business plans should include investments in human resources, just as they include capital investments. People support the accomplishment of organizational objectives, and the need for enhancing employees' abilities through education should be recognized in the planning process. Consequently, the organization's training specialists and human resource professionals should work closely with business strategists and organizational planners to formulate and fund learning systems.

11. Organizations should be open to new training processes incorporated into new work structures. For instance, computer training at home can prepare mothers with school-age children to reenter the work force, perhaps working at home after completing the training. Organizations short of labor can use financial incentives to encourage pension-eligible workers to stay on the job, perhaps working part-time and receiving training that prepares them for different types of jobs with the organization.

12. Organizations should take a more proactive approach to retraining as a national need. Government and private industry need to unite in an effort to ensure continuous learning and skills development and thereby prepare the American work force to compete effectively in the global economic environment. Corporations need to invest more in our educational systems, from grade school through college, to ensure

that available workers, minorities in particular, will have the skills to meet future human resource needs.

13. Employee development should be synchronized with the changing needs of the business environment and with changing job requirements. For instance, organizations need action-learning methods to help managers learn how to handle struggling projects, lead heterogeneous work groups, implement reorganizations, and understand foreign cultures.

14. Organizations should analyze the projected demographic changes in the work force of the future. Possible gaps between existing employees' skills and future skills requirements, and between future requirements for numbers and types of people and the availability of these people in the labor market, should be considered. Organizations need work-force management strategies for selecting, reducing, training, and retraining the work force.

15. Studying and anticipating trends, and formulating responses that ensure that employees are ready to meet customers' needs, can have an effect beyond an individual company's success. This endeavor, well conducted by many companies, can have significant positive effects on the competitiveness of the American work force and the American economy.

References

American Society for Training and Development. (1986). *Employee training in America: A comparative assessment of training and development:* Vol. I. *National survey of training and development executives.* Alexandria, VA: American Society for Training and Development.

Bardwick, J. (1986). *The plateauing trap.* New York: Amacom.

Belbin, E. (1958). Methods for training older workers. *Ergonomics, 1,* 207–221.

Belbin, R. M. (1970). The discovery method in training older workers. In H. L. Sheppard (Ed.), *Towards an industrial gerontology.* Cambridge, MA: Schenkman, 1970.

Blotnick, S. (1985). Midcareer changes. *Forbes, 135,* 140–141.

Bové, R. (1987, March). Retraining the older worker. *Training and Development Journal, 41*, (3), 77–78.

Bureau of National Affairs. (1987). *A comparative study of corporate training costs.* Washington, DC: Bureau of National Affairs.

Caldwell, D. F., & O'Reilly, C. A. (1985). The impact of information on job choices and turnover. *Academy of Management Journal, 28*, 934–943.

California Employment Training Panel (1987). *Report to the Legislature.* Sacramento: State of California.

Casner-Lotto, J., & Associates (1988). *Successful training strategies: Twenty-six innovative corporate models.* San Francisco: Jossey-Bass.

Condon, M. (1984). The ins and outs of displacement. *Training and Development Journal, 38*, 60–65.

Cyert, R. M., & Mowery, D. C. (Eds.) (1987). *Technology and employment: Innovation and growth in the U.S. economy.* Washington, DC: National Academy Press.

Deming, W. E. (1987, February). Western managers must make drastic changes. *Executive Excellence*, p. 1.

DuBois, L. (1981). *Career and family in middle men and women.* Unpublished doctoral dissertation, Adelphi University.

Ference, T., Stoner, T., & Warren, F. (1977). Managing the career plateau. *Academy of Management Review, 2*, 602–612.

Fisher, S. (1985). The adult learner. In W. R. Tracey (Ed.), *Human resources management and development handbook* (pp. 1395–1403). New York: Amacom.

Hall, D. T. (1985). Project work as an antidote to career plateauing in a declining organization. *Human Resource Management, 24*, 271–292.

Hickey, J. V. (1987). *Brightening the job prospects of displaced workers: General Electric Company's Columbia, Maryland, Re-Employment Center.* Scarsdale, NY: Work in America Institute.

Hill, R. E., & Miller, E. L. (1981). Job change and the middle seasons of a man's life. *Academy of Management Journal, 24*, 114–127.

Korman, A. K. (1988). Career success and personal failure: Mid- to late-career feelings and events. In M. London & E. M. Mone (Eds.), *Career growth and human resource strategies* (pp. 81–94). Westport, CT: Quorum.

Korman, A. K., & Korman, R. W. (1980). *Career success/ personal failure: Alienation in management.* Englewood Cliffs, NJ: Prentice-Hall.

Latack, J. C., & Kaufman, H. G. (1988). Termination and outplacement strategies. In M. London & E. M. Mone, *Career growth and human resources strategies* (pp. 289–313). Westport, CT: Quorum.

Lawler, E. E., III, & Ledford, G. E., Jr. (1987, February). Skill-based pay: A concept that's catching on. *Management Review*, 46–51.

Leana, C. R., & Feldman, D. C. (1988). Individual responses to job loss: Perceptions, reactions, and coping behaviors. *Journal of Management, 14,* 375–390.

Lee, C. (1983). Retraining America: Solutions or sugar pills? *Training, 20,* 22–29.

Lee, C. (1986, October). Training profiles: The view from ground level. *Training,* 67–69.

Leider, R. J. (1974). Why a second career? *Personnel Administrator, 19,* 40–45.

Levinson, D. J. (1986). A conception of adult development. *American Psychologist, 41,* 3–13.

Levinson, D. J., Darrow, C. N., Klein, E. B., Levinson, M. H., & McKee, B. (1978). *The seasons of a man's life.* New York: Knopf.

London, M. (1983). Toward a theory of career motivation. *Academy of Management Review, 8,* 620–630.

London, M. (1985). *Developing managers: A guide to motivating and preparing people for successful managerial careers.* San Francisco: Jossey-Bass.

London, M. (1987). Employee development in a downsizing environment. *Journal of Business and Psychology, 2,* 60–73.

London, M. (1988). *Change agents: New roles and innovation strategies for human resources professionals.* San Francisco: Jossey-Bass.

London, M. (1989). *Managing the training enterprise: High-quality employee training at a cost the organization can afford.* San Francisco: Jossey-Bass.

London, M., & Bray, D. W. (1984). Measuring and developing young managers' career motivation. *Journal of Management Development, 3,* 3–25.

London, M., & MacDuffie, J. P. (1987, November). Implementing technological innovations. *Personnel*, 26–38.

London, M., & Mone, E. M. (1987). *Career growth and survival in the workplace*. San Francisco: Jossey-Bass.

Lowy, A., Kelleher, D., & Finestone, P. (1986, June). Management learning: Beyond program design. *Training and Development Journal*, *40*, 34–37.

Mandel, T. F. (1987). *Corporate education and training: Investing in a competitive edge*. Palo Alto, CA: SRI International.

Manz, C. C., & Sims, H. P., Jr. (1987). Leading workers to lead themselves: The external leadership of self-managing work teams. *Administrative Science Quarterly*, *32*, 106–129.

Marlatt, G. A., & Gordon, J. R. (1980). Determinants of relapse: Implications for the maintenance of behavior change. In P. O. Davidson & S. M. Davidson (Eds.), *Behavioral medicine: Changing health life styles* (pp. 410–452). New York: Brunner/Mazel.

Marx, R. D. (1982). Relapse prevention for managerial training: A model for maintenance of behavior change. *Academy of Management Review*, *7*, 433–441.

Mintz, F. (1986, October). Retraining: The graying of the training room. *Personnel*, 69–71.

Mumford, A. (1987). Action learning. *Journal of Management Development*, *6*, 3–4.

Organization and Strategy Information Service (OASIS) (1986). *Linking organization to strategy*. New York: The Hay Group, Inc.

Parker, N. (1987, October). *Personnel Philosophies at Delta Airlines*. Paper presented at the Symposium on Emerging Issues, Hopewell, NJ.

Piore, M. J., & Sabel, C. F. (1984). *The second industrial divide*. New York: Basic Books.

Plous, F. K., Jr. (1985). *Advanced employee training in high technology at Xerox Corporation*. Scarsdale, NY: Work in America Institute.

Rosen, N. A., Williams, L. K., & Foltman, F. F. (1965). Motivational constraints in an industrial retraining program. *Personnel Psychology*, *18*, 65–79.

Rosow, J. (Sept. 1987). *Declining employee morale: Corporate crisis*. Paper presented at the Symposium on Emerging Issues, Hopewell, NJ.

Rosow, J. M., & Zager, R. (1988). *Training—The competitive edge: Introducing new technology into the workplace.* San Francisco: Jossey-Bass.

Sheppard, H. L. (Ed.). (1970). *Towards an industrial gerontology.* Cambridge, MA: Schenkman.

Stout, S., Slocum, J. W., Jr., & Cron, W. L. (1987, August). *Dynamics of the career plateauing process.* Paper presented at the annual meeting of the Academy of Management, New Orleans.

"Switch Rather Than Stew." (1985). *Training and Development Journal, 29,* 10.

Taylor, M. (1986). Learning for self-direction in the classroom: The pattern of a transition process. *Studies in Higher Education, 11,* 55–72.

Tosi, H., & Tosi, L. (1986, Winter). What managers need to know about knowledge-based pay. *Organizational Dynamics.*

U.S. General Accounting Office. (1987, March). *Dislocated workers: Local programs and outcomes under the Job Training Partnership Act.* GAO/HRD-84-41. Washington, DC: U.S. Government Printing Office.

U.S. Office of Personnel Management. (1981, October). *Federal personnel manual.* Inst. 271. Washington, DC: U.S. Government Printing Office.

Vaillant, G. E. (1977). *Adaptation of life.* Boston: Little, Brown.

Van Velsor, E., & Musselwhite, W. C. (1986, August). The timing of training, learning, and transfer. *Training and Development Journal, 40,* 58–59.

Wanous, J. P. (1981). *Organizational entry.* Reading, MA: Addison-Wesley.

Work in America Institute. (1978). *Midcareer perspectives.* Scarsdale, NY: Work in America Institute.

Work in America Institute. (1980). *The future of older workers in America.* Scarsdale, NY: Work in America Institute.

Work in America Institute. (1985). *Training for new technology: Part II. Toward continuous learning.* Scarsdale, NY: Work in America Institute.

Work in America Institute. (1987). *Training for new technology: Part IV. The continuous learning/employment security connection.* Scarsdale, NY: Work in America Institute.

10

Socialization, Resocialization, and Training: Reframing the Research Agenda

Daniel C. Feldman

Historically, researchers in the areas of training and socialization have been concerned both with the ways individuals learn their jobs and the ways they adjust to new organizations. These two groups of researchers have brought very different perspectives to bear on the organizational entry process, however, and have focused on very different aspects of this transition.

Training has traditionally been defined as "the formal procedures which a company utilizes to facilitate learning so that the resultant behavior contributes to the attainment of the company's goals and objectives" (McGehee & Thayer, 1961, p. 10). This definition highlights several features of training that have been very salient for researchers and practitioners in this area. Training has been very concerned with the individual as the unit of analysis. The dependent variable of greatest interest has been work-related behavior; the independent variable of greatest interest has been individual knowledge, or learning. The context of learning that has been most widely studied is the

Note: The author wishes to acknowledge the helpful comments of Irwin L. Goldstein, Raymond A. Katzell, Walter Nord, and Cynthia Stohl.

formal training program provided by the corporation's professional training staff.

Socialization has traditionally been defined as "an organizationally directed process that prepares and qualifies individuals to occupy organizational positions" (Caplow, 1964, p. 16) or "the manner in which an individual learns that behavior appropriate to his position in a group through interaction with others who hold normative beliefs about what his role should be and who reward or punish him for correct or incorrect actions" (Brim, 1966, p. 3). While socialization research has examined the learning of work-related behavior to some extent, it has been more centrally concerned with the attitudes and values of new employees and with how newcomers learn their roles. Socialization research has also focused more closely on the informal ways individuals learn about their work settings, and the impact that other members of the work group have on that learning. Whereas training research has been most concerned with individuals' abilities to perform routine work tasks, socialization research has focused more deeply on individuals' conformity to or deviance from the demands of the organization, and even on whether conformity to expectations uniformly contributes to organizational effectiveness.

Over the past fifteen years, scholars in training and socialization have become much more aware of, and concerned with, the research topics and findings of each other. Consequently, the research questions that each group of scholars are asking are becoming more theoretically interesting and practically important. This chapter explores more fully the ways in which the training and socialization literatures can be integrated for an understanding of how newcomers learn their jobs and adjust to organizations.

The chapter is divided into three sections.

The first section of the chapter explores several areas in which socialization research has informed or expanded the traditional focus of training research: (1) the impact of learning values, attitudes, and social behavior on the learning of work-related behaviors; (2) the impact of the training group and the work-group setting on the learning of work-related behaviors; (3) the role of informal training by peers, supervisors, and mentors in newcomers' learning; (4) the consideration of adaptation and innovative behavior as outcomes of training and socialization programs; (5) the impact of prior socialization experiences (either organizational or occupational) on newcomers' openness and willingness to learn; and (6) the difference between resocialization and retraining, on the one hand, and initial socialization and training, on the other. For each of these six areas, past research findings are summarized and integrated, and future avenues for research are identified.

The second section examines the ways in which training programs have become, in many cases, the main socialization process for new employees. Traditionally, training programs have only been a part (and often a minor part) of the socialization process. Today, with increasing frequency, training programs have become the main crucible for the setting of individual expectations about the job, the major stimulus to the creation of group norms, and the greatest source of hard data for attributions about the company. The implications of this shift in the role of training programs are explored, both in terms of future research and in terms of the design and implementation of training programs in practice.

The third section explores the expanded role that training programs are being asked to play in the management of human resources in organizations. Over the past fifteen years, training has been used as a means of converting employees to the corporation's ideology (for example, "positive personnel practices," training in "union prevention"), as a reward for past good performance (as opposed to training for remediation), as a career development tool, as a test for promotion, and as an outplacement device. This widening domain of the use of training programs has important consequences, not only for the types of research that should be conducted but also for the training of trainers in organizational settings. Reframing important research questions in the light of our knowledge of socialization should help researchers and practitioners alike better understand the dynamics of training programs and more effectively design and implement those programs.

Integrating Socialization and Training Research

Several topics have been studied by both training and socialization scholars, but in six areas, in particular, socialization research has substantially informed or expanded the traditional focus of training research. Below, each of these six areas is considered in turn, both with an eye to synthesizing previous research and an eye to identifying fruitful avenues for future investigation.

The Impact of Learning Values, Attitudes, and Social Behavior on the Learning of Work-Related Behavior. Researchers in socialization have long been aware that organizational socialization involves the transformation of several aspects of newcomers' behaviors, values, and attitudes (Van Maanen, 1976; Schein, 1968). More recently, however, the notion of multiple socialization processes has emerged to explain the interactions among the learning of work tasks and the other types of learning that occur during socialization (Feldman, 1981). Feldman suggests that there are three relatively distinct sets of changes in employees during socialization: changes in the development of work skills and abilities, changes in the acquisition of appropriate role behaviors, and changes in adjustment to the work group's norms and values.

Feldman's theory also suggests that progress through the three different kinds of socialization occurs at different speeds and depends on different sets of organizational contingencies. For instance, socialization to the task is highly dependent on the selection system's ability to pick newcomers reliably, the formal training program, and performance appraisal. In contrast, socialization to the role is more dependent on the employee's expectations of the organization and on his or her ability to manage intergroup and outside-life conflicts, while socialization to the group is dependent on individual needs and values and informal interactions with peers and supervisors. Feldman further suggests that each type of socialization process leads to different sets of behavioral and affective outcomes. Mastering work skills and abilities is hypothesized to have the strongest influence on performance of routine job activities, general satisfaction, and turnover. Adjustment to the group is hypothesized to have the strongest influence on cooperative behavior and job involvement.

In general, empirical research that has tested the notions of multiple socialization processes and stage models has lagged behind theoretical work (Feldman, 1976a; Fisher, 1986). Nevertheless, some consistent findings suggest the ways in which other types of socialization influence learning about the job itself.

First, becoming adjusted to a group seems to be strongly related to employees' abilities to learn their jobs. For instance, in a study of hospital employees' socialization, Feldman (1977) found that newcomers felt that until they could trust co-workers, they could not find out information essential to doing their jobs well, especially information about the idiosyncratic preferences of supervisors and about shortcuts around administrative procedures. In Feldman's study, acceptance by the group preceded task mastery by about three months.

Second, becoming adjusted to the role seems to be the socialization process that takes the longest to complete. Graen, Orris, and Johnson (1973) found that new clerical employees spent decreasing amounts of time over the first sixteen weeks learning their tasks, but increasing amounts of time trying to manage role conflict. This is consistent with other models of socialization (Feldman, 1976a; 1981; Porter, Lawler, & Hackman, 1975; Van Maanen, 1976), which suggest that role-conflict resolution does not occur until the metamorphosis (or change and acquisition) stage.

One likely explanation for this finding can be found in the work of Hollander (1958) on idiosyncrasy credit. Hollander suggests that group members generate idiosyncrasy credit by being good group citizens — that is, by generally conforming to the expectations of the group and by contributing effectively to the attainment of group goals. Individuals expend these credits when they deviate, either by failing to comply with group norms or by performing poorly at work. New group members generally have not had the opportunity to build up a balance of idiosyncrasy credits and therefore do not have much latitude to negotiate role conflict upon entry. Once newcomers have established themselves as solid performers and good group members, however, they may be given more slack to resolve some of these role conflicts (Feldman & Arnold, 1983; Feldman, 1984).

Unfortunately, we know much less about the impact of newcomers' attitudes and values on openness and willingness to learn work tasks during socialization. Socialization researchers have documented that attitudes and values toward organizations change upon entry (Adler & Shuval, 1978; Fisher, 1986; Weiss, 1977; Sylvia & Pindur, 1978), but how those global value and attitude changes affect openness to learning is much less clear. In general, a more fruitful approach to this question involves a more microscopic reframing of the research on values and attitudes toward training.

For example, while socialization researchers have examined realistic job expectations as an important antecedent to individual adjustment to organizations (Wanous, 1981; Premack & Wanous, 1985), the whole issue of expectations about training itself has to be explored more fully. Some organizations sell their training programs as a major inducement to join, and they create very high expectations of those programs in recruits' eyes. Whether or not the jobs themselves live up to expectations, false expectations of training programs may indeed have strong negative consequences on performance in training programs and tenure in an organization.

Lewicki's (1981) work on organizational seduction is nonempirical, but it is also suggestive of the types of changes in attitudes and values that can occur during training. Organizational seduction frequently occurs in high-status organizations and includes four major elements: selecting individuals who ideologically fit in with the organization's goals; providing newcomers with ready access to status symbols and high-status managers; providing newcomers with challenging, involving work that highly stimulates them; and providing new recruits with an extremely pleasant work environment and pay incentives to satisfy their needs for comfort. Lewicki suggests that the seductive organization first selects employees who are psychologically ready to accept its values and then provides them with challenging tasks that not only increase the attractiveness of their jobs but also decrease their stress and dissatisfaction with their workloads and work hours. Empirical research is needed to test these hypotheses, as well as to examine how attitudes and values change in less intense training settings. Regardless of whether the hypothetical syndrome of organizational seduction holds up under empirical investigation, its four main components probably do play major roles in shaping new recruits' values and attitudes toward training.

Social Context of Training. A second area of training that socialization researchers have been exploring is the social context of training. While most training research has focused on how the individual absorbs new information and on his or her cognitive processes, socialization researchers have been studying the impact of the work group and the training group on individual learning.

Central to this approach has been Van Maanen's (1978) typology of "people-processing strategies." Van Maanen identifies seven dimensions of social interactions along which company training and socialization programs can be arrayed (1978, pp. 21–28):

1. Formal-informal: extent to which newcomers' status is made explicit; segregation of newcomers from veterans
2. Individual-collective: whether newcomers are trained/socialized one by one, or in groups
3. Sequential-nonsequential: extent to which new recruits must pass through a series of discrete steps to obtain full status (e.g., probationer, apprentice, junior partner)
4. Fixed-variable: extent to which newcomers know in advance when their probationary status will end
5. Tournament-contest: the degree to which newcomers are identified as "fast track" employees soon after entry

6. Serial-disjunctive: whether newcomers are trained by their job predecessors or by professional staff not in their home unit
7. Investiture-divestiture: the degree to which the training and socialization programs reaffirm newcomers' self-confidence or strip it away

Van Maanen suggests that strategies for people processing do have a major impact on the attitudes, beliefs, and performance of new recruits. His article, though, raises two important empirical questions: Are these seven people-processing strategies independent, or do they co-occur in regular patterns? What systematic impact do these strategies have on the attitudes, values, and behaviors of newcomers?

Jones (1986) used a sample of one hundred MBAs to answer these questions. His results suggest three clusters of people-processing strategies: investiture-divestiture and serial-disjunctive; sequential-nonsequential and fixed-variable; and individual-collective and formal-informal (Jones did not examine the tournament-contest dimension). Jones found that the collective-formal-sequential pattern (what he calls the "institutionalized strategy") leads to poorer affective adjustment to organizations and less innovative behavior than the "individualized" approach.

What these results suggest is that the more newcomers an organization is trying to socialize at once, the more formal and distancing the training becomes. Moreover, these two strategies of people processing often have countervailing effects on recruits' attitudes and behavior. The collective strategy creates less positive affect among new recruits toward the organization and generates less innovative behavior, but it does generate the greatest cohesion among new recruits. The individualized strategy produces more innovative behavior in new recruits, but it also generates the most uncertainty and role confusion for newcomers.

For the future, Van Maanen's typology and the subsequent research suggest the possibility of developing some sort of "fit" model of people-processing strategies and outcomes of training. The classes of behavior and attitudes that researchers may be interested in predicting are speed of learning, innovative behavior, performance of routine tasks, and affect toward the organization. The independent variables of interest could be desirability of new job, level of performance demanded (Fisher, 1986), perceived legitimacy of organization demands (Schein & Ott, 1962), and heterogeneity of skills and attitudes among recruits. One could hypothesize, for instance, that the "institutional" mode of socializing recruits would be most effective when new recruits had homogeneous skills and attitudes, when the legitimacy of the organization's demands was high, and when the organization was most interested in the quick learning of routine tasks (for example, among clerks and blue-collar workers). In contrast, one could hypothesize that the "individualized" approach would be most effective when there was heterogeneity of recruits' skills and attitudes and when the level of performance demanded was very high but the organization wanted to generate both positive affect toward itself (perhaps to reduce turnover) and more innovative behavior (say, among middle managers).

Van Maanen's research also suggests a variety of questions for training practitioners: How much segregation of new recruits from veterans is helpful to training, and how much is dysfunctional? Does a long probationary period serve any useful function, in terms of motivation or performance? Does the training of new recruits by their job predecessors actually impede their learning of certain behaviors, especially innovative ones? Does divestiture, in building cohesion among cohort groups, have long-term consequences for attitudes toward the organization and intention to remain? All these questions about the social environment of training need to be consciously addressed.

The other side of the group-dynamics issue—how group dynamics in a training cohort influence individual learning—has received very little attention. Two research streams in particular, however, can be fruitfully applied to the understanding of this question. The first stream is represented in the job-design literature. The work of Hackman and Oldham (1980) suggests that the design of the work itself (here, the training) and the composition of the group (here, the training cohort) influence the level of effort and knowledge brought to the learning of new jobs. One could hypothesize that new members would exert the most effort in training when the training itself was characterized by high levels of skill variety, task identity, task significance, autonomy, and feedback. Group-composition factors that can be hypothesized to influence individual learning positively are small size, a high degree of interaction among trainees, and homogeneity of skill levels at entry.

The second stream of research that can help illuminate the group-dynamics issue is represented in the social psychological research on group cohesiveness. The literature suggests that cohesiveness among training cohorts will be greatest when there are high levels of interaction (Festinger, Schachter, & Back, 1950), when the trainees share the same goals or cooperatively set the goals of training (Lott & Lott, 1965), and when they have similar attitudes and values upon entry (Aronson, 1976). Nevertheless, whether high cohesiveness leads to high productivity depends on whether there is trust and friendliness between workers and management (Whyte, 1955a; Trist & Bamforth, 1948) and on whether the jobs themselves are boring and tedious (Arnold & Feldman, 1986; Golembiewski, 1962; Seashore, 1954).

Thus, in terms of the role group dynamics play in facilitating (or impeding) learning, the following three factors seem to consistently emerge as important: whether the people-processing strategies used for trainees are "institutionalized" or "individualized," whether the work itself is challenging, and whether the training cohort has sufficient homogeneity of entry-level skills and attitudes to become cohesive. Theoretically, this could result in $8(2^3)$ possible patterns of group dynamics; for brevity, let us consider two of these scenarios. In the first, the "institutionalized" approach engenders a hostile attitude among trainees toward the organization. When the work is unchallenging and the group is cohesive, the trainees become cohesive against exerting effort on learning. In the second scenario, the institutionalized approach again engenders a hostile attitude among trainees toward the organization, but when the work is challenging and the group is cohesive, the trainees become motivated to prove themselves as a group to the trainers and veterans.

Unfortunately, not much empirical work has been done on the impact of group dynamics on training. Most of what is speculated about here is extrapolated from theoretical pieces, on the one hand, and social psychology laboratory experiments, on the other. Much more work is needed for an understanding of the interpersonal dynamics of training, both between trainers and trainees and among trainee cohorts.

Impact of Informal Training by Peers, Supervisors, and Mentors. Socialization research has made more salient the impact of informal training on how much, and in what ways, newcomers learn about their organizations. A great deal of what new recruits learn is learned through informal interactions with peers, supervisors, and mentors outside the context of formal training.

Research suggests that formal training programs often fail to pitch their material at the appropriate level of difficulty and job specificity (Feldman, 1988). Some organizations do an inadequate job of diagnosing recruits' individual strengths and weaknesses, or they do not adequately identify what job skills or knowledge will be needed for various jobs. As a consequence, many organizations provide training at the lowest common denominator — training from which everyone, regardless of specific job assignment, can learn. Too often, though, the material is so broad and unspecific that new recruits fail to see any usefulness in the training exercises. Such "generic training" provides neither enough useful information nor enough feedback and sense of accomplishment. (Lubliner, 1978; McGarrell, 1984; St. John, 1980).

Consequently, informal interactions with supervisors, peers, and mentors play an important role in filling the gaps left by formal training and orientation.

Louis, Posner, and Powell (1983) found in their research that formal off-site residential training was available to only 35 percent of their respondents, and formal on-site orientation was available to only 64 percent of their respondents. On a scale of 1 to 5 of "helpfulness," formal training and orientation were rated 3.08 and 3.18, respectively. In contrast, interactions with peers, supervisors, and senior co-workers were available to 89 percent, 87 percent, and 75 percent of new recruits, respectively. Moreover, these interactions were all rated more helpful to newcomers (3.96, 3.52, 3.79) than were formal training and orientation. Louis, Posner, and Powell (1983) also examined the relationships between various socialization practices and affective variables (job satisfaction, organizational commitment, and intention to stay). Off-site residential training had the strongest relationship to these three affective variables (average $r = .41$), followed by interactions with peers, supervisors, and co-workers (average $r = .27$), and formal orientation (average $r = .26$).

Three areas for future research and improved practice are suggested by these studies of the role of informal training and orientation on newcomers' learning.

First, it is clear that supervisors play a critical role in facilitating the transfer of learning from formal training programs to the back-home setting (Feldman, 1976b; Van Maanen & Schein, 1979), but the exact processes by which supervisors accomplish this liaison are much less certain. Several explanations (not mutually exclusive) exist for this phenomenon. Eden and Shani (1982) report some empirical evidence that a "Pygmalion effect" may be operating in some training programs: A supervisor who has positive expectations about how a subordinate can perform and communicates those expectations to the subordinate may actually facilitate the subordinate's performance. The work of Weiss (1977) indicates that subordinates' imitation of supervisors' behavior and social learning plays an important part in the transfer of learning. Weiss also found that the more the manager was viewed as competent and successful by the subordinate, the more the subordinate behaved similarly to the supervisor. Schein (1978) and Kram (1985) suggest that supervisors and mentors can facilitate newcomers' learning and adjustment by coaching them on the organization's political climate, by forcing newcomers to stretch themselves to their greatest abilities, and by protecting them from senior managers for their early mistakes. Which of these processes may create the greatest transfer of learning, and why, needs further investigation.

Second, the research is fairly consistent that peer and co-worker relationships also play a vital part in filling the gaps between formal training and the "real world" (Feldman, 1977; Louis, Posner, & Powell, 1983). As with the nature of supervisors' facilitation, the exact processes by which peers and co-workers accomplish this task are much less clear. Feldman (1980b) and Van Maanen (1984) suggest that co-workers play an interpretive and filtering function. Senior co-workers give new recruits frameworks with which to integrate seemingly disparate pieces of information, historical data or company "myths" that put new information into context, and a "view from the front" on what parts of the training are critical to attend to, what parts should be ignored, and what information is really needed for effective performance on the job. Kram (1985) focuses more on the ways peers and senior co-workers meet the social and esteem needs of newcomers. Peers may be able to fulfill some roles that neither trainers nor supervisors can: someone to talk to about career strategies or doubts, someone to provide self-affirmation, someone with whom to discuss feelings and emotional reactions, and someone who can also serve as a friend or confidante outside the workplace. Whichever roles peers play in facilitating, impeding, or redirecting the transfer of learning, this research suggests the need for more attention to the way newcomers are assigned to work partners (Van Maanen, 1975) and work groups (Feldman, 1977).

Third, research on the role of informal interactions in newcomers' learning suggests that we need a better understanding of how different organizational strategies of training may relinquish responsibility to or fuel the motivation of the informal network for accomplishing the tasks of the formal structure. Previous studies suggest that too much generic training, information overload, lack of adequate follow-up, and information irrelevance all contribute to the need of newcomers to turn to the informal system for concrete, specific information (Lubliner, 1978; McGarrell, 1984; St. John, 1980). Another issue relevant to both research and practice is the consequences of the "one shot" mentality of many training and orientation programs (Feldman, 1988). There is often a tendency for organizations to load their training and orientation efforts into some sort of "cram" course. Such a program, particularly when it is not supplemented by follow-up training or assessment, forces newcomers to turn to the informal network to make sense of, sort out, and rank in importance the material that has been presented.

Training research has sensitized practitioners and scholars alike to the need to design learning experiences that facilitate the transfer of knowledge. Socialization research suggests the need for increased investigation of, and attention in practice to, the ways informal interactions facilitate or impede the transfer of learning.

Adaptation and Innovation as Outcomes of Training and Socialization. The most frequently used dependent variables in training research have been tests of job knowledge and measurement of newcomers' performance on routine job tasks. Socialization research suggests that the study of how employees learn to perform innovatively is an equally important issue to consider. The whole question of replication versus nonreplication in training and socialization has been addressed from three perspectives.

First, from the prescriptive perspective, several scholars have noted that complete replication of newcomers' performance in the mold of veteran co-workers' performance may not increase organizational effectiveness and, indeed, may decrease it. Van Maanen (1976) writes that the socialization process is often deemed unsuccessful if it produces an overconformer, while Whyte (1956) refers to overconformity as "regrettable socialization" and Dubin (1959) refers to overconformers as "institutional automatons." Schein (1968) distinguishes among three basic responses to socialization: rebellion (the rejection of all values and norms), conformity (the acceptance of all values and norms), and creative individualism (the acceptance of pivotal values and norms, and the rejection of all others.) Schein

(1968, p. 10) writes that creative individualism is what organizations should be encouraging, for conformity "moves the organization toward a sterile form of bureaucracy."

Second, researchers on socialization have explored the job, organizational, and individual-difference variables that may influence newcomers' openness to or opportunities for innovative behavior. At the organizational level, Goffman (1961) and Etzioni (1961) suggest that total organizations (those that control all aspects of a person's life, such as boot camps) and coercive organizations (those that depend on punishment to ensure individuals' compliance) allow few opportunities for individuals to be proactive. At the level of job characteristics, Nicholson (1984) suggests that job discretion and job novelty— in Hackman and Oldham's (1980) terms, autonomy and skill variety— are the task dimensions most likely to encourage noncustodial responses. At the level of individual differences, self-esteem (Weiss, 1977), self-efficacy (Jones, 1986), locus of control (Rotter, 1966), and career stage (Nicholson, 1984) all influence individuals' openness to experimentation.

Third, some empirical research has examined the antecedents of innovative behavior, as well as the relationship of innovative behavior to other outcomes of socialization. For example, Feldman (1976a) found that mastery of the task, perceptions of equity between performance and evaluation, and role clarity were all antecedents of innovative behavior. Jones (1986) found that institutionalized socialization tactics (for example, divestiture) led to less innovative role definition than did individualized tactics, and that innovative behavior was strongly correlated with positive affective outcomes.

As Fisher (1986) notes, however, conformity may be a functional and desirable outcome in some socialization settings but not in others: "Innovation on the part of bank tellers, grocery baggers, or members of a marching band may be unnecessary at best, and harmful at worst" (p. 112). Training researchers have generally assumed replication as a given "good," just as socialization researchers have assumed innovation to be beneficial. Therefore, much more empirical research is needed to identify the constellations of organizational, job, and

individual-difference variables for which innovation as an outcome makes the most sense, theoretically as well as practically.
Furthermore, we need to examine, at a much more molecular
level, what aspects of formal and informal training facilitate or
inhibit innovative behavior in newcomers. At the molar level, it
appears that institutionalized training is more likely to stifle
experimentation than individualized training is, but research
on the issue to date has focused almost entirely on overall
organizational socialization, and not on training design characteristics per se.

The whole question of adaptation and innovation, as
outcomes of training and socialization, raises another important issue: the extent to which the absorption of newcomers into
an organization can provide training or developmental experiences for job incumbents. The socialization literature suggests
that organizational entry is an underdeveloped and under-
utilized opportunity for professional growth for veteran workers. Feldman (1976b, 1980b), Brett (1984), and Kram (1985)
suggest that the arrival of newcomers provides an organization
with opportunities to develop the people already working there.
Feldman notes that the addition of new work-group members
gives the organization an opportunity to reallocate tasks, as
much along individual preferences as possible, and to consider
work-redesign projects that capitalize on different employees'
comparative strengths. Brett writes that job entry provides
"break points," or opportunities for "unfreezing" from old routines. Kram's research indicates that serving as mentors to newcomers can provide an array of professional and personal rewards to veteran workers. Protégés can provide their mentors
with solid technical support on work projects, as well as with a
sense of what Levinson and his colleagues (1978) call "gener-
ativity"—the feeling among older workers that they have knowledge and expertise worth being taught to others.

A related issue that needs additional study is the process
by which groups of newcomers modify and change the behavior
of the trainers or agents of socialization (Graen, Orris, and
Johnson, 1973). Implicit in the idea of innovation and role
negotiation is change in the behavior, values, and attitudes of

trainers and socialization agents. We would especially expect these changes when the newcomers to an organization far out-number the trainers (as in MBA programs), in total organizations (such as in long-term health care facilities), and in organizations that give newcomers some reward or punishment power over trainers (such as in organizations where trainees' evaluations of trainers are considered seriously in pay and promotion decisions). Thus, while the research evidence is consistent that training and socialization are mutual-influence processes, we know much less about the extent and mechanics of trainees' impact on trainers.

Impact of Prior Socialization Experiences on Newcomer Will-ingness to Learn. Training and socialization scholars alike have researched the impact of newcomers' "base rate" characteristics on their adjustment to organizations. From the training per-spective, that research has largely focused on accurately gauging what newcomers have already learned about their jobs and on planning training that advances job knowledge and job perfor-mance beyond that point. In contrast, the socialization liter-ature has mainly focused on the impact of prior socialization on willingness to learn and has focused more closely on individual attitudes and values.

Most of the research on this topic has been on the impact of professional and occupational training on the attitudes, val-ues, and expectations of new recent graduates. Representative of this type of research study are Becker, Geer, Hughes, and Strauss's (1961) book on medical school education and Van Maanen's (1983) article on managerial socialization and gradu-ate education. Extrapolating across case studies, several charac-teristics of training itself seem to be consistently related to the amount of influence that occupational training has over the attitudes and values of students. These characteristics are phys-ical separation of students from practitioners in the early phases of training; disjunctive socialization (training done by professional staff, and not by job predecessors); collective so-cialization of large numbers of students; desirability of occupa-tion, in terms of financial and status rewards; length of training;

homogeneity of values, achieved through self-selection for training; and frequent interactions among students, fostered by task-interdependent learning assignments.

A second approach to prior socialization is represented by Van Maanen's (1984) notion of "chains of socialization." Van Maanen writes that most of the attention in organizational socialization has been on what socialization agents do to bring about abrupt shifts in newcomers' skills, knowledge, and values; consequently, researchers have paid insufficient attention to how much of organizational socialization is a subtle process and how much of the process consists of recruits' making only minor modifications in their behavior and attitudes from job setting to job setting. These chains of socialization are strongly forged in professional or occupational training, and they are merely filed, rather than resoldered, as individuals change organizations.

The concept of chains of socialization is intriguing, but, as Van Maanen notes, empirical evidence on this question is largely lacking. Research here has either focused on how students change during occupational training or on how recent graduates adjust to their first organizations. Very little longitudinal, empirical research follows recruits from time of entry into occupational training through their first organizational experiences. A notable exception is Schein's (1975) work on "career anchors," which examines how employees reassess their skills and aptitudes over time, in light of a series of job experiences in the real world. An important empirical research question is how individuals modify their skills training and attitudes from educational settings to job settings.

A third approach to the impact of prior socialization on organizational training and socialization is found in the work of Van Maanen and Barley (1984) on "occupational communities." They argue that occupational communities, regardless of status or professionalism, bring about a common focus among their members on work procedures, social relations, and perceptions of career success. An important contribution of this approach is that it focuses attention on the issue of how and when organizations can channel newcomers' energies away from the "cosmopolitan" concerns of the occupation and toward the "local" concerns of the firm (Gouldner, 1957). Van Maanen and Barley (1984) suggest that such factors as organizational complexity, control over innovation and technology, and amount of managerial power all influence the degree to which newcomers can be oriented to local procedures and values. Consideration of how organizations can co-opt newcomers away from their professional concerns (and of how occupational training forewarns or inoculates individuals against organizational influence) is critical to a richer understanding of transfer-of-learning issues.

An additional important research question, in this regard, is how organizations use selection as a way to obviate the need for either further training or socialization. Organizations may send out different messages to attract different types of workers (Stohl, 1986). The research on selection interviews, for instance, has long suggested that recruiters are likely to recommend candidates who are demographically similar to themselves and who meet their own stereotype of a good employee, in terms of style and appearance (Webster, 1964; Schmitt, 1976; Arvey & Campion, 1982). Van Maanen's (1984) research on chains of socialization suggests that organizations may be using selection as a means of choosing candidates with the same "culture of orientation," candidates who will need very little training or socialization to adjust. This tendency may explain, for instance, why some corporations (and universities) recruit from a small number of educational programs; they are already heavily staffed with graduates of these programs, and newcomers can be absorbed more readily.

Feldman (1976b) notes that organizations vary in where they put the most emphasis in socialization programs. His research indicates that organizations put most energy into *recruitment and selection* of highly educated employees (accountants, doctors, lawyers, professors), and at the highest levels of the organizational hierarchy, where the cost of hiring the wrong applicant or the consequences of choosing the wrong candidate are greatest. In contrast, organizations put more energy into *training and development* of employees who have relatively low skill levels, or who are at the lowest levels of the organization (or both). Feldman's research suggests that this either-or strategy —

attention to selection, or attention to training—misses the point. Researchers and practitioners need to be concerned both with the selection of members of occupational communities into organizations and with their adjustment to organizations, regardless of employees' perceived levels of professionalism.

Different Nature of Resocialization and Retraining. Historically, both training and socialization research have concentrated on the teaching of skills, attitudes, and values upon entry, but more and more attention is currently being paid to the resocialization and retraining of individuals in organizations. If previous socialization experiences have a major impact on current training efforts, as already suggested, then it is equally important to examine the chains of socialization within organizations.

In a longitudinal study of eighty managerial employees in a consumer products corporation, Feldman and Brett (1983, 1985) compared the entry experiences of new hires and job changers in learning their jobs and adjusting to their new settings. They documented several notable differences between the two groups.

1. New hires were often given some time to get up to par, but transferred and promoted employees were expected to "hit the floor running." They were expected to take charge immediately, and to perform at the same high level where they were performing before the change.

2. Most new hires were given some formal training for their new jobs, and they were encouraged to seek help when they needed it. In contrast, most organizations viewed job changers as needing less training for their new positions. These managers were expected to pick things up as they went along, even when the new jobs bore little relationship to the old ones.

3. Frequently employees were promoted or transferred so quickly on fast-track career paths that they were given new jobs, with increased responsibility, before they had mastered their old jobs. Often these managers felt out of control as they realized they were responsible for products or services about which they knew virtually nothing.

4. Because most new hires were coming right out of

school, their co-workers expected them to feel somewhat disoriented. Co-workers anticipated that these new employees would have some self-doubts, and co-workers more readily offered social support to them. While job changers also felt uncertain or alone in their new positions, their co-workers were less likely to be attuned to their anxiety or tension.

5. Finally, one special challenge to promoted and transferred employees was learning how to behave appropriately in their new settings. Job changers often had to unlearn norms, attitudes, values, and behaviors of the old settings, which were inappropriate to the new jobs. This need to unlearn was most pronounced among employees who were moving geographically between headquarters and field operations.

While the different experiences of new hires and job changers have been documented, there has been much less research on differences in the training provided to these two sets of employees. In practice, it is clear, organizations are putting more energy into training employees as they move from technical to managerial jobs and at other important career transitions, but there is much less empirical evidence on how organizational strategies for retraining differ from those for entry-level training.

The whole issue of unlearning is another important research topic that needs to be addressed. We know that job changers do go through an unfreezing or unlearning stage, but we know much less about the organizational or situational factors that cue employees to the need to unlearn and about the individual-difference variables that facilitate or impede unlearning. Brett (1984) suggests that such factors as task novelty, context novelty, changes in job discretion, knowledge about the performance of the prior incumbent, and levels of self-esteem and anxiety are critical.

The focus of research on training traditionally has been on how individuals learn job content and procedures. The socialization literature, particularly in examining resocialization, has reframed the research question to consider how employees undergoing job transitions cope with new tasks and new social environments. The term *coping strategies* means actions that individuals take to reduce uncertainty, reestablish routines, and exert control (Beehr & Newman, 1978; Folkman & Lazarus, 1980). When the differences between new hires and job changers are reframed in terms of coping, several interesting issues emerge.

Feldman and Brett (1983, 1985) found that new hires and job changers faced different opportunities and constraints in coping with new jobs; consequently, they used different coping strategies. New hires were more constrained from being proactive in changing their actual work environments, having not yet proved themselves in the organization; therefore, they were more likely to seek task help, job-related information, and social support in order to adjust. In contrast, job changers had more opportunities to restructure or redesign their work environments, but they were also expected to demonstrate higher performance soon after entry; consequently, job changers were significantly more likely to work longer hours and somewhat more likely to delegate and change work procedures. The nature of the relationship between coping and adjustment was also different for new hires and for job changers (Brett, Feldman, & Weingart, 1987). For new hires, high initial adjustment stimulated additional seeking of feedback. New hires who "hit the floor running" were then able to capitalize on their early adjustment and probe more deeply into their job activities and into how they were performing. In contrast, job changers sought additional feedback only as a last resort. They were more afraid that asking for help might stimulate others to view them as inept or insecure. They were also more concerned about losing face if their requests for help were rejected, about inadvertently revealing potentially damaging information about themselves, and about exposing themselves to negative feedback.

The examination of coping, in the context of training and socialization, also suggests two new directions for research on feedback. Training research has historically conceptualized feedback as data given to trainees that indicate their progress in learning or their standards of performance. The socialization literature suggests that feedback is a scarce resource, both to trainers and to trainees, and that it has costs as well as benefits associated with it (Ashford & Cummings, 1983). Much more empirical research is needed to discover the circumstances under which supervisors are willing to give feedback and trainees are willing to seek it.

A second direction for future research involves broadening the conceptualization of feedback. More attention needs to be paid to cognitive feedback, as opposed to outcome feedback (Jacoby, Mazursky, Troutman, & Kuss, 1984). Cognitive feedback describes how and why the desired outcome has or has not been achieved, while outcome feedback merely indicates whether the desired goal (such as a quota) is met. Researchers have noted that cognitive feedback is especially valuable to employees because it helps them identify the contingencies between their behavior and effective performance in different situations (Feldman & Weitz, 1988; Jones & Gerard, 1967; Weitz, Sujan, & Sujan, 1986). More empirical research is also needed on the differences between feedback seeking through monitoring and feedback seeking through inquiry. Most of the research discussed here has looked only at overt actions taken by newcomers to obtain information from peers or supervisors (inquiry). We know much less, though, about how trainees unobtrusively infer how they are performing by comparing their performance to that of others or by interpreting others' reactions to them (monitoring).

Training as Socialization

As the role and the scope of training in organizations have expanded, training has become an increasingly major part of the socialization process. For some entry-level managers, training programs often last three to six months, and the content of these programs goes far beyond teaching newcomers work skills. More and more, training has become the setting where perceptions and expectations about the organization are formed, where norms about social behavior are developed, where corporate values and ideology are communicated, and where individuals formulate their career paths. Indeed, in many cases, training has gone beyond being part of the socialization process and has become synonymous with it.

Regardless of whether training and socialization become isomorphic, it is clear that the overall training program plays a major role in how individuals make sense of and adjust to their new job settings. In this section, we will examine two major ways in which this may occur: attributional processes and norm development.

Attributional Processes. A central issue in the socialization and training literatures is the question of how new recruits learn *how* to learn and *what* to learn (Fisher, 1986). Even in highly structured training programs, such as medical schools, students report that a major task in their first few weeks is reaching consensus about what and how to study (Becker, Geer, Hughes, & Strauss, 1961). The problems of what to learn, and from whom to learn it, are especially salient to individuals who are not in structured training programs. These newcomers often report that they must identify what parts of their informal training are relevant and should be taken seriously (Fisher, 1986).

By the term *attributional processes* we mean the processes used by newcomers to determine which parts of their environments they should carefully attend to, and the processes used by newcomers to infer the nature of an organization from its training program. Thus, training programs play two roles in newcomers' attributions: They cue newcomers to salient aspects of their work environments, and they frame how newcomers interpret the seemingly random events about them (Salancik & Pfeffer, 1978; Van Maanen & Schein, 1979).

Very little empirical work has been done either on the aspects of training that particularly cue newcomers' attention to features of the organization or on what inferences trainees make from those cues. Theoretical and descriptive writing suggests several important features, however:

- Amount of bureaucracy: Cues newcomers to the organization's concern with rules and regulations; enables inferences

about whether the organization is employee-oriented, concerned with innovation, or efficient
- Choice of trainers: Cues newcomers to supervisory style,
  interpersonal style, norms of dress, timeliness; enables inferences about the importance of the training function in
  the organization, preferred leadership styles, modes of self-
  presentation
- Difficulty of training material: Cues newcomers to complexity of jobs, expected workload; enables inferences about
  pressure in the organization and number of work hours
  expected
- Punitiveness of training program: Cues newcomers to management style, use of punishment versus rewards as motivational tool; enables inferences about the level of trust in
  the organization and the competitiveness of the climate
- Custodial versus individualized training: Cues newcomers
  to organizational emphasis on predictability, teamwork,
  amount of differentiation tolerated among trainees; enables
  inferences about the importance of peer relationships, tolerance for deviance, concern with individual needs and
  desires.

Different constellations of features in training programs
are likely to cue trainees into different aspects of their work
environments and lead them to draw different inferences.
Custodial, bureaucratic, punitive training programs, for instance, may encourage a "get along by going along" predisposition. In contrast, an individualized, nonbureaucratic, non-
punitive training program may encourage an experimental
stance toward the job. Much more research is needed to identify
other aspects of training programs that may play a major role in
attributional processes, as well as how they do so.

Attributional processes are even more complicated when
newcomers enter an organization collectively in a formal training program (as is true in many educational programs and many
entry-level managerial and professional training programs).
Trainees are isolated from most insiders, with the exception of
the trainers; they typically have very little access to others for

information. Consequently, the trainees are likely to talk among themselves, to figure out what critical events in the training program mean and what implications these events have for how trainees should behave in the organization. Newcomers in these settings generate a "social construction of reality" (Berger & Luckman, 1966; Weick, 1977) — that is, together they generate a version of reality that makes the most sense of their current experiences, in the light of their past experiences. This perceptual reality later takes on a life of its own, regardless of the hard data; the "enacted" environment gets reified (Louis, 1980).

There is perhaps no other area of socialization research in which statistical evidence is both so lacking and so needed. Theoretical writing and case studies suggest that training and socialization programs are the crucible in which attributions and versions of reality are generated, and yet there is virtually no empirical research on these issues, in large part because these theories and concepts are too global to be testable, as formally presented. Nevertheless, if these cognitive approaches to socialization and training are to move beyond the status of general frameworks or meta-assumptions, then reframing these research questions in terms of some testable, middle-range theories becomes especially critical (Merton, 1957; Feldman, 1980a).

Norm Development. Training also serves as socialization by providing the setting and mechanism for the development of group norms. If newcomers enter the organization alone or receive only informal training, then training really has very little impact on the learning of norms. Most newcomers, however, go through some type of formal training in a group when they first enter an organization. The training program is where important group norms are developed and where the boundaries of acceptable behavior are delineated. There are at least six reasons why training programs provide such fertile ground for norm development (Feldman, 1984).

First, norms that facilitate group survival or task success are often set by the leader of the group or other powerful group members (Whyte, 1955b). These norms are set by explicit statements by supervisors and give newcomers at least one version of how to "make it" in the organization. In training programs, trainers offer newcomers pieces of advice to follow, both in the program and in the back-home setting, which will help them survive in their new jobs.

Second, critical events in the training program can often establish important precedents. For instance, when participants in the program are chastised for lateness or for dress or for some other form of self-presentation, trainees learn what the central, distinctive values of the group are. By the use of sanctions, trainers also make clear to newcomers what the boundaries of acceptable behavior are (Feldman, 1984).

A third reason why training programs have a major influence on norm development is that the first behavior pattern to emerge in a group often sets subsequent group expectations. For example, when the training program is marked by very formal interaction between supervisors and subordinates, trainees continue to behave in the same way when they start their jobs in the back-home setting. Norms that develop through this kind of primacy often simplify or make predictable the behavior that is expected of newcomers. Newcomers do not have to decide how to behave in certain classes of situations and can more easily avoid potentially embarrassing situations (Feldman, 1984).

Fourth, as noted earlier, an organization often hires people from the same set of schools, or other institutions, that powerful members of the dominant coalition come from. The training program then emphasizes to the newcomers the distinctive ways in which the new setting is similar to the old setting. The organization capitalizes on the relatively homogeneous sets of experiences of the newcomers and shows them how to turn shared values into expected behaviors in the organization (Feldman, 1984).

Fifth, training programs play a vital role in identifying deviant behavior (and group deviants). In a training program, behavior that is considered unacceptable to the group (either for task reasons or social reasons) is punished. In some cases, a deviant will be identified—a person whose behavior is so irritating, embarrassing, or threatening that the group censures him or her (Hackman, 1976). Even after the training program is over, newcomers vividly remember the lessons learned from the deviant. Moreover, once the deviant newcomer leaves the training setting, he or she may continue to be scapegoated, as a reminder to others.

Sixth, training programs perform the important function of creating and maintaining diversity among group members (Bales & Slater, 1955; Hackman, 1976). For instance, a training group may have one member whom others expect to break the tension when tempers become too hot, another to take care of the "creature" needs of the group (for example, by making arrangements for meals), and a third to keep accurate notes or maintain files. None of these roles entails formal duties, but they do involve activities that the group must accomplish and that it parcels out among its members (Feldman, 1984). Even when recruits leave training, many continue to perform the same functions for their cohorts in the organization.

In terms of future directions for study, the research agenda needs to be reframed to investigate norm development in the context of organizational training programs. Much of what we know about group norms comes from laboratory experiments in social psychology (Shaw, 1981) or from case studies (Whyte, 1955a, 1955b). There are also numerous, and excellent, studies of how norms develop in professional schools (Becker, Geer, Hughes, & Strauss, 1961) and in intensive occupational training programs (for example, Van Maanen's 1975 work on police). What is missing, though, is an analysis of how norms develop in organization-run (as opposed to profession-run or occupation-run) training programs.

There is also a relative lack of information about the job or situational factors that facilitate (or inhibit) the carryover of norms from training to back-home settings. Extrapolating from Van Maanen and Schein (1979), though, one might expect the greatest carryover of norms in the following circumstances:

- When the training is provided for individuals crossing functional boundaries (learning fundamentally new skills and job duties)

- When performance in the training program is likely to determine a person's fitness for promotion
- When the people-processing strategies are custodial in nature
- When the nature of the work is seen to involve high levels of risk for the newcomer or his or her clients and peers
- When the training is provided by past job incumbents, rather than by a professional training staff.

In terms of practice, the issues of norm development and carryover suggest the need for trainers to be more sensitive to how newcomers interpret and react to sanctions in the training program. Punishment in training programs is frequently conceived of in terms of extinguishing incorrect skill knowledge or job behaviors (Dentler & Erikson, 1959); less frequently do trainers attend to the more general lessons trainees learn from sanctions.

Development of New Theory, Methodology, and Practice

In the past fifteen years, there have been significant advances in our understanding of the entry of individuals into organizations, both from the training perspective and from the socialization perspective. Much remains to be learned, however. In this concluding section, we will explore some important future considerations for the integration of training and socialization research during the decade ahead. We will consider three sets of issues here, in particular: the development of new theory, the development of new research methodology, and the development of new practices of training and socialization in organizations.

New Theory. While there has certainly been more integration of the training and socialization perspectives in examinations of organizational entry in the past fifteen years, much of that work has been done in integrative literature reviews (Fisher, 1986), theoretical articles (Feldman, 1981), and comparative case studies (Van Maanen, 1984). What is noticeable is the lack of simultaneous attention to both training and socialization questions in single research studies (especially empirical ones).

Particularly since 1980, the research in socialization has seemed to swing more and more toward understanding the roles and norms of newcomers, and more and more away from understanding their learning of job content. At the same time, training research (especially that conducted in laboratory settings) has steadily controlled for the effects of the socialization aspects of training, focusing its attention directly on the cognitive processes involved in learning and on the measurement of learning or behavioral changes. Each set of researchers is aware of the findings of the other and dutifully cites them as "caveats to the present study" or "directions for future research," but rarely are these exhortations for integration heeded in practice.

For this situation to change, some reframing of the research agenda is needed on both sides. From the socialization perspective, the proliferation of new terms, concepts, and frameworks seems at times like an end in itself. There has been too much approach, and not enough arrival (Feldman, 1980). To have more theoretical impact, greater consideration of middle-range theories is needed (Merton, 1968; Hempel, 1966; Weick, 1971). These middle-range theories would be characterized by the following characteristics: concepts close enough to observable data for empirical testing of propositions to occur; sets of testable, related hypotheses; hypotheses dealing with limited sets of social phenomena; and theories cutting across micro and macro problems (Merton, 1968). In short, socialization research must demonstrate more consolidation of conceptual definitions and more integration of micro and macro hypotheses to advance our understanding about organizational entry.

The other theoretical issue that socialization research needs to address more carefully is how the learning of a job interacts with the learning of a role and of group norms. In many ways, in their desire to demonstrate that entry involves much more than learning a job, socialization researchers have increasingly ignored that aspect of entry, focusing instead on the learning of attitudes and values. The pendulum needs to swing back somewhat to considering the job-content issues of socialization more closely. A theory that purports to explain entry without explaining job learning is as impoverished as a theory that explains entry only by job learning.

From the training perspective, it is now critical for researchers to explicitly address the social environment and organizational context of training activities. This does not necessarily mean abandoning the core of training research; rather, it means more careful attention to variables that have previously been ignored or controlled for. For example, what systematic differences occur between individual training and group training? What differences occur in learning when training is conducted by past job incumbents, rather than by a professional training staff? How do the learning processes of job changers differ from those of new hires? What are the different consequences between "divesting" and "investing" training climates? What aspects of a training group facilitate or inhibit the transfer of learning? Rather than generating additional ways to excluding these questions from study, training research explicitly needs to research how these context factors interact with formal training to help or hinder individual learning.

A second broad theoretical question that training researchers need to consider is the active role trainees play in their own learning. In the conventional training research paradigm, the notion of activity has been conceptualized in terms of letting trainees practice concepts presented in lecture. The socialization research suggests a different set of questions: When will employees seek training? Why do employees fail to seek potentially useful feedback? Under what circumstances do employees turn to peers and informal contacts for help, instead of to supervisors or others officially in charge of training? How do employees learn to cope? Implicitly, training research has conceptualized the newcomer as a relatively passive agent with, if not a tabula rasa, at least a relatively uncluttered schema. The socialization research suggests that research in the training area should be reframed to consider the active role that newcomers play in their own learning and the ways in which previous training interacts with current training to influence new learning.

New Methodology. In many ways, the different methodologies of training research and socialization research have reinforced the divergent paths these literatures have taken. Socialization research has been largely nonempirical and has grown through the accumulation of theoretical pieces and detailed or provocative case studies. There has been some empirical longitudinal research (Vroom, 1966; Fisher, 1985) and some empirical cross-sectional research (Feldman, 1976a; Jones, 1986); by and large, however, the field has been neither data-dominated nor data-driven. In contrast, training research has been largely experimental, originally in the lab but more recently in the field. Control groups and pre- and postdata are regularly included. There are some widely accepted theoretical frameworks (for example, reinforcement theory), and research studies that flesh out and refine those frameworks constitute the bulk of the published research. If the integration of socialization and training research is to be accomplished at the theoretical level, as suggested here, then the research methodologies and techniques must also be modified, to some extent.

The first major change, from the socialization perspective, must be made in sampling. The knowledge base in socialization relies too much on individuals in a small handful of occupations—police officers, nurses, military recruits, engineers, and graduate professional students (Fisher, 1986). Very few studies examine more than one job or organization at a time. Moreover, in many studies occupational and organizational socialization are confounded ("learning to be a doctor" versus "learning to get through medical school"). Researchers have to be much more innovative in the choice of samples and much more persistent in gaining access to a broader array of subjects, especially those out of graduate school.

Second, socialization research needs many more longitudinal studies, mainly because (apart from the problems of retrospective bias) researchers are missing the opportunity to study individuals who do not make it successfully through the socialization process (Athanasiou, 1971). Moreover, researchers may attribute differences among successive cohorts to socialization processes, when many of these differences may be due to initial sample nonequivalence (Fisher, 1986).

Third, socialization research needs to move away from its almost exclusive reliance on qualitative data and researchers' ability to "go native" (Fisher, 1986). A recent step in this direction is the combination of various data-collection techniques — open-ended questions with loosely structured interviews (Schein, 1978), participant observation with structured questionnaires (Van Maanen, 1975); open-ended interviews with structured questionnaires (Feldman, 1976), and closed-ended interviews with structured questionnaires (Feldman & Brett, 1983). Such middle-ground data-collection techniques will allow socialization researchers to communicate more readily with one another, build on the findings of their colleagues, and facilitate the use of their findings by scholars outside their own domain.

From the training perspective, attention to the social environment and organizational context of training activities will also force some redirection of research methodology, although this will not be so dramatic as the shift required in socialization research. On the issue of sampling, training researchers need to sample contexts as well as subjects. Training research could be sampling different types of trainers, different sizes of training groups, different types of trainees (new hires, transfers, promotions), and different types of training climates to get a better understanding of how formal training interacts with its environment to influence individual learning. Along the same lines, training research could expand its measurement of dependent variables beyond individual job learning and the performance of routine tasks.

Training research has been well served by its lab and field experiments. For better understanding of the impact of context factors on learning, however, more qualitative research methods may be needed. For instance, to understand the impact of custodial versus individualized training on new recruits, data may need to be collected through observation, open-ended interviews, and survey questionnaires. Unfortunately (as socialization researchers have long been aware), many of the contextual influences on organizational entry are not readily tractable to experimental measurement at this point.

Training research could also benefit from longer-term studies of employees' learning. For example, it would be useful to measure transfer (or decay) of learning over time in the back-home setting, as well as the social and organizational factors that influence it. Similarly, longitudinal research would be helpful in discovering how the informal network modifies, reinforces, or counteracts the lessons of formal training.

New Practices. The integration of training and socialization research has led to a parallel process in the realm of practice. Training departments are being asked to broaden their scope well beyond their initial mission of remediating employees' deficiencies and preparing employees for new job assignments.

Consider the varieties of additional ways that training has been used in organizations over the past fifteen years. Training is being used to present the firm's ideology and values to managers and newcomers alike. Training is also being used as a reward. Employees are sent to training programs in luxurious settings, not for remediation or preparation, but as a reward for past performance. In some corporations, training is used as a test for promotion or as a sort of "tournament" (Rosenbaum, 1979) in which the best performers can be identified. Training is also being used as a means of reenergizing plateaued performers, as a precursor to demotion, and as a halfway house for outplacement candidates (Feldman & Weitz, 1988).

The increased pressure on trainers comes not only from corporations but also from society. Training programs are being asked to help compensate for corporations' past discriminatory actions, to deal with demographic and social trends (late enterers and part-time workers), to help workers adjust to new technology, and to resettle employees who have been laid off (see Chapter Nine).

Employees themselves are also turning to trainers, to deal with their career concerns (Feldman, 1985). Employees now hope—or demand—that corporations will help them identify their career goals, help them change careers, or help them find jobs better suited to their interests and motivation. Trainers are playing a major role in these activities.

The expansion of training into all these new areas presents new opportunities, as well as potential difficulties. On the positive side, the enlarged role of training departments has moved them into more mainstream positions in human resource departments and in corporations as a whole. They have moved beyond their narrow niche, to take on tasks that are central to the core functions of the organization and that create strong links with other units in the firm. The nature of the work they do has become more interesting, and the social policy consequences of that work have become significantly greater. On the negative side, trainers are being asked to perform duties for which they may not be especially well trained themselves, or for which they may have no real aptitude: personal counseling, placement counseling, making selection and promotion decisions, advocating (or opposing) social policy–based human resource programs, outplacement advising, career pathing, and so on. Moreover, many of the activities that training departments are taking on are less profit-generating than the traditional activities. Thus, as training groups accrue more and more activities farther away from their traditional turf, they also generate less revenue to justify and support their expanded mission.

In many ways, the prospects that face training practitioners are much like those that face their colleagues in training research. As the training function moves into the twenty-first century, scholars and practitioners alike will have to find a delicate series of balances: between integrating their work with other areas and losing their separate identity; between expanding their traditional areas of expertise and losing their distinctive competence; between accommodating the demands of others and becoming swamped by them; and between becoming jacks of all trades and masters of none.

References

Adler, I., & Shuval, J. T. (1978). Cross pressure during socialization for medicine. *American Sociological Review, 43,* 693–704.

Arnold, H. J., & Feldman, D. C. (1986). *Organizational behavior*. New York: McGraw-Hill.

Aronson, E. (1976). *The social animal*. San Francisco: Freeman.

Arvey, R. D., & Campion, J. E. (1982). The employment interview: A summary and review of recent research. *Personnel Psychology*, *35*, 281–322.

Ashford, S. J., & Cummings, L. L. (1983). Feedback as an individual resource: Personal strategies of creating information. *Organizational Behavior and Human Performance*, *32*, 370–398.

Athanasiou, R. (1971). Selection and socialization: A study of engineering student attrition. *Journal of Educational Psychology*, *62*, 157–166.

Bales, R. F., & Slater, P. E. (1955). Role differentiation in small groups. In T. Parsons, R. F. Bales, J. Olds, M. Zelditch, & P. E. Slater (Eds.), *Family, socialization, and interaction process* (pp. 35–131). New York: Free Press.

Becker, H. S., Geer, B., Hughes, E. C., & Strauss, A. L. (1961). *Boys in white*. New Brunswick, NJ: Transaction Books.

Beehr, T. A., & Newman, J. E. (1978). Job stress, employee health, and organizational effectiveness: A facet analysis, model, and literature review. *Personnel Psychology*, *31*, 665–700.

Berger, P., & Luckman, T. (1966). *The social construction of reality: A treatise in the sociology of knowledge*. New York: Anchor Books.

Brett, J. M. (1984). Job transitions and personal and role development. In K. M. Rowland & G. R. Ferris (Eds.), *Research in personal and human resources management* (Vol. 2) (pp. 155–185). Greenwich, CT: JAI Press.

Brett, J. M., Feldman, D. C., & Weingart, L. R. (1987). *Coping behavior and adjustment: New hires and job changers*. Working paper, University of Florida, Graduate School of Business.

Brim, O. G. (1966). Socialization through the life cycle. In O. G. Brim & S. Wheeler (Eds.), *Socialization after childhood* (pp. 1–49). New York: Wiley.

Caplow, T. (1964). *Principles of organization*. San Diego, CA: Harcourt Brace Jovanovich.

Dentler, R. A., & Erikson, K. T. (1959). The functions of deviance in groups. *Social Problems*, *7*, 98–107.

Dubin, R. (1959). Deviant behavior and social structure: Communities in social action. *American Sociological Review, 24,* 147–164.

Eden, D., & Shani, A. B. (1982). Pygmalion goes to boot camp: Expectancy, leadership, and trainee performance. *Journal of Applied Psychology, 67,* 194–199.

Etzioni, A. (1961). *A comparative analysis of complex organizations.* New York: Glencoe Press.

Feldman, D. C. (1976a). A contingency theory of socialization. *Administrative Science Quarterly, 21,* 433–452.

Feldman, D. C. (1976b). A practical program for employee socialization. *Organizational Dynamics, 5,* 64–80.

Feldman, D. C. (1977). The role of initiation activities in socialization. *Human Relations, 30,* 977–990.

Feldman, D. C. (1980a). On research in organizational socialization: The case for middle-range theory. In C. Pinder & L. Moore (Eds.), *Middle-range theory and the study of organizations* (pp. 315–325). Boston: Martinus Nijhoff.

Feldman, D. C. (1980b). A socialization process that helps new recruits succeed. *Personnel, 57,* 11–23.

Feldman, D. C. (1981). The multiple socialization of organization members. *Academy of Management Review, 6,* 309–318.

Feldman, D. C. (1984). The development and enforcement of group norms. *Academy of Management Review, 9,* 47–53.

Feldman, D.C. (1985). The new careerism: Origins, tenets, and consequences. *The Industrial Psychologist, 22,* 39–44.

Feldman, D. C. (1988). *Managing careers in organizations.* Glenview, IL: Scott, Foresman.

Feldman, D. C., & Arnold, H. J. (1983). *Managing individual and group behavior in organizations.* New York: McGraw-Hill.

Feldman, D. C., & Brett, J. M. (1983). Coping with a new job: A comparative study of new hires and job changers. *Academy of Management Journal, 26,* 258–272.

Feldman, D. C., & Brett, J. M. (1985). Trading places: Managing employee job changes. *Personnel, 62,* 61–65.

Feldman, D. C., & Weitz, B. A. (1988). Career plateaus reconsidered. *Journal of Management, 14,* 69–80.

Festinger, L., Schachter, S., & Back, K. (1950). *Social pressures in informal groups.* Palo Alto, CA: Stanford University Press.

Fisher, C. D. (1985). Social support and adjustment to work: A longitudinal study. *Journal of Management, 11*, 43–57.

Fisher, C. D. (1986). Organizational socialization: An integrative review. In K. Rowland & G. Ferris (Eds.), *Research in personnel and human resources management* (Vol. 4) (pp. 101–145). Greenwich, CT: JAI Press.

Folkman, S., & Lazarus, R. S. (1980). An analysis of coping in a middle-aged community sample. *Journal of Health and Social Behavior, 21*, 219–239.

Goffman, E. (1961). *Asylums*. New York: Doubleday.

Golembiewski, R. T. (1962). *The small group*. Chicago: University of Chicago Press.

Gouldner, A. (1957). Cosmopolitans and locals: Toward an analysis of latent social roles. *Administrative Science Quarterly, 2*, 281–306.

Graen, G., Orris, J. B., & Johnson, T. (1973). Role assimilation processes in a complex organization. *Journal of Vocational Behavior, 3*, 395–420.

Hackman, J. R. (1976). Group influences on individuals. In M. D. Dunnette (Ed.), *Handbook of industrial and organizational psychology* (pp. 1455–1525). Skokie, IL: Rand-McNally.

Hackman, J. R., & Oldham, G. R. (1980). *The design of work*. Reading, MA: Addison-Wesley.

Hempel, C. G. (1966). *Philosophy of natural science*. Englewood Cliffs, NJ: Prentice-Hall.

Hollander, E. P. (1958). Conformity, status, and idiosyncrasy credit. *Psychological Review, 65*, 117–127.

Jacoby, J., Mazursky, D., Troutman, D., & Kuss, A. (1984). When feedback is ignored: Disutility of outcome feedback. *Journal of Applied Psychology, 69*, 531–545.

Jones, E. E., & Gerard, H. B. (1967). *Foundations of social psychology*. New York: Wiley.

Jones, G. R. (1986). Socialization tactics, self-efficacy, and newcomers' adjustments to organizations. *Academy of Management Journal, 29*, 262–279.

Kram, K. E. (1985). *Mentoring at work*. Glenview, IL: Scott, Foresman.

Levinson, D. J., Darrow, C. N., Klein, E. B., Levinson, M. H., & McKee, B. (1978). *The seasons of a man's life.* New York: Knopf.

Lewicki, R. J. (1981). Organizational seduction: Building commitment to organizations. *Organizational Dynamics, 10,* 5–21.

Lott, A. J., & Lott, B. E. (1965). Group cohesiveness as interpersonal attraction: A review of relationships with antecedent and consequent variables. *Psychological Bulletin, 64,* 259–307.

Louis, M. R. (1980). Surprise and sense making: What newcomers experience in unfamiliar organizational settings. *Administrative Science Quarterly, 25,* 226–251.

Louis, M. R., Posner, B. Z., & Powell, G. N. (1983). The availability and helpfulness of socialization practices. *Personnel Psychology, 36,* 857–866.

Lubliner, M. (1978). Employee orientation. *Personnel Journal, 57,* 207–208.

McGarrell, E. J., Jr. (1984). An orientation system that builds productivity. *Personnel Administrator, 29,* 75–85.

McGehee, W., & Thayer, P. W. (1961). *Training in business and industry* (2nd ed.). New York: Wiley.

Merton, R. K. (1957). *Social theory and social structure.* New York: Free Press.

Merton, R. K. (1968). *Social theory and social structure* (2nd ed.). New York: Free Press.

Nicholson, N. (1984). A theory of work-role transitions. *Administrative Science Quarterly, 29,* 172–191.

Porter, L. W., Lawler, E. E., & Hackman, J. R. (1975). *Behavior in organizations.* New York: McGraw-Hill.

Premack, S. L., & Wanous, J. P. (1985). A meta-analysis of realistic job preview experiments. *Journal of Applied Psychology, 70,* 706–719.

Rosenbaum, J. E. (1979). Tournament mobility: Career patterns in a corporation. *Administrative Science Quarterly, 24,* 220–241.

Rotter, J. B. (1966). Generalized expectancies for internal versus external control of reinforcement. *Psychological Monographs, 80,* 1–26.

St. John, W. D. (1980). The complete employee orientation program. *Personnel Journal, 59,* 373–378.

Salancik, G. R., & Pfeffer, J. (1978). A social information processing approach to job attitudes and task design. *Administrative Science Quarterly, 23*, 224–253.

Schein, E. H. (1968). Organizational socialization and the profession of management. *Industrial Management Review, 9*, 1–16.

Schein, E. H. (1975). How career anchors hold executives to their career paths. *Personnel, 52*, 11–24.

Schein, E. H. (1978). *Career dynamics: Matching individual and organizational needs.* Reading, MA: Addison-Wesley.

Schein, E. H., & Ott, J. S. (1962). The legitimacy of organizational influence. *American Journal of Sociology, 67*, 682–689.

Schmitt, N. (1976). Social and situational determinants of interview decisions: Implications for the employment interview. *Personnel Psychology, 29*, 79–102.

Seashore, S. (1954). *Group cohesiveness in the industrial work group.* Ann Arbor: University of Michigan, Institute for Social Research.

Shaw, M. (1981). *Group dynamics* (3rd ed.). New York: McGraw-Hill.

Stohl, C. (1986). The role of memorable messages in the process of organizational communication. *Communication Quarterly, 34*, 231–249.

Sylvia, R. D., & Pindur, W. (1978). The role of leadership in norm socialization in voluntary organizations. *Journal of Psychology, 100*, 215–220.

Trist, E. L., & Bamforth, K. W. (1948). Some social and psychological consequences of the longwall method of coal-getting. *Human Relations, 4*, 1–38.

Van Maanen, J. (1975). Police socialization: A longitudinal examination of job attitudes in an urban police department. *Administrative Science Quarterly, 20*, 207–228.

Van Maanen, J. (1976). Breaking in: Socialization to work. In R. Dubin (Ed.), *Handbook of work, organization, and society* (pp. 67–130). Skokie, IL: Rand-McNally.

Van Maanen, J. (1978). People processing: Strategies of organizational socialization. *Organizational Dynamics, 7*, 18–36.

Van Maanen, J. (1983). Golden passports: Managerial socialization and graduate education. *The Review of Higher Education, 6*, 435–455.

Van Maanen, J. (1984). Doing new things in old ways: The chains of socialization. In J. L. Bess (Ed.), *College and university organization* (pp. 211–247). New York: New York University Press.

Van Maanen, J., & Barley, S. R. (1984). Occupational communities: Culture and control in organizations. In B. Staw (Ed.), *Research in organizations* (Vol. 6) (pp. 287–365). Greenwich, CT: JAI Press.

Van Maanen, J., & Schein, E. H. (1979). Toward a theory of organizational socialization. In B. Staw (Ed.), *Research in organizational behavior* (pp. 209–264). Greenwich, CT: JAI Press, 1979.

Vroom, V. H. (1966). Organizational choice: A study of pre- and postdecision processes. *Organizational Behavior and Human Performance, 6,* 36–49.

Wanous, J. P. (1981). *Organizational entry.* Reading, MA: Addison-Wesley.

Webster, E. C. (1964). *Decision making in the employment interview.* Montreal: McGill University, Industrial Relations Center.

Weick, K. E. (1971). Middle-range theories of social systems. *Behavioral Science, 19,* 357–367.

Weick, K. E. (1977). Enactment processes in organizations. In B. Staw and G. R. Salancik (Eds.), *New directions in organizational behavior* (pp. 267–300). Chicago: St. Clair.

Weiss, H. M. (1977). Subordinate imitation of supervisor behavior: The role of modeling in organizational socialization. *Organizational Behavior and Human Performance, 19,* 89–105.

Weitz, B. A., Sujan, H., & Sujan, M. (1986). Knowledge, motivation, and adaptive behavior: A framework for improving selling effectiveness. *Journal of Marketing, 50,* 174–191.

Whyte, W. F. (1955a). *Money and motivation.* New York: Harper & Row.

Whyte, W. F. (1955b). *Street corner society.* Chicago: University of Chicago Press.

Whyte, W. H., Jr. (1956). *The organization man.* New York: Simon & Schuster.

11

Training the International Assignee

Simcha Ronen

As a result of extensive migration and shifting socioeconomic trends, few Western nations can claim a culturally homogeneous workforce. Ethnic, religious, racial, and linguistic issues within these countries challenge individual citizens to be more culturally sensitive and to communicate better if they are to get along effectively. The business environment unquestionably raises these same challenges, both within and among organizations. Moreover, these challenges become still more difficult as national borders become increasingly porous and as the cultures that organizations face grow more and more diversified.

These global trends, in turn, produce yet another challenge: Effective communication between cultures requires skills for both long- and short-term interactions. Certain forces affect long-term interactions, however, in two ways, simultaneously. These forces encourage cooperation between business associates from diverse cultural backgrounds; at the same time, the same forces also hinder and constrain such cooperation.

Consider the following example: An international assignee (IA) is sent from his headquarters to a host-country subsidiary. There he encounters his counterpart, the local manager. The IA sees that the local manager shares one of his two goals: the multinational corporation's success. At the same time, the local manager has other goals, too—among them, the success of his particular subsidiary. The IA will no doubt make attributions about the host-country manager's dual agenda. This is a common, routine process. But is the IA properly equipped to make attributions about other emotional, cognitive, and value sets that may affect the host-country manager's behavior? After all, this manager belongs to (or is affiliated with) various groups or levels of society. He is a member of his family, his professional peer group, his company, his ethnic or religious group, and his nation. Each of these groups may contribute different perceptual sets, cognitive paradigms, codes of behavior, and expectations. Moreover, the IA may have to interact successfully during the assignment with various individuals representing all these reference subgroups, individuals who may or may not share the same business goals. In dealing with these complex issues, the IA often feels as if he must possess the patience of a diplomat, the zeal of a missionary, and the linguistic skill of a United Nations interpreter. Of course, few international assignees are so inherently gifted. Under such circumstances, the multinational corporation has two fundamental choices. One choice is to recruit extraordinary candidates to fill international assignments or, alternatively, to compromise on the available candidates from within the organization. This choice presents the calculated risk of a high failure rate. The second choice requires the use of the classic staffing model provided by our field and the modest application of it to the challenge at hand.

This chapter employs the latter approach. Following the classic model, I shall undertake the following tasks: to identify the behavioral characteristics of a successful international assignee (job description); to identify the optimal skills necessary for the assignment (job analysis); and to evaluate the training techniques available for developing such skills.

The biggest obstacle to pursuing these tasks is the limited quantity and quality of pertinent empirical research literature. Latham (1988) concludes in his review that interest in conducting empirical research on cross-cultural training has declined in North America since the late 1960s and 1970s. Mendenhall and Oddou's (1985) review is also discouraging, concluding that our knowledge of the cognitive dynamics of the IA cross-cultural adaptation process is quite limited. Still, I have tried to benefit from whatever research is available and from various reviews, such as the monumental handbook compiled by Landis and Brislin (1983). I have also tried to benefit from the knowledge of related fields. Nevertheless, I was forced periodically to supplement the gaps with my own speculations and suggestions.

This chapter attempts to answer the following questions.

1. Why is there a need to develop training programs for international assignees?
2. What is the task, and what is the behavior that must be developed? What are the necessary skills? What are the training goals?
3. Who should be trained? What should the processes of recruitment and selection contribute? Who are the candidates?
4. How (and by what techniques) can we best achieve our training goals?
5. By whom should the IA be trained? What should be the trainers' qualifications?
6. When should the various training techniques be applied?

I shall now address these questions one by one.

Why the Increased Need for Training?

Two major concerns account for the proliferation of articles and reports on staffing issues related to selecting and training IAs. The first concern involves the trend toward an increase in the number of international assignees, despite companies' efforts to hire host-country nationals. (This trend also holds true for reverse expatriates — foreign managers who temporarily join the headquarters staff.) The second concern derives from consistent (although at times sporadic) reports about the high failure rate among international assignees. Let us start by reviewing the reasons for the potential increase in the need for IAs. Ideally, the following list will serve three purposes: to explain the rationale for this chapter; to energize our colleagues

into pursuing much-needed research in this area; and to provide a framework for identifying performance criteria.

- Increased global competition
- Rapid transfer of technology
- Shorter product life cycles
- Decentralized organizations
- Advancement in functional areas
- Complexity of overseas duties
- Host-country requirements
- Local ethnocentric attributes
- Cost of failures

Now let us examine these reasons one by one.

Increased global competition forces American corporations
to manage their production processes, service functions, and
marketing efforts more effectively. This task is often perceived to
be best achieved by direct action from headquarters.

The *rapid transfer of technology*—including technical skills
and production technology—and the rapidity with which such
technology becomes obsolete prompts headquarters to take
energetic initiative to instruct and modernize subsidiaries' operations. The transfer of technology requires IAs to be mobile and
adaptable.

Shorter product life cycles necessitate centralized or highly
coordinated efforts on research and development and product
design. This coordination often results in sending experts into
the field to speed up adaptation to new specifications.

Decentralized organizations result from the complexity of
controlling and monitoring subsidiary operations, with a consequent delegation of responsibility to individual subsidiaries or
to regional headquarters. To maintain some level of control and
influence, the home-country headquarters must send its representative to the host country.

Advancement in functional areas has a consequence similar
to the one resulting from the increasing number of subsidiaries.
In addition, host-country governments (mainly in the Third
World) often require multinational corporations to develop

high-technology production locally, which in turn prompts headquarters to send experts in various functional areas to instruct and develop local personnel.

The *complexity of overseas duties* provides yet another reason for training IAs. In addition to their more traditional tasks—providing technical and functional expertise to the local subsidiary management—IAs are increasingly perceived by locals as having other roles. Such roles include representing headquarters in various matters that are not necessarily within the international assignee's own expertise. Examples include company strategy, human resource policy, rationales for decisions, and so forth. To compound the difficulty of this complex role, the IA must often explain or protect home-country national viewpoints. Such a multiplicity of roles challenges almost everyone.

Host-country requirements are changing and increasing complexity. For example, Third World countries present greater and greater requirements to multinational corporations in terms of financial commitment, utilization of human resources, and share of ownership. Labor-intensive operations were once attractive to multinational corporations; now, many host-country work forces regard them as a manifestation of exploitation. Local governments now want advanced technology and increased training of their work forces. In addition, local managers want greater autonomy, which further complicates the international assignee's task (Pazy & Zeira, 1985). IAs cannot escape these issues and must be prepared to deal with them.

Local ethnocentric attributes require a similar sort of training. In many host countries, antagonism toward foreigners further aggravates the task. It can also complicate the family life of the IA.

The *cost of failures* (casualties) is perhaps the most dramatic evidence for why IA training is necessary. Although high rates of early return are reportedly common, the literature refers to very few (and, at times, regrettably outdated) field reports. For example, one of the main sources, Tucker (1974), reported that the rate of managers' premature return from assignments in some Middle Eastern nations was about 50 percent. Even those who completed their terms did not always function effectively. Paige and Martin (1983) report that among the teachers sent to North African nations, approximately 75 percent experienced extreme psychological and/or physical difficulties. The researchers attribute these results to inadequate training programs and poor trainers. Tung (1982) reports a 15 percent rate of recall or dismissal among U.S. companies responding to a survey.

Note, however, that not all failures return. Some IAs persist and do not appear in such reports, yet they remain costly to the multinational corporation in terms of reputation and financial risk. As in other areas, such as quality control and improved technology, multinational corporations should aim at zero failure. It should be emphasized, in particular, that the benefit of reducing international assignees' failures is enormous. One leading multinational corporation executive recently estimated that the expenses incurred by an IA during the first year abroad equal four times that person's yearly salary.

Tung's (1982) study is informative, although it is not a representative sample, on account of a low return rate for the survey. Tung found that the correlation between a rigorous level of selection and training and the expatriates' failure rate for U.S. companies was − .63. (It was − .47 for European and − .34 for Japanese companies.) In other words, the availability of a rigorous selection and training program significantly reduced the incidence of expatriates' inability to function effectively in foreign environments.

Finally, the cost of failures—whether through voluntary return, recall, or dismissal—is difficult to estimate. The potential negative effects are dramatic: loss of goodwill, reduction in effectiveness, and other long-term harm to the subsidiary. The effects on the returning manager and his or her family can also be devastating. To improve the international assignee's effectiveness, a training program is necessary. Before proceeding, however, we should first review the task components for the IA.

Training Goals

Through the training process, we attempt to create systematic change and development of the knowledge, skills, and attitudes required for effective performance (Goldstein, 1980; Latham, 1988; Wexley & Latham, 1981). Identifying the behavior necessary to effective job performance — that is, establishing job criteria — is the single most important input to training plans. This process of identifying behavior can be achieved through a variety of means (Schneider & Schmitt, 1986).

In our case, however, this task is not easy. The traditional source of information, a job description and analysis, is mostly unavailable. Most often lacking is the definition of the job from the viewpoint of management. Although the functional task of the IA is relatively clear — after all, he or she was selected for experience and technical skills — skills constitute only one aspect of the job requirements. For this reason, managers' performance evaluations tend to be unreliable and vague. Such evaluations are completed both at the home office and in the field. Lacking a job description from the home office, however, host-country supervisors evaluating IAs simply rely on their own expectations and subjective choices of characteristics. Such evaluations provide only minimal information necessary for identifying skills, characteristics, traits, and behaviors that account for overall performance ratings. This process could be partially enhanced if the available performance ratings at least represented a wide-scale range. On the contrary, the only available hard data on performance comes from the lowest portion of this scale — that is, from the failures.

Other sources of information regarding job descriptions are international assignees' own reports (usually after completion of assignments) and host-country managers' reports. These reports present a grim view of the field. Still, we can make some general statements related to the selection of IAs and their performance. (See for example, Harris & Harris, 1972; Hays, 1971, 1974; Howard, 1974; Ivancevich, 1969; Miller, 1972a, 1972b; Tung, 1981, 1987). These statements justify some propositions for further analysis of the international assignee's task.

Proposition 1: The IA who has failed in an assignment (returned prematurely) had a good track record in the job before assignment overseas. Alternative explanations may also be surmised from this statement. For example, technical skills used in the home country were insufficient for effectively carrying out the technical duties abroad; failure resulted from other factors in the work environment; failure resulted from factors associated with life external to the job; premature return was not a result of performance but rather of a spouse's or children's reaction to living overseas.

Proposition 2: From reports of headquarters personnel, host-country nationals, and returning expatriates, it appears that a manager's relational abilities (interpersonal skills, adaptation to local culture, and so on) account for the difference between failure and success. High relational proficiency increased the rate of successful completion of missions. Unfortunately, very few companies recognize the importance of this factor. In short, personal adaptation to new environments (physical, social, cultural, and so on) requires skills and motivations unrelated to the job at home.

Proposition 3: International assignees with previous overseas experience were more likely to succeed in their foreign assignments. This was true even when the country of early experience differed from the country of current assignment. Apparently, an exposure to a wider range of cultural environments provides a socialization process that helps to create a diversity of values and to encourage more efficient adaptation to foreign surroundings. This process may influence an individual's cognitive set, but it also seems to have a lasting effect on his or her personality.

Hays (1971) reports a correlation of $-.43$ between number of years before age twenty spent abroad and the authoritarianism-dogmatism scale. Managers' successful and effective performance points to a few possible conclusions: Cultural adaptability is a learned (socially acquired) skill; people with high skills in this area succeed in overseas assignments; individuals may exhibit not only good relational skills but also a high level of motivation to experience diverse cultures and to derive satisfaction from them. This hypothesis is based on the assertion that the successful desired behavior is a function of both the skills necessary and the motivational level. Hays (1971) indicates that American companies no longer depend on foreign-reared individuals to fill positions abroad. He observes that, in the past, multinational corporations focused on locating and attracting sons of diplomats and business expatriates with considerable early life experience abroad. With the current trend of promotion from within (and the need for high functional-technical training), such a practice is no longer possible. The fact remains that exposure to a multicultural socialization process improves the candidate's chances for success in a foreign assignment.

Proposition 4: Most companies use technical skills and professional competence as the major variables in selecting IAs. Generally, these are the most easily identifiable task requirements. From the corporate viewpoint, this trait may seem easily available, while the other skills are either difficult to ascertain or, worse yet, are still considered unimportant by headquarters executives. Another possibility is that, from the viewpoint of the personnel staff, this selection process provides a low-risk alternative (Miller, 1977).

These four propositions are confirmed throughout the available literature. The main conclusion we can draw is that one of the most pertinent areas contributing to the effective performance of the IA — and by far the most lacking in attention from the present training (and selection) programs — concerns relational abilities and intercultural adaptability. A detailed analysis of this area is therefore necessary.

Relational Abilities and Multiculturalism

One of the main issues emerging from the reported data is the importance of cross-cultural sensitivity and intercultural competence (sometimes refered to as *multiculturalism*). To function effectively in a new culture, individuals must exhibit behavior that reflects appropriate personal characteristics, of both a cognitive and an affective nature.

Three tasks are immediately apparent at this stage of our analysis: first, to survey all the characteristics reported in the literature that represent cross-cultural sensitivity and intercultural competence; second, to categorize them into meaningful clusters; and, third — and perhaps most difficult — to describe these characteristics in terms of trainable behaviors and abilities. These tasks should facilitate the early identification of

Exhibit 11.1. Attributes of Success in Overseas Assignment.

Perseverance	Managerial ability	Resourcefulness
Empathy	Organizational ability	Creativity
Courtesy and tact	Administrative skills	Responsibility
Respect	High motivation	Alertness
Interest in nationals	Overseas experience	Desire to go abroad
Flexibility	Display of respect	Interest in foreign
Adaptability	Listening skills	cultures
Patience	Confidence	Intellectual curiosity
Tolerance	Frankness	Belief in mission and
Initiative and energy	Kindness	job
Openness	Communication skills	Willingness to change
Nonjudgmentalness	Ability to deal with	Spouse's positive
Sincerity and integrity	stress	opinion
Emotional stability	Tolerance for	Adaptability of spouse
Nonethnocentrism	ambiguity	and family
Positive self-image	Political sensitivity	Willingness of spouse
Independence	Integrity	to live abroad
Outgoingness and	Dependability	Stable marriage
extraversion	Industriousness	
Experience in	Variety of outside	
company	interests	
Technical skills and	Youthfulness	
knowledge	Imagination	

potential candidates who possess these abilities and should also simplify the training and developmental processes necessary to develop those abilities. Combined, these tasks will facilitate the desired behavior when the IA starts his or her challenging new job.

The formidable task of identifying the training goals of an effective preparatory program for an IA can be surmised from Exhibit 11.1.

This list derives from various publications, many of which are reported in Kealey and Ruben (1983). These studies report findings on four groups of overseas professionals: Peace Corps volunteers, overseas businesspeople, technical assistance personnel, and military personnel. (See Arensberg & Niehoff, 1971; Brislin, 1981; Cleveland, Mangone, & Adams, 1960; Detweiler, 1975; Dinges, 1980; Gudykunst, Wiseman, & Hammer, 1977; Guthrie & Zektick, 1967; Harris, 1973; Harris & Moran, 1979;

Hautaluoma & Kaman, 1975; Hawes & Kealey, 1980; Hays, 1972; Howard, 1974; Ivancevich, 1969; Kealey, 1978; Maretzski, 1965; Mezingo, 1974; E. Miller, 1977; V. Miller, 1979; Mumford, 1975; Ruben, 1980; Ruben & Kealey, 1979; Russell, 1978; Schwartz, 1973; Thompson & English, 1964; Yellen & Hoover, 1973.)

As long and comprehensive as Exhibit 11.1 may appear, the attributes listed keep reappearing in various publications. To suggest appropriate training techniques for the potential IA, we must analyze and organize this list.

Two steps seem appropriate: first, to categorize the attributes into underlying dimensions along some rational consideration; and, second, to include in each category or dimension the higher-order attributes that seem to include lower-level attributes. In addition, the guiding principle for that process should be our present knowledge of attributes that can be operationalized in behavioral terms. This armchair process is, of course, inferior to the optimistic statistical predictive model. In the current absence of a comprehensive data base for relating individual scores on each attribute and for rating individual performance, however, we can only resort to extrapolation from other fields of applied research.

Note two important aspects of Exhibit 11.1. At this stage of research, it is difficult to distinguish clearly between behavioral descriptions that are optimally associated with effective performance criteria, on the one hand, and, on the other hand, the abilities one should possess in order to acquire the desired behavior through experience and training. The conceptualizations in the list therefore include both kinds of features. Moreover, the list also includes, under a separate category, attributes that are associated with the individual's motivational state. These attributes have been greatly neglected. Furthermore, they can be ascertained at the stage of selecting a candidate. Therefore, they deserve a separate analysis.

The second aspect is related to the purpose of creating the list. Although our task here is to develop training goals, the properties listed are equally appropriate for the selection process. The two tasks—selection and training—are no doubt closely interrelated, especially in the case of the IA candidate.

There are two reasons for the interrelation of these tasks. First, many companies have yet to develop any structured training programs. Second, even when training is not available, most companies are also negligent about applying a rigorous selection procedure that includes variables other than technical skills.

Categorizing the Attributes of Success

The following categorization of training needs is an attempt to produce a comprehensive structure of suitable dimensions. Planning for a particular program, of course, should benefit from well-established principles in the training field. First, one should resort to the needs assessment methodologies useful for designing training system (Prien, Goldstein, & Macey, 1987) and content validity models (Goldstein, 1980). The second step is the selection of the candidates and the analysis of the individual training needs.

Few companies have initiated rigorous surveys to assess training needs associated with improving effectiveness among IAs. Unfortunately, corporations that do so rarely report their findings publicly. One firm, however, reported its findings in the literature (Dotlich, 1982). Honeywell, Inc., launched a survey to identify such needs. The company surveyed 347 managers who lived abroad or traveled regularly, plus 55 local executives who interacted with foreign managers. Two quotations from the interviews are indicative of this survey (p. 28):

> Time as a cultural value is something which we don't understand until we are in another culture. It took me six months to accept the fact that my staff meeting wouldn't begin on time and more often would start thirty minutes late and nobody would be bothered but me.

> Communication can be a problem. I had to learn to speak at half the speed I normally talk.

The most important result of the survey was the conclusion that increased levels of training are necessary in international management, both for top headquarters executives (Pazy & Zeira, 1983) and for IA candidates. (Pazy and Zeira, 1983, address some of the issues associated with the changes in parent organizations.) This survey reached the following recommendations regarding IAs:

- Improve the selection process
- Provide extensive culture-specific information
- Provide general cultural information on values, assumptions, and so on
- Provide self-specific information, including identification of one's own cultural paradigms, such as values and beliefs that shape perceptions about others
- Provide language training.

American executives from various multinational corporations have reported their perceptions of the factors contributing to expatriates' failures to function effectively in foreign environments (Tung, 1982). In ascending order of importance, the factors are the following:

- Inability of manager's spouse to adjust to a different physical or cultural environment
- Inability of manager to adjust to a different physical or cultural environment
- Other family-related problems
- Manager's personal or emotional immaturity
- Manager's inability to cope with the larger responsibility posed by overseas work
- Manager's lack of technical competence for the assignment
- Lack of motivation to work overseas.

To categorize the training needs previously mentioned, we can be guided by field surveys (Dotlich, 1982; Tung, 1982), various suggestions for cross-cultural training applications (Triandis, 1983; Warren & Adler, 1977), the attributes listed in

Exhibit 11.2. Categories of Attributes of Success.

Job Factors
  Technical skills
  Acquaintance with host-country and headquarters operations
  Managerial skills
  Administrative competence
Relational Dimensions
  Tolerance for ambiguity
  Behavioral flexibility
  Nonjudgmentalism
  Cultural empathy and low ethnocentrism
  Interpersonal skills
Motivational State
  Belief in the mission
  Congruence with career path
  Interest in overseas experience
  Interest in the specific host-country culture
  Willingness to acquire new patterns of behavior and attitudes
Family Situation
  Willingness of spouse to live abroad
  Adaptive and supportive spouse
  Stable marriage
Language Skills
  Host-country language
  Nonverbal communication

Exhibit 11.1, and, in particular, Hays's (1971) review. We end up with five categories: job-related factors, relational dimensions, motivational state, family situation, and language skills. The relative importance of each category is difficult to establish. Returning IAs and managers' evaluations, however, do offer some information in this regard, as reported earlier. Unfortunately, the lack of systematic evaluation of such data renders speculative any statement about the relative importance of these dimensions in contributing to an international assignee's level of effectiveness.

Exhibit 11.2 summarizes the categories now delineated.

Job Factors

Most multinational corporations rely on the candidate's technical skills in applied functional areas (production, marketing, finance, data processing) as the only criterion for selection. Without question, competency in the functional area is the initial requirement and should be the first step in the selection process, but job factors also include managerial skills, particularly administrative competence.

Note, too, another way in which international assignments differ from local domestic transfers. Host-country personnel expect IAs to represent headquarters policies and practices. IAs are often perceived by host-country personnel as potential resource persons for information on headquarters procedures and strategies. Moreover, IAs may have to defend such policies. A thorough knowledge of home-office structure and policies, as well as knowledge of the company's international operations, is highly desirable. Particularly in many Third World countries, the international assignee's credibility may be related to his or her connections with appropriate headquarters authorities or to ability to secure needed information and resources.

Relational Dimensions

This area has received the most attention in the literature on the selection, preparation, and performance of IAs (see Adler, 1974; Hays, 1971; Hammer, Gudykunst, & Wiseman, 1978; Howard, 1974; Ivancevich, 1969; Miller, 1972a, 1972b, 1977; Paige & Martin, 1983; Porter & Samovar, 1976; Ruben, Askling, & Kealey, 1977). We have already noted that this area most often accounts for the international assignee's success or failure, at the same time that headquarters executives most thoroughly ignore it. This category is the most difficult to conceptualize because of the various and numerous properties reported in the literature that could fall under this heading (see Exhibit 11.2). Furthermore, this category includes properties that range from deeply rooted personality characteristics (such as extraversion or emotional stability) to more transient socialized value systems (such as ethnocentrism) to incidental behavior resulting from the interaction of the individual with immediate environmental conditions (courtesy, initiative, interest in locals).

To examine this category and form meaningful subcategories, I have chosen to follow the approach underlying the available literature on assessing future managerial potential: the assessment-center technique. The rationale for this choice is based on four reasons: First, the assessment center considers present abilities, rather than effective target behavior expected in the future managerial job. Second, assessment is based on manifestations of exhibited behavior (that is, although abilities are assessed, they are evaluated through observed behavior in simulated conditions). Third, most of the dimensions evaluated are of the relational type and are observed in group-simulated interactions. Fourth, some of the major training techniques that capture desired behavior are of the experiential type, techniques that involve ground rules similar to those used in the group simulations in assessment centers.

Accordingly, I have reduced the approximately thirty properties associated with the relational ability (see Exhibit 11.1) to five dimensions. The major abilities in the relational category are tolerance for ambiguity, behavioral flexibility, nonjudgmentalism, cultural empathy and low ethnocentrism, and interpersonal skills. Let us now examine these abilities one by one.

Tolerance for Ambiguity. This attribute is related to the candidate's ability to survive effectively in a new environment that introduces continuous uncertainties. It enables him or her to resist stressful situations and, ideally, to react to challenging moments with resourcefulness and creativity. This ability is, of course, necessary for any top executive in the home office. It is all the more crucial in the overseas environment, since the international assignment includes not only the uncertainty of the immediate functional task but also social, political, and economic surprises.

Behavioral Flexibility. Candidates with behavioral flexibility can vary their behavior according to immediate requirements. Such individuals are alert to social cues and are capable of altering their responses and adapting effectively to the environment with independence and confidence.

Nonjudgmentalism. The frame of reference by which human beings evaluate other people and events results from their personalities and value systems. Whether about esthetic or moral issues, the socialization process and culture itself provide us with subjective yardsticks. There are, however, individual differences in the intensity of convictions about such issues, as well as in the intensity with which such judgments are expressed. The potential to become more effective in one's communication with others and, moreover, the ability to function cooperatively are related to such intensity. Higher exposure to varied cultures lowers individuals' thresholds for accepting others' beliefs, esthetic evaluations, and norms.

Cultural Empathy and Low Ethnocentrism. Ethnocentrism is an individual's predisposition to attribute superiority to members of his or her ethnic or national group, as well as to that group's values, norms, and achievements, while rejecting or condescending to members of other groups and their values, norms, and achievements. A low ethnocentric attitude is desirable for an individual in a foreign culture. It appears as tolerance for diverse behaviors and norms, empathy toward local beliefs and customs, political sensitivity, courtesy, and—if possible—even kindness.

Interpersonal Skills. Skills that enable effective interpersonal communication also foster intercultural sensitivity. One has to be patient, respectful, capable of listening, and alert to various stimuli from individuals and events. For example, one should be sensitive to the limitations of one's own language and be willing to compromise by talking more slowly or using a simpler vocabulary. Some researchers have asserted that an outgoing (extraverted) personality is more appropriate to working in a foreign environment.

Motivational State

A separate discussion of the motivational states is important, for three reasons. First, certain aspects of the topic reappear in the literature. For example, Miller and Cheng (1977) found that, among both American and West German expatriate managers, the predominant factors in accepting an overseas assignment were opportunities to enhance one's career, financial remuneration, the appeal of serving abroad, and encouragement from others. Second, certain motivational states can be discerned at an early stage and can be used to represent minimum cutoff points for selection. Third, some motivational aspects are necessary for facilitating an effective training program and, if identified, can probably be enhanced through appropriate reinforcements.

The most pertinent attributes in this category are belief in the mission, congruence with career path, interest in overseas experience, interest in the specific host-country culture, and willingness to acquire new patterns of behavior and attitudes.

Belief in the Mission. This is a dimension that concerns the congruence between an individual's and an organization's goals. The candidate should feel that he or she is sent to a necessary position and that he or she will serve both the multinational corporation and its interests abroad. In Hackman and Oldham's (1980) terms, this is the perception of task significance.

Congruence with Career Path. One of the main obstacles to the effectiveness of an IA abroad is his or her doubt that the assignment contributes to his or her future career. Lack of long-term headquarters strategy, and especially the reluctance of many multinational corporations to use assignees' international skills and knowledge, have left many returning managers out of the race for promotions. The "grapevine" often denigrates such assignments, and the result is an unmotivated IA.

Interest in Overseas Experience. Desire to go abroad and experience the opportunities unique to travel, as well as intercultural curiosity and desire for adventure, are helpful in motivating the IA to accept and persevere in the overseas task.

Interest in the Specific Host-Country Culture. Multinational corporations operate largely in diversified countries. For this reason, candidates vary in the interest they express toward overseas experience. The host countries themselves vary in terms of language, level of industrialization, geography, and climate. Zeira and Harari (1979) have demonstrated that host-country managers are highly sensitive to international assignees' attitudes and expect them to demonstrate interest in the local culture. Another factor, also applicable to other categories, is that financial remuneration and cost-of-living adjustments may differ significantly from one country to another. Even such factors as the availability of appropriate education for the assignee's children can influence attitudes toward the whole country.

Willingness to Acquire New Patterns of Behavior and Attitudes. This dimension, inherent both in the experience abroad and in potential training programs, can be an important catalyst when it supports the experience. Concomitantly, it is a great hindrance when it is lacking.

Family Situation

Now we come to one of the most significant concerns reported by returning assignees (particularly early returners) regarding their overseas experience. This concern is the adaptability of the spouse and children to the new environment. In fact, this aspect has been reported as the major reason for failure to complete international assignments.

The spouse's willingness to live abroad should be discerned fully before departure. If the spouse and the children feel reluctant to live overseas, their reluctance may later become detrimental to the assignee's ability to survive. The family's desire to live abroad, particularly in the target country, is essential. At present, few multinational corporations provide an acquaintance visit for the whole family.

A mutually supportive family is similarly necessary for living overseas. It provides the resilience that the IA needs during a time of stress and daily life challenges. Tales about families that break up after repatriation have become appallingly prevalent.

Language Skills

This category appears continually in the literature. The emphasis is on the host-country language. For example, Zeira and Bani (1981) report that managers from European host-country organizations prefer locals as top executives but will accept expatriates if they are fluent in the local language and are sensitive to the silent (nonverbal) language. Even an initial acquaintance with simple daily terms, however, has proved helpful. Continual learning of the language during the term abroad is most desirable.

Acquaintance with nonverbal communication is also crucial. Although host-country personnel and the general public tend to forgive foreigners for ignorance of subtle customs and nonverbal cues, IAs must be familiar with basic local expressions in order to survive. Misinterpreting nonverbal messages by attributing to them "self-evident" home-country meanings may be devastating.

Methods and Techniques for Intercultural Training

If we accept the assertion that culture is one of the most important ways in which humans adapt to their environment (Triandis, 1983), and if we also accept the notion that cultural variations exist among different societies, then the issue of an individual's preferred culture is related only to the incident of birth. All cultures are equally appropriate and valuable. This is one of the messages that individuals preparing to encounter another culture should consider. Moreover, if culture is a result of an extended adaptation process, then it is deeply rooted in the particular society. It is transmitted to its members through the early socialization process. It provides norms of behavior, a value system for evaluating events and objects, and a means of judging right from wrong. The alien who visits a different culture must either comply with it or be rejected. These notions are the basic premise underlying the need for intercultural training. The uniqueness of an unfamiliar culture may reflect differences in patterns of social interactions, patterns of decision making, esthetic preferences, and attributes that grant prestige or status.

A challenging task in learning about a foreign culture—especially when the newcomer takes on a professional capacity—is to distinguish between the essential and the superficial elements of a culture. What will locals expect from the visitor? Some aspects of social behavior (such as recognizing religious taboos) are mandatory, whereas ignorance of the niceties (such as aspects of local attire) tend to be forgivable. The IA's effectiveness may decline drastically if he or she is unfamiliar with certain essentials—for example, nonverbal behavior.

On the basis of the categories of attributes describing the successful IA, we now turn to a summary of the available training techniques that will encourage development or acquisition of these attributes. Table 11.1 presents a summary of these techniques and their purposes.

Didactic-Informational Training

This technique employs a classroom lecture style, printed material, videotapes, and movies. The technique is relatively economical and easily administered. Three major areas can be effectively covered by this technique.

Acquaintance with Host-Country Environment. This concerns information about the host country, its geography, demographics, climate, political system, economy and industrialization, resources, history, customs, religion, labor force and institutions, and generalized habits and customs. Such information is sometimes referred to as *area studies*.

Table 11.1. Training Techniques.

Method	Technique	Purpose
Didactic-Informational Training	• Lectures • Reading material • Videotapes • Movies	Area studies, company operation, parent-country institutions
Intercultural Experiential Workshops	• Cultural assimilators • Simulations • Role playing	Culture-general, culture-specific negotiation skills; reduce ethnocentrism
Sensitivity Training	• Communication workshops • T groups • Outward-Bound trips	Self-awareness, communication style, empathy, listening skills, nonjudgmentalism
Field Experiences	• Meeting with ex-IAs • Minicultures • Host-family surrogate	Customs, values, beliefs, nonverbal behavior, religion
Language Skills	• Classes • Cassettes	Interpersonal communication, job requirements, survival necessities

Acquaintance with Company Operations. The candidate should be introduced to the company's organizational chart, communication system, strategic decision-making process, and, particularly, the international operation.

Information About Parent Country and Institutions. This involves lectures and selected reading about parent-country institutions, environment, resources, labor force, and selected topics in organizational behavior. This material enables the candidate to represent his or her society credibly and to provide a means for comparing information in the host-country environment. This information is usually neglected as superficial and even trivial, but it has important value to candidates when it is needed. Without question, the spouse should also acquire the information referred to here.

Intercultural Experiential Workshops

This technique employs cultural assimilators, simulations, and role playing. Experiential involvement of these sorts forces the individual to apply affective and cognitive processes to behavioral manifestations. These training workshops should be structured to include both general cultural and culture-specific experiences. General cultural experiences aim to sensitize the candidate to general variations in intercultural settings, while culture-specific experiences aim to acquaint the IA with the target environment. The candidate experiences diversity in such areas as values, norms, customs, dress, and interpersonal communication styles.

Sensitivity Training

This approach, which began with the human potential movement during the 1960s, has received conflicting reactions for its applicability to improving organizational effectiveness. It appears appropriate, however, as a preparatory stage for intercultural training. The purpose of sensitivity training is to allow candidates to explore their own interpersonal styles and their underlying values and attributions. In particular, participants experiment with and explore their listening ability, selective interpersonal perceptions, cognitive paradigms, reactions to feedback, and predispositions toward judgmental attitudes. They are encouraged to investigate their behavior during direct confrontations, to reevaluate their beliefs and value systems, and to learn to be more expressive about their feelings.

Like any technique, sensitivity training has advantages and disadvantages. Its advantages are that it provides an opportunity for internalization, self-understanding, and openness that may augment the benefits of later intercultural experiential workshops. Its disadvantages are that it may prompt candidates to adopt values and norms of openness and confrontation that are not universal. If carried too far, these values may hinder rather than help the candidate. Still, the underlying assumption is that increased self-awareness will enhance an individual's empathy and acceptance of other cultures, norms, and values. Increased sensitivity to individual differences should transfer to accepting cultural differences and should improve effective communication in intercultural settings, thus increasing behavioral flexibility. One of the main purposes of sensitivity training is to learn how to learn and, in the long run, to benefit from intercultural communication workshops.

Field Experiences

Most companies allow the IA (and his or her spouse) to visit the prospective country for a week or two. The trip abroad usually aims at initial preparation for the extended stay. Such a trip is essential, should be well prepared for, and should be extended, as necessary. The contributions of peers and host-country managers are of course invaluable. I would like, however, to emphasize two other kinds of field experiences.

Meetings with Ex-IAs. Meetings with ex-IAs should take place in these colleagues' homes, and not at working lunches or meetings. Ideally, the visit should be a family event, thus allowing for more intimate interaction. At times, such visits will require travel to other cities or states. Despite the related costs, these meetings should be encouraged.

Simulated Host-Country Experiences. This form of training has two types. First, there are *minicultures*. An unexplored yet promising experience is available to candidates in the home country. The circumstances vary, but the most common approach involves an extended visit to a microcultural environment within the home country. The United States is blessed with a multitude of ethnic groups, many of which form suburban communities that maintain their original cultures and languages. Such minienvironments may offer an opportunity for increased cultural awareness. A second approach, using *a host-family-surrogate*, promises to offer an exciting yet nonthreatening experience that can be arranged easily in the home country. A family similar in its composition to the IA's, but typical of the target country's ethnic background, is hired to host the IA family. The stay should be extended long enough for the guest family to experience day-to-day living. The hosts may introduce their visitors to typical living customs and habits while understanding the guests' cognitive set. Because the hosts speak English, however, the learning experience is both challenging and nonthreatening, thus enhancing both the exchange of cultural information and open communication.

Language and Communication Skills

It should be self-evident that the IA's proficiency in the host-country language is invaluable. Nevertheless, since many IAs cannot reach fluency by the time they start their assignment, any level of proficiency is preferable to none at all. IAs will find day-to-day encounters more difficult and frustrating without fundamental language skills. Moreover, inability to use the local language will limit and distort their experiences of the host country from the outset.

Assessing Training Effectiveness

Earlier in this chapter, we saw a list of training needs based on the barest of sources, such as IAs' self-reports, home countries' and host countries' executive surveys, and analysis of reasons for casualties. The challenge before us now is research to establish whether such training programs are actually related to effective job performance and, further, to determine whether training scores in these areas should be included in the criteria for selecting candidates (Goldstein, 1980). Two main issues are relevant.

One is related to the relative effectiveness of the particular training techniques; the other, to the degree of transfer of skills from the training setting to the task environment. In terms of particular training techniques, there is an accumulation of literature that allows some generalizations. A few landmarks should be mentioned. Triandis, Feldman, Weldon, and Harvey (1975) observe that, as a result of particular socialization processes, people may develop attributional processes and selective perceptions that lead them to distrust people and the environment. They call this phenomenon *ecosystem distrust*. One training technique, the cultural assimilator (Fiedler, Mitchell, & Triandis, 1971; Triandis, Feldman, Weldon, & Harvey, 1974), can be employed to train such people and promote understanding of cultural (or subcultural) differences, to facilitate cooperation between members of different cultures. It was used successfully by O'Brien and Plooij (1977). For an excellent review of cultural assimilators and intercultural sensitizers, see Albert (1983). More recently, there has been an effort to compare documentary (informational) to interpersonal training methods (Earley, 1987). The two methods seem comparable. For maximum effect, they should be used cumulatively.

The second issue confronting the designer of an intercultural training program pertains to the transfer of training. Although no direct results from research on intercultural training programs are available, we can point to conclusions in other areas of training that suggest that organizational and environmental factors facilitate or constrain positive transfer of training. I wish to emphasize here that the organizational factors that are the most relevant and that require linking are, as Hall (1986) suggests, the executive training program's management-succession process and the corporate strategy. This recommendation for linking, however, given the present state of affairs, is farfetched.

Who Should Train IAs?

The qualifications of an effective intercultural trainer cannot be described on the basis of the research literature, simply because there is none. Kohls's (1984) review and summary, however, provide some guidance. From the training techniques described earlier, and through transfer from other areas of instruction, we can surmise certain basic requirements.

The literature on attitudinal change and its behavioral consequences offers two models. One promotes the notion that adoption of new attitudes will result in the change to the desired behavior. The other suggests that specific behaviors can be modeled and imitated, and that attitudes will then change and be generalized to a larger field of associated behaviors. We expect an effective trainer—or the designer of a training program—to be familiar with these alternative models and to apply the appropriate sequences to the selected technique.

Accordingly, the trainer should be familiar with the desired behaviors through personal experiences abroad. He or she should have internalized the process of adaptation to a foreign environment and therefore be able to project it to the candidates and be empathetic about such experiences. The trainer should also feel personally enthusiastic and positive toward new experiences, especially the experience of encountering a new culture. Familiarity with cultural differences is of course essential. When applicable, so is a comprehensive knowledge of the target country and its specific culture.

If the starting point of every intercultural training is familiarity with and awareness of one's own culture, social norms, and personal value system, then the trainer should be well acquainted with these also. A clear understanding of American ways and mores, and of how they differ from other cultures, is essential.

Finally, I wish to emphasize the process orientation of most techniques. Effective interpersonal skills and one-to-one working ability are the effective trainer's most powerful tools. For further elaboration on ethical issues involved in the training process, as well as on the trainer's professional ability, see Paige and Martin's (1983) excellent review.

When to Train What

The scope of this chapter does not allow complete development of a model indicating the interaction between time sequence, training technique, and desired cognitive, affective, or behavioral changes. An optimal model requires an analysis of each stage and of its length and consequences, plus a thorough delineation of the various simulations and techniques. Nevertheless, it is possible to make a few important points.

First, no sequence of training programs is possible unless IA candidates are selected early enough. The personnel department should alert the multinational corporation's policymakers to the importance of early selection. IAs themselves may request delay in departure, if they are properly advised and mentored by personnel managers. Furthermore, staff executives in the human resources function should prepare files of alternative available training programs, and consultants should ensure prompt counseling for all candidates. Most multinational corporations are very efficient in designing remuneration and compensation packages for their international assignees. Candidates' training needs are equally significant and deserve equal attention.

Second, one stage of training that rarely receives notice takes place after the IA arrives and has begun his or her initial adaptation. This stage should be left neither to the individual IA nor to the host country; it should be institutionalized by the parent company's international division.

Finally, a word of caution concerning the initial stage of the training program: The IA's spouse should be integral to most processes, from selection all the way to the on-site socialization process.

Dilemmas in Intercultural Training

In 1982, the Academy of International Business selected the first recipient of an award for the International Business Leader of the Year. The recipient, Jacques G. Maisonrouge, senior vice-president, IBM Corporation, and chairman of the board, IBM World Trade Corporation, stated in his address (1983) that a deserving individual "has demonstrated either in his career or writings that while remaining attached to his national roots — even patriotic — he has managed to rid himself of the prejudices acquired during his early childhood years" (p. 141).

Intuitively we cannot help agreeing with Maisonrouge. Moreover, most of the techniques aimed at improving an individual's intercultural competence through training are related to the adoption of new behavior. This in turn presumably leads to changes in attitudes, values, and beliefs. Consider the assertion of Paige and Martin (1983): "It is not the normal condition of human beings to be culturally relativistic, appreciative of contradictory beliefs and behavioral systems, or nonjudgmental when confronted with alternative cultures" (p. 44).

It appears that we now face a theoretical dilemma—one we should investigate further. Raising the level of intercultural sensitivity means that the individual becomes more tolerant of other value systems, more accepting of unfamiliar behavior, and more empathetic to other beliefs and social norms. To achieve this nonethnocentric attitude, we must change the beliefs and value systems that the individual has acquired during his or her socialization process. Nevertheless, early socialization also contributes to the individual's identity, perception of truth and reality, and preferred ways of thinking and behaving. An individual chooses or accepts his or her reference groups, which reinforce these beliefs and value systems. Can multicultural training threaten the individual with the loss of personal identity? Can it confuse the individual's self-concept or threaten the support of his or her peer groups? (See Adler, 1974; Geertz, 1963; Kuhn, 1962; Mestenhauser, 1981; Paige & Martin, 1983.) To what extent can multicultural training be threatening and stress-provoking? Many individuals resist and experience stress when forced to expose personal tendencies like rigidity, fear of failure, and argumentativeness. It is not surprising that individuals often resent exposing their biases and prejudices— qualities that may appear during training—and wish to avoid confrontations.

Let us now consider another dilemma in the training process. One training goal is to acquaint the candidate with the host-country culture. He or she is expected to become familiar with its geography, climate, and level of industrialization. To prepare for effective interpersonal communication, the candidate learns about its attitudes, beliefs, value systems, and various personality traits. Under these circumstances, however, one can easily fall into overgeneralization and even resort to stereotyping (Gudykunst & Hammer, 1983). Generally speaking, various aspects of training tend to increase the individual's arousal level, while the overarching goal of training is to reduce potential stress and apprehension.

Conclusions

This overview of training for the international assignee focuses on the current and future need (and opportunity) for research into these issues. Most staffing organizations' models and theories are violated by multinational corporations' selection and training practices with overseas candidates. Among the problematic practices are the following:

- Absence of a realistic preview of the assignment
- Role ambiguity in the assignment
- Role conflict in the task
- Inadequate performance evaluation, which, even when it does exist, does not cover many aspects of the real field requirements
- Absence of career-succession plans for IAs
- Repatriation problems — often the rule, not the exception
- Performance criteria expressed in terms of personality characteristics as well as behavior
- No clear differentiation between predictors (skills) and criteria (performance) ratings.

What are some of the reasons given by most multinational corporations for not training IAs, and why do these corporations resort mainly to a domestic model for the selection process? Reasons that multinational corporations give for not using training programs include the following:

- Immediate need for appointment
- Lack of candidates
- Lack of trainers
- Smaller population for organized training
- Lack of long-range planning
- Lack of awareness of training needs

- Doubt that IAs are trainable
- Lack of research to verify the success of training
- Low contribution of overseas assignments to career paths
- Exclusive importance of technical skills
- Ethnocentrism within corporate headquarters.

The message intended in this chapter is also that of all who encounter a culturally diverse work force, whether in the extreme case (across national boundaries) or between sub-cultures (within national borders). The case of ethnic diversity is obvious. Less obvious but still relevant are the implications that arise, for example, from the predictions made by Goldstein and Gilliam (in press) and Cascio and Zammuto (1987) concerning demographic changes in the work force: In the future, work organizations will need to depend on populations that will include increasing numbers of minorities, women, and older workers. Another growing trend—the establishment of dual-country, joint ventures—also points to the need to include cross-cultural training in any program for executive development.

Finally, we should give credit to the formidable task the IA faces and the inherent conflict in his or her task: Some aspects of the home-country organization's goals may conflict with the local subsidiary's goals, while at the same time the home-country organization's goals may also conflict with those of the host-country government (see, for example, the conflict matrix in Ronen, 1986). Small wonder that most IAs face a massive, complex, and often ambiguous task in their overseas assignments. Training the IA does not solve his or her fundamental dilemma, let alone predict the final outcome, but training does give the IA at least a fighting chance. The alternative is simply to search for individuals who, in addition to competence in functional areas and managerial skills, possess the patience of a diplomat, the zeal of a missionary, and the linguistic skill of a United Nations interpreter.

References

Adler, P. (1974). Beyond culture identity: Reflections upon cultural and multicultural man. *Topics in Culture Learning, 2,* 23–41.

Albert, D. (1983). Intercultural sensitizer or cultural assimilator: A cognitive approach. In D. Landis & R. W. Brislin (Eds.), *Handbook of intercultural training* (Vol. 2) (pp. 186–217). Elmsford, NY: Pergamon Press.

Arensberg, C. M., & Niehoff, A. H. (1971). *Introducing social change: A manual for community development* (2nd ed.). Hawthorne, NY: Aldine.

Brislin, R. W. (1981). *Cross-cultural encounters.* Elmsford, NY: Pergamon Press.

Cascio, W. F., & Zammuto, R. F. (1987). *Societal trends and staffing policies.* Denver: University of Colorado Press.

Cleveland, H., Mangone, G., & Adams, J. (1960). *The overseas Americans.* New York: McGraw-Hill.

Detweiler, R. (1975). On inferring the intentions of a person from another culture. *Journal of Personality, 43*, 591–611.

Dinges, N. (1980). Interdisciplinary collaboration in cross-cultural social science research. In M. P. Hamnet & R. Brislin (Eds.), *Research in culture learning: Language and conceptual studies* (pp. 136–143). Honolulu: University Press of Hawaii.

Dotlich, D. L. (1982, October). International and intracultural management development. *Training and Development Journal, 36*, 26–31.

Earley, P. C. (1987). Intercultural training for managers: A comparison of documentary and interpersonal methods. *Academy of Management Journal, 30*, 685–698.

Fiedler, F. E., Mitchell, T. R., & Triandis, H. C. (1971). The culture assimilator: An approach to cross-cultural training. *Journal of Applied Psychology, 55*, 95–102.

Geertz, D. (1963). The integrative revolution: Primordial sentiments and civil politics in the new states. In C. Geertz (Ed.), *Old societies and new states: The quest for modernity in Asia and Africa.* New York: Free Press.

Goldstein, I. L. (1980). Training in work organizations. *Annual Review of Psychology, 31*, 229–272.

Goldstein, I. L., and Gilliam, P. (in press). Training and work populations in the year 2000. *American Psychologist.*

Gudykunst, W. B., & Hammer, M. R. (1983). Basic training and design: An approach to intercultural training. In D. Landis &

R. W. Brislin (Eds.), *Handbook of intercultural training* (Vol. 1) (pp. 118–154). Elmsford, NY: Pergamon Press.

Gudykunst, W. B., Wiseman, R., & Hammer, M. R. (1977). Determinants of a sojourner's attitudinal satisfaction. In B. Ruben (Ed.), *Communication yearbook* (Vol. 1) (pp. 352–370). New Brunswick, NJ: Transaction.

Guthrie, G., & Zektick, I. (1967). Predicting performance in the Peace Corps. *Journal of Social Psychology, 71,* 11–21.

Hackman, J. R., & Oldham, G. R. (1980). *Work Redesign.* Reading, MA: Addison-Wesley.

Hall, D. T. (1986). Dilemmas in linking succession planning to individual executive learning. *Human Resource Management, 25,* 235–265.

Hammer, M. R., Gudykunst, W. B., & Wiseman, R. L. (1978). Dimensions of intercultural effectiveness: An exploratory study. *International Journal of Intercultural Relations, 1,* 99–110.

Harris, J. (1973). A science of the South Pacific: An analysis of the character structure of the Peace Corps volunteer. *American Psychologist, 28,* 232–247.

Harris, P. R., & Harris, D. L. (1972). Training for cultural understanding. *Training and Development Journal, 26,* 8–10.

Harris, P. R., & Moran, R. T. (1979). *Managing cultural differences.* Houston: Gulf Publishing.

Hautaluoma, J. E., & Kaman, V. (1975). Description of the Peace Corps volunteers' experience in Afghanistan. *Topics in Culture Learning, 3,* 79–96.

Hawes, F., & Kealey, D. (1980). *Canadians in development.* Ottawa: Canadian International Development Agency.

Hays, R. D. (1971). Ascribed behavioral determinants of success-failure among U.S. expatriate managers. *Journal of International Business Studies, 2,* 40–46.

Hays, R. D. (1972). The executive abroad: Minimizing the behavioral problems. *Business Horizons, 4,* 87–93.

Hays, R. D. (1974). Expatriate selection: Ensuring success and avoiding failure. *Journal of International Business Studies, 28,* 25–34.

Howard, C. G. (1974). Model for the design of a selection program for multinational executives. *Public Personnel Management, 3*, 138–145.

Ivancevich, J. M. (1969). Selection of American managers for overseas assignments. *Personnel Journal, 48*, 190–193.

Kealey, D. J. (1978). *Adaptation to new environments.* Unpublished paper, Canadian International Development Agency, Ottawa.

Kealey, D. J., & Ruben, B. D. (1983). Cross-cultural personnel selection of criteria, issues, and methods. In D. Landis & R. W. Brislin (Eds.), *Handbook of intercultural training* (Vol. 1) (pp. 155–175). Elmsford, NY: Pergamon Press.

Kohls, R. *Intercultural training: Don't leave home without it.* Washington, DC: SIETAR, 1984.

Kuhn, T. S. (1962). *The structure of scientific revolutions.* Chicago: University of Chicago Press.

Landis, D., & Brislin, R. W. *Handbook of intercultural training* (Vols. 1, 2, 3). Elmsford, NY: Pergamon Press.

Latham, G. P. (1988). Human resource training and development. *Annual Review of Psychology, 39*, 545–582.

Maisonrouge, J. (1983). Address to the Academy of Management.

Maretzski, T. W. (1965). Transition training: A theoretical approach. *Human Organization, 24*, 128–134.

Mendenhall, M., & Oddou, G. (1985). The dimensions of expatriate acculturation: A review. *Academy of Management Journal, 10*, 39–47.

Mestenhauser, J. A. (1981). Selected learning concepts and theories. In G. Althen (Ed.), *Learning across cultures.* Washington, DC: National Association for Foreign Student Affairs.

Mezingo, T. P. (1974). *The development of an attitude-measuring device for improvement of selection/screening of U.S. personnel for overseas duty.* Unpublished M.A. thesis, Naval Postgraduate School, Monterey, CA.

Miller, E. L. (1972a). The overseas assignment: How managers determine who is to be selected. *Michigan Business Review, 24*, 12–19.

Miller, E. L. (1972b). The selection decision for an international assignment: A study of the decision maker's behavior. *Journal of International Business Studies, 3*, 49–65.

Miller, E. L. (1977). Managerial qualifications of personnel occupying overseas management positions as perceived by American expatriate managers. *Journal of International Business Studies, 8,* 57–68.

Miller, E. L., & Cheng, J.L.C. (1977). *A factor-analytic study of the circumstances that influenced the decision to accept an overseas assignment across German and American expatriate managers.* Paper presented to the 37th annual meeting of the Academy of Management, Orlando, Florida.

Miller, V. A. (1979). *The guidebook for international trainers in business and industry.* New York: Van Nostrand Reinhold.

Mumford, S. J. (1975). *Overseas adjustment as measured by a mixed standard scale.* Paper presented to the meeting of the Western Psychological Association, Sacramento, CA.

O'Brien, G. E., & Plooij, D. (1977). Comparison of programmed and prose culture training upon attitudes and knowledge. *Journal of Applied Psychology, 62,* 499–505.

Paige, R. M., & Martin, J. N. (1983). Ethical issues and ethics in cross-cultural training. In D. Landis & R. W. Brislin (Eds.), *Handbook of intercultural training* (Vol. 1) (pp. 36–80). Elmsford, NY: Pergamon Press.

Pazy, A., & Zeira, Y. (1983). Training parent-country professionals in host-country organizations. *Academy of Management Review, 8,* 262–272.

Pazy, A., & Zeira, Y. (1985). Compatibility of expectations in training parent-country managers and professionals in host-country organizations. *International Studies of Management and Organizations, 15,* 75–93.

Porter, R. E., & Samovar, L. A. (1976). Communicating interculturally. In L. A. Samovar & R. E. Porter (Eds.), *Intercultural communication: A reader* (2nd ed.). Belmont, CA: Wadsworth.

Prien, E. P., Goldstein, I. L., & Macey, W. H. (1987). Multidomain job analysis: Procedures and applications. *Training and Development Journal, 41,* 68–72.

Ronen, S. (1986). *Comparative and multinational management.* New York: Wiley.

Ruben, B. D. (1980). Communications, games, and simulations: An evaluation. In R. E. Horn & A. Cleaves (Eds.), *The guide to simulation games for education and training.* Newbury Park, CA: Sage.

Ruben, B. D., Askling, L. R., & Kealey, D. J. (1977). Cross-cultural effectiveness. In D. S. Hoopes, P. B. Pedersen, & G. W. Renwick (Eds.), *Overview of intercultural education, training, and research* (Vol. 1). Washington, DC: Society for Intercultural Education, Training, and Research.

Ruben, B. D., & Kealey, D. (1979). *Behavioral assessment of communication competency and prediction of cross-cultural adaptation.* Ottawa: Canadian International Development Agency.

Russell, P. W. (1978). *Dimensions of overseas success in industry.* Unpublished doctoral thesis, Colorado State University.

Schneider, B., & Schmitt, N. (1986). *Staffing organizations* (2nd ed.). Glenview, IL: Scott, Foresman.

Schwartz, P. A. (1973). Selecting effective team leaders. *Focus, 2,* 2–8.

Thompson, C. P., & English, J. T. (1964). Premature return of Peace Corps volunteers. *Public Health Reports, 79,* 1065–1073.

Triandis, H. C. (1983). Essentials of studying cultures. In D. Landis & R. W. Brislin (Eds.), *Handbook of intercultural training* (Vol. 1) (pp. 82–117). Elmsford, NY: Pergamon Press.

Triandis, H. C., Feldman, J. M., Weldon, D. E., & Harvey, W. M. (1974). Designing preemployment training for the hard-to-employ: A cross-cultural psychological approach. *Journal of Applied Psychology, 59,* 687–693.

Triandis, H. C., Feldman, J. M., Weldon, D. C., & Harvey, W. M. (1975). Ecosystem distrust and the hard-to-employ. *Journal of Applied Psychology, 60,* 44–56.

Tucker, M. (1974). *Screening and selection for overseas assignments: Assessments and recommendations to the U.S. Navy.* Denver: Center for Research and Education.

Tung, R. L. (1981). Selection and training of personnel for overseas assignments. *Columbia Journal of World Business, 16,* 68–71.

Tung, R. L. (1982). Selection and training procedures of U.S., European, and Japanese multinationals. *California Management Review, 25,* 57–71.

Tung, R. L. (1987). Expatriate assignments: Enhancing success and minimizing failure. *Academy of Management Executive, 1,* 117–126.

Warren, D., & Adler, P. (1977). An experiential approach to instruction in intercultural communication. *Communication Education, 26,* 128–134.

Wexley, K. N., & Latham, G. P. (1981). *Developing and training human resources in organizations.* Glenview, IL: Scott, Foresman.

Yellen, T.M.I., & Hoover, M. W. (1973). *In-country experience: Navy personnel stationed in Greece.* Washington, DC: Naval Personnel Research and Development Laboratory, Washington Naval Yard.

Zeira, Y., & Bani, M. (1981). Attitudes of host-country organizations towards MNCs' staffing policies: A cross-country and cross-industry analysis. *Management International Review, 21,* 38–47.

Zeira, Y., and Harari, E. (1979). Host-country organizations and expatriate managers in Europe. *California Management Review, 21,* 40–50.

PART FOUR

Commentaries on
the Training Issues

12

A Historical Perspective
on Training

Paul W. Thayer

McGehee and Thayer's classic book was published in 1961, and in the almost three decades that have passed, much has happened to change the field of training. This chapter will concentrate on the changes described in the preceding chapters and will not attempt to give a comprehensive view of all the changes that have taken place. Instead, my job will be to look at each chapter and contrast what is said there with what was extant thirty years ago.

As an aid to the reader, this review will follow the same order as the chapters. Since historical treatment is given in several of them, that material will not be repeated here. At the end, some general impressions will be given of how far we have come and of whether progress has been made.

Training Needs Assessment

Thirty years ago, McGehee and Thayer (1961) found little in the way of systematic thinking about needs analysis. They cited Mahler and Monroe (1952), who provided survey data showing that only about one company in ten used any sort of systematic approach to determining training needs. What there was concentrated on operations or task analysis, with some recognition that one should do a "man analysis" to ensure that training did not teach what was already known (since that time, the latter expression has properly become *person analysis*). There was, however, little concern with what is known about individual differences, as psychologists use the expression, or organizational analysis. The latter was not unknown but received attention primarily in human resource planning, which might or might not involve the training activities of the organization.

Although current data similar to those of Mahler and Monroe (1952) are not available, it is clear that the need for needs assessment is well recognized, even though many training activities are still initiated and maintained because someone thinks they are a good idea, or because other organizations are using particular training techniques. That practice, one fears, will always be with us.

Chapter Two, by Ostroff and Ford, represents a major step forward in training needs assessment. Although the authors' trinity implicitly recognizes that different levels of analysis are necessary, their treatment gives the trainer and training researcher the framework to do more sophisticated and interlocking needs analyses. The expansion to twenty-seven cells, resulting from three levels of training content, three organizational levels, and three levels of application, makes explicit the many kinds of information needed. It also clarifies the interrelationships among different kinds of information and suggests to the trainer data to be collected that might otherwise not occur to him or her. There is good reason to be optimistic about the future of needs assessment, if this new framework is used.

Utility Approaches to Evaluation

There is no reference to utility analysis in McGehee and Thayer (1961). There are two references to Brogden and Taylor's (1950) work on the "dollar criterion," in one discussion of the possibility of converting managerial performance records to dollar values and in another discussion of possible ways to combine criteria into a single index. There is also a lengthy discussion of the overemphasis on training costs, without regard to a consideration of the profitability of the training endeavor. Finally, there is a lengthy plea for evaluation of training and an expression of dismay over the apparent acceptance by managers that training is a given good. McGehee and Thayer (1961) said at that time, "Evaluation of training in industry is in much the same category as Mark Twain placed the weather" (p. 256).

In the intervening years, it has become clear that managers will not always accept training as a given good, and that they may cut back training activities when business is bad or when other investments must be made. Several colleagues have found that, despite top managers' protestations to the contrary, human resources and research are expendable, and human resources research is especially so.

Careful attention to the material in Chapter Three, by Cascio, should place those responsible for training in a more defensible position, not only for existing programs but also for obtaining additional funding to expand the training enterprise in an organization. Cascio's chapter not only brings us up to date, with regard to utility analysis in its various forms, but also takes us into some cost-accounting procedures with which almost all trainers and training researchers have little familiarity. He also provides us with several ways of expressing the gains from effective training, including monetary benefits, percentage increases in output, reductions in the size of the work force, and concomitant dollar savings in payroll costs. Undoubtedly, some managers will take some convincing about the legitimacy of these methods, but Cascio's approaches to the problem take us a long way toward competing more effectively for organizational resources and being less vulnerable to cutbacks when business is bad.

Training Evaluation

Arvey and Cole, in Chapter Four, point out that recent training texts give relatively brief treatment to evaluation designs. Thirty years ago, there were fewer designs available, and evaluation was so rare that McGehee and Thayer (1961) were reluctant to spend too much time on them, for fear of scaring off training professionals. Thirty pages were devoted to evaluation, most of them on criterion-measurement issues. Eight pages were used to discuss four simple designs: measures after training, with no control group; measures before and after training, with no control group; measures after training, with a control group; and measures before and after training, with a control group. There was no discussion of statistical issues.

The reader must remember that training evaluation at that time typically involved no more than the administration of a "happiness" questionnaire at the end of training. The use of those four simple designs, which involved suitable criteria, was unusual. Kirkpatrick's (1959, 1960) work on levels of criteria had just been published. Time-series designs were unheard of. Discussions of power came in other guises. Although ANOVA and ANCOVA were commonly used in laboratory studies, they were rare in the training literature.

Although exposure to different designs and measurement issues is common today, Arvey and Cole point out that little has been published to help us measure change. They give us an updated discussion of the statistical issues involved in measuring the change that results from training interventions. Their presentations of alternative statistics, power, reliability, alpha, beta, and gamma change in self-report measures, and latent-variable statistics clearly indicate how far we have come in the last thirty years.

Training the Human Information Processor

McGehee and Thayer (1961) remarked on management's ignorance of the learning process and how such ignorance blocks efficient training. The inclusion of two chapters on learning processes in a book on training was revolutionary. They pointed out that there were two major groups concerned with learning, the trainers and the learning theorists, and that communication between the two groups was rare. They then tried to teach trainers something about the learning process. Although their approach was eclectic, it relied heavily on the behavioristic tradition. Research on thinking and cognitive processes was relatively new. Thus, there was discussion of motivation, reinforcement, massed versus spaced practice, knowledge of results, reward and punishment, whole versus part learning, overlearning, individual differences, and transfer issues.

If one looks at many modern training texts (Goldstein, 1986; Wexley & Latham, 1981), the treatment of learning is not too different. Although knowledge of cognitive processes is being introduced into the field of training in technical reports (Cormier, 1984), only now are we seeing the introduction of cognitive processes into training texts. Chapter Five, by Howell and Cooke, takes us a long way in that regard. It will be hard to write training texts in the future without the use of such cognitive expressions as *declarative knowledge, procedural knowledge, automaticity, schema, scripts,* and *frames.* Learning strategies, expert systems, heuristic processing, trouble shooting, and judgments and decision making will be common topics. As John Campbell (1988) points out, instructional psychology is beginning to have its impact on training. Research studies and theory in ergonomics, information processing, instructional psychology, and various cognitive processes are about to revolutionize the training literature, to the benefit of the enterprise.

Applications of Ability Taxonomies

McGehee and Thayer (1961) devoted fewer than three pages to learning and individual differences. They referred to a summary of studies in the *Handbook of Human Engineering Data* (1952), which indicated that "learning can be affected by such variables as age, sex, motivational state, and capacities of the individual such as intelligence [and] motor abilities" (p. 166). Goldstein (1986) and Wexley and Latham (1981) spend six and five pages, respectively, on this topic and devote much of their discussion to the potential importance of ATI. McGehee and Thayer (1961) also noted that the evidence concerning learning rates and various abilities was not clear, adding, "Studies relating learning rates on specific tasks to scores of relatively pure factor tests would give us considerable insight into this problem area" (p. 166). Obviously, they were aware of the early work of

Fleishman and his colleagues (for example, Fleishman & Hempel, 1956) and were hopeful that it would bear considerable fruit.

Fleishman and Mumford, in Chapter Six, show that it has. Chapter Six clearly shows how far that work has come in thirty-three years but also illustrates how a sustained program of research is required for such advances. The implications of that work remain for John P. Campbell and Kenneth N. Wexley to comment on in the remainder of this volume, but it is clear that training will benefit in major ways through applications of ability taxonomies—assigning people to training, training for required skills, using optimal learning strategies for people at different stages of skills acquisition, matching content with abilities, and designing training.

Behavioral Approaches

Chapter Seven, by Latham, contains a fairly complete history of various approaches to learning and training. Thirty years ago, B. F. Skinner was best known in training circles for his revival of teaching machines and his attempt to employ behavioristic principles in training. Other applications of operant techniques had not occurred. Albert Bandura's effecting of a rapprochement between behaviorism and cognition did not occur until 1969. How different things are today! Few trainers would not acknowledge the effectiveness of behavior modeling as a training technique. For example, the need for practice in supervisory techniques, not just lectures on them, is now accepted, even though that need should have been recognized long ago. Unfortunately, supervisory behaviors were not regarded as skills needing practice in the same way that operating a lathe or running a milling machine was a skill needing a great deal of practice. That lesson has not yet been fully learned, but the points made by Latham may help us accept it.

Behavioral approaches to training have had other important effects. Few training researchers, for example, would not point to the value of multiple-baseline designs to get around the problems of random assignment required by classic research designs. Although the effectiveness of the early applications of behaviorism was (as is true of the effectiveness of all new approaches) greatly exaggerated, there is a great deal in the approach to recommend it, if it is carefully and properly applied. Komaki, Waddell, and Pearce (1977), for example, offer an excellent example of how operant analysis of a task or work setting can contribute substantially to the solution of a work or safety problem. Many other benefits have been derived from behavioral approaches to learning and training. Looking back, Latham gives us a much clearer view of how all that has come about.

Aging and the Training and Learning Process

Although it was recognized thirty years ago that older workers might be slower learners, the training or retraining of older workers was not a priority. The work force was large, the post–World War II generation would be entering the work force in the near future, and compulsory retirement was the order of the day. There were many common misconceptions about older people: that they could not learn new skills, had poor memories, and that their intelligence levels declined after their early twenties, so that older workers could not produce as much as younger, strong people. Rapid changes in technology were not yet upon us, and so retraining at any age was less important. Indeed, it was not uncommon for organizations to replace workers as new technology came along, rather than retrain current employees.

Sterns and Doverspike, in Chapter Eight, show how the aging of the work force, the elimination of compulsory retirement, and rapid technological innovation have changed things. Today, we simply must have a better understanding of older workers and of how to train them. In addition, many large corporations appear to espouse a lifetime employment philosophy, making the training and retraining of older workers essential.

Sterns and Doverspike contribute a good deal to our understanding of older workers and their training. It is interesting to note that, while older workers are somewhat slower, they are not different from younger workers (or even children) in the way they learn or with regard to the conditions that facilitate or retard learning. Chapter Eight does much to challenge the conventional wisdom of some experts in adult learning.

Career Growth

Thirty years ago, the concepts of career planning, career growth, career paths, and career counseling were unheard of. Training was regarded as the formal procedures used by organizations to facilitate the development of appropriate behaviors for the attainment of organizational goals. While there was a recognition of the value of matching personal and organizational goals, the emphasis was on the latter, and some formal attempts were designed to bring the former in line with the latter. While job rotation might have been an acknowledged way of grooming young managers for higher positions, it was not considered to be training.

Chapter Nine, by London and Bassman, shows that all that has changed in many organizations. Formal career development programs have become standard. Career paths and systems for guiding people through them are common. Organizations now recognize the value of retraining, rather than replacing. Unions and top managers now cooperate in the retraining of employees. Indeed, the responsibilities of training departments have been enlarged to include these functions. Research is in progress on ways to enhance the acceptance and implementation of such programs. Times have changed, indeed.

Socialization, Resocialization, and Training

As Feldman observes in Chapter Ten, traditional views of training were not concerned with the socialization process; they were concerned with teaching appropriate work-related behaviors in furtherance of organizational goals. Social or group norms, while acknowledged, were often regarded as impediments to training, and especially to transfer of training. Training today is a major force in socializing the individual, and Feldman points to a number of implications of that change.

Researchers in training and socialization ignored or were unaware of each other until about fifteen years ago. Now, trainers are becoming aware of the impact of the group and the training setting on the learning of new behaviors and on the role of informal training by peers and mentors. (Indeed, mentoring has become the latest "fad" in the training literature; one hopes that sufficient good research will be done to save it from the usual fate of fads.) Trainers are beginning to recognize the impact that occupational socialization has on learning and organizational socialization.

Training has also taken on a new role, something that began about thirty years ago and has become commonplace. Training is now often given as a reward, as recognition of advancement within the organization. Partly because of tax legislation, the conduct of sales and management conventions has become a training function, emphasizing even more the reward component of some training. The opportunity for training directors to interact with top managers is considerably greater than it was thirty years ago, when training was something that new employees, especially blue-collar employees, received. Feldman gives many examples of the changes that the socialization role has brought to training. It is clear that the training department has many different functions today. The opportunities for both success and failure are great.

Training the International Assignee

Thirty years ago, there would have been little reason for a chapter like Ronen's. We were just beginning to hear about multinational corporations. The U.S. State Department was concerned with training its employees for overseas assignments, but their roles and their need to interact with local officials were considerably different from the role of international assignees. The military had its problems in this area, but it often took its culture with it, so that adjustment problems were not so severe as for the international assignee of today.

Chapter Eleven describes the many problems that confront multinational organizations and presents some suggestions for their solution. Ronen's concluding comments are pessimistic, however. Even today, too few organizations modify their human resource staffing models so as to train international assignees effectively. Ronen also points to the fact that our work force is becoming marked by increasing cultural diversity. Unless that is recognized, training and development of employees at all levels will fail to confront the problems that will arise.

Some Impressions

If McGehee and Thayer's (1961) book were to be written today, it would be vastly different. Writing it would be both easier and harder. It would be easier because so much more is known about the learning and training process. Finding information of value to the trainer would be easy. The usable yield from a literature search would be quite high.

Thirty years ago, Bill and I read hundreds of pieces, in the hope that there might be some useful information in articles on education or training. We read absolutely anything that sounded as if it had the remotest connection with training. I estimate that we discarded about 90 percent of what we found, because it was primarily opinion. Solid data and well-conducted studies were rare. Extrapolation from laboratory studies was necessary because there were so few good training studies done in the field.

Conditions today are very different. There are many good studies and theoretical approaches, and there is much sound advice about research designs and statistical analyses. We now have a much better fix on the conditions that enhance or inhibit learning and transfer. We are not as naïve as we used to be. We used to believe, for example, that giving managers insight through laboratory training was sufficient for marked behavioral change. We now know that supervisory skills need practice and reinforcement, like other skills. We are also just beginning to understand and study the various environmental inhibitors and facilitators for transfer of training to the work setting.

Given all this new knowledge, it would be easier to write a new version of our 1961 book. At the same time, it would be harder, because there is so much to cover. The present volume clearly shows how the functions of the training department have expanded in scope. Training and development now cover the entire employee spectrum, from the least skilled to the highest echelons of management. The changing makeup of the work force with regard to gender, ethnicity, social background, and age provides challenges to the training and development specialist that have never been known before. The expansion of organizations into the international scene requires totally new approaches to the training and development of some portions of the work force. Social and legislative changes add to the pressures for change.

Rapid changes in technology will also have marked effects on the training and development function. As Howell and Cooke point out in Chapter Five, the increasing automation of production will require more and more employees to be trained in trouble shooting and problem solving. Simple skills development and practice in production procedures will be a thing of the past. We have much to learn about the development of these skills, but we must move quickly to remain competitive. Add to this the changes in the social structure of the work setting, and we have much more to learn and apply.

Given all these changes, it is clear that training and development are or should be major corporate functions today. Opportunities to have a substantial impact on the organization are much greater than ever, and the methods to demonstrate that impact are now on hand. Convincing top managers of that imperative will not be easy, since training departments still have a bad image to overcome. Again, the opportunities for success and failure are both very great. It is my hope that trainers will attend to the many lessons contained in the foregoing chapters. The odds for success will be enhanced if they do.

References

Brogden, H. E., & Taylor, E. K. (1950). The dollar criterion— applying the cost-accounting concept to criterion construction. *Personnel Psychology, 3*, 133–154.

Campbell, J. P. (1988). Training design for performance improvement. In J. P. Campbell & R. J. Campbell (Eds.), *Productivity in organizations* (pp. 177–215). San Francisco: Jossey-Bass.

Cormier, S. (1984). *Transfer of training: An interpretative review.* Arlington, VA: Army Research Institute.

Fleishman, E. A., & Hempel, W. E. (1956). Factorial analysis of complex psychomotor performance and related skills. *Journal of Applied Psychology, 40,* 90–104.

Goldstein, I. L. (1986). *Training in organizations: Needs assessment, development, and evaluation* (2nd ed.). Moneterey, CA: Brooks/Cole.

Handbook of human engineering data (1952). Medford, MA: Tufts College Institute of Applied Experimental Psychology.

Kirkpatrick, D. L. (1959). Techniques for evaluating training programs. *Journal of the American Society of Training Directors, 13,* 3–9, 21–26.

Kirkpatrick, D. L. (1960). Techniques for evaluating training programs. *Journal of the American Society of Training Directors, 14,* 13–18, 28–32.

Komaki, J. L., Waddell, W. M., & Pearce, M. G. (1977). The applied behavior-analysis approach and individual employees: Improving performance in two small businesses. *Organizational Behavior and Human Performance, 19, 337–352.*

Mahler, W. R., & Monroe, W. H. (1952). *How industry determines the need for and effectiveness of training.* New York: The Psychological Corporation.

McGehee, W., & Thayer, P. W. (1961). *Training in business and industry.* New York: Wiley.

Wexley, K. N., & Latham, G. P. (1981). *Developing and training human resources in organizations.* Glenview, IL: Scott, Foresman.

13

The Agenda for
Theory and Research

John P. Campbell

Given his overall goals, the editor's needs analysis suggested that the behavioral performance objectives for this chapter would be to describe how the present volume contributes to the current development of training theory and research and to comment on its implications for future research and theory. With considerable grace, the editor did not do a person analysis and ask embarrassing questions about required KSAs for being an author, or about glaring needs for author retraining. Consequently, the principal objectives of this chapter are to discuss the contributions of this volume to more useful formulations of issues pertaining to training design, training methods, and training research. Another objective is to offer comments on where things seem to be pointed for the future and on whether the direction should be changed, altered, or elaborated upon.

Some Assumptions

The context of this discussion assumes certain things to be true. First, the general consensus seems to be that the state of training research and theory is much improved from what it was fifteen to twenty years ago (Campbell, 1988; Goldstein, this volume; Latham, 1988). Such areas as behavior modification, social learning theory, and cognitive models of decision making and problem solving have provided an infusion of new ideas and methods. Prescriptions for training design have become much more sophisticated, and a lot more empirical research has been conducted on various training issues. While the marketing of training programs may still be faddish, training theory and research are no longer dull.

Second, the general question of whether training programs with reasonable objectives and reasonable designs will produce positive results in the direction of the objectives has been answered affirmatively. Training and development interventions constitute independent variables that have considerable potential for bringing about change in individual behavior and performance. The question is not whether training works but how, why, and for what. A corollary is that asking whether training or selection is the more powerful intervention, for purposes of increasing performance, is not a useful question. In general, questions of this form (for example, ability versus motivation) are misleading and unhelpful. Certainly, both are important, and it is both the sum of their main effects and their interaction that should be investigated.

Third, it is assumed that most readers accept the notion that job performance is multidimensional. Further, a training program is hardly ever directed at affecting total job performance. Training objectives are virtually always more circumscribed than that. Consequently, using a measure of "overall" job performance as a dependent variable for assessing training effects can be a misleading, if not dangerous, thing to do. In general, the construct validity of the dependent variable — or the criterion problem, as it pertains to training evaluation and research — has not been given much attention.

Finally, while the *Annual Review of Psychology* has published four chapters on training and development and seven chapters on instructional psychology, with virtually no acknowledgment of one by the other, there is much more similarity in the educational and occupational training contexts than the lack of contact between the two would imply.

Implications for Current Issues

The chapters in this volume speak to issues in training design, training evaluation, theory-based training methods, and specific training problems of critical importance. What are the principal implications of these chapters for how we do both basic and applied research on training problems?

Certainly, as noted by Ostroff and Ford (Chapter Two), stating training needs in terms of individual performance is not the same thing as stating them in terms of work-group performance or unit performance. Going from one level to another may result in different training content (for example, to include or not to include cross-training on different jobs, training in task coordination, and so on) or may dictate different criteria with which to assess training's effects. The level must be consistent across the different parts of the training intervention, or the differences must be made explicit and accounted for in terms of functional similarity, degree of interaction, and functional dependence. Mixing levels is reminiscent of asking, or training, for A (for example, individual task performance) but rewarding B (for example, improved coordinated group task performance) (Kerr, 1975). Training research can also suffer from an unexplicit mixing of levels, as when two methods are compared but each focuses on behavior at a different level (for example, modeling versus team building), or when group incentives are used to manipulate the level of the individual learner's self-efficacy. Such level checking should become part of everyone's research design activity in the future. Among other things, it would help prevent the use of group or unit indexes to evaluate the results of training directed at individual performance needs.

The confusion over levels also has implications for how utility analyses should be used and interpreted in the training context. That is, the meaning of Y in SD_Y cannot be passed over lightly. As already noted, any given training program is probably not directed at every major component of total performance, and if Y represents total performance, then changes in Y may be a function of a number of things in addition to training.

Attributing all the change in Y to a training program requires a particularly well-controlled experimental design. Given this caveat, perhaps the most important implication of Chapter Three's analysis of the utility problem is that, for many typical situations, the effect size required to yield a positive return on a training investment is quite small. Compared to other investments, most personnel program interventions are relatively inexpensive, and it does not take much of a training-produced change to yield a positive return. This has also been shown to be true with respect to personnel selection (Boudreau, 1984), and industrial and organizational psychology should probably do a better job of communicating this information to nonpsychologists. In fact, we need to develop an effective training program for teaching people what this kind of utility analysis means. The program should have minimal prerequisites and should teach a basic understanding of the rationale and mechanics of the Cronbach and Gleser model and of SD_Y estimation methods.

One nagging worry generated by Chapter Three is illustrated by the following syllogism: (1) Training programs should be rigorously evaluated, in terms of documenting whether they produce a positive return, because managements demand it. (2) From the capital budgeting perspective, benefits must be stated in terms of tangible, measurable changes in cash flows. (3) If dollar measures of tangible benefits in a dollar metric are not feasible, then evaluation of the program is not possible, and the program cannot be justified; therefore, the training program should not be implemented. The first two statements are made in Chapter Three. Although Cascio does not do so and gives examples to the contrary, drawing the conclusion in the third statement seems all too "rational," in which case the decision of whether to use training interventions would be driven not by training needs but by the availability of certain kinds of bottom-line outcome measures. March and Simon (1958) described this issue some time ago when they noted that decision making gravitates toward situations where outcomes are most easily quantifiable.

If the magnitude of change in Y that is required to produce a nonzero positive return is usually quite small, then Chapter Four's discussion of power issues is especially relevant. Maximizing power to detect small differences, and to help overcome the limitations imposed by small sample sizes, is absolutely critical. Chapter Four focuses on a very concrete issue and provides a very clear portrayal of the commonalities and dissimilarities among alternative experimental designs. It should significantly increase the efficiency with which future investigators use pretest information.

In contrast to the well-structured implications of Chapter Four, the discussion in Chapter Six is far-reaching, a bit radical, and more than a bit mind-boggling in its implications for training theory and research. After an excellent review of their efforts to more completely specify a basic taxonomy of cognitive, psychomotor, physical, and sensory abilities, Fleishman and Mumford propose some very different ideas for how knowledge of ability taxonomies and the ability requirements of both job and training tasks can be used in training design. Their discussion assumes the validity of their proposed interaction between stages of learning and ability determinants of performance, the most important of which is that general abilities diminish and specific abilities increase in importance as learning progresses.

Given this kind of interaction, Fleishman and Mumford make two very innovative proposals. First, abilities should not be assumed to be entirely stable traits; indeed, they may be trainable. Consequently, if an analysis of training task requirements shows that abilities A, B, and C are highly correlated with performance during training, then perhaps people should be trained (pretrained?) on these abilities before job training begins. If general cognitive ability is related to early performance, and if specific spatial or psychomotor abilities are required later in training to achieve final form, then so be it. We should consider pretraining on both general and specific abilities. This is a very environmentalist position and not one that is frequently found in the instructional psychology or training and development literature.

Second, the design of training content for improving task performance should be a function of the ability requirements —

that is, the learner's performance on the training content (as manifested by exercises, quizzes, and instructors' evaluations) should show the expected correlations with the appropriate abilities at each stage, or the content should be changed to achieve the appropriate correlation pattern. This comes very close to arguing that validity of a particular course structure is not supported by data showing that it promotes higher achievement and retention than alternative course designs, but by data showing the appropriate correlations with abilities. Both of these ideas are the converse of the conventional wisdom. Campbell, Daft, and Hulin (1982) have argued that asserting the converse and exploring its implications is frequently a very useful way of getting out of a conceptual rut. It is what has given us the notion of validity generalization (F. L. Schmidt, 1981, personal communication); Fleishman and Mumford use it here to give us a new way to look at the role of abilities, the design of treatments, and the nature of their interactions. It invites a great deal of research on these issues, the outcomes of which should be extremely valuable.

While not as revolutionary as Fleishman and Mumford's chapter, Chapter Seven by Latham (behavioral approaches), and Chapter Five, by Howell and Cooke (cognitive approaches), are informative and provocative. Each one should be a source of new research ideas in a variety of basic and applied contexts. Both chapters try to create something of an adversarial relationship between things behavioral and things cognitive. This must have been just for its entertainment value, because the two chapters, when looked at closely, do not address quite the same set of issues; if anything, their prescriptions for training research and training design are complementary, not competitive.

My reasons for drawing this conclusion are as follows. The behavioral approach, as Latham applies it, is really trying to prescribe the crucial learning events (the generic instructional methods) that will best lead to mastery of a certain class of performance objectives; that is, modeling followed by practice followed by feedback are the preferred learning events, so long as these events incorporate the appropriate capabilities. For example, if the objective is to be able to deal effectively with conflict among subordinates, then the capability is not mastery of the facts concerning conflict resolution; rather, it is mastery of the behavioral skills necessary to mediate conflict among subordinates verbally, face to face. The important training problems portrayed in Chapter Seven deal with leadership and supervisory skills, behavioral dysfunctions, the self-management of one's own behavior in general, and executive or managerial self-development in particular. For it all to work, the performance objectives (learning points) must be correctly described, and the training content must match the objectives.

Howell and Cooke's portrayal of the cognitive information-processing model is an account of the learning process and an attempt to describe how mastery is achieved or not achieved via effective or ineffective information processing. Consequently, there is much discussion of attentional processes, encoding of information, memory parameters, mental models (such as schemata) of knowledge structures, and problem-solving processes. The training objectives of interest have much more to do with improving problem solving, decision making, and cognitive skills in general than the interpersonal and self-management skills that Latham worries about. A common element is the need for the most useful kind of task analysis. The specification of learning points by people doing behavioral modeling, and the cognitive task analysis described by Howell and Cooke, are virtually identical in function. They are both descriptions of what an expert performer would do, or of what a successful trainee should be able to do.

If we put these two chapters together, in terms of their prescriptions for future research in training and development, we also get a very complementary set of ideas. Consider the following: Latham argues that if we use the precepts of social learning theory, then we will make liberal use of modeling, guided practice, and feedback to promote mastery of interpersonal skills, effective self-management, and the elimination of specific dysfunctional behavior. Considerable research should be directed at designing learning events that require responses that map the desired behavioral skill as closely as possible. We should also pay close attention to the motivational elements in trainee behavior and conduct a lot of research on self-efficacy and outcome expectancies (for example, how to assess them and how to change them), both as antecedents of trainees' behavior and as products of training. Social learning theory and its descendants (Kanfer & Gaelick, 1986; Kanfer & Ackerman, in press) focus on learner motivation in ways that the information-processing models of cognitive psychology do not.

If we are motivated by Howell and Cooke's chapter, we will define what is to be learned via cognitive task analyses that describe what the expert or competent performer does—that is, as Glaser (1982) has noted, we must be able to specify what competent performance is—for example, what competent or expert technical performance is for a computer systems analyst or tax accountant. Protocol analysis will be heavily relied on. Once we have described what the expert does, we must specify, to some degree, the structure of the knowledge and the cognitive skills that must be mastered to enable expert performance. Here, such questions arise as whether problem-solving skills are general or domain-specific (Larkin, McDermott, Simon, & Simon, 1980). If the structure of knowledge and skill can be specified, then our attention shifts to the trainee, and we must ask whether the individual has learned a mental model that maps the desired knowledge structure appropriately. For the sake of more effective training, we need a good deal of domain-specific research on how best to encode new knowledge and skill for purposes of retention, retrieval, and transfer. Deficiencies in the mental model, or in the strategies used to apply the knowledge structure to performance problems, should then be identified. In this regard, research in instructional psychology has focused on developing a number of procedures for modeling errors, as illustrated by the DEBUGGY algorithm (Burton, 1982), such that remedies for performance errors can be incorporated into the training program.

Let us say that we have applied these notions to designing better training for the research design performance of I/O psychologists. We would then devote attention to giving a much more complete specification of what expert designers of I/O research do. For example, in what form do they state research questions? Next, our accumulated collective wisdom must be used, to give the best possible description of the required knowledge structure. For example, should everyone "know" the contents of Chapters Two, Three, and Four in this volume? For purposes of storage in memory, what is the best mental representation of that knowledge? Finally, can we model the most frequent errors in research design (for example, emphasizing Type I error and forgetting about Type II error) and inoculate the learner against them?

In sum, operant models, social learning theory, and cognitive psychology can all contribute to our understanding of training issues, and they really speak to different sources of variation in training effects. The well-trained I/O psychologist should have a well-developed mental model for each. If that were true, researchers would be more likely to be able to act on the suggestions in Chapters Five and Seven.

A good example of an attempt to use the available research, theory, and prevailing practice to describe the knowledge structure pertaining to a particular problem is Chapter Eleven, on training people from one country to successfully fulfill job assignments in another. To the limit allowed by the current state of knowledge, Chapter Eleven lays out the objectives for such training and then summarizes all we currently know about what the training content should be and what methods should be used to teach it. The chapter is a model that should be applied to as many different training problems as possible. It very clearly illustrates what we already know and what we need to find out (still a considerable amount). The format of Chapter Eleven could profitably be used to summarize the prevailing objectives, content, and instructional methods for critical training problems such as decision making, problem solving, various aspects of leadership, mechanical trouble shooting, electrical trouble shooting, using desktop computers, and so on. In fact, a volume consisting of a collection of such summaries would be an enormously valuable resource for the training enterprise, both for research and for practice. After such a volume was created, it would be a straightforward matter to revise and expand it.

Chapters Eight and Nine (on aging and career growth, respectively) speak to the interactive effects of two broad parameters—chronological age and career age—on training objectives and training content. One comes away from these two chapters with the conclusion that we still do not know much about either area. Consequently, both chapters are best viewed as road maps for where to direct our research efforts. Given the impending movement of the baby boom cohort into middle age, as well as the increasing research support for the study of aging, such guidance should prove valuable. In Chapter Eight, Sterns and Doverspike certainly point to the need to improve the specification of the kinds of job content that are susceptible to aging effects and the kinds that are not. When performance components are affected by age, how can that effect be obviated? Will it be by providing more practice, or by developing different work techniques? What role does motivation play? The prototypical experiment by Salthouse (1984), in which older subjects maintained their keyboard speed by means of a greater span of anticipation for impending keystrokes, deserves to be imitated.

The problem of maintaining a productive and satisfying career is even more ill structured than the age × performance issue. Chapter Nine outlines the problem in some detail and provides a schematic model of the parameters that organizations and individuals should worry about. For example, the model strongly suggests that individuals will almost certainly experience job loss, career plateau, or some other kind of mid-career crisis. How can organizations and individuals best deal with such events? London and Bassman suggest that one way is by motivating individuals to define such problems in particular ways (for example, a career plateau can be a stimulus for learning new skills) and by providing support for maintaining such a viewpoint. The parameter of career motivation is hypothesized to be central to effective career self-management. The basic ingredients of career motivation are career resilience, career insight, and career identity. A number of research questions will revolve around the relationship of these three variables to positive career outcomes; whether they are best viewed as state or trait and how appropriate changes in them can be generated through training or job redesign. The London and Bassman model is very comprehensive and suggests a number of applied research problems relevant to training. Psychologists interested in career issues would do well to study it.

Finally, everything that has been said so far reflects an "other things being equal" view of training issues and problems. Feldman's excellent chapter on socialization issues provides a good dose of reality. Everyone is reminded that trainees do not just fall out of some great trainee bin in the sky; they probably have rather long and varied histories, which have created certain attitudes, values, and behaviors relative to specific training experiences. Their previous socialization may have been in support of or in conflict with the specific goals of a training program and with the methods used to implement it. Also, a great deal of past, present, and future training is carried out informally and may or may not support the formal training efforts. Furthermore, since people are often trained in groups, the impact of the group's dynamics on training outcomes may be considerable. "Failure to replicate" may be due to the formation of different group norms in different training groups. Finally, training programs, in addition to pursuing their formal objectives, almost always serve as socialization devices themselves. For example, a skills-training course may inadvertently teach trainees a lot about the supportive or unsupportive management climate in the organization, about whether performance standards are high or low, and about what kinds of performance appraisal will be forthcoming. A multitude of critical research questions are laid out in Chapter Ten, and they reflect issues that we should all think about. For example, how can we best determine whether the socialization process has led to informal training goals that are in direct conflict with the goals incorporated in the training design? What does the program teach besides its mandated objectives? How does the socialization process influence learners' self-efficacy or need achievement? In sum, without knowing the effects of the socialization process, we may not be able to draw the correct conclusions about training effects.

Implications for the Future

While there is very little to criticize in the foregoing chapters, the training and development world is not perfect, and a few discordant notes must be mentioned. The points to be made here are primarily definitional and pertain more to the literature in general than to the foregoing chapters in particular.

Definitional Issues. There is a certain amount of semantic and syntactical confusion regarding a number of training-relevant concepts. Some of the confusions are easier to deal with than others. Among the former is the use of the term *aptitude-treatment interactions (ATIs)*. It appears several times in this volume but virtually never in the context of an actual illustration of an ATI. In general, the ATI is often confused with situations in which there is a main effect for the treatment factor (for example, the new training program makes more of a difference compared to the old) and the aptitude measure has a positive relationship with the training achievement, but there is no interaction. Consider the six situations illustrated in Figure 13.1.

In each case, there are two treatments, or training programs (I and II); some measure of training-produced effects (Y); some measure, or composite measure, of individual differences, commonly referred to as the aptitude (X); and the regression of the criterion on the aptitude measure within each training group. In (A), there is no correlation between aptitude and achievement, and no mean differences are produced by the two treatments. In (B), there is a positive relationship between the predictor and the criterion within each training group, but there is still no difference in effects produced by the two methods. In (C), there is a difference in payoff in favor of method A but no correlation between the aptitude and the criterion. In (D), there are two main effects: Treatment A produces a consistently higher payoff for everybody, and the higher the score on the aptitude, the higher the payoff. (E) is the same as (D) except that the regression of payoff on aptitude is not the same for the two training groups. In situations (A), (B), (C), (D), and (E), the

Figure 13.1. Six Hypothetical Examples of the Regression of Training Payoff on Individual Aptitude for Two Different Training Programs.

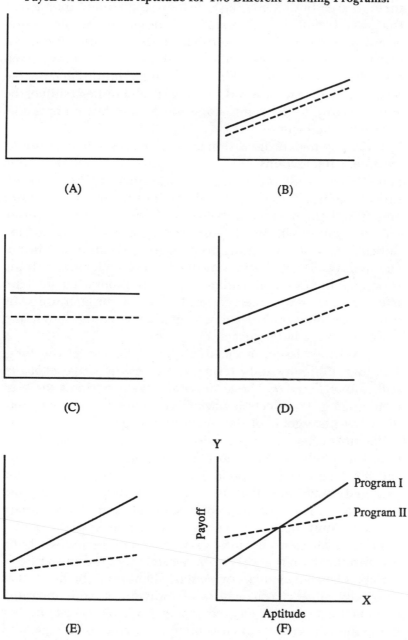

(A)

(B)

(C)

(D)

(E)

(F)

Y

Payoff

Program I

Program II

Aptitude

X

organization would maximize payoff by giving the same treatment to everybody. Only in (F) is there the kind of interaction
that would result in differential assignment of people to programs on the basis of aptitude. This particular situation is not
discussed by any of the authors in the present volume. Interestingly, the suggestion by Fleishman and Mumford that people
be pretrained on the aptitude variable itself implies a shift of the
entire picture to the right, along the X axis, but no aptitude-
treatment interaction.

   An up-to-date discussion of current research on aptitude-
treatment interactions can be found in Ackerman, Sternberg,
and Glaser (1988) and in Kanfer, Ackerman, and Cudeck (in
press). Campbell (1988) makes the point that an ATI worthy of
attention is the interaction between the degree of prerequisite
knowledge and skill already possessed by the individual and the
difficulty level of the training program. (For example, maybe not
all supervisors should have the same kind of leadership training
program.) In any event, we should be clear about what are main
effects and what are interactions. In the current literature, the
former are often talked about as if they were the latter, and
research on the latter goes begging.

   Another issue, more difficult to address, is the long-
standing ambiguity of the terms *aptitude, ability, developed ability,
skill,* and *performance.* The term *performance* is perhaps the least
troublesome. It reflects behaviors or actions that contribute
directly to the goals of the institution, organization, or individual; it is what the organization wants to pay for (see Campbell, Campbell, & Associates, 1988). *Skills* are task-domain-
specific cognitive, perceptual, psychomotor, physical, or interpersonal capabilities that are acquired through training and
instruction. In the training context, *aptitudes* and *abilities* have
relevance only because they help predict or explain performance; they have no intrinsic value in and of themselves, but a
major difficulty has always been the state-versus-trait nature of
variables labeled *aptitudes* or *abilities.* Should they be defined as
relatively stable characteristics of individuals, with measurement methods developed accordingly? Or is *ability* just another
name for *achievement,* which is quite amenable to change, and

which must be linked to specifications of domains of content? Another issue is how to treat the traditional distinctions between *cognitive abilities* and *personality traits.* Are they really two entirely different domains? This is not the place to take up such arguments; the interested reader is referred to Ackerman (in press), Henry and Hulin (1987), Humphreys (1974), and Messick (1987).

A more manageable issue for the training literature is a strong suggestion that researchers and practitioners be very explicit about how they view the aptitude variable in the ATI. Do they intend that such variables be viewed as stable or dynamic? trainable or untrainable? under what conditions? If the theory is clearly stated, and if measurement is consistent with the theory, then arguments about what the results mean will be more useful. For example, a bit more explicitness in Chapter Six would have helped in this regard. Also, in a number of the chapters, authors use the term *ability* when they clearly mean *skill,* as just defined. Perhaps there should be a set of standards for definitions of such terms.

Substantive Issues. This author hopes that he is not the only one to see it this way, but both the recent training and development literature (for example, Latham, 1988) and some of the chapters in this volume suggest a shift in the way that future literature could be organized. In the past, the paradigm has been to review research results around "methods," such as programmed instruction, computer-assisted instruction, management development, sensitivity training, and so on. In the future, such reviews should center more and more on the substantive training objective. For example, what does the literature tell us about how to teach certain kinds of interpersonal skills, electronic trouble shooting, or computer literacy?

If such a change occurred, it would highlight at least two other directions for training research. First, in the post–Industrial Revolution era, are there generic training needs that should be identified, and should their population frequencies be described? Argyris (1964) spoke to this issue a number of years ago, when he argued that virtually everyone is so interpersonally incompetent that a strong training response is a necessity if organizations are ever to function in a mature way. What are some others? What are the real generic training needs for major segments of our work force? What are reasonable ways to meet them? A second implication is that if we want to get into the business of establishing generic training needs and training strategies, then analyses of expert or competent performance, and descriptions of knowledges, skills, and abilities in terms of the required "structure" of knowledge and skill, become critical.

Very recently, there has been a renewal of interest in learners' motivation (Noe, 1986; Latham, 1988; Campbell, 1988), and both Chapters Seven and Ten should stimulate still more interest. We simply should pay much more attention to the following areas:

- Trainees' goals and their correspondence or conflict with program goals
- The variability and extent of self-efficacy before and during training
- The self-regulatory behavior of trainees
- The cognitions of trainees regarding the instrumentality of training programs for obtaining desired outcomes
- The reinforcement and punishment contingencies that actually exist
- The dispositional characteristics of learners with respect to mastery versus performance needs (Dweck, 1986)
- The socialization and group processes that influence trainees' goals, self-efficacy, and instrumentality judgments.

Everyone intuitively appreciates that motivational effects can completely swamp the potential benefits of improved instructional design. It is time to investigate them more systematically, and on a large scale.

Finally, it has always seemed the case that the term *training research* is virtually synonymous with *evaluation research*. However, the field has matured past the point where we must be so consumed by the question Does it work? or Does it pay? It is time for questions such as: What learning content, and which learning events, best promote mastery of being able to use goal setting with subordinates? What should be the content of a training program in managerial problem solving, and how should it be structured? What elements of a training group influence individual self-efficacy? It is the investigation of theory-driven substantive issues like these that will advance training and development, not more and more summative evaluation. Pursuit of both basic and applied research along such lines, as well as a breaking down of barriers between I/O psychology and instructional psychology, is in our future and will enhance the intrinsic value of training and development as a place to investigate human behavior.

References

Ackerman, P. L. (in press). Within-task intercorrelations of skilled performance: Implications for predicting individual differences. *Journal of Applied Psychology*.

Ackerman, P. L., Sternberg, R. J., & Glaser, R. (Eds.) (1988). *Learning and individual differences: Advances in theory and research*. New York: W. H. Freeman.

Argyris, C. (1964). *Integrating the individual and the organization*. New York: Wiley.

Boudreau, J. W. (1984). Decision theory contributions to HRM research and practice. *Industrial Relations, 23*, 198–217.

Burton, R. R. (1982). Diagnosing bugs in a simple procedural skill. In D. Sleeman & J. S. Brown (Eds.), *Intelligent tutoring systems*. Orlando, FL: Academic Press.

Campbell, J. P. (1988). Training design for performance improvement. In J. P. Campbell, R. J. Campbell, & Associates (Eds.), *Productivity in organizations* (pp. 177–215). San Francisco: Jossey-Bass.

Campbell, J. P., Campbell, R. J., & Associates. (1988). *Productivity in organizations*. San Francisco: Jossey-Bass.

Campbell, J. P., Daft, R. L., & Hulin, C. L. (1982). *What to study: Generating and developing research questions*. Newbury Park, CA: Sage.

Dweck, C. S. (1986). Motivational processes affecting learning. *American Psychologist, 41,* 1040–1048.

Glaser, R. (1982). Instructional psychology: Past, present, and future. *American Psychologist, 37,* 292–305.

Henry, R. A., & Hulin, C. L. (1987). Stability of skilled performance across time: Some generalizations and limitations on utilities. *Journal of Applied Psychology, 72,* 457–462.

Humphreys, L. G. (1974). The misleading distinction between aptitude and achievement tests. In D. R. Green (Ed.), *The aptitude-achievement distinction.* New York: McGraw-Hill.

Kanfer, F. H., & Gaelick, L. (1986). Self-management methods. In F. H. Kanfer & A. P. Goldstein (Eds.), *Helping people change: A textbook of methods* (3rd ed.). Elmsford, NY: Pergamon Press.

Kanfer, R., & Ackerman, P. L. (in press). Motivation and cognitive abilities: An integrative/aptitude-treatment interaction approach to skill acquisition. *Journal of Applied Psychology.*

Kanfer, R., Ackerman, P. L., & Cudeck, R. (Eds.) (in press). *Abilities, motivation, and methodology: The Minnesota Symposium on Learning and Individual Differences.* Hillsdale, NJ: Erlbaum.

Kerr, S. (1975). On the folly of rewarding A, while hoping for B. *Academy of Management Journal, 18,* 769–783.

Larkin, J. H., McDermott, J., Simon, D. P., & Simon, H. A. (1980). Expert and novice performance in solving physics problems. *Science, 80,* 1335–1342.

Latham, G. P. (1988). Human resource training and development. *Annual Review of Psychology, 39,* 545–582.

March, J. G., & Simon, H. A. (1958). *Organizations.* New York: Wiley.

Messick, S. (1987). Structural relationships across cognition, personality, and style. In R. Snow & M. Farr (Eds.), *Aptitude, Learning, and Instruction: Vol. 3. Conative and Affective Process Analysis.* Hillsdale, NJ: Erlbaum.

Noe, R. A. (1986). Trainees' attributes: Neglected influences on training effectiveness. *Academy of Management Review, 11,* 736–749.

Salthouse, T. A. (1984). Effects of age and skill in typing. *Journal of Experimental Psychology, 113,* 345–371.

14

Contributions to
the Practice of Training

Kenneth N. Wexley

The push for the effective training and retraining of American workers is more critical than ever before. The influence of such things as overseas competition, new technology, and the changing nature of American employees has made the practice of training an important vehicle for enhancing the productivity of the U.S. work force.

In my opinion, there are four practical issues that must be dealt with if the training is really to be an effective means of increasing our nation's productivity. First, too often training programs get their start in organizations simply because the program was well advertised and marketed, or because "other organizations are using it." It makes no sense for organizations to adopt expensive and time-consuming training programs just to "keep up with the Joneses." Instead, training practitioners need an approach for assessing their organization's training needs that both works and is practical to use.

A second practical issue concerns the design of training programs. Quite frankly, at this time, we know relatively little about designing training programs. Most of what is done falls more in the category of "art" than the category of "technique based on rigorous empirical research." We need to know more about selecting trainable trainees, choosing the best combination of methods and techniques depending on what is being

487

trained, and maximizing trainees' learning and positive transfer.

The third practical issue is the changing nature of the American work force. For example, we need to be concerned with retraining older blue-collar workers for jobs in the high-technology, service, and information sectors. It has been estimated that employers will have to retrain office workers five to eight times during their careers in the near future. We need better methods of training American workers for overseas assignments as well as for work in foreign-owned companies here at home.

The fourth practical issue is the question of evaluating the effectiveness of training programs. The typical approach in the past has been to review a program with one or two vice-presidents at the corporate office, various managers in the field, and perhaps a group of former trainees. If there is consensus that the training program has been worthwhile, it continues to be implemented until it becomes all but institutionalized. Unfortunately, all of this is done on the basis of opinion. In the end, nobody really knows whether the training achieved the objectives for which it was designed. These practices cannot continue! We need to develop the methodology to determine both the degree to which our training programs are improving employee job performance and their utility from a cost/benefit standpoint.

After reviewing the ten chapters in this volume from the practitioner's perspective, I am impressed with both the quantity and quality of the suggestions presented that can be implemented by I/O psychologists specializing in personnel training and development. Here, as I review each chapter, it will become evident that I feel that each one contains something valuable for the practitioner, despite the fact that certain of these chapters (for example, Chapters Two and Ten) were definitely written more for the researcher than for the practicing I/O training specialist.

In Chapter Two, Ostroff and Ford contend that the emerging literature in organizational psychology on levels of analysis can readily be applied to training needs assessment. Specifically, these authors suggest that practitioners would be better off handling training needs assessment by using a twenty-seven-cell matrix than by following more traditional methods. Basically, their approach expands on organizational, task, and person analyses by suggesting that each of these three areas be viewed at three levels of analysis: organizational, subunit, and individual. Moreover, they argue that constructs (or conceptual variables) relevant to each of the nine cells on the front face of their twenty-seven-cell matrix should be identified, defined, measured, and interpreted. This means that practitioners should consider measuring such conceptual variables as goals, objectives, values, and time orientation when performing organizational analyses; measure the technical environment and situational constraints when doing task analyses; and conduct skills inventories and climate assessments when conducting person analyses. To accomplish this, Ostroff and Ford suggest that practitioners follow five guidelines or steps: identify the level(s) of analysis relevant to the current needs assessment, identify the conceptual variables of interest for the appropriate level(s) of analysis, develop causal pathways or models that link variables within and across levels of analysis, measure variables and interpret results at the appropriate level(s) of analysis, and, use the levels-of-analysis perspective to guide training design and evaluation strategies.

From the practitioner's viewpoint, too many pages in Chapter Two are devoted to such inapplicable concepts as isomorphism, bond strength, parts and wholes, and unity of theory. Later, when it is time to discuss how the various conceptual variables (for example, time orientation and climate) are to be operationalized and interpreted, the reader is told that this step is complex and beyond the scope of the paper. Take, for example, time orientation. We are told that organizations address issues of the scheduling, coordination, and allocation of time differently, that subunits differ on spans or intervals for receiving definitive feedback about their work, and that individuals have their own time conceptions. As a practitioner, I would find it useful to know how to operationalize these variables, but I am not told how my findings could be used to identify training needs. Let us say that a hypothetical organization schedules, coordinates, and allocates time rather quickly. This organization's sales department receives rapid feedback about its behavior and results. In addition, about one-quarter of its salespersons possess a "fast" time conception, while the rest display a "slow" conception. What should the practitioner do with all this information, in terms of needs assessment?

Reading Chapter Two, I had the impression that the authors were suggesting that the conceptual variables in *all nine* cells need to be measured and interpreted. From a practical standpoint, it was important to learn from steps one and two that only certain levels of analysis, as well as conceptual variables relevant to the purpose of the needs assessment, should be included. This suggestion helps to minimize the time, effort, and personnel that any needs assessment entails. The question here is how one knows which of the nine cells to include and exclude in the needs assessment. For instance, suppose a training needs assessment is intended for teams of ten individuals manufacturing paper, where each team member will be expected to perform all the team's tasks. It is not clear in Chapter Two why anything more than individual-level task analysis would be needed. True, there may be some interactions between members of different teams; but can it not merely be included in the individual-level task analysis? It is not clear to practitioners whether this example should also entail analyses at the subunit and organizational levels, nor is it clear what specific conceptual variables should be assessed. Moreover, the notion of developing a causal pathway or model that would link variables within and across levels of analysis seems to have limited applicability and practicality for the practitioner, since it is not clear how this causal pathway can be used.

On the positive side, Chapter Two suggests to the practitioners that they be careful not to automatically restrict themselves to the individual level of analysis when conducting task and person analyses, nor to the individual and subunit levels of analyses when conducting organizational analyses. This unfreezing of our traditional ways of thinking is good. Finally, Ostroff and Ford propose conceptual variables for inclusion in a needs assessment. For instance, I particularly liked their citing the use of a framework for identifying situational constraints, not just at the individual level but also at the subunit and organizational levels. This will help practitioners realize that performance deficiencies at the individual, group, or organizational levels often should not be remediated through training. Practitioners should also benefit from Ostroff and Ford's suggestion that we consider goals, values, and objectives, not only of the organization as a whole but also of its various subunits and individual workers. This idea certainly needs reemphasis.

Chapter Three makes an important contribution by discussing utility analysis from an entirely new and unique perspective. In the past, utility formulas have given practitioners ways and means to evaluate the end results of their training programs in economic terms. In Chapter Three, Cascio discusses how utility approaches can also be used as a first step in deciding which of several proposed investment opportunities should be pursued. Since all organizations have limited financial resources, training professionals need to demonstrate ahead of time that proposed training programs will yield an impressive return on investment, in comparison with other investment opportunities. Chapter Three provides training professionals with a new, three-step approach to this task and demonstrates how this approach can be applied to a hypothetical goal-setting and feedback program. Cascio also shows how practitioners can take account of additional factors, such as attrition of employees, decay in the strength of training effects over time, the effects of discounting, and the effects of training multiple cohorts. From the practitioner's perspective, Cascio's chapter is ideal in that it presents something new, helpful, and applicable.

Chapter Four, by Arvey and Cole, deals with a question that more I/O practitioners have asked themselves: What is the correct way to evaluate change? Until now, this has been an extremely complex and confusing issue for practitioners and researchers alike. Arvey and Cole do an excellent job of comparing several traditional statistical methods of evaluating change, in terms of the effects of power and unreliable measures, and they demonstrate which methods are best. For years, training practitioners have been unsure of whether to collect both posttest and pretest measures. Organizational practitioners have also been unsure of how to evaluate training programs and frequently have been forced to resort to using small sample sizes, self-report criterion measures, and/or nonequivalent groups. Alternate-ranks assignment (based on pretest measures) used with ANCOVA is an excellent recommendation for handling the problem of small sample sizes, as is the use of the "retrospective pretest" with self-report measures. Finally, it is interesting to note that many training specialists have incorrectly assumed that gain-score analysis or ANCOVA could compensate for having nonequivalent groups at pretest. Arvey and Cole's chapter straightens out this misconception and briefly suggests three alternative procedures. Nevertheless, since the problem of using nonequivalent groups is so frequently encountered by training practitioners, and since gain-score analysis and ANCOVA are not solutions, the authors should have provided more detail and examples of how to use latent-variable models to handle this situation.

In Chapter Five, Howell and Cooke point out that the nature of work has undergone dramatic changes over the past decade, because of the impact of computer technology. Given these changes, work requirements at all levels have become more demanding, in the cognitive sense. For training practitioners, this implies that workers will need to learn and refine somewhat different skills than they have in the past. The new cognitive skills involve such things as being a better diagnostician, creating appropriate mental models for handling the complex processes under one's control, increasing attentional capabilities, and improving one's monitoring and problem-solving skills. Howell and Cooke answer the question "What do we know about human cognition that is of potential value in the design and implementation of training programs for work settings?" To my knowledge, this important question has not been adequately addressed in any previous training books or articles. Therefore, this chapter makes a unique and important contribution to training practitioners.

From the practitioner's viewpoint, however, the chapter is somewhat overwhelming and perplexing, because it is loaded with numerous ideas, concepts, and theories. It is difficult for the practitioner to decipher which topics are immediately applicable to the design of training programs, and which are based on conjecture. Nevertheless, there are certain parts of this chapter that all training professionals should learn about before designing another instructional program. Most important, the authors point out the need for conducting cognitive task analyses, and they offer several analytical frameworks that can be used. Howell and Cooke make it clear that, as the first step, training designers must identify the overall objectives of the tasks to be trained and decompose them into elements that have meaning for the learner and for what is currently known about underlying cognitive processes. Only after doing a cognitive task analysis can the training designer decide what elements will be trained, and in what order. Chapter Five also provides valuable ideas on improving short- and long-term memory; training people in the formation and use of efficient conceptualizations or mental models of tasks, systems, and processes; improving learners' skills in diagnosing, at any given stage during training, what they still do not know; teaching general problem-solving strategies; and knowing when to provide outcome feedback, process feedback, and no feedback at all.

Many ideas presented by Fleishman and Mumford in Chapter Six are quite meaningful for training practitioners. Most important, the authors point out that one needs to consider learners' characteristics as essential ingredients of instructional system design. More specifically, Fleishman and Mumford contend that the reliable and valid measurement of ability requirements, by means of their MARS methodology, can prove useful for instructional purposes, in several ways. Even in the most carefully designed training program, there is not likely to be one-to-one correspondence between required abilities and training activities. This finding is quite important and clearly suggests that, to get a comprehensive view of learners' characteristics, training practitioners must consider both the job environment and the training environment. Such information can be used for decisions about whether to select individuals for training. It can also be used for assigning people to alternative training programs, so that the ability requirements of training match individual ability profiles. Clearly, Fleishman and Mumford's approach provides training specialists with a useful method for tackling these objectives.

As the authors themselves recognize, learners' characteristics consist of all the knowledge, skills, abilities, and other characteristics needed for learning and task performance in particular training and job situations. MARS is certainly an excellent method for determining the abilities needed by trainees. It allows practitioners to identify the abilities required for training tasks, as well as to assess trainees' characteristics. In its current state, however, MARS is inadequate as a vehicle for identifying the job-specific knowledge, skills, and other characteristics needed for targeted areas of job performance. This deficiency is acknowledged by the authors, and measures are being taken to rectify it. For instance, additional behaviorally anchored rating scales that assess such characteristics as driving, typing, and persuasion are currently being added to the taxonomy. Further, as part of the five-step MARS procedure conducted at the task level, additional job-specific abilities not shown in the taxonomy are being specified. Despite all this, practitioners will have to continue using other approaches, to make certain that all of the specific job knowledge, skills, and personal characteristics that need to be addressed during training are identified.

Fleishman and Mumford do an excellent job of reviewing previous research on skills acquisition, from a pragmatic viewpoint. On the basis of this review, the authors suggest that practitioners focus on training general abilities and knowledge during the initial stages of skill learning. They say that certain generic abilities can be improved, that the design of training should differ as a function of trainees' levels of ability, and that learning will be optimized when training interventions provide explanation, modeling, active practice, and feedback. The latter point ties in nicely with Latham's comments in Chapter Seven, concerning Bandura's social learning theory.

Latham's chapter focuses the reader's attention on several behaviorally based training approaches that have proved effective in organizations. Chapter Seven offers practitioners a theoretical explanation of why behavior modeling, self-management strategies, programmed instruction, and training through positive reinforcement have proved so effective. Specifically, such training methods such as behavior modeling and self-management are based on Bandura's social learning theory, which, unlike behaviorism, is eclectic in that it recognizes the existence of cognitive as well as behavioral factors in learning. Such training methods as programmed instruction and positive reinforcement are grounded in behaviorism and are based on operant principles of conditioning. When these techniques have been found effective, such cognitive factors as goal setting, self-efficacy, and outcome expectancy have been involved. All this suggests that practitioners cannot ignore the contents of the "black box," and that training programs have to affect trainees' behavior as well as their cognitions.

Some of Latham's speculations regarding future directions for training have important implications for practitioners. First, training methods that focus both on behavior and on cognition (for example, behavior modeling), thereby bridging theoretical gaps, are quite effective. Second, it is advisable to select trainees who already have self-efficacy and outcome expectancy or else somehow to improve these cognitions at the start of training. Third, computer-based training is advisable, because it can be expected to reduce training time and adjust to individual differences in learning rates. Fourth, the use of mild punishment should automatically be rejected by training practitioners; instead, the effects of punishment should be studied further. Finally, practitioners should take note of Latham's prediction that the training of employees in self-management strategies will become more critical as organizations reduce the number of their managers.

Considering the growing numbers of middle-aged and older workers in the American labor force, Chapter Eight, by Sterns and Doverspike, focuses on an important training issue: optimizing the training and retraining of older workers. From the practitioner's viewpoint, the most perplexing aspect of this chapter is the authors' conception of the term *older*. Sterns and Doverspike begin by reviewing five general approaches to the classification and definition of the older worker. They conclude that, for training purposes, the life-span approach is particularly useful. This approach emphasizes individual differences in aging by recognizing that behavioral changes can occur at any point in the life cycle. If this is so, and if the chronological age of the learner is not the significant influence on performance, then how are training designers supposed to identify ahead of time which particular trainees are going to behave during training as if they were "older"? In all likelihood, it will be extremely difficult to identify these individuals before the training is designed. If this is true, then why must unique principles of learning be incorporated into training programs for "older" adults? Instead, it seems that these are sound training principles that practitioners should incorporate into all training programs for all trainees.

On the one hand, Sterns and Doverspike advocate the life-span conception of aging. On the other hand, they cite several studies suggesting that older individuals may require longer training times and may make more errors, even though they may be able to perform at the same level as younger individuals once they have reached proficiency. From the practitioner's viewpoint, it is unclear how one should handle the training of adults forty and older who are covered by the Age Discrimination in Employment Act of 1967. The life-span approach suggests that we not treat them differently as a group, because individual differences among trainees (regardless of chronological age) account for most of the variance in learning. Conversely, other research suggests that we should do such things as provide slower presentation rates, longer periods for completing diagnostic tests, and longer periods for study. The chapter does not say clearly enough how practitioners should handle these types of applied issues.

Three points in Sterns and Doverspike's chapter are particularly interesting and helpful to the practicing I/O psychologist. First, the authors point out that recent research has demonstrated continued cognitive growth and development well into the late older-adult period. This contradicts the common-sense notion that there is some optimal point in the life span for acquiring new information. Second, the chapter provides quite a few learning principles that should be incorporated into the design of training programs that involve older workers. Third, on-the-job training programs continue to be the most popular training method in American organizations and government-sponsored programs. Nevertheless, the authors warn, power-relationship problems may occur when younger employees are asked to train older ones.

From the practitioner's viewpoint, Chapter Nine, by London and Bassman, has both shortcomings and strengths. Its major shortcoming stems from the fact that the authors attempt to discuss the components of and the relationships among all the individual and organizational processes that affect training and retraining. The reader is likely to ask, "Where am I? Where is this chapter taking me now?"

Despite these shortcomings, the chapter has many interesting and important training prescriptions for practitioners who are interested in motivating and maximizing the continuous learning of midcareer employees. It also includes numerous up-to-date examples of organizational practice. Perhaps the most useful part of this chapter is the authors' conception of career motivation as consisting of three principal domains—resilience, insight, and identity—and their ideas of how training programs can be designed especially for midcareer employees, to improve their career motivation. Useful training suggestions are also given for increasing career resilience, insight, and identity.

London and Bassman's discussion of adults' learning processes ties in nicely with the chapter by Sterns and Doverspike. Both chapters provide clear ideas on how to maximize learning on the part of older adults. The most pragmatic prescriptions offered by London and Bassman entail having older employees discover for themselves the answers to problems, as opposed to using traditional didactic methods; allowing them to design and structure learning experiences for themselves; and using relapse prevention as a means of maximizing positive transfer, by sensitizing trainees to the likelihood of future failure and developing their coping strategies for dealing with failure.

The authors also list a host of useful things that organizations can do to motivate continuous learning. In addition to certain obvious things, such as tuition assistance and labor-management agreements, the authors recommend skill- and knowledge-based pay systems, the development of mastery paths, the training and rewarding of supervisors for developing and counseling older employees, and the involvement of top-level managers in training (beyond mere verbal statements of support).

Feldman's chapter focuses on integrating the socialization and training literatures for a better understanding of how newcomers learn their jobs and adjust to their organizations. This chapter is quite interesting, but more from the standpoint of its suggestions for future research than from the practitioner's perspective. This is certainly because the socialization and resocialization literature to date is theoretical and speculative rather than empirical. Despite this limitation, there are certain parts of Feldman's chapter that I/O practitioners can apply to organizations.

From the practitioner's viewpoint, Feldman's chapter points out several important research findings that can be readily used in designing training programs for the socialization of newcomers and the resocialization of incumbents. First, trainees need to get adjusted to and trust their co-workers and supervisors before they can really start concentrating on learning the details of their new jobs, and learning their new roles takes the longest. Second, how new recruits are processed can have a profound influence on the attitudes and behaviors that they learn during socialization. (Interestingly, individual socialization tends to provide more innovative behaviors while generating more role uncertainty and confusion; the socialization of large groups of newcomers, however, results in fewer innovative behaviors and fewer positive feelings toward the organization but greater cohesiveness among trainees.) Third, new recruits frequently learn more from informal interactions with supervisors, peers, and mentors than they do from training and orientation programs, because the formal programs are too easy, too broad, and too general. In other words, rigorous need assessment is required to pitch programs at the appropriate level of complexity for trainees.

One of the most provocative parts of Feldman's chapter concerns the question of whether it is better to generate innovativeness or conformity on the part of newcomers. The answer depends on the organization's culture and the specific job involved. In general, training specialists have traditionally assumed that replication is the best way to orient newcomers. Chapter Ten questions this assumption and offers intriguing suggestions for how innovation can be fostered. Finally, Feldman points out several noticeable differences in the ways practitioners have handled the training of new hires versus job changers, as well as differences in the coping strategies and constraints of these two groups. Although more prescriptive research is needed in this area before definite conclusions can be reached, it certainly makes one think about possible differences between the socialization of newcomers and the resocialization of job changers.

The final chapter, by Ronen, focuses on the important practical question of how best to train an international assignee (IA), who will be sent from corporate headquarters to a foreign country. From the practitioner's perspective, Ronen does an excellent job of clearly explaining why there is a need to train IAs, what the goals of training should be, who should be trained, what training techniques should be used, how training goals can best be achieved, and when various training techniques should be used.

Many practitioners will probably be surprised to learn about the high incidence of failure among IAs working for multinational corporations. Many practitioners would suspect, as I did, that the careful selection of IAs—based on their experience, technical skills, previous performance, and expressed interest in working for a host-country subsidiary—would, combined with a brief orientation, be sufficient to ensure their success. Ronen's chapter strongly suggests that this approach is insufficient. Instead, IAs need to be trained in several important categories, and this intercultural training must be accomplished through a variety of methods.

Ronen points out that trainers, too, should be carefully selected, on the basis of their own adaptation to foreign environments and their ability and willingness to model desired behaviors for IA trainees. In addition, Ronen says that IAs need to be chosen and trained well in advance of their assignments, and again after they arrive in their host countries and start their initial adaptation. Most organizations probably conduct IA training only in the United States. Ronen's recommendation of training after arrival in the host country is probably an excellent approach toward maximizing positive transfer of learning.

Unfortunately, very little empirical research has been conducted to date on cross-cultural training. Consequently, many of Ronen's ideas (as the author acknowledges) are derived from reported experiences of IAs and from various articles and reports. Nevertheless, these ideas are excellent, from the practitioner's viewpoint, and they deserve additional field research.

In conclusion, I feel strongly that this volume on training and career development will make a significant contribution to the future practice of I/O psychology. The editor and the authors are to be congratulated for their fine work.

Name Index

Subject Index

A

Abilities: aspects of, 183–255; assessing, 220–221; and associative interference, 229–230; background on, 183–185; and basic skills and remediation, 239–241; categories of, identifying, 195–201; concept of, 194; and concept-identification performance, 213–215; conclusion on, 241–242; and course-content variables, 186, 188–189; defining, 193–195, 482–483; evaluating descriptive system for, 203–209; generic, developing, 230–234; history of taxonomies of, 461–462; implications of, 230–241; importance of, 185–191; and job-level use, 217; in job performance, 216–219; and late-stage learning, 225–228; at learning stages, 222–228; measuring, 197, 201–205; and part-whole task relationships, 228–229; and perceptual-task performance, 211–212; and performance dimensions, 217–218; practice issues for, 493–494; and psychomotor performance, 210–211; and reasoning performance, 212–213; research agenda for, 473–474; and retention, 229; and sequencing of training, 234–238; skill acquisition linked to, 221–230; and task-level use, 218–219; task re-

quirements linked with, 209–216; taxonomic issues for, 190–193; taxonomy of requirements for, 193–203; and training design, 238–239; and training requirements, 216–221; for training tasks and materials, 219–220; and validity-generalization issues, 215–216

Accountability, impact of, 13–14

ACT model, and comprehension, 131–132

Active participation, by aging trainees, 312

Activity learning, for aging trainees, 307–308

Adults, learning processes of, 343–348. *See also* Midcareer workers

Advanced organizers: as instructional concept, 17; and knowledge, 169–170

Age Discrimination in Employment Act (ADEA) of 1967, 300–301, 496

Aggregation of responses: and interpretation, 34, 48, 56; and operationalization, 33, 35, 37, 43, 48

Aging trainees: aspects of, 299–332; attributes of, 303; background on, 299–300; chronological/legal view of, 300–301; and cognitive training, 313–317; conclusions on, 325–326; defining, 300–306; functional view of, 301–302; history of training and, 463–464; individual differences in, 305–306,

515

cept of, 136–137; in education, 142–144

Individual level of analysis: and climate, 47; concept of, 30; and goals, 39; in levels-of-analysis model, 35, 36–37, 41; and situational constraints, 43–44; and skills, 45–46; and technical environment, 42–43; and time orientation, 41

Industrial gerontology, concept of, 299. *See also* Aging trainees

Industrial-organizational (I/O) psychology: and behaviorism, 259–263; and evaluation, 274; future of, 276–277, 279, 285, 286; practice issues for, 488, 489, 491, 496, 498, 500; research agenda for, 476–477

Inferences, in cognitive model, 132–133

Information processing: cognitive models for, 125–129; depth of, 129–130, 233; model of, 126–127. *See also* Cognitive models

Instruction: computer-managed, 280–281; intelligent computer-assisted, 137, 142–143, 144, 167–169; programmed, 266–268, 280–281, 309. *See also* Learning and cognitive issues

Instructional Quality Inventory, 160

Instructional system design, impact of, 12

Instructional System Development (ISD), and cognitive models, 124, 161

Intelligence: changes in, and aging, 316–317; and training, 231–232

International assignees (IAs): aspects of training, 417–453; attributes of, 425, 426, 430; background on, 417–419; categories of training for, 428–436; conclusions on, 446–447; evaluating training for, 441–442; failures by, 421–422, 423–424; family situation of, 435–436; field experiences for, 440–441; goals of train-

ing, 422–425; history of, 465–466; issues in training, 444–446; job factors for, 430–431; language skills of, 436, 441; methods for training, 436–441; motivational state of, 434–435; multiculturalism of, 424–428; need increasing for, 419–422; and practice issues, 499–500; relational abilities of, 424, 425–428, 431–433; research agenda for, 477; role complexity for, 421, 447; sequence of training for, 443–444; trainers for, 442–443

Interpersonal skills, in international assignees, 433

Interpretation, and levels of analysis, 33–34, 35, 37, 47–48, 55–56

Isomorphic constructs, in levels-of-analysis model, 38–47

Isomorphism, and conceptualization, 30–31, 35, 37

J

Japan: international assignees from, 422; training and retraining in, 65

Job factors, for international assignees, 430–431

Job level, use of abilities at, 217

Job loss, and midcareer change, 339

Job performance: abilities in, 216–219; and utility analysis, 77–78

Job Training Partnership Act (JTPA) of 1982, 301, 360

Judgment, and human factors psychology, 154–159

K

Knowledge, and advanced organizers, 17, 169–170

Knowledge elicitation, issue of, 161–163

Multiple processes: concept of, 136, 137; and task analysis, 138–142

Multiplicative rule, in decision making, 155–156

N

Needs assessment, training: aspects of, 25–62; background on, 25–26; conclusions on, 56–57; framework for, 26–27; history of, 457–458; implications of, 48–56; and levels-of-analysis components, 29–34; literature review on, 26–29; model of, 34–48; and organizational change, 366–367; practice issues for, 487, 488–491; research agenda for, 471; and task characteristics, 215; and training issues, 6, 12, 13, 15

Net present value, in utility analysis, 69, 71, 80–81

Nonequivalent groups, evaluation of, 109–111, 113

Norms: carryover of, 403–404; and socialization, 401–404, 405–406

Null hypothesis, testing, and statistical power, 97–98

O

Occupational communities, and socialization, 393–394

Older Americans Act, Title V of, 301

Older workers. See Aging trainees

Operant conditioning: in behaviorism, 258, 261; and programmed instruction, 266, 267; and punishment, 281; and reinforcement, 269; and social learning theory, 265

Operationalization, and levels of analysis, 32–33, 35, 37, 47–48

Operations analysis. See Task analysis

Organization and Strategy Information Service (OASIS), 365, 374

Organizational analysis: concept of, 26–27; in levels-of-analysis model, 36–44

Organizational level of analysis: and climate, 46; concept of, 30; in levels-of-analysis model, 35, 36–37, 38–40; research for, 49–51; and situational constraints, 44; and skills, 45; and technical environment, 42

Organizational seduction, and socialization, 381–382

Organizations: aging by, 304–305; change in, and retraining, 362–367; as learning systems, 64; and midlife crisis, 338–339; recommendations for, 368–371

Organizing: advanced, for learning, 17, 169–170; by aging trainees, 312; and memory, 130–131, 164–165

Outcome expectancy, future of, 278

P

PAQ methodology, and human factors, 148

Part-whole distinction: and abilities, 228–229; and conceptualization, 32, 35, 37

Pay, skill-based, and retraining, 355–356

Payoffs, expected, in utility analysis, 73–76

Peers, socialization by, 388

People-processing strategies, and socialization, 382–384

Perceptual tasks, and abilities, 211–212

Performance: ability dimensions of, 210–219; concept of, 482

Person analysis: concept of, 27; in levels-of-analysis model, 36, 44–47

Positivism, and behaviorism, 258

Posttest-only design, uses of, 92, 98–102, 104–105, 109–110, 112

Power: in compared designs, 98–100; concept of, 96; factors affecting, 96–97; and null hypothesis test-